Foreign in a Domestic Sense

WITHDRAWN

AMERICAN ENCOUNTERS/GLOBAL INTERACTIONS
A series edited by Gilbert M. Joseph and Emily S. Rosenberg

This series aims to stimulate critical perspectives and fresh interpretive frameworks for scholarship on the history of the imposing global
presence of the United States. Its primary concerns include the deployment and contestation of
power, the construction and deconstruction of
cultural and political borders, the fluid meanings
of intercultural encounters, and the complex interplay between the global and the local. American Encounters seeks to strengthen dialogue and
collaboration between historians of U.S. international relations and area studies specialists.

The series encourages scholarship based on
multiarchival historical research. At the same
time, it supports a recognition of the representational character of all stories about the past and
promotes critical inquiry into issues of subjectivity and narrative. In the process, American Encounters strives to understand the context in
which meanings related to nations, cultures, and
political economy are continually produced,
challenged, and reshaped.

Foreign in a Domestic Sense

Puerto Rico, American Expansion,

and the Constitution

Edited by Christina Duffy Burnett and Burke Marshall

Duke University Press   Durham/London 2001

© 2001 Duke University Press
All rights reserved
Printed in the United States of America on acid-free paper ∞
Typeset in Minion by Keystone Typesetting, Inc.
Library of Congress Cataloging-in-Publication Data appear
on the last printed page of this book.
The chapter by José Julián Álvarez González was
originally published in a different form in
Journal on Law and Inequality 17 (1999): 359.

To my late grandfather, Francisco Ponsa Feliú
C. D. B.

Contents

Preface

Para ser digno y libre, ¿a quién esperas?

Lo serás, si es que quieres, cuando quieras.

—Luis Muñoz Rivera, "A Cualquier Compatriota" (1887)

As this book was nearing completion, the debate over the future of the island of Puerto Rico, one of five U.S. territories, took a puzzling turn. Suddenly, we learned (from political leaders on the island and in Congress) that it was, perhaps, "too soon" to resolve the problem of Puerto Rico's colonial status. Although the island had been a colony for half a millennium—and an American colony since the end of the nineteenth century—now, on the verge of the twenty-first, it seemed untimely, to some, for the island's colonial existence to come to an end. The reason? Puerto Rico's electorate had recently participated in a "status plebiscite" (a nonbinding referendum offering several status options), and a slight majority had cast a befuddling vote: "none of the above." This inscrutable result suggested to many that the issue of Puerto Rico's colonial status was best left untouched. A friend to whom I tried to explain the plebiscite laughed when I told her of the winning non-option. "Isn't that a vote for the status quo?" she asked. And I, unable myself to believe it (or perhaps to accept it), responded that the issue was more complicated than it seemed. I hoped.

Puerto Rican patriot Luis Muñoz Rivera would, if he were here, shake his head in wonder. "To have dignity and to be free," he wrote of his people in 1887, "for whom are you waiting? You will be so, if that is what you want, whenever you want it." That was over one hundred years ago, and the status quo at the time was four centuries of Spanish colonial rule. Over the course of the last of those centuries, Puerto Rico had gained and lost varying degrees of local self-government and representation in the Spanish Parliament innumerable times, as the island's fate had fallen victim to Spain's tempestuous domestic politics and the disintegration of her overseas empire. Muñoz Rivera had (understandably) grown impatient, and that was still more than a decade before U.S. troops landed on the shores of the southern Puerto Rican town of Guánica, on the 25th of July 1898. Their arrival effected a transition, in the words of one scholar, "from Spanish Colony to American Possession." General Nelson A. Miles professed, on behalf of the people of the United States, to come "bearing the banner of freedom," but the dawn of the twentieth century, like the dawn of the twenty-first, was apparently too soon for this freedom to be fully bestowed upon the people of Puerto Rico.

That Muñoz Rivera had grown impatient with his own people suggests that perhaps something more complicated was afoot than the mere imposition from above of an imperialist government against the will of the people. The people, his words seem to tell us, were in some sense complicitous in their own colonization. The same is said today, though not always with the same tinge of frustration that is evident in Muñoz Rivera's poetic chiding. Puerto Rico is a colony, it is conceded, but this, for now, is the "will of the people," expressed by them in the exercise of their inalienable right to self-determination. This consent, it is argued, renders the colonial reality more complicated (not as easy to denounce, in other words) than it would be if the United States were still simply imposing an imperialist government from above, against the popular will.

Without a doubt, it is complicated. But "more" so? When was imperialism simple? Is there really a simple distinction between the imposition from above of an unwanted colonial regime and the inability of the colonial subjects to agree on a path toward decolonization? Can the lingering divisions among colonized people ever be fully separated from the inherent divisiveness of a regime imposed from above? Are these not at some point mutually constitutive? One might say, looking at the result of the 1998 plebiscite, that the people of Puerto Rico exercised their inalienable right to self-determination, and a majority of them—fully 50.3 percent, to be exact—chose to remain a colony. One might also say, however, that the oldest strategy for governing recalcitrant subjects—divide and conquer—was subtly at work.

A long-overdue and commendable reluctance on the part of the United States to impose an unwanted solution upon Puerto Rico's colonial problem has become indistinguishable from a less commendable willingness to do nothing at all about the problem, now well cloaked in the unimpeachable rhetoric of noninterference with the principles of "self-determination" and the "will of the people." This inaction rests on flawed premises: that Puerto Rico's status problem is somehow untouched by the actions and inactions of the people of the United States and their government; that this problem has no real consequences for them.

This book is inspired by a desire to impeach this unimpeachable rhetoric, to expose these flawed premises. Respecting the right of self-determination is not the same as doing nothing (or, as is more common when it comes to the United States's relationship with its territories, knowing nothing). Rather than fostering self-determination, doing nothing further divides the nearly four million United States citizens—yes, United States citizens—who live in Puerto Rico, thereby ensuring that this island remains a colony. And a situation in which four million U.S. citizens are colonial subjects does not just *have* consequences for this nation—it *is* the dire consequence of the United States's unfinished flirtation with imperialism.

When Spain ceded Puerto Rico, Guam, and the Philippines to the United States in 1898, the question of their status—one headline called it "the question of the hour"—galvanized the nation; its leading legal scholars represented just one among numerous groups who readily engaged in the urgent debate over the future of these new "possessions." The people of the possessions themselves were conspicuously absent from this debate. Today, the reverse is true. Now it is the people of the metropolis whose voices are conspicuously absent from a debate that consumes political life in the re- maining colonies. Yet voices from the mainland are desperately needed. The impasse in the debate over the status of the U.S. territories is due largely to their peoples' fear and uncertainty over how, precisely, the mainland would respond to change. A principal aim of this book is thus to lure American legal scholars back to the unresolved problem of territorial status in the United States, reminding them (and asking them to remind others) that the "question of the hour" is now the question of a century, and none the less urgent for it.

The essays collected in this volume reflect the belief that a rigorous scholarly examination of the United States's complicated colonial problem has a crucial role to play in its resolution. The book focuses heavily on constitutional analysis because U.S. constitutional jurisprudence—most notably the *Insular Cases* of 1901—is the source of the colonial status in which the territories are still trapped. Such an examination requires careful and constructive dialogue, inclusive of participants from the territory and the mainland, and respectful of all points of view. We have tried hard to achieve that here. It also requires faith—faith that the people of Puerto Rico do want dignity, equality, and an end to their colonial dilemma. I have no doubt that they do, although I suspect that there are many Puerto Ricans (I among them) who, like Muñoz Rivera, have often been puzzled by the majority's apparent choices. But it is crucial to remember—as the essays in this book remind us—that the people of Puerto Rico are not the only ones confronted with a decision, though they, at least, are aware of it.

The people of the United States, though most are *not* aware of it, confront a decision as well. They continue to be complicitous in a vestigial colonialism. The "anti-imperialists" of the turn of the century, after all, warned of consequences we live with today: The United States continues to exercise sovereignty over people (now its own citizens) denied equal membership in the Union; the colonial system that many warned would betray the nation's commitments to freedom and equality endures. (In the words of one Supreme Court Justice at the time, this would create an "utterly revolting" situation.) And because apathy and ignorance will not make the situation disappear, our contributors ask once more: What kind of a nation are we? What kind of a nation ought we to be? This collection of essays is inspired by the hope that in another hundred years, on the bicentenary of the Spanish-American War, someone will pick up this book and look back, to a time long ago, when we reexamined the living legacy of an imperialist past and the anti-imperialists finally had their day.

This project grew out of a conference I organized at Yale Law School marking the centenary of the Spanish-American War, entitled "Foreign in a Domestic Sense: Reflections on the Centenary of the United States' Acquisition of Puerto Rico," which took place on March 27–29, 1998. Twelve of the seventeen essays in this book are revised and expanded versions of presentations given at that conference. (The essays added subsequently include the Introduction and the chapters by Mark S. Weiner, Brook Thomas, Juan Perea, and Rogers M. Smith.) I express my heartfelt gratitude to the many individuals and institutions who made that event possible, among them: co-sponsors Dean Anthony T. Kronman of Yale Law School and Dean Antonio García Padilla of the University of Puerto Rico School of Law; Yale Law School Dean of Students Natalia Martín and her assistant Brooke Goolsby; Judge José A. Cabranes of the Court of Appeals for the Second Circuit; my classmate and co-organizer Damon J. Hemmerdinger; moderators Rogers M. Smith, Burke Marshall, Judith Resnik, Akhil Reed Amar, and Owen Fiss; and Raymond Craib and my husband, D. Graham Burnett, curators of *Insular Visions 1898,* an exhibit on the Spanish-American War at Yale's Sterling Memorial Library that opened the conference. Dean Kronman saw the project through from beginning to end, dedicating to it an extraordinary amount of time, energy, and resources; he also secured additional financial support from the law school that enabled me to devote several months after graduation to editing this volume. Judge Cabranes, with his keen sense of good mentorship, provided essential guidance throughout, generously sharing his wisdom on all matters Puerto Rican. Others, too many to name here, contributed their time and efforts, and I am deeply grateful to them all.

I am indebted to the contributors to this book, both those who participated in the conference and expanded their presentations into essays for publication and those whose pieces we were fortunate to add subsequent to the conference to round out the historical component of the book. I am especially grateful to Sanford Levinson, whose continued work on the topic of territories and American expansion includes revisions to the latest edition of his constitutional law casebook, *Processes of Constitutional Decision-making* (with Akhil Reed Amar, Jack Balkin, and Paul Brest), for the inclusion of material on the *Insular Cases*. Herbert W. Brown III gave this project support and encouragement from the beginning, as did series editor Gil Joseph. My sister Nicole provided invaluable research assistance, and my sister Adriana kept me honest with her invariably tough questions. To Valerie Millholland and Pam Morrison at Duke University Press, and to Chris Mooney, who applied his considerable talents to preparing the index, I am thankful for their infinite patience and hard work.

My coeditor, Burke Marshall, is a role model and an inspiration. To my parents, Edda Ponsa Duffy and Lawrence E. Duffy, I owe more than I can repay. And to my husband, Graham, thank you. *A nadie te pareces. . . .*

C. D. B.

Between the Foreign and the Domestic: The Doctrine of Territorial Incorporation, Invented and Reinvented

Christina Duffy Burnett and Burke Marshall

The phrase that entitles this book, and which describes the constitutional status of the "territories" of the United States, appeared in an opinion of the United States Supreme Court much noted in its time, and crucial to the period of United States imperialism a century ago, but almost forgotten since then: *Downes v. Bidwell.*[1] This was one of a series of decisions known as the *Insular Cases,* which in 1901 gave legal sanction to the colonization of islands taken by the United States at the close of the Spanish-American War: Puerto Rico, Guam, and the Philippines.[2] In those cases, the Supreme Court held that these islands were neither "foreign" countries nor "part of the United States." Instead, they were something in between: in the words of Justice Edward Douglass White, whose concurrence in *Downes* would eventually be adopted by a unanimous Supreme Court, they were "foreign to the United States in a domestic sense."[3] They had not been, he explained, "incorporated" into the United States upon their acquisition from Spain, but were, in the phrase the Court would later adopt, "unincorporated territories,"[4] belonging to—but not a part of—the United States.

Over the course of the twentieth century, these and a number of other territories would find themselves in relationships with the United States that might well be described as "foreign in a domestic sense," though each in a different sense. Today the so-called unincorporated territories include the Commonwealth of Puerto Rico, the Commonwealth of the Northern Mariana Islands, Guam, the U.S. Virgin Islands, and American Samoa. These islands have a combined population of approximately 4 million, 3.8 million of whom live in Puerto Rico. Although each of the U.S. territories has a different status—by which we mean its particular relationship to the United States—they have several features in common: Congress governs them pursuant to its power under the Territorial Clause of the U.S. Constitution;[5] none is a sovereign independent country or a state of the Union; people born in the territories are U.S. citizens, or, in the case of American

Samoa, U.S. "nationals"; all are affected by federal legislation at the sole discretion of Congress; none has representation at the federal level.[6] In addition, they share varying levels of dissatisfaction with their current relationships to the mainland, still colonial despite gradually increased levels of local self-government.[7] In the Commonwealth of Puerto Rico, dissatisfaction with the status quo is one of the few areas of consensus in an otherwise acrimonious status debate; even the party that advocates the continuation of "commonwealth" status has long sought to replace the current status with an "enhanced" or "perfected" version.[8]

The *Insular Cases,* decided between 1901 and 1922, invented and developed the idea of unincorporated territorial status in order to enable the United States to acquire and govern its new "possessions" without promising them either statehood or independence. Over time, however, the *Insular Cases* and the unusual status they invented have led in turn to a curious reversal: now, many of the U.S. citizens who live in the territories *themselves* reject both statehood and independence, the options denied the inhabitants of the territories by the *Insular Cases* at the turn of the last century. No one today defends the colonial status sanctioned by these cases, yet the idea of a relationship to the United States that is somewhere "in between" that of statehood and independence—somehow both "foreign" and "domestic" (or neither)—has not only survived but enjoys substantial support. A territorial status born of colonialism has been appropriated by colonial subjects. Justice White's rhetorical flourish is therefore doubly suitable as a title: in a historical sense, the curious juxtaposition of the foreign and the domestic captures the essence of the much-aligned status imposed "from above" on the former Spanish colonies in 1901; in the current context, the same phrase embodies a crucial feature of some decolonizing solutions now proposed "from below."

What has happened to being somewhere in between "foreign" and "domestic" that has made it so desirable to so many? Many residents of the territories gravitate toward the idea of a status in between statehood and independence and struggle to implement it on their own terms—why? And why, at the same time, do so many others adamantly oppose these efforts, insisting that only statehood or independence can provide a truly noncolonial solution to the territories' status dilemma?

The essays in this book confront these and related questions concerning territorial status; about half of them address the U.S. territories generally, while the rest focus on the largest and most populous, Puerto Rico. The principal aim of this book is to examine the history, content, and implications of the idea that certain statuses within the United States's constitutional framework are appropriate only for certain groups of people in certain geographical locations. A crucial but long-neglected chapter in the narrative of the United States's development as a nation, the story of the U.S. territories—those invisible American colonies—and their unusual and widely misunderstood relationship to the United States challenges our understanding of who "we, the people" are, and questions cherished assumptions about our principles of liberal constitutional government and our ideals of citizenship, federalism, sovereignty, representation, and equality.

Our introduction roughly mirrors the structure of the book, tracing a trajectory from the historical context (sections 1 and 2), to more specific questions of constitutional jurisprudence (sections 2 and 3), to related issues of sovereignty, citizenship, culture, and national identity (sections 3 and 4). We begin with a brief discussion of the historical context of the *Insular Cases,* and then take a closer look at two of these cases, *Downes v. Bidwell* and *De Lima v. Bidwell.*[9] Turning then to Puerto Rico, we provide an overview of the debate over the island's current status, emphasizing the central role that constitutional questions play in that debate. Moving finally from the constitutional to the normative, we offer some observations concerning the preconditions to a sound resolution of the status dilemma. We conclude with a summary of the chapters.

History and Expansion: 1898

The "Spanish-American War" of 1898, a short-lived conflict both in time and in American memory, lasted from the explosion of the U.S.S. *Maine* in the Havana harbor on February 15, 1898, to the signing of the Treaty of Paris on December 10 of that year.[10] The war took place as a broader debate unfolded in the United States over whether the nation could—and should— become an imperialist power. Victory over Spain presented the United States with the opportunity to try its hand at some European-style colonial governance. Defeated, Spain ceded to the United States the islands of Cuba and Puerto Rico in the Caribbean, and Guam and the Philippines in the Pacific. Although Congress had previously disclaimed any intention to take permanent sovereignty over Cuba, no such bar existed with respect to Puerto Rico, Guam, or the Philippines.[11] In the words of Article IX of the Treaty of Paris: "The civil rights and political status of the native inhabitants of the territories hereby ceded to the United States shall be determined by the Congress."[12]

Not knowing quite what to do with these new "possessions" and the culturally and racially different peoples who inhabited them, the United States held
onto them while a debate between "imperialists" and "anti-imperialists"
raged on. This "fervent controversy . . . led to a flood of controversial
literature, phrase-making in and out of Congress, and to a bitterness which
almost threatened to resemble the controversies over the Fugitive Slave Law
and the Missouri Compromise. . . . The election of 1900 largely turned
upon the so-called issue of Imperialism."[13] The presidential race between
William McKinley and William Jennings Bryan cast the debate in terms of
the catchy (but somewhat misleading) question of whether the Constitution
"followed the flag," with Bryan arguing that it did, and McKinley insisting
that it need not.[14]

As we discuss in more detail below, to ask whether the Constitution
followed the flag was in effect to ask whether, if these territories were to be
kept under U.S. sovereignty, they must eventually be granted statehood. The
United States already had territories, of course, and the Constitution did
not entirely "follow the flag" to any of them. Rather, Congress exercised
nearly absolute, or "plenary," power over territories under the Territorial
Clause of the Constitution, which gives Congress "power to dispose of and
make all needful rules and regulations respecting the territory or other
property belonging to the United States,"[15] without any requirement that
such territory have representation in the national government. In this sense,
the labels "imperialist" and "anti-imperialist" are not entirely accurate:
many anti-imperialists did not object to the acquisition of territories per se,
or to their quasi-colonial governance under the Territorial Clause. Instead,
they objected to the idea that arose with respect to the former Spanish
colonies: that Congress could subject them to *permanent* territorial status,
without intending ever to admit them into the Union as full and equal
member states. (Most anti-imperialists, rejecting the idea of permanent
territories, also rejected the idea of statehood for the former Spanish colonies, and urged instead that they be granted independence.)[16] The "imperialists," on the other hand, insisted that not all territories must follow the
pattern established by the Northwest Ordinance of 1787, whereby they had
evolved through several stages culminating in statehood. Some territories,
they argued, could be held indefinitely, as colonies, to be dealt with in
whatever way Congress saw fit. The imperialist mood of the time was captured in essay titles such as "How Great Britain Governs Her Colonies" and
"The Rights of a Conqueror." The mood was contagious; with the election
of McKinley, the voters sanctioned imperialism.[17]

Even then, however, it remained unclear whether the United States could—constitutionally—keep colonies indefinitely. No matter how readily the general public took to the idea of possessing colonies, the constitutional question could not be fully resolved until the Supreme Court stepped in. In the meantime, the United States went ahead and governed the new territories. In Puerto Rico, it established first a military government, and then a colonial civil government, created as in prior territories by an organic act, in this case the Foraker Act of 1900.[18] This government was headed by an American governor appointed by the president of the United States. Six appointed American department heads, together with five persons born in Puerto Rico, composed the nonelective Executive Council, one of two legislative chambers. The other, a House of Representatives, consisted of thirty-five elected representatives from Puerto Rico. The Foraker Act did not grant the inhabitants of Puerto Rico U.S. citizenship. Nor, it turned out, did the Act "incorporate" the island into the United States.

THE SCHOLARLY DEBATE

Before the debate on imperialism reached the Supreme Court, numerous civic and political leaders weighed in with views on the constitutional dilemma presented by the newly acquired territories and their inhabitants. The stature of the participants in this debate—former U.S. president Benjamin Harrison, the presidents-to-be of Harvard University and the University of Chicago, and prominent professors, deans, judges, and attorneys— suggests the widespread recognition at the time that the new territories raised questions of profound significance for the future of the American nation. The dozens of articles appearing in law reviews alone contained a wealth of arguments concerning such fundamental issues as the purposes and advantages of a written constitution; the meaning of the phrase "United States"; the distinction between the status of territories and the status of their inhabitants; the differences between civil and political rights; the distinctions between "citizens," "nationals," and "aliens"; and more.

The most frequently cited contributions to this debate were five articles that appeared in the *Harvard Law Review* between 1898 and 1899.[19] Each contains an invaluable analysis of territorial status throughout the history of the United States, but the central question they addressed—and the one the Supreme Court would take up thereafter—was whether the phrase "United States" includes territories. Two concluded that it does, two that it does not.[20] The fifth, an article by future Harvard president Abbott Lawrence Lowell entitled "The Status of Our New Possessions—a Third View," seemed to fall somewhere in between. In this article, Lowell made the novel argument that some territories are part of the United States and others not. This argument, further developed by Justice White in his concurrence in *Downes v. Bidwell* two years later, would become the doctrine of territorial incorporation.

Lowell characterized his "third view" as a compromise between the two "opposing theories" that had been "very ably advocated" by his peers: C. C. Langdell and James Bradley Thayer on the one hand, and Carman F. Randolph and Simeon E. Baldwin on the other.[21] Langdell and Thayer had advocated a version of the imperialist position: they argued that the "United States" excludes territories, and that the new territories could therefore be governed as colonies if Congress so chose. Randolph and Baldwin, in contrast, had advocated a version of the anti-imperialist view, whereby all areas under American sovereignty become a part of the United States upon acquisition.

Lowell, on the other hand, saw the issue as a matter of discretion: "[T]he incorporation of territory in the Union, like the acquisition of territory at all, is a matter solely for the legislative or the treaty-making authorities," he wrote.[22] Thus distinguishing between the "incorporation" of territory and its "acquisition," Lowell argued that Congress alone can determine whether to incorporate a territory into the United States, and he noted that Congress had not done so with respect to Puerto Rico, Guam, or the Philippines. This was clear, he argued, from the language of the Treaty of Paris, which had left the "civil rights and political status of the native inhabitants" of these islands up to Congress.[23] Thus these islands were not a part of the United States, and might never be. The decision was up to Congress, and Congress alone.[24]

Subtle and persuasive as Lowell's legal arguments were, they were driven in large part by somewhat less subtle views of Anglo-Saxon superiority, to which he devoted little space in his law review articles but which he expressed at greater length elsewhere.[25] In this, he agreed with all four of his peers, imperialist and anti-imperialist alike. His views on race, along with his views on the constitutional status of territories, would find support among the Justices of the Supreme Court.[26]

Expansion and Constitution: A Closer Look at Downes v. Bidwell

_en in 1901 the Supreme Court finally turned to the question of the new _ries, the Justices disagreed as vigorously as the nation's leading legal _ had done. The *Insular Cases* of 1901 have been seen by many as the most controversial decisions of the Court since *Dred Scott.* "This grave question," wrote one contemporary commentator, "confronts us inexorably, and a true or false answer is sure incalculably to affect our future civilization."[27] A "judicial drama of truly Olympian proportions,"[28] was how another commentator described these cases some years later; in the words of a more recent account, the *Insular Cases* "helped shape national identity and secure a unique place in history for the Fuller Court."[29] But they also caused a great deal of confusion, even among the Justices themselves. In *Downes v. Bidwell,* generally considered the most important of the *Insular Cases* (because it produced the most detailed exposition of Justice White's doctrine of incorporation), the Court found itself so far from consensus that it produced five separate opinions. Three of these agreed with the specific holding, and two dissented, but not one garnered a majority in its reasoning. The complexity of this case—and its importance for understanding the status of unincorporated territories—requires that we examine it in some detail.

THE JUDICIAL DEBATE

Downes arose out of a dispute between a businessman by the name of Samuel Downes, operating through the firm of S. B. Downes & Company, and the customs collector of New York. The collector had charged Downes a duty of $659.35 on a shipment of oranges from Puerto Rico under the Foraker Act, which had authorized duties on Puerto Rican goods of up to 15 percent of those charged on goods from foreign countries. This reduced duty was thus not the exact equivalent of a duty on "foreign" goods, yet it meant Puerto Rico was being treated differently from other areas in the United States, as no duty at all would have been charged on goods originating elsewhere in the "United States."

Downes paid the duty under protest and later challenged it in court. The question ultimately presented to the Supreme Court was whether the requirement set forth in the Uniformity Clause of the Constitution—that "all duties, imposts and excises . . . be uniform throughout the United States"[30]—applied to Puerto Rico, in which case the duty would have been unconstitutional. To answer this question, the Court first turned to the same question the *Harvard Law Review* articles had addressed, though in slightly narrowed form: whether Puerto Rico was part of the "United States," for purposes of the Uniformity Clause. The Court held that it was not.

Justice Henry Billings Brown's opinion "for the Court" was not joined by any of the other Justices.[31] Brown took the position that the phrase "United

States" does not include the territories and, therefore, that the Uniformity Clause—the terms of which cover only the United States—does not apply to territories unless Congress chooses to apply it by legislation, which it had not done in the case of Puerto Rico. Justice White wrote a concurrence, joined by Justices George Shiras and Joseph McKenna, in which he echoed Abbott Lawrence Lowell's argument that some territories are part of the United States and others not.[32] Puerto Rico was among the latter, he explained, and it was for this reason that the Uniformity Clause did not apply to the island. (White agreed with Brown that Congress could apply the requirement of uniformity by legislation, but that it had not done so in this case.) Justice Horace Gray wrote a third and very brief concurrence in which he agreed with the substance of White's opinion; he emphasized simply that any territory taken by cession from a foreign sovereign must undergo a transition before becoming part of the United States.[33]

The dissenters, who included Chief Justice Melville Weston Fuller and Justices David Brewer, Rufus Wheeler Peckham, and John Marshall Harlan, argued that the phrase "United States" includes all territories subject to American sovereignty, without exception, and that the Uniformity Clause applies to them all, including Puerto Rico. They wrote two dissenting opinions: the first, written by the Chief Justice, was joined by all the other dissenters; in addition, Justice Harlan wrote a dissenting opinion of his own.[34]

In his opinion for the Court, Justice Brown set forth what has come to be known as the "extension theory."[35] According to this theory, Congress has sole discretion over whether to "extend" the Constitution to the territories, because they are not part of the United States. Governmental action in the territories, Brown reasoned, is limited only by certain fundamental prohibitions. In order to identify these prohibitions, he explained, one must look primarily to the distinction between "natural" and "artificial" rights: the former are protected everywhere and at all times, while the latter are "peculiar to our system of jurisprudence" and protected only within the "United States."[36] Brown thus relied on a distinction between the limits on congressional action in the territories, derived generally from fundamental principles of natural justice, and the limits applicable to governmental action within the United States, which are spelled out in the Constitution.[37]

Although his opinion has been characterized as a theory of wholly extra-
nal governmental power, Justice Brown did note that a few con-
ovisions containing fundamental limitations apply every-
he territories. "To sustain the judgment in the case under

consideration," he wrote, "it by no means becomes necessary to show that none of the articles of the Constitution apply to the island of Porto Rico. There is a clear distinction between such prohibitions as go to the very root of the power of Congress to act at all, irrespective of time or place, and such as are operative only 'throughout the United States' or among the several states."[38] Brown did not provide an exhaustive list of either of these categories, but as examples of the former, he listed the constitutional prohibitions against bills of attainder, ex post facto laws, and titles of nobility.[39] The requirement of uniformity, in any case, was not among these universally applicable limitations, and so could be disregarded outside the "United States."

Justice White in his concurrence was among the first to suggest that Justice Brown's opinion had authorized entirely extraconstitutional governmental power over the territories. Distinguishing his own view, White wrote: "In the case of the territories, as in every other instance, when a provision of the Constitution is invoked, the question which arises is, *not whether the Constitution is operative, for that is self-evident, but whether the provision relied on is applicable.*"[40] In fact, this reasoning is very similar to Brown's, for Brown too acknowledged that all constitutional provisions expressing fundamental prohibitions are operative everywhere. The difference between their views arises in the next step in White's analysis. The determination of whether a given provision is applicable, White explained, "involves an inquiry into the situation of the territory and its relations to the United States."[41] Contrary to Brown, who placed all territories in the same category—that is, outside the United States—White placed some in this category and others within the United States. In his view, the *status* of a given territory—specifically, whether that territory has been "incorporated" into the United States—is the key factor in a case-by-case analysis of which constitutional provisions constrain governmental action there.

Rather than elaborate on the precise meaning of "incorporation," Justice White devoted most of his opinion to defending the idea that Congress has sole discretion over whether and when to incorporate—whatever that might mean. Thus, despite the central role of the idea of incorporation in White's opinion, the consequences of incorporation remained unclear. Moreover, despite White's attempt to distinguish himself from Brown by insisting that the Constitution is operative everywhere and at all times, his doctrine of incorporation proves difficult to distinguish from Brown's so-called extension theory. As far as unincorporated territories were concerned, the theories looked exactly the same: In either scenario, these territories were not considered part of the "United States," and only certain fundamental constitutional prohibitions constrained governmental action there.

Skeptical of Justice White's distinction between categories of territories, the dissenters refused to concede that incorporation meant anything at all. "Great stress is thrown upon the word 'incorporation,' " wrote Chief Justice Fuller, "as if possessed of some occult meaning, but I take it that the [Foraker Act] made Porto Rico, whatever its situation before, an organized territory of the United States. Being such, and the act undertaking to impose duties by virtue of clause 1 of § 8, how is it that the rule which qualifies the power does not apply to its exercise in respect of commerce with that territory?"[42] To the dissenters, the issue was simple: if Congress could impose upon Puerto Rico a civil government, and regulate commerce with it, then the island must be a part of the United States, and the Uniformity Clause must apply there.

Skeptical also of distinctions between fundamental or natural and artificial rights, the dissenters characterized *both* Justice Brown's and Justice White's opinions as theories of extraconstitutional governmental power. Justice Harlan was particularly emphatic in this criticism. "It will be an evil day for American liberty," he warned in his separate dissent, "if the theory of a government outside of the supreme law of the land finds lodgment in our constitutional jurisprudence. No higher duty rests upon this court than to exert its full authority to prevent all violation of the principles of the Constitution."[43]

Justice Harlan's impassioned language proved less persuasive to his brethren on the Court than it has to most students of the *Insular Cases* since. Thus a majority of the Justices confirmed that the United States could acquire and govern new territories unhindered by certain otherwise applicable constitutional restrictions—and unencumbered by any implicit commitment eventually to grant these places and their peoples full membership in the Union.

Scholarship on the *Insular Cases* has focused primarily on the former consequence—the inapplicability of constitutional provisions. Hence the question of whether the Constitution "follows the flag" has persisted over time as the preferred shorthand for describing the holding in these cases. Put in more technical legal terms, the question is whether the Constitution applies *"ex proprio vigore"* or of its own force to unincorporated territories. According to this account, the holding that Puerto Rico was not part of the United States stood for the broader proposition that the Constitution did not "follow the flag" or apply *ex proprio vigore* to the unincorporated territories. The colonial status of Puerto Rico and the other unincorporated territories has therefore been attributed primarily to Congress's so-called plenary power over these territories.[44]

This interpretation of the cases is rooted not least of all in the Justices' own characterizations of each other's views. As described above, Justice White took Justice Brown to task for espousing the idea that the Constitution is not operative everywhere and at all times, while the dissenters criticized all of the Justices in the majority for precisely the same reason. Similarly, scholarly accounts of the *Insular Cases* have conflated the question of whether a territory is "incorporated" with the question of whether the Constitution "applies" there, as in this representative account: "[T]he doctrine [of incorporation] asserts that the domestic territories are of two kinds: 'incorporated' and 'unincorporated. . . .' Since such incorporated territories are infant or incipient States, the federal Constitution, including the Bill of Rights, fully applies to them."[45]

Yet this way of framing the issue—by connecting the idea of incorporation to the applicability of the Constitution—is perhaps not the best way to capture the full significance of the doctrine of incorporation. Indeed, this way of framing the issue is somewhat misleading. As noted earlier, the Constitution had never "followed the flag" to any of the territories.[46] Some of its provisions had, to be sure, but even then it was not clear that these applied *ex proprio vigore,* as opposed to being in force via congressional legislation or by "inference and the general spirit" of the Constitution.[47] True, the *Insular Cases* established that even fewer constitutional provisions applied in unincorporated territories (such as the requirement of uniformity).[48] Yet other provisions—most notably those concerning representation at the federal level and the guarantee of a republican form of government—had never "applied" in any territory. Moreover, Congress had always exercised plenary power over territories under the Territorial Clause: as the Supreme Court had explained, "The people of the United States, as sovereign owners of the National Territories, have supreme power over them and their inhabitants";[49] Congress, by virtue of its plenary power, could make "a void act of the Territorial legislature valid, and a valid act void."[50]

To say that "the federal Constitution, including the Bill of Rights, fully applies" to incorporated territories is thus somewhat inaccurate; it is also to lose sight of the real distinction between incorporated and unincorporated territories—and of why it is plausible to say that the *Insular Cases* sanctioned imperialism. Why, for instance, is it more imperlialistic to withhold uniformity, as *Downes* did with respect to unincorporated territories, than to withhold representation in the federal government, as had always been the case in all territories? Why, in other words, were only the new territories *colonies*?

They were, and the reason lay in the relationship between incorporation and "incipient statehood." The idea that Congress had discretion over whether to incorporate a territory freed Congress from any suggestion that it must follow the pattern established by the Northwest Ordinance of 1787 whereby all territories had evolved through various stages of increasing self-government culminating in statehood. The discretion not to incorporate a territory made clear not only that the acquisition of territory need never lead to statehood (or, for that matter, to independence) but also that Congress could postpone a decision concerning the ultimate status of a territory altogether.[51]

This holding simply rejected a long-standing *assumption* that territorial status must, eventually, lead to statehood.[52] Nothing in the Constitution, after all, actually requires Congress to make a state out of a territory. The *Insular Cases*, however, transformed that long-held assumption into a congressional power to make an affirmative commitment to grant statehood at some future date—a commitment effected by means of the *incorporation* of a territory. Conversely, the withholding of incorporation from certain territories now functioned as the equivalent of an explicit denial of the promise of statehood. By using incorporation as the basis of an affirmative constitutional distinction between two categories of territories, Justice White separated those to which Congress had promised a final status from those from which Congress had withheld any promise at all.

Congress, it should be noted, already exercised other forms of plenary power over entities that would never be states—namely, the District of Columbia and Indian tribes.[53] The status of these entities, however, while bitterly contested, was not left entirely unresolved. Contrary to their (concededly unenviable) situation, the unincorporated territories were denied even the promise of any final status, either within the constitutional framework or outside of it. They were subjected not only to an unequal condition but also to absolute uncertainty concerning their ultimate status—uncertainty about who they were, where they belonged, and what their future held. Their fate was left to the sole discretion of Congress: Congress could eventually commit to grant them statehood; it could change its mind entirely and release them into independence; or it could postpone the decision forever. The withholding of a commitment to a final, permanent status thus was what truly distinguished the new territories from the old. It was a difference not of degree but of kind. It meant that Congress could now employ the *means* of colonial government toward an *end* other than statehood—that is, as an end in itself. Thus American imperialism was born of a deferred decision.[54]

EMPIRE BY DEFERRAL

The tremendous uncertainty inherent in this unprecedented status was captured by Chief Justice Fuller in an oft-quoted passage in his dissent in *Downes:* "[T]he contention seems to be that, if an organized and settled province of another sovereignty is acquired by the United States, Congress has the power to keep it, like a disembodied shade, in an intermediate state of ambiguous existence for an indefinite period. . . ."[55] Indeed, the contention was precisely that. In Justice White's words: "The result of what has been said is that while in an international sense Porto Rico was not a foreign country, since it was owned by the United States, it was foreign to the United States in a domestic sense, because the island had not been incorporated into the United States, but was merely appurtenant thereto as a possession."[56]

This passage is frequently cited for language that captures the paternalistic tenor of White's rhetoric—"owned," "appurtenant," "possession"—but its references to "the international sense" and "the domestic sense" shed even greater light on the status of the new territories. Denied a place both within the United States and outside of it, Puerto Rico, and the other new territories by implication, became foreign *relative to* states and incorporated territories, and domestic *relative to* foreign countries.

A comparison of cases dealing with these different contexts illustrates the point. *Downes* concerned the former (the domestic context); *De Lima v. Bidwell* dealt with the latter (the foreign or international context).[57] In *De Lima,* the plaintiff had challenged duties imposed on a series of shipments of sugar from Puerto Rico to the United States, after the ratification of the Treaty of Paris but before passage of the Foraker Act. These had been imposed under the Dingley Act, which provided for duties on goods shipped to the United States from "foreign countries." In *De Lima,* the Court held that Puerto Rico was not a "foreign country" for purposes of the Dingley Act and, hence, that the duties were invalid.

The apparent inconsistency between *Downes* and *De Lima* was vigorously criticized.[58] How could Puerto Rico *both* not be a "foreign country" *and* not be part of the "United States"? Critics included eight of the nine Justices of the Fuller Court itself—only Justice Brown joined the majority in both cases, while his eight colleagues switched sides from *De Lima* to *Downes.* Yet Brown's opinions were consistent; indeed, the key to understanding the doctrine of incorporation lies in understanding how they were consistent. Combined, Brown's opinions in *De Lima* and *Downes* capture the innovation in the *Insular Cases* even better perhaps than Justice White's famous concurrence in *Downes* does by itself.

In adhering to the view that the new territories were neither foreign countries nor part of the United States, Justice Brown rejected a simple distinction between the foreign and the domestic. Exclusion from these two categories—the United States and foreign territory—did not mean exclusion from all categories. It meant inclusion within the boundaries of what might be called the United States's *sphere of sovereignty.* Lacking the right words to describe territory subject to U.S. sovereignty but not a part of the United States, Brown referred to the new territories as "domestic," but at the same time sought to expand that category by distinguishing between domestic territory as a whole and the narrower subcategory of the United States proper. Accordingly, Justice Brown rejected the notion that either the Dingley Act or the Uniformity Clause should apply to such places. The former applied by its terms to foreign countries, the latter to the United States. The Foraker Act, in contrast, was uniquely intended for the territory to which it applied—Puerto Rico—a territory squarely within the United States's sphere of sovereignty but not within the United States.

Curiously, the dissenting opinion in *De Lima,* written by Justice McKenna and joined by Justices Shiras and White (the same three who signed onto White's concurrence in *Downes*), described this challenge to the boundary between foreignness and domesticity far more clearly than Justice Brown did, even as these dissenters insisted that Puerto Rico must be treated as a "foreign country" under the Dingley Act. McKenna wrote:

> Settle whether Porto Rico is "foreign country" or "domestic territory," to use the antithesis of the opinion of the court, and, it is said, you settle the controversy of this litigation. But in what sense, foreign or domestic? Abstractly or unqualifiedly—to the full extent that those words imply—or limitedly, in the sense that the word foreign is used in the customs laws of the United States? If abstractly, the case turns upon a definition, and the issue becomes single and simple, presenting no difficulty, and yet the arguments at bar have ranged over all the powers of government, and this court divides in opinion. If at the time the

duties, which are complained of, were levied, Porto Rico was as much a foreign country as it was before the war with Spain; if it was as much domestic territory as New York now is, there would be no serious controversy in this case. If the former, the terms and the intention of the Dingley act would apply. If the latter, whatever its words or intention, it could not be applied. Between these extremes there are other relations, and that Porto Rico occupied one of them and its products hence were subject to duties under the Dingley Tariff act can be demonstrated.[59]

Undoubtedly Brown would have agreed with most of this passage, short of the conclusion that Puerto Rico's products "hence were subject to duties under the Dingley Tariff act." For Brown, it was precisely because Puerto Rico had a relationship to the United States *between the extremes* that Congress must legislate specifically for Puerto Rico, rather than rely on the Dingley Act. The dissenters' criticism of Brown thus seems misplaced, both because they, not Brown, forced Puerto Rico into the "foreign" category, and because they overlooked the more important antithesis in Brown's opinion: an antithesis not between foreign and domestic, but between the domestic broadly conceived—that within the United States's *sphere of sovereignty*—and the more narrow domestic subcategory of the United States itself.

It may be that these three dissenters (the fourth, Justice Gray, wrote his own brief opinion in *De Lima* as well as in *Downes*) overlooked the extent of their agreement with Justice Brown because he used the term *domestic* to describe Puerto Rico's status in *De Lima,* although evidently he meant, as they did, that Puerto Rico occupied a status between the extremes of the domestic and the foreign. In any event, the real source of their disagreement with Brown concerned the narrower question, posed by the facts in *De Lima,* of what would be the consequences of Congress's failure to legislate with respect to a particular subject matter—in this case tariffs—immediately following the ratification of a treaty of cession. Brown concluded that tariffs applicable to foreign countries would cease to apply to conquered territory until Congress provided for new ones, while McKenna, Shiras, and White reasoned that the formerly applicable tariffs would continue to apply until they were replaced with legislation such as the Foraker Act. Thus these four Justices reached an agreement as to the holding in *Downes,* for that case involved congressional legislation that none of them doubted Congress had the power to enact with respect to the new territories. Yet Brown's rejection in *De Lima* of the idea that the new territories should simply be treated as foreign countries until Congress got around to legislating for them arguably reflects a better understanding of the consequences of the new category, or at least a more rigorous application of it. White's concurrence in *Downes*, in turn, may be the view ultimately embraced by the Court largely because the word *incorporation* more successfully captured the idea of the domestic broadly conceived—of a sphere of sovereignty distinct from and extending beyond the boundaries of the United States.

Walter LaFeber has argued that the *Insular Cases* were a crucial step in the transformation in constitutional thought between 1890 and 1920 that "resolved the terrible tension emerging between the new foreign policy and the traditional Constitution by separating the two." In LaFeber's view, the idea that the United States could conduct foreign affairs unrestrained by constitutional provisions gradually took hold during this period, and the *Insular Cases* contributed to this "false separation of foreign and domestic affairs" by "ratifying McKinley's conquests and by allowing the United States government to rule the conquered as it saw fit."[60] LaFeber's account (one somewhat reminiscent of the idea of the Constitution following the flag) rests in part on the premise that the government of a conquered people properly belongs in the category of foreign affairs—only by assuming this can one conclude that these cases contributed to the separation of the Constitution from foreign policy. Yet as we have seen, not only were the several Justices of the Fuller Court who took sides with the imperialists at pains to demonstrate that the Constitution remained in force wherever the United States exercised sovereignty (if only with respect to its most basic guarantees), but they also strongly questioned the false separation between foreign and domestic affairs. As Justice McKenna put it in his dissent in *De Lima*, "to set the word foreign in antithesis to the word domestic proves nothing."[61]

The other four Justices—those who joined Justice Brown in the majority in *De Lima* and dissented in *Downes*—took issue with the constitutionality (not to mention the desirability) of this liminal category of territory. They rejected this third view, as Lowell had described it, of the new territories' status, which subjected them to U.S. sovereignty but excluded them from equal membership in the Union. In their view, what followed from *De Lima*'s holding that the territories were not foreign was the conclusion that the territories were part of the United States. A reasonable conclusion, one would have thought. Nevertheless, a liminal category of territories subject to U.S. sovereignty was precisely what the *Insular Cases* made possible. To argue that the holdings in *Downes* and *De Lima* were inconsistent is to overlook *how* they made imperialism possible.

The *Insular Cases* and subsequent Supreme Court opinions would apply a case-by-case inquiry to determine which constitutional provisions and federal laws apply to which unincorporated territories, thus developing and clarifying the first feature of Justice White's doctrine—that fewer constitutional protections limit governmental action in unincorporated territories.[62] However, the case law would shed little light on the meaning of incorporation itself, thus leaving open many questions concerning this second feature of his doctrine. In 1917, the Jones Act would confer U.S. citizenship, though not representation, upon the residents of Puerto Rico (an action taken by Congress without consulting the Puerto Rican people).[63] The Supreme Court would explain soon thereafter that U.S. citizenship had not incorporated the island into the Union, and would use this opportunity to establish that incorporation requires the express intent of Congress.[64] Beyond that, the Supreme Court has not elaborated on the scope of Congress's discretion with respect to the final status of unincorporated territories. The dispute over the precise content of this power is at the heart of today's status debate. The central questions in this dispute—must Congress decide, at some point, what to do about a territory's final status, and may Congress implement a final, noncolonial status other than statehood or independence?—continue to divide the people of Puerto Rico, to whom we now turn.

Constitution and Membership: Puerto Rico and the Legacy of the Insular Cases

A century after the status of the new territories occupied center stage in American political and scholarly discussions, the issue and the colonies it affected have long faded from the national stage, but the debate rages on in the territories themselves. In Puerto Rico, discontent with the island's current status is well-nigh universal, but the island is deeply divided both as to what the island's status ought to be instead and as to what, constitutionally, it may be.

It is widely agreed that both Congress and a majority of the inhabitants of the territory must consent to any resolution to the current colonial situation and that the terms of a transition out of the current status must be acceptable to both sides. There is also little dispute that an agreement to implement either statehood or independence would not run afoul of the Constitution, although there are a number of questions concerning the requirements of a transition into either of these options, such as whether an independent Puerto Rico could retain U.S. citizenship for its people, or whether a state of

Puerto Rico could remain officially bilingual, as the island has been for most of the past century. Similar questions apply to the options in between statehood and independence: it is not clear, for instance, whether any status other than statehood could guarantee U.S. citizenship for people born in Puerto Rico, nor is it clear whether any status other than independence could guarantee that Spanish would remain one (or the) official language of the island. But the intermediate options raise additional questions, since the idea of a permanent, nonterritorial status that is neither statehood nor independence—nor any of the other options provided for in the Constitution—is without precedent in American federalism, and necessarily involves much constitutional terra incognita.

THE DEBATE OVER COMMONWEALTH STATUS

Puerto Rico's transition into "commonwealth"[65] status in 1952 raised these questions in a debate that continues today. Four years earlier, the island had for the first time elected its own governor, choosing the man who conceived of the island's commonwealth status, Luis Muñoz Marín.[66] The founder and leader of the Popular Democratic or "Commonwealth" Party, Governor Muñoz Marín went on to win repeated reelections, remaining in power until he chose not to run for a fifth term in 1964. The transition into commonwealth status officially began when President Truman signed Public Law 600 authorizing a constitutional convention.[67] That convention, in turn, led to the approval in a 1952 referendum of the Constitution of the Commonwealth of Puerto Rico and the new status by a vote of 76.4 percent. This result inaugurated the Commonwealth, but did not put an end to the status debate.

The Commonwealth of Puerto Rico has been described in several judicial opinions, including Supreme Court decisions, as "sovereign over matters not ruled by the [federal] Constitution."[68] Whether this means the island ceased to be an unincorporated territory, and what "matters" exactly the federal Constitution "rules," remain the sources of considerable disagreement.[69] At the heart of this disagreement is the language of the preamble to Public Law 600, to the effect that that law authorized a relationship between island and mainland "in the nature of a compact."[70]

According to the "compact theory," P.L. 600 and the 1950–52 process terminated Puerto Rico's territorial status, unincorporated or otherwise, replacing it with a mutually binding "bilateral compact" which ended Congress's absolute sovereignty over the island under the Territorial Clause, and thus purged the relationship of its colonial attributes.[71] The contrary view holds that P.L. 600 and the process it authorized did not and could not end Puerto Rico's colonial status, because P.L. 600 is a federal law, and is thus repealable by Congress without Puerto Rico's consent.[72] According to this view, Congress could not, even if it wanted to, *permanently* relinquish its nearly absolute sovereignty under the Territorial Clause, except by implementing another status specifically provided for in the Constitution, by amending that document, or by granting a territory independence.[73]

Supporters of the compact theory insist that the adoption of the Constitution of Puerto Rico was itself a sovereign act of the people of Puerto Rico and, as such, that it effected a transfer of sovereignty from Congress which Congress may not rescind. In response, opponents of the compact theory insist that if this "sovereign act" required the authorization of a higher sovereign, it merely represented a delegation of powers of self-government by that higher sovereign. Thus, goes this argument, the relationship may resemble a compact (as the preamble to P.L. 600 acknowledges), but it cannot be a binding agreement, and is therefore still colonial.

This debate continues unabated. The answers to these unresolved questions have important implications with respect to the future of the island. If it is possible for the United States and Puerto Rico to enter into such a truly binding compact—whether or not this happened in 1952—then it may be possible to create a status other than statehood or independence that is not subject to congressional power (and repeal) under the Territorial Clause and thus, arguably, not colonial. If this is not possible, then it would seem that the only way out of the colonial predicament is statehood, independence, or a constitutional amendment. The disagreement is not merely "political": differing views about what is constitutionally possible shape the different views about what is desirable.

Despite this continued disagreement, events subsequent to 1952 (including Supreme Court case law concluding that the Territorial Clause is still the source of Congress's power over Puerto Rico)[74] led to an increasing consensus that whatever the island became in 1952, it did not cease to be some kind of colony of the United States, and that whatever its level of "sovereignty," it is not enough.

The events of 1952 did put an end to the debate at the United Nations, at least for a time. Upon the approval of commonwealth status, at the request of Governor Muñoz Marín, the United States sought to cease transmitting information on Puerto Rico to the United Nations' Decolonization Committee under Article 73(e), which requires administering powers to transmit information on non-self-governing territories.[75] The argument was, of course, that Puerto Rico was no longer a non-self-governing territory—precisely the issue that was disputed. The governor's request initiated an effort that culminated in November of 1953 with the General Assembly's decision that the United States could indeed cease transmitting Article 73(e) reports on Puerto Rico. In theory, this resolved the matter in the international arena. The process, however, further fanned the flames of the debate about the true nature of Puerto Rico's status.[76] Moreover, the process did not put an end to what has been described by one scholar as Governor Muñoz's "gnawing feeling" that Puerto Rico remained a colony of the United States.[77] These doubts led the Commonwealth Party to initiate a vigorous and lasting effort to "perfect" or "enhance" the status achieved in 1952. Efforts to implement these enhancements have thus far encountered the obstacle of a largely indifferent Congress and the opposition of territorial groups who favor statehood or independence, largely because of their own "gnawing feeling" that anything in between will always be colonial.

"ENHANCED" COMMONWEALTH

Proponents of enhanced commonwealth have put forward a slate of desiderata that reveal a vast gap between the current arrangement and a suitably noncolonial status, among them: a grant, by Congress to Puerto Rico, of sovereignty greater than that of a state (but not independence); a promise of permanent union with the United States (but not statehood); a guarantee of U.S. citizenship for persons born in Puerto Rico now and in the future; local control over areas traditionally under federal control, such as immigration and foreign trade; a grant of power for the local government selectively and unilaterally to nullify federal laws on a case-by-case basis; an unambiguous statement by Congress to the effect that the relationship between the United States and Puerto Rico is in the form of a binding compact, alterable only by mutual consent.[78] In short, enhanced commonwealth could be described as a modern-day confederate state or a nation within a nation; its proponents call it the "best of both worlds."

The goal of this combination of features is, put simply, to enable Puerto Rico to maintain a separate national identity, with its distinctive culture and language, and to foster its international personality and economic growth, while preserving U.S. citizenship and deeply entrenched ties (themselves also cultural and economic) to the United States. Under this arrangement, the applicability of constitutional provisions (and federal laws) would still be subject to a case-by-case analysis, but now primarily by Puerto Rico's government.

There can be no doubt that many Puerto Ricans like this idea, regardless of its feasibility. In 1967, an option defined as commonwealth status "with authorization for further development" won a local nonbinding plebiscite with 60.5 percent of the vote, compared to 38.9 percent for statehood and 0.39 percent for independence. A second nonbinding plebiscite in 1993 yielded a narrower victory for enhanced commonwealth, this time with 48.6 percent of the vote, against 46.3 percent for statehood and 4.4 percent for independence. A third nonbinding plebiscite in 1998, discussed in more detail below, yielded a victory for an enigmatic "none of the above" option.

When the first two plebiscites did not lead to congressional action, the legislature of Puerto Rico requested clarification from Congress concerning whether the 1993 plebiscite had had a binding effect and, if so, what steps should follow.[79] In response, the relevant congressional committees made clear that they would not consider the results of a plebiscite to be binding unless Congress first approved the options offered on the ballot.[80] They suggested also that the "enhancements" to commonwealth status might be constitutionally unacceptable, a plausible but contested claim.[81]

This congressional assertion of a prerogative to define the options of a binding plebiscite echoes the imperialist premises implicit in any claim of congressional power over Puerto Rico's fate. At the same time, there is a strong argument that, since Congress must agree to any solution that requires a continuation of U.S. sovereignty (along with a permanent guarantee of U.S. citizenship), congressional agreement to the options *prior* to a plebiscite would save the people of Puerto Rico the grief of an emotionally draining and politically divisive vote that might result in a status not acceptable to Congress—as, by some accounts, has happened every time Puerto Rico has voted on the matter since 1967. This was, in part, the reasoning behind the controversial "Young bill," first introduced in 1996 by Representative Don Young, a Republican from Alaska, and designed to authorize a congressionally sponsored plebiscite with options acceptable to Congress. The Young bill passed by one vote in the House on March 4, 1998, but died in the Senate several months later.[82]

It would be difficult to exaggerate the divisions the Young bill caused. As originally introduced, the bill did take a clear position, as Puerto Rico had urged Congress to do for so long, concerning which status options would be acceptable to Congress. Its position, however, ruled out commonwealth status altogether, causing immediate and overwhelming opposition to the bill on the island, primarily (though not only) on the part of the Commonwealth Party.[83] The ultimate result of the political maneuvering that followed was a bill offering three status options: statehood; commonwealth without "enhancements"; and independence/free association.[84]

The Young bill in its final form remained unacceptable to supporters of enhanced commonwealth status, mainly the Commonwealth Party. They argued that, by leaving out the enhanced commonwealth option (which had, after all, prevailed in previous plebiscites), the bill failed to respect the people's right of self-determination. This, combined with the inclusion of the far less attractive status quo version of "commonwealth" (along with several other aspects of the bill's wording), led to widespread charges that the Young bill was slanted in favor of the statehood option.[85] The response of the bill's supporters to these objections was that a number of features of enhanced commonwealth are, simply, constitutionally impermissible; that the bill represented what Congress would accept (based on what is constitutional); and that if the lack of enhancements to commonwealth status would lead the people to prefer statehood, this would be the appropriate consequence of a ballot offering accurate definitions of truly viable status options. Because the bill died in the Senate, Congress's official position on the status issue remains unresolved.

Frustrated by the demise of the Young bill, the pro-statehood government held a third nonbinding plebiscite in December 1998. The options on that ballot included: independence; "free association" (this time as a status distinct from independence); statehood; commonwealth (again without enhancements); and "none of the above."[86] The government loosely modeled the options on those provided by the Young bill rather than consulting with the other political parties. That decision, and the wording chosen to describe the "commonwealth" option, led the Popular Democratic Party to oppose this plebiscite as well, urging voters to protest it by choosing "none of the above." While, by some accounts, the government's definition of *commonwealth* shined the unforgiving light of truth on the colonial status quo (thus giving the people a chance to express their opinion on the status quo, rather than on the "best of both worlds" version of commonwealth that had been presented in prior plebiscites), by other accounts this definition improperly distorted the status quo, once again trying to force a vote for statehood. Either way, that option did not do well. A mere 0.06 percent of the electorate voted for the (unenhanced) commonwealth option, while 50.3 percent chose "none of the above," and 46.6 percent opted for statehood. "Free association" and independence split the remainder.

What did this result mean? The mainland media dramatically oversimplified the matter by reporting a victory for the status quo. And in truth, nothing would change with "none of the above." Yet if this were the whole truth, the results of the December 1998 plebiscite would be, above all, heartbreaking, for until that moment, a divided electorate had at least agreed in its rejection of the current colonial status. The choice, though, was arguably just the opposite: an emphatic rejection of yet another futile exercise—another nonbinding referendum for which Congress, once again, had failed to approve the options, and which it would therefore be likely to ignore. Thus, even as the mainland wondered at Puerto Rico's inability to make up its mind, Puerto Ricans once again began to wait for Congress to make up its mind.

Membership and Recognition: Beyond the Legacy?

The seemingly irreconcilable divisions in Puerto Rico's status debate are the result not only of disagreements about the constitutionality of the options but also about their desirability. A resolution of the question of constitutionality would bring one much closer to understanding the options for decolonization, but not all the way there. The normative questions embedded in the status debate concern the kinds of trade-offs that distinct racial, ethnic, and cultural groups ought to be able to make in order to maintain their association with a larger polity while asserting and protecting their distinctive identities.

RECOGNITION VERSUS REPRESENTATION

In the case of Puerto Rico, this question is raised in starkest form in the context of voting and representation, because a status in between statehood and independence, no matter what its advantages, would not include equal representation at the federal level for U.S. citizens living in Puerto Rico (unless this were implemented via constitutional amendment). This is one example of an acknowledged limit on Congress's power to prescribe a status for territories: the states' federal representation may not be diluted, and only states, and to a limited extent the District of Columbia, have a right to federal representation.

Under the intermediate statuses now sought, equal federal representation would be traded for the combination of greater local sovereignty and permanent association to the mainland described above. In this scenario, some form of nullification power over federal laws would presumably make up for the lack of representation. Many see the price in this trade-off as too high: they consider the idea of remaining U.S. citizens without equal representation in the federal government as colonial, even if this comes with a reduced level of federal sovereignty and a high level of local sovereignty. Many others see in such increased local sovereignty, with the kind of group recognition it would imply, a cure for the colonial attributes of the lack of representation at the federal level.

This disagreement poses an extremely difficult challenge in the context of American liberalism. On the one hand, groups emerging from a colonial status have an especially strong moral claim to official government recognition, on *their* terms. (Colonial status, of course, is a form of "group recognition" too.) On the other hand, group recognition is in tension with the ideals of liberalism whenever it involves the sacrifice of rights and privileges ordinarily associated with citizenship. The embodiment in law of different statuses for different racial, cultural, and ethnic groups strays dangerously far from the principle of individual equality before the law, and must be judged in that context as well.

In other words, whereas the arguments of the imperialists of the turn of the century—that the cultural integrity and economic development of the mainland must be fostered at the expense of its colonies—have long been discredited, today few would argue with the idea that the cultural integrity and economic development of the *colonies* must be fostered. The risk, of course, is that this would once again come at the expense of a group—though now only a subgroup within the colony, made up of those who, by voting either for statehood or independence, continue to reject the idea of partial, unequal membership in any nation.

This tension, between a colonial group and the subgroups within it, reveals one of the most intractable problems of the status debate: discerning the "will of the Puerto Rican people." Appeals to the right of self-determination and the will of the Puerto Rican people embody extremely important principles, to be sure, and denote essential preconditions in the process of decolonization. Yet they also beg the most difficult questions of the status debate, for to accept that a group of U.S. citizens living under federal sovereignty may exchange representation (or any other right or privilege associated with U.S. citizenship) in return for greater local sovereignty— and that this may be done over the opposition of a minority within that group—is to accept an arrangement for that group that would not be acceptable for U.S. citizens living in a state.

Perhaps such an arrangement is the best solution to the island's unique colonial dilemma; perhaps Puerto Rico's differences do, after all, demand a different system of government. Yet as long as that system involves federal sovereignty and American citizenship, the United States has an obligation to evaluate it according to those principles that ordinarily apply to its "own" citizens. It must not again rely on what seems good enough for "other" people. The latter, after all, looks suspiciously like the reasoning that sanctioned colonialism a century ago.

In Puerto Rico, any of the numerous views on status involves enormously complex commitments; a constructive conversation about status must not oversimplify them. The debate on status reaches its lowest point when one group is accused of being willing to jettison its culture, or another of being willing to dispense with true equality, or another of yielding to an inflexible vision of national identity. In fact, Puerto Ricans are confronted with impossibly difficult choices imposed upon them by centuries of colonial domination. It is quite likely that all Puerto Ricans wish to preserve their culture, ensure true equality, and nurture a communal identity, and that they disagree as to how best to achieve this combination of goals. Accusations to the contrary debase the discussion of status. That these desires sometimes seem contradictory, or that their content varies from party to political party, is not the result of one side's desire to sabotage the other's vision. It is the result of a colonial legacy that has produced conflicting identities, conflicting desires, and conflicting commitments, and situated those conflicts in a complex network of legal forms, precedents, and principles. With this legacy in mind, we hope with this book to make a contribution toward a constructive conversation, and toward the long-awaited resolution to the status question.

Summary of Chapters

José A. Cabranes paves the way for a dialogue about territorial status with a historical overview of the relationship between Puerto Rico and the United States during the past century. Identifying those easily forgotten areas of consensus in Puerto Rico's status debate, he approaches the explosive topic of territorial status with his observations on that "political expletive," the word *colonialism*. Noting that the term can be informative as well as pejorative, and choosing to use it in the former sense, he reminds us that the idea of colonialism is useful simply because it points toward common ground, since *all* of the political camps of Puerto Rico seek *de*colonization.

Mark S. Weiner provides a rich account of the intellectual atmosphere that made U.S. colonialism possible, in an analysis that explores a concept he calls "ethno-juridical discourse." Moving beyond the claim that law can be an instrument for the pursuit of racist aims, Weiner argues that race and law are mutually constitutive concepts. In this account, the idea that the Anglo-Saxon race was superior to other races—an idea at the root of the turn-of-the-century desire to govern territories without admitting them into the Union—was entangled with the idea that Anglo-Saxon culture was especially suited for lawmaking and state-building. This reasoning justified colonialism not simply with the idea that whites were superior, but rather that they were superior at *governing*—a notion clearly on the minds of the justices in the *Insular Cases.*

Brook Thomas's contribution locates the events of the turn of the century in the context of a transformation in the United States's conception of itself as a nation. He describes the events surrounding the Spanish-American War as part of a fundamental transition from an idea of the United States as a "compact of contracting entities" to that of a "corporate model of a nation-state," whereby, somehow, the "United States" ceased to be a plural term; *they* became *it.* Thomas explains the role of the metaphor of "incorporation" in this process, and in doing so, shows how metaphor generally (and, in *Downes,* the metaphor of incorporation specifically) facilitates legal transformation by maintaining the appearance of continuity.

A similar interest in the power of language informs Efrén Rivera Ramos's analysis of the category of "unincorporated territories." Unmasking the colonial aims of this category, Rivera draws attention to another way in which legal rhetoric facilitates transformation, in this case by maintaining the appearance of neutrality. As Rivera sees it, the creation of the "unincorporated territory" not only was a questionable strategy based on illegitimate claims to sovereignty, but has long been discredited, and must no longer be cited in the debate on territorial status. He calls on Congress simply to renounce its absolute sovereignty over these territories, wrongly claimed and unjustifiably upheld in the *Insular Cases,* and to proceed with a solution to Puerto Rico's status on the basis of a recognition of the island's sovereignty.

This reminder that the status debate must contend with the *Insular Cases,* be they an illegitimate obstacle or a binding precedent (or, distressingly, both), provides a transition into Sanford Levinson's discussion of the place of the *Insular Cases* in the canon of constitutional law—or rather, their lack of a place there, an oversight that Levinson decries and addresses here. Levinson's analysis offers something valuable and unusual: a review of the wealth of material on pre-1898 territorial history that we find in *Downes.* By discussing the key role of the *Insular Cases* in the broader history of American territories, Levinson points the way toward a revisionist account of American constitutional history.

Juan Perea's contribution also locates the *Insular Cases* within the broader history of the United States, in this case its previous attempts to withhold full membership from racial "others" while exercising sovereignty over them nevertheless. Perea describes how racist attitudes against Mexicans caused resistance to their admission as full members in the nation, at the same time that their lands were readily annexed. Perea uses this precedent to shed light on the legal reasoning in *Downes* and the later treatment of Puerto Ricans.

In the next essay, E. Robert Statham Jr. then argues that those previous instances were perhaps analogous but also different in important ways. Statham identifies a framework for understanding what happened in 1898–1901 that distinguishes these territorial acquisitions from their precursors. The difference, in short, was that the rationale for expansion had changed from some notion of growth to an idea of power. While territorial acquisition had been part of a process of domestic growth until 1898, from that point on the United States seems to have decided it was finished "growing," even as it acquired more territory. The reason for this change, Statham explains, was that the acquisitions of 1898 crossed an imaginary line dividing diversity of the tolerable kind from diversity of an unacceptable sort. "Growth" could accommodate the former; only imperialism could handle the latter.

Gerald L. Neuman closes Part I with a synthesis of two centuries of territorial jurisprudence, laying the groundwork for the legal and constitutional specificities that we encounter when we turn to the case of Puerto Rico in Part II. His account proposes dividing territorial jurisprudence into a number of phases, with two major approaches evolving throughout these phases. The "membership" approach recognizes a privileged relationship to the constitutional project for some individuals or locales under the government's sovereignty—one might call them "members." The second approach, or "mutuality of obligation" approach, requires that a claim of sovereignty be justified by the enjoyment of corresponding constitutional rights and limits for all; that is, all who are subject to a nation's sovereignty must be full members in it. According to this framework, the *Insular Cases* represent a version of the "membership" approach, denying membership to the inhabitants of territories under American sovereignty. Asking whether this may have created "parallel" constitutional systems, one for members and another for territorial (and other) nonmembers, Neuman challenges the assumption that we are governed by a unified constitutional document.

Mark Tushnet's essay opening Part II picks up where Neuman's leaves off. If this nation has created parallel systems—indeed, even if a territorial majority demands a parallel system—is this the course we should pursue? Should the nation accede to a territorial majority's claim to partial membership? After all, as Tushnet points out, that local majority may in turn be a minority on the national stage. And if the nation should accede, would this be consistent with the ideals of liberal political theory on which the United States is founded? By addressing these questions, Tushnet takes up the crucial issue of the United States's obligation to define its own position in response to conflicting claims among territorial groups.

In the two essays that follow, Juan R. Torruella and José Trías Monge engage these questions by addressing the constitutional implications of the intermediate status options at issue in Puerto Rico's debate. Their pieces are best read together, as they in many ways set forth the two principal positions on the constitutional questions of Puerto Rico's status debate. Torruella's rigorous and exacting analysis identifies the specific constitutional parameters that define and limit the available status options, while Trías's imaginative and learned account calls into question the validity of such limits. Their respective views on what is desirable stem largely from their different readings of the Territorial Clause of the U.S. Constitution: recognizing the absence of direction in the vague words of this clause, Trías turns for guidance to models from the international arena; Torruella seeks his guidance from the text of the Constitution as a whole.

Roberto Aponte Toro joins this discussion along lines similar to those of Trías, proposing that Puerto Rico's status dilemma be resolved in the context of international alternatives to American federalism. Although he briefly considers some of the constitutional principles that might stand in the way of certain alternatives for Puerto Rico, Aponte's inspiration derives from elsewhere; he sees currently evolving notions of sovereignty, citizenship, and the nation-state as alternatives preferable to a strict reading of the requirements of traditional American federalism.

José Julián Álvarez González shares Aponte's concern with the limitations of the American federalist system in fulfilling the needs of Puerto Rico, but rather than an exploration of alternatives, his piece is a rigorous critique of the specific alternative of statehood. Focusing on cultural concerns instead of economic ones, and particularly on the problem of language, Álvarez argues that the American federalist system poses not merely limitations but great dangers for the survival of Puerto Rico's native Spanish language. In Álvarez's view, the "equality" of statehood means the inequality and destruction of Spanish, and ultimately of Puerto Rico's identity. That, he argues, is no equality at all.

Ángel Ricardo Oquendo also addresses the problem of cultural survival, but rejects the project of debating status options per se. In his view, rather than debate any given status, the options themselves should take shape around already existing and nearly universal consensus on several key issues: Puerto Ricans of all persuasions, Oquendo argues, want both a permanent relationship with the United States and official recognition of their distinctness from other Americans. Accepting these premises, he says, we should simply explore which relationship will best serve these goals. His essay does so in the context of the work of political theorists including Jürgen Habermas, John Rawls, Michael Walzer, and Charles Taylor.

The closing chapters, by Richard Thornburgh and Rogers Smith, turn to a recent controversy in Puerto Rico over the existence and nature of "Puerto Rican citizenship," a debate which exemplifies the historical contingency of claims to particular national identities. The events they address concern an instance of self-imposed "exclusion," in which a leading Puerto Rican political figure, Juan Mari Brás, renounced his U.S. citizenship and declared himself a "citizen of Puerto Rico." The underlying question: is there such a thing as a "citizen of Puerto Rico" who is not a U.S. citizen? The answer, according to the local Supreme Court, was yes, but the U.S. State Department disagreed.

Locating this debate within the context of Puerto Rico's constitutional and legal status, Thornburgh insists that any dialogue on the content of the citizenship of territorial residents, and thus on territorial status, must consider what the various alternatives imply about the structure of the Union. By examining the light that American federalism sheds on Mari Brás's claim, Thornburgh engages in the status debate as other mainland Americans should: by confronting the implications that a parallel system, to use Neuman's terms, would have for the nation as a whole.

In his thoughtful closing essay, Rogers Smith evaluates the same issue by returning to history, addressing the debate over Puerto Rican citizenship by exploring its legal sources, and examining their implications for Mari Brás's claim. While not questioning the force of what he sees as a strong moral claim to a distinct Puerto Rican citizenship, Smith questions the local Supreme Court's legal basis for recognizing that citizenship: the Foraker Act of 1900, which denied Puerto Ricans U.S. citizenship, calling them "citizens of Porto Rico," even as it established congressional sovereignty over them— and all of this on the basis of Puerto Ricans' supposed racial inferiority. This, Smith argues, is a less than ideal source for a claim to Puerto Rican citizenship.

This last essay encompasses many of this volume's principal themes: that the debate on the status of unincorporated territories must not ignore the lessons of history; that it must contend with the American constitutional and legal context in which it has evolved; that the moral and legal claims in the debate are distinct but inextricably linked and mutually influential; that there remain in this debate many unresolved tensions and opposing views; and that these opposing views, deeply rooted and passionately held, require a careful and honest engagement, even as they militate against easy answers. A careful and honest engagement—but no easy answers—is what we have to offer in this book.

Notes

We thank Jesse Furman and Andrew Zimmerman for their comments on earlier drafts of this introduction.

1   182 U.S. 244 (1901). Today, the "U.S. territories" include Puerto Rico, the U.S. Virgin Islands, Guam, the Northern Mariana Islands, and American Samoa. The United States also exercises sovereignty over a number of unpopulated islands. See GAO, Report to the Chairman, Committee on Resources, House of Representatives, *U.S. Insular Areas: Application of the U.S. Constitution* (November 1997); Stanley K. Laughlin, *The Law of United States Territories and Affiliated Jurisdictions* (1995); Arnold Leibowitz, *Defining Status: A Comprehensive Analysis of U.S. Territorial Relations* (1989).

2   There has been some inconsistency in scholars' identification of which opinions belong under the rubric of the *Insular Cases,* but *Downes* is always on the list, and is universally recognized as the leading case in the series. See "A Note on the *Insular Cases*" in this volume.

3   *Downes,* 182 U.S. at 341–42. The case in which the Court unanimously and expressly adopted Justice White's reasoning was *Balzac v. Porto Rico,* 258 U.S. 298 (1922). *Balzac* is generally agreed to be the last in the series of the *Insular Cases.*

4   Justice White himself did not use the term *unincorporated;* rather, he spoke of "incorporation" and mentioned "disincorporation." Eventually, those territories which had not been incorporated became known as "unincorporated" territories.

5   Art. IV, sec. 3, cl. 2: "The Congress shall have Power to dispose of and make all needful Rules and Regulations respecting the Territory or other Property belonging to the United States."

6   Some territories, including Puerto Rico, have non-voting "representatives" in the House; others have no presence in Congress at all. On the territories' presence in Congress, see Abraham Holtzman, "Empire and Representation: The U.S. Congress," *Legislative Studies Quarterly* 11 (1986): 249.

7   See, e.g., Leibowitz, supra note 1, at 40–45.

8   See, e.g., "Proposal for the Development of Commonwealth," adopted by the governing board of the Popular Democratic Party (PDP), October 15, 1998 (on file with author); see also José Trías Monge, *Puerto Rico: The Trials of the Oldest Colony in the World* (1997), at 124–35, for an account of the PDP's efforts to enhance commonwealth status since the 1950s.

9   182 U.S. 244 and 182 U.S. 1 (1901).

10   On this period, see David Trask, *The War with Spain in 1898* (1981); Julius Pratt, *Expansionists*

of 1898: The Acquisition of Hawaii and the Spanish Islands (1959); Robert L. Beisner, *Twelve against Empire: The Anti-Imperialists, 1898–1900* (1968). For the Treaty of Paris, see *Treaty of Peace between the United States and the Kingdom of Spain, U.S. Statutes at Large* 30 (1899): 1754.

11   *Joint Resolution for the Recognition of the Independence of the People of Cuba, U.S. Statutes at Large* 30 (April 20, 1898): 738, at 739 (the "Teller Amendment"). See also *Neely v. Henkel,* 180 U.S. 109 (1901) (discussing the United States's temporary exercise of sovereignty over Cuba).

12   Treaty of Paris, supra note 10, art. IX, at 1759.

13   Frederic R. Coudert, "The Evolution of the Doctrine of Territorial Incorporation," *American Law Review* 60 (1926): 801. (An abridged version of this article appears in *Columbia Law Review* 26 (1926): 823.) Coudert and his colleagues at the renowned international law firm Coudert Brothers were the plaintiffs' attorneys in *De Lima* and *Downes.*

14   The imagery of the Constitution following the flag had already been employed in other constitutional and political debates. It echoed, for instance, the rhetoric of antebellum debates over the status of slavery in the territories, in which Southerners, led by John Calhoun, had insisted that the Constitution "followed the flag" to the territories as part of the broader argument that slavery could not be prohibited by Congress in territories (see, e.g., Alfred Brophy, Note, "Let Us Go Back and Stand upon the Constitution: Federal-State Relations in *Scott v. Sandford,*" *Columbia Law Review* 90 (1990): 192, at 205–6), as well as rhetoric used in debates over the expansion of trade (i.e., "trade follows the flag") (see Brook Thomas's essay in this book).

15   See supra note 5.

16   See, e.g., H. Teichmueller, "Expansion and the Constitution," *American Law Review* 30 (1899): 202; see generally Beisner, supra note 10; Christopher Lasch, "The Anti-Imperialists, the Philippines, and the Inequality of Man," *Journal of Southern History* 24 (1958): 319.

17   Lebbeus R. Wilfley, "How Great Britain Governs Her Colonies," *Yale Law Journal* 9 (1900): 207; "The Rights of a Conqueror," *Legal Times* 109 (1900): 217. That McKinley's victory gave the presidency to the imperialists is beyond debate, though the view that his support for imperialism was considered the deciding factor by the electorate has been questioned. See Thomas A. Bailey, "Was the Presidential Election of 1900 a Mandate on Imperialism?" *Mississippi Valley Historical Review* 24 (1937): 43.

18   *U.S. Statutes at Large* 31 (1900): 77.

19   Carman F. Randolph, "Constitutional Aspects of Annexation," *Harvard Law Review* 12 (1898): 291; Simeon E. Baldwin, "The Constitutional Questions Incident to the Acquisition and Government by the United States of Island Territory," *Harvard Law Review* 12 (1899): 393; C. C. Langdell, "The Status of Our New Territories," *Harvard Law Review* 12 (1899): 365; James Bradley Thayer, "Our New Possessions," *Harvard Law Review* 12 (1899): 464; Abbott Lawrence Lowell, "The Status of our New Possessions—A Third View," *Harvard Law Review* 13 (1899): 155.

20   The former were Randolph and Baldwin; the latter, Langdell and Thayer.

21   Lowell, supra note 19, at 156.

22   Ibid. at 176.

23   Ibid. at 170–72.

24   Note that Lowell was writing before Congress instituted a civil government in Puerto Rico via the Foraker Act, supra note 18. In *Downes,* Justice White would not only echo Lowell's argument but would also conclude that the Foraker Act had not incorporated Puerto Rico.

25   See Abbott Lawrence Lowell, "The Colonial Expansion of the United States," *Atlantic Monthly*

83 (1899): 145. Rogers Smith's essay in this book compares Lowell's dry legal reasoning in the *Harvard Law Review* with his more racially charged rhetoric in the *Atlantic Monthly.*

26   Our discussion in the next section will not focus directly on race, but we share the view of several of the essays that follow that race and cultural difference played a central role in the debate over imperialism.

27   Teichmueller, supra note 16, at 202.

28   Charles Warren, *The Supreme Court in United States History* (1924), cited in Jaime B. Fuster, "The Origins of the Doctrine of Territorial Incorporation and Its Implications Regarding the Power of the Commonwealth of Puerto Rico to Regulate Interstate Commerce," *Revista Jurídica Universidad de Puerto Rico* 43 (1974): 259, at 263 n. 6.

29   Owen M. Fiss, *Troubled Beginnings of the Modern State, 1888–1910,* vol. 8 in *History of the Supreme Court of the United States,* ed. Stanley N. Katz (1993), at 226.

30   *United States Constitution,* art. I, sec. 8, cl. 1.

31   *Downes,* 182 U.S. at 247 (Brown, J.). For accounts of the *Insular Cases* that include some of the relevant biographical details about the Justices, see Fiss, supra note 29, and Juan R. Torruella, *The Supreme Court and Puerto Rico: The Doctrine of Separate and Unequal* (1985), at 40–84.

32   *Downes,* 182 U.S. at 287 (White, J., concurring).

33   Ibid. at 344 (Gray, J., concurring).

34   Ibid. at 347 (Fuller, C. J., dissenting) and 375 (Harlan, J., dissenting).

35   See, e.g., Efrén Rivera Ramos, "The Legal Construction of American Colonialism: The Insular Cases, 1901–1922," *Revista Jurídica Universidad de Puerto Rico,* 65 (1996): 225, at 269; Torruella, supra note 31, at 53; Coudert, supra note 13, at 809.

36   *Downes,* 182 U.S. at 282.

37   Ibid. at 280 and 282–83.

38   Ibid. at 276–77.

39   Ibid. at 277.

40   Ibid. at 292 (emphasis added).

41   Ibid. at 293.

42   Ibid. at 373.

43   Ibid. at 382.

44   Most scholars make reference to the "flag" phrase simply to evoke the contemporary rhetoric; a few have observed that this way of framing the question is not the best way to describe the substance of the opinions in the *Insular Cases.* See, e.g., Fiss, supra note 29, at 228; Leibowitz, supra note 1, at 19. However, other scholars use the "flag" rhetoric and the corresponding idea of *ex proprio vigore* applicability of the Constitution to explain the central issue in the *Insular Cases.* See, e.g., Marybeth Herald, "Does the Constitution Follow the Flag or Can it be Separately Purchased and Sold?," *Hastings Constitutional Law Quarterly* 22 (1995): 707, at 708. One scholar, represented in this book, has objected to an alternative formulation of the question, arguing that the central issue in the *Insular Cases* was precisely whether the Constitution applied *ex proprio vigore* (or followed the flag) to the new territories. See Rivera Ramos, supra note 35, at 269 (criticizing Chief Justice Taft's formulation of the question [following Justice White] in *Balzac v. Porto Rico,* 258 U.S. 298, 312 [1922]).

45   Fuster, supra note 28, at 264.

46   For an exhaustive account of the constitutional status of nineteenth-century territories, published just after the decisions in the first seven *Insular Cases* and including a supplement on these opinions, see Henry Wolf Biklé, "The Constitutional Power of Congress over the Territory of the United States" (Supplement), *American Law Register* 49 (1901): v–120.

47 See, e.g., *Late Corporation of the Church of Jesus Christ of Latter Day Saints v. United States,* 136 U.S. 1, 44 (1890) (*Mormon Church*) (explaining that Congress would be subject to fundamental constitutional limitations in the territories, "but these limitations would exist rather by inference and the general spirit of the Constitution from which Congress derives all its powers, than by any express and direct application of its provisions"); *Thompson v. Utah,* 170 U.S. 343, 349 (1898) (citing *Mormon Church*).

48 Subsequent case law has held that the Sixth Amendment right to a trial by jury does not apply to unincorporated territories, and it has subjected these territories to differential treatment under the Constitution and federal laws. See *Hawaii v. Mankichi,* 190 U.S. 197 (1903) (holding that Sixth Amendment right to trial by jury did not apply to Hawaii between its cession and its incorporation); *Dorr v. U.S.,* 195 U.S. 138 (1904) (Sixth Amendment trial by jury did not apply to Philippines); *Balzac v. Porto Rico,* 258 U.S. 298 (1922) (same for Puerto Rico); *Califano v. Torres,* 435 U.S. 1 (1979) (per curiam) (upholding denial of SSI benefits to residents of Puerto Rico); *Harris v. Rosario,* 446 U.S. 651 (1980) (per curiam) (upholding lower rates of AFDC assistance in Puerto Rico than in states).

49 *Murphy v. Ramsey,* 114 U.S. 15, 44 (1885).

50 *Thompson,* 170 U.S. at 348 (citing *National Bank v. Yankton,* 101 U.S. [11 Otto] 129, 133 [1879]); *Mormon Church,* 136 U.S. at 43 (same).

51 Unincorporated territories were, of course, denied not only a promise of statehood but also of independence. The latter was equally objectionable, though it was not what distinguished the new territories from previous U.S. territories.

52 See, e.g., *McAllister v. United States,* 141 U.S. 174, 187–88 (1891) (explaining that lack of tenure of territorial court judges was justified in part by the fact that territorial status was temporary); *Snow v. United States,* 85 U.S. 317, 320 (1873) (explaining that territories are in a "term of pupilage"); *Pollard's Lessee v. Hagan,* 44 U.S. 212, 224 (1845) (describing territorial governments as "temporary territorial governments"); *Loughborough v. Blake,* 18 U.S. (5 Wheat.) 317, 324 (1820) (explaining that territories are in "state of infancy advancing to manhood, looking forward to complete equality"). The pattern of governance set forth by the Northwest Ordinance of 1787 and implemented throughout the nineteenth century established that statehood would ensue soon after the population of a territory was sufficiently large (and sufficiently assimilated into the "Anglo-Saxon" mainstream). For a similar emphasis on the effects of the *Insular Cases* on ultimate status, see Arnold Leibowitz, "Trying to Gain Dignity and Maintain Culture," *Revista Jurídica de la Universidad Interamericana de Puerto Rico,* vol. 17 (1982): 1, at 8 ("[W]hat was at issue was whether the usual pattern of territorial evolution leading toward Statehood [as set forth in the Northwest Ordinance] would be changed."); José A. Cabranes, *Citizenship and the American Empire: Notes on the Legislative History of the United States Citizenship of Puerto Ricans* (1979), at 50 ("[T]he Court made it possible, in time, for the nation to accept the principle of self-determination free of the suggestion that statehood was the inevitable destiny of the new colonial territories.").

53 See, e.g., *United States Constitution,* art. I, sec. 8, cl. 17 (District of Columbia); *United States v. Kagama,* 118 U.S. 375 (1886) (Indian tribes).

54 This deferral, it should be noted, was also different from, and more harmful than, the postponement of *admission* itself—which had been common in prior territories. By inventing the idea that "incorporation" (as distinct from "acquisition") stood for the commitment to eventual statehood, the Court made possible not only the deferral of admission but the deferral of any congressional decision at all with respect to a final status—a deferral that, in the case of Puerto Rico and Guam, is now entering its second century.

55   *Downes,* 182 U.S. at 372. Fuller continued: "and, more than that, that after it has been called from that limbo, commerce with it is absolutely subject to the will of Congress, irrespective of constitutional provisions." This second clause suggests that Fuller thought that even incorporation might not require the applicability of the Uniformity Clause. This point is arguable; Justice White's opinion had not gone so far, though perhaps Fuller's point was that the case-by-case analysis White had proposed could lead to this result. In any case, Fuller's observation that Puerto Rico would be trapped "like a disembodied shade" eloquently summed up the greatest damage that *Downes* inflicted on the new territories.

56   Ibid. at 341–42.

57   182 U.S. 1. The term "incorporation" actually made its first appearance in the *Insular Cases* in Justice McKenna's dissent in *De Lima,* in which he was joined by Justices Shiras and White. See ibid., at 200.

58   See, e.g., Charles E. Littlefield, "The Insular Cases" (Parts 1 and 2), *Harvard Law Review* 15 (1901–2): 169 (1), 281 (2); and, more recently, Torruella, supra note 31, at 53 n. 202. But see [James Bradley Thayer] J. B. T., "The Insular Tariff Cases in the Supreme Court," *Harvard Law Review* 15 (1901–2): 164. Justices Gray and Harlan explicitly criticized the apparent inconsistency of Justice Brown's opinions. See Justice Gray's dissent in *De Lima,* 182 U.S. at 220, and Justice Harlan's dissent in *Downes,* 182 U.S. at 386.

59   *De Lima,* 182 U.S. at 200.

60   Walter LaFeber, "The Constitution and U.S. Foreign Policy: An Interpretation," *Journal of American History* 74 (1987): 695, at 707, 714.

61   *De Lima,* 182 U.S. at 200.

62   With respect to Puerto Rico, see, e.g., *Balzac,* 258 U.S. 298 (Sixth Amendment right to trial by jury does not apply); *Torres v. Puerto Rico,* 442 U.S. 465 (1979) (Fourth Amendment applies, either directly or via the Fourteenth Amendment); *Examining Board v. Flores de Otero,* 426 U.S. 572 (1976) (due process and equal protection guarantees apply, either through the Fifth or the Fourteenth Amendment); *Calero-Toledo v. Pearson Yacht Leasing Co.,* 416 U.S. 663 (1974) (due process guarantees apply, either through the Fifth or the Fourteenth Amendment). For a discussion of this case law, see Torruella, supra note 31, at 100–115.

63   See generally Cabranes, supra note 52.

64   *Balzac,* 258 U.S. at 311.

65   This status is known in Spanish as the *Estado Libre Asociado,* which literally translated means "Free Associated State." Contrary to what this phrase suggests, Puerto Rico's relationship to the United States is not one of "free association." The United States does have relationships with several freely associated republics. These are independent countries which have entered into treaties of free association with the United States. See Leibowitz, supra note 1; Howard Loomis Hills, "Compact of Free Association for Micronesia: Constitutional and International Issues," *International Lawyer* 18 (1984): 583.

66   A concise account of these events appears in Trías Monge, supra note 8, at 107–18.

67   *U.S. Statutes at Large* 64 (1950): 319.

68   See, e.g., *Posadas de Puerto Rico Associates v. Tourism Co.,* 478 U.S. 328 (1986); *Alfred L. Snapp & Son v. Puerto Rico,* 458 U.S. 592 (1982); *Rodríguez v. Popular Democratic Party,* 457 U.S. 1 (1982); *Calero-Toledo,* 416 U.S. 663.

69   Certainly some of this disagreement arises out of similar statements by the Court even before 1952, describing the island's unequivocally colonial government with terms such as "autonomous," "quasi-sovereign," and "commonwealth" even while it still had an appointed governor. See *Puerto Rico v. Shell Co.,* 302 U.S. 253, 261–62 (1937): "The aim of the Foraker Act and the

Organic Act was to give Puerto Rico full power of local self-determination with an autonomy similar to that of the states and incorporated territories. . . . The effect was to confer upon the territory many of the attributes of *quasi*-sovereignty possessed by the states—as, for example, immunity from suit without their consent. . . . 'A body politic'—a commonwealth—was created" (citations omitted).

70 "Be it enacted by the Senate and House of Representatives of the United States in Congress assembled, that, fully recognizing the principle of government by consent, this Act is now adopted in the nature of a compact so that the people of Puerto Rico may organize a government pursuant to a constitution of their own adoption." Preamble, Public Law 600, supra note 67.

71 For arguments in favor of the compact theory, see, e.g., Arnold H. Leibowitz, "The Applicability of Federal Law to the Commonwealth of Puerto Rico," *Georgetown Law Journal* 56 (1967): 219; Rafael Hernández Colón, "The Commonwealth of Puerto Rico: Territory or State?," *Revista del Colegio de Abogados de Puerto Rico* 19 (1959): 207; Calvert Magruder, "The Commonwealth Status of Puerto Rico," *University of Pittsburgh Law Review* 15 (1958): 1.

72 For arguments against the compact theory, see Torruella, supra note 31, at 144–200; Grupo de Investigadores Puertorriqueños, *Breakthrough from Colonialism: An Interdisciplinary Study of Statehood* (1984), at 1300–2; Carlos Soltero, "Is Puerto Rico a 'Sovereign' for Purposes of the Dual Sovereignty Exception to the Double Jeopardy Clause?" *Revista Jurídica de la Universidad Interamericana de Puerto Rico* 28 (1994): 183, at 194–97.

73 Independence is of course "provided for" by the Constitution as well, to the extent that that document empowers the federal government to enter into relations with foreign sovereigns.

74 See *Harris*, 446 U.S. 651.

75 On these events at the United Nations, see Trías Monge, supra note 8, at 121–24; Torruella, supra note 31, at 160–66.

76 See the discussion in Torruella, supra note 31, at 144–200. Torruella reviews the evolution of commonwealth status with an emphasis on the federal government's usually ambiguous and often contradictory statements on Puerto Rico's status.

77 I borrow here from Trías Monge. See supra note 8, at 116.

78 These features have been elements of a number of proposed bills and recommendations addressing the status issue since 1952. See ibid. at 124–35. See also "PDP Proposal," supra note 8.

79 H. Conc. R. 62, adopted by the Legislature of Puerto Rico, December 14, 1994. On the first two plebiscites, see Trías-Monge, supra note 8, at 130–35.

80 See, e.g., letter to Hon. Roberto Rexach Benítez, President of the Senate of the Commonwealth of Puerto Rico, and Hon. Zaida Hernández Torres, Speaker of the House of the Commonwealth of Pueto Rico, from Rep. Don Young, Chairman, House Committee on Resources; Rep. Ben Gilman, Chairman, Committee on International Relations; Rep. Elton Gallegly, Chairman, Subcommittee on Native American and Insular Affairs; and Dan Burton, Chairman, Subcommittee on the Western Hemisphere, February 29, 1996, at 4 (on file with author).

81 Ibid. at 3–4. See also *Report together with Additional Views [to Accompany H.R. 856]*, Rept. 105–31, 105th Cong., 1st sess., at 23–30; *Report together with Additional and Dissenting Views [To Accompany H.R. 3024]*, Rept. 104–713, 104th Cong., 2d sess., at 16, 18–23, 29–30.

82 *United States–Puerto Rico Political Status Act*, H.R. 856, 105th Cong., 2d sess. (1998). The Senate thereafter held a series of "workshops" on Puerto Rico's status, but issued only a resolution on the matter. See *The Puerto Rico Self-Determination Act*, S. 472, and S.R. 279, 105th Cong., 2d sess. (1998).

83 See H.R. 3024, 104th Cong., 2d sess. (1996) (offering two options: [1] statehood; and [2]

independence or free association under a "separate sovereignty" option). Independence and "free association" appeared under one option because each of these statuses is, in effect, independence; under "free association," Puerto Rico would become a separate, sovereign, and independent nation, and would enter into a treaty of free association with the United States. See Hills, supra note 65.

84   On "independence/free association" as one option, see note 83.

85   This criticism was fueled by the fact that Puerto Rico's "resident commissioner," the island's elected but non-voting representative in the House, an advocate of statehood and former pro-statehood governor, supported the Young bill.

86   See "Puerto Rico's Still-Cloudy Future," Editorial, *Tampa Tribune,* December 29, 1998, at 8. As mentioned above (at note 83), "free association" is a form of independence. It was included as a separate option on this ballot perhaps because the idea is gradually gaining currency in Puerto Rico.

I. History and Expansion

Some Common Ground

José A. Cabranes

It is now a century since the war that brought Puerto Rico under the American flag—the war that John Hay described (in a famous letter to his friend and political ally Theodore Roosevelt) as "the splendid little war; begun with the highest motives, carried on with magnificent intelligence and spirit, favored by that fortune which loves the brave."[1] In this volume we commemorate that "splendid little war" and renew a conversation on the subject that, a century ago, convulsed American politics and the Supreme Court—the constitutional law and politics of national identity. This was serious business in 1898, and it is serious business today.

Our terms of discourse will consist largely of constitutional doctrine and political theory. But my task is on a less grandiose plane. It is merely to recall that national identity is inevitably shaped less by *theory* than by *history*. And colonial peoples are, everywhere and always, exquisitely sensitive about the history of their relationship to the metropolitan state—a history of which others may be blissfully ignorant, but a history which the colonial people live and breath every single day.

Understandably, the colonial people's vision of the future will be greatly affected by their view of the past, maybe as much as by abstract notions of equality and freedom. Accordingly, we do well to take seriously the observation of the late Richard Pares of Oxford University, a student of British colonial history, that in these matters "[g]ood history cannot do so much service as money or science; but bad history can do almost as much harm as the most disastrous scientific discovery in the world."[2]

It is the common experience of all colonial peoples—not merely the experience of the Puerto Ricans—to feel that history has dealt them an inadequate hand. There is no such thing as colonialism that is not accompanied by an acute and deeply felt sense of historical aggrievement—feelings of having long been subordinated, slighted, ignored, and marginalized.

Expressions of anger or frustration on this score, by friend or foe of the metropolitan state, should surprise no one; they are in the nature of things, commonplace and perfectly understandable. Powerlessness is what colonialism is all about. And decolonization in all its varieties—whether it is national independence, autonomy or free association, or political integration into the metropolitan state on the basis of equality—is everywhere supposed to be the antidote to this historical political impotence.

So it is that even well-intentioned political initiatives and good-faith statements of common interest, conveyed without a full appreciation of historical context, can cause confusion and agitation in many sectors of a colonial society. And when the dust settles, persistent hostility and frustration, or worse, may be all that remains.

Because my comments concern history and our terms of discourse, in an effort to identify some common ground among all the participants in this debate I pause for a moment to dwell on a word that I have already used, and one which we will hear often in any discussion of Puerto Rico's history and its future—*colonialism.*

Americans, whose country was born of anticolonial struggle, often (and understandably) cringe at the word *colonialism* when it is applied to United States history or practice—they react with surprise, and even irritation, in those rare instances when they are required to think about the people of the overseas territories of the United States. This reaction to the word *colonialism* is understandable, because the term became a bad word in the past half century; it was made a bad word by those who successfully revolted against colonialism, and also by the propaganda machinery of the Soviet Union, which during the Cold War ceaselessly attacked the Western powers on account of their overseas territories.

In a striking example of the politics of language, the word *colonialism* became in our time a political expletive. Most Americans have come to think that colonialism is something nasty and mean by definition, something that may be attributable to certain European states but certainly not to the United States.

So when the word *colonialism* is uttered to describe some aspects of the American Century, it tends to raise more than a brow or two. All the more reason, therefore, to try to speak plainly about our history and avoid the confusion that frequently accompanies the use of this word as a cliché and an epithet. I, for one, do not use it in this pejorative sense.

Speaking plainly and honestly about our history requires us to acknowledge, without rancor and without embarrassment, that *colonialism* is a simple and perfectly useful word to describe a relationship between a powerful metropolitan state and a poor overseas dependency that does not participate meaningfully in the formal lawmaking processes that shape the daily lives of its people.

Colonialism is a useful term for our purposes especially because it is *decolonization* that is, in truth, the animating force behind each of the major political camps in Puerto Rico today. However much they may each disagree with this point, however much they may differ in their choice of means—and however much they attack the authenticity or legitimacy of their adversaries—Puerto Ricans do share a common goal of seeing Puerto Rico evolve, by mutual consent, toward a greater measure of control over its own destiny. For a great many, this means statehood or some form of political autonomy. For others, far fewer in number, independence. Crucially, even those who favor the island's present commonwealth status have consistently demonstrated their own dissatisfaction with the status quo, and their leaders have repeatedly proclaimed their desire for greater autonomy and self-government.[3]

In short, it is fair to say that *all* of Puerto Rico's political movements seek to chart a path toward a postcolonial future, whatever form it may take. The central political problem of Puerto Rico remains, as ever, decolonization and how it is to be fully achieved.

So for all the differences in outlook that emerge from any discussion of decolonization in Puerto Rico, it bears emphasizing that a remarkably broad consensus for change and constitutional reform exists in Puerto Rico. There is some common ground as to ends, if not as to means.

In recent years, Puerto Rico's postcolonial destiny has been in the news again, reappearing on Washington's radar screen as it does periodically whenever a major election or plebiscite is in the offing. In March 1998, the U.S. House of Representatives adopted, by a margin of only one vote, a bill sponsored by Representative Don Young of Alaska, the Republican chairman of the House Resources Committee, Speaker Newt Gingrich, and Resident Commissioner Carlos Romero Barceló of Puerto Rico (the island's only representative in Congress). The Young bill, which was supported by President Clinton and most House Democrats, would establish a long-term process for consulting the electorate of Puerto Rico on its choice of a permanent political status.

To most Americans, the vote in the House came as a surprise. Nowadays the subject of Puerto Rico's political status is obscure and difficult to understand. Indeed, the treatment of the issue by some elements of the media and some celebrity commentators was confused and full of conceit, revealing an embarrassing ignorance of the history of the United States. The issue was often handled facetiously, regarded as trivial or even silly. All in all, what little discussion there was of the subject seemed to me unworthy of serious commentators on public affairs.

This was not always so. From the hindsight of a hundred years it may be difficult to believe, but at the turn of the century the future of Puerto Rico and the Philippines, and their relationship to the United States, were subjects of the greatest significance to all Americans. It dominated the presidential campaign of 1900, and it precipitated constitutional litigation described by John W. Davis as "the most hotly contested and long continued duel in the life of the Supreme Court."[4] Another prominent lawyer of the time, Frederic R. Coudert, reported that these cases had caused more turmoil on the Supreme Court than any case since *Dred Scott.*[5]

Why was this so? Because then, far more so than now, the question of Puerto Rico's political status was understood to raise basic questions of national identity—the national identity of the Puerto Ricans, for sure, but also the national identity of the United States.

The "paramount issue" of the presidential election of 1900—what today we would call the "hot button issue" of the campaign—was, according to William Jennings Bryan and the Democratic Party platform of that year, "imperialism" and, in particular, the decision of the McKinley administration and Congress to retain indefinitely the insular territories extracted from Spain in the Treaty of Paris of 1898, which ended the Spanish-American War.[6]

Whether these territories would be regarded as "part of the United States" or as colonies in the European imperial tradition, and how the people of these territories, including Puerto Rico, would be treated under the American flag, were reduced to the famous question, "Does the Constitution follow the flag?"[7] The political division on this question was between (on the one hand) the advocates of a "large policy" or imperialism, advocated most vigorously by the heroic Republican candidate for vice president, Theodore Roosevelt, and (on the other hand) those like Bryan and the Democratic Party who claimed that the Constitution of the United States had no room for territories whose people could be held indefinitely in a position of political subordination.

From the beginning, the debate on imperialism revealed many contradictions and ironies. Some of the anti-imperialists, who argued against annexation of these insular territories, were not advanced thinkers but merely racists, who had nothing but contempt for the Filipinos and the

Puerto Ricans and simply wanted to have nothing to do with them. And it was often the proponents of colonialism who showed respect for these island peoples and who expressed the hope that they would become a part of the United States.

In 1900, McKinley and Roosevelt resoundingly trounced William Jennings Bryan and the Democrats, thereby resolving the "paramount" political issue of the campaign in favor of imperialism.[8] Within months, the Supreme Court followed, blessing the American colonial experiment in the now largely forgotten *Insular Cases*.[9] The Court did so by answering (in effect) that the Constitution did not "follow the flag." To simplify greatly, the Court held that Puerto Rico and the other new insular territories were not "foreign territory," but it also held that they were not "a part of the United States" for all constitutional purposes.

The constitutional theory enunciated by the *Insular Cases,* known as the doctrine of territorial incorporation, had been devised in the *Harvard Law Review* in 1899, in an article by Abbott Lawrence Lowell, then a professor of government and soon to become president of Harvard University.[10] The doctrine of territorial incorporation recommended by Lowell and adopted by Justice Edward Douglass White (and, in due course, by the whole Court) held that "whilst in an international sense [Puerto] Rico was not a foreign country, since it was . . . owned by the United States, it was foreign to the United States in a domestic sense because the island had not been incorporated into the United States, but was merely appurtenant thereto as a possession."[11]

In sum, Congress was empowered by the Court "to locally govern at discretion."[12] In other words, the United States could hold Puerto Rico and the other insular territories indefinitely, without ever making them "a part of the United States" and without holding out the promise of eventual statehood or according their people the full panoply of constitutional rights enjoyed by the citizens of the states.

The Supreme Court decisions in the *Insular Cases* of the turn of the century, which determine the fate of Puerto Rico to this very day, prompted the great Irish-American political sage of the turn-of-the-century tabloids, Mr. Dooley, sarcastically to articulate one of the most enduring, and most quoted, rules of American constitutional adjudication (and I translate now from the New York Irish of Mr. Dooley): "[N]o matter whether the constitution follows the flag or not, the supreme court follows the election returns."[13]

The doctrine of territorial incorporation has survived for a century. It is fair to say that it was devised in order to make colonialism possible. Ironically, this constitutional doctrine, by recognizing Congress's plenary authority to determine the status of "unincorporated" territories such as Puerto Rico, also made possible great and innovative political changes over time—changes that reflected the social, economic, and political development of the island, and reflected also the democratically expressed aspirations of its people.

There can be little doubt that change came slowly, too slowly in the views of virtually all Puerto Ricans. In the flush of war and the rush for empire, the desperately poor people of one of Spain's most neglected colonies had been promised, by the commanding general of the American invading forces, "the fostering arm of a nation of free people, whose greatest power is in its justice and humanity to all living within its fold." They had been assured that the object of American rule would be to "promote your prosperity and to bestow upon you the immunities and blessings of the liberal institutions of our government."[14]

By this standard, most Puerto Ricans have counted the first half century of American rule, from 1898 until 1948, as a disappointment. Puerto Rico's governors were appointed by the president of the United States, and it was not until 1946 that President Truman appointed a Puerto Rican to that position. Under two "organic acts" passed by Congress in 1900 and 1917, Puerto Rico's local government was patterned generally on those of the mainland territories and states, but from 1900 until 1917 the Puerto Rican electorate voted only for the lower house of a bicameral legislature, with significant power vested in an appointed upper chamber. It was not until 1917 that Puerto Ricans were accorded an elected senate and made citizens of the United States. And during this first half century, their acute and widespread poverty knew little relief.

A painful, but accurate, snapshot of Puerto Rican society during the first half century of colonial rule was provided by the great American journalist John Gunther in 1941, in one of his famous *Inside* books—*Inside Latin America* (and I quote only a bit of his devastating portrait):

> I plodded through the streets of San Juan, and I took a brief trip or two into the countryside. What I found appalled me.
>
> I saw rickety squatter houses perched in garbage-drenched mud. . . .
>
> I saw native villages steaming with filth—villages dirtier than any I ever saw in the most squalid parts of China. . . .
>
> I saw, in short, misery, disease, squalor, filth. It would be lamentable enough to see this anywhere. It would be shocking enough in the

remote uplands of Peru or the stinking valleys of the Ganges. But to see it on American territory, among people whom the United States has governed since 1898, in a region for which our federal responsibility has been complete for 43 years, is a paralyzing jolt to anyone who believes in American standards of progress and civilization.[15]

It was not until the election of the populist and charismatic Luis Muñoz Marín as governor, in 1948—with his determination to transform Puerto Rico by attracting capital investments from the mainland and by massive efforts to attack poverty and to lift standards of living—that Puerto Rico began its rise from abject misery and its concomitant movement toward political empowerment of the Puerto Rican people.

Although Puerto Rico remains relatively poor—with a per capita income of just $8,000 per year compared with $26,000 per year in the mainland[16]—it is certainly no longer the grim and pitiable place that John Gunther described more than half a century ago. It can now fairly be described as part of "the first world."

This economic transformation coincided with the growth of a vibrant, if sometimes tumultuous, democracy. Muñoz, the centenary of whose birth Puerto Ricans also commemorated in 1998, turned away from advocacy of national independence and became the architect and prime mover of a distinctive form of decolonization—a distinctive political and constitutional formula—based on "autonomy." This political status, known in Spanish as the *Estado Libre Asociado de Puerto Rico,* and in English as the Commonwealth of Puerto Rico, was purposely designed to avoid either independence or statehood, and to evoke the idea of dominion status familiar in the evolving British Commonwealth of Nations.

Muñoz's populist and transformative economic and social policies coincided with the adoption of this new political status in 1952, which he consistently promoted as one based on mutual consent—the consent of the people of Puerto Rico as well as the consent of the Congress of the United States—and one destined to evolve over time toward greater self-government. Advocates of both statehood and independence vigorously dissented, viewing the commonwealth arrangement as a subordinate constitutional status.

Notwithstanding his controversial vision, Muñoz could have retained power indefinitely, in the tradition of other Latin American political leaders of his day. Instead, he deliberately surrendered personal power in 1964 after sixteen years at the helm. In so doing, he reinforced and institutionalized the island's democratic tradition.

It is precisely because the roots of this democratic political culture have

penetrated so deeply in Puerto Rico that a process of *democratic* decolonization, initiated by Muñoz Marín, is possible. Indeed, what sets Puerto Rico
apart from virtually all other places that have "decolonized" is precisely this:
In Puerto Rico, there is well-nigh universal agreement that change will
come, if at all, only through the use of the ballot—and only by mutual
consent.

There is indeed some common ground in Puerto Rico: As noted earlier,
there *is* a firm consensus for change. The vigorous debate on the island's
political status is over which vision of the future to embrace. But there is
little question that, in the last analysis, it is largely the Puerto Ricans themselves who will shape their postcolonial destiny and complete the work of
political empowerment begun by Luis Muñoz Marín. Successive U.S. administrations have clearly indicated that they are prepared to support the
firmly and democratically expressed aspirations of the people of Puerto
Rico. I have no doubt that, in time, these aspirations will win the support of
the people of the United States, for whom self-determination and democracy are sacred words.

In the meantime, Puerto Ricans of all persuasions will have to come to
terms with the fact that American political processes—by design—are slow
and cumbersome. And they will have to recognize that even victorious
political movements achieve their objectives only through prolonged advocacy of their cause in Washington. Nothing happens automatically under
the American political system. Delays and frustrations are inevitable. But
no one, in my view, should assume that Puerto Rican aspirations are destined to be spurned by mainland Americans, once the political process has
run its course.

With this in mind, and with the history of the past century as a backdrop,
we are afforded an opportunity to resume the exploration of national identity that galvanized a great public debate a century ago. We thus embark
upon an inquiry that an earlier generation of Americans understood to be
as much about the United States as about Puerto Rico. But today we do so
with a confidence that Puerto Ricans and all Americans share a common
devotion to democratic principles—to majority rule and to the rule of law.
An inquiry informed by these principles is one that is well worth undertaking, as Puerto Ricans and all Americans look back on a century of social and
economic transformation and begin to contemplate what a new century
holds in store.

The public debate on this question will mirror, to a large extent, the
debate that has dominated the public life of Puerto Rico for decades. The

debate will be divisive, as always; Puerto Ricans take politics very seriously, and even while many argue that Puerto Rico lacks political influence, Puerto Ricans themselves are Herculean political infighters.

For all the divisiveness of the debate, we would do well to recall that, as I have emphasized, there is indeed some common ground here: There is the common feeling of political weakness and marginality; there is the common yearning for change; there is the common aspiration for the empowerment of the people of Puerto Rico; there is the common good faith of the competing movements and their leaders; and there is the common longing for the Puerto Ricans to stand upright and unbowed.

Notes

1 Frank Freidel, *The Splendid Little War* (1958), at 3.

2 Richard Pares, "The Revolt against Colonialism," in *The Historian's Business and Other Essays*, ed. R. A. and Elisabeth Humphreys (1961), at 82.

3 See, e.g., Rafael Hernández Colón, *La Nueva Tesis: Estrategia para el Desarollo Integral de Puerto Rico* (1979); José Trías Monge, *Puerto Rico: The Trials of the Oldest Colony in the World* (1997).

4 John W. Davis, "Edward Douglass White," *American Bar Association Journal* 7 (1921): 378.

5 See *Scott v. Sandford,* 60 U.S. (19 How.) 393 (1857); Frederic R. Coudert, "The Evolution of the Doctrine of Territorial Incorporation," *American Law Review* 60 (1926): 801, at 840.

6 See Julius W. Pratt et al., *A History of United States Foreign Policy,* 4th ed. (1980), at 187–88; see also Thomas A. Bailey, "Was the Presidential Election of 1900 a Mandate on Imperialism?," *Mississippi Valley Historical Review* 24 (1937): 43.

7 Coudert, supra note 5, at 801.

8 See Pratt, ibid.; Bailey, supra note 6.

9 See, e.g., *Downes v. Bidwell,* 182 U.S. 244, 341–42 (1901) (White, J., concurring); see also *Rassmussen v. United States,* 197 U.S. 576 (1905) (Alaska); *Dorr v. United States,* 195 U.S. 138, 149 (1904) (Philippines); *Hawaii v. Mankichi,* 190 U.S. 197 (1903) (Hawaii); *Balzac v. Porto Rico,* 258 U.S. 298, 305 (1922) (Puerto Rico).

10 See Abbott Lawrence Lowell, "The Status of Our New Possessions—A Third View," *Harvard Law Review* 13 (1899): 155.

11 *Downes,* 182 U.S. at 341–42.

12 Ibid. at 290.

13 Finley Peter Dunne, *Mr. Dooley on the Choice of Law,* ed. E. J. Bander (1963), at 52.

14 *Documents on the Constitutional History of Puerto Rico* (1964), at 55 (quoted in Trías Monge, supra note 3, at 30); see also Bailey W. and Justine Whitfield Diffie, *Porto Rico: A Broken Pledge* (1931), at 3.

15 John Gunther, *Inside Latin America* (1941), at 423.

16 Lucinda Harper, "Puerto Rico Offers Mixed Merits as State," *Wall Street Journal,* March 16, 1998, at A2.

Teutonic Constitutionalism:
The Role of Ethno-Juridical Discourse
in the Spanish-American War

Mark S. Weiner

Jurisprudence is the general part of adjudication, silent prologue
to any decision at law.—Ronald Dworkin, *Law's Empire*

There are people in the world who do not understand any form of
government . . . [and] must be governed.—Sen. Albert J. Beveridge,
"Our Philippines Policy"

In the following discussion, I examine the ideological foundations of the
Spanish-American War—and the subsequent legal decisions that established the peculiar constitutional status of the island of Puerto Rico— from
a perspective broadly influenced by the emerging scholarly movement
known as the cultural studies of law. Scholars associated with the cultural
studies of law seek to use the multidisciplinary methods associated with
British and American cultural studies in their analysis of legal history and
contemporary legal issues. One of the special concerns of cultural studies is
the social and political analysis of rhetoric, and I address that concern here
through an analysis of the rhetoric of citizenship.[1] Specifically, I argue that
the global American empire that emerged after 1898, and in whose shadow
the people of Puerto Rico continue to live today, was based on a discrete
type of civic language. I call this civic language "ethno-juridical discourse."[2]
Ethno-juridical discourse was a way of characterizing the proper boundaries of civic life in which the concepts of race and law were mutually
constitutive; it was a normative political idiom in which the questions
"What is race?" and "What is law?" were fundamentally interconnected.
This language drew upon two seemingly distinct vocabularies for its lexi-
con, that of jurisprudence and that of anthropology, blending them in such
a way that the two were indistinguishable from one another. I believe ethno-
juridical discourse has been a fundamental though previously unrecog-

nized fact of the legal and intellectual history of United States citizenship, forming a basic conceptual building block of modern notions of civic membership.[3]

The character of ethno-juridical discourse has changed over time, following the history of social scientific thought more generally. The form of ethno-juridical discourse central to the Spanish-American War was based on a type of social scientific analysis known as the "Teutonic origins thesis" of American government. Proponents of this thesis claimed that the greatest American legal achievements found their spiritual origin in the free and strong warrior peoples of ancient Germany described by Tacitus in the *Germania*. In making this claim, Teutonic origins scholars characterized Anglo-Saxons as a people with a special genius for law and for state-building; they described the state and legal order itself as Anglo-Saxon in character; and they portrayed dark-skinned peoples as incapable of legality and thus essentially criminal. This racial-legal vision was central to the Spanish-American War in two respects: first, it undergirded the thought of those political leaders who pushed the United States into the conflict; second, it formed the logical basis for the legal decisions that followed in the wake of the Treaty of Paris. To show this intellectual unity, I juxtapose one of those leaders and one of those decisions, showing how they share a common mode of ethno-juridical thought. The political leader is Senator Henry Cabot Lodge, blue-blood Bostonian politician, influential advocate of U.S. imperialism, and early student of the Teutonic origins thesis, a man whose life underwent many changes but whose soul was bound together by a consistent ethno-juridical vision. The decision is *Downes v. Bidwell* (1901), one of the *Insular Cases* (1901–04), the series of Supreme Court decisions that determined the constitutional status of Hawaii, Puerto Rico, and the Philippines and that left Puerto Rico "foreign in a domestic sense."[4] I believe the ethno-juridical worldview Lodge advanced was the distinctive jurisprudential vision of *Downes* and the *Insular Cases,* the "silent prologue" to the legal decisions whose consequences are examined throughout this volume.

Henry Cabot Lodge and the Anglo-Saxon State

A brief history of the Spanish-American War might trace the following narrative.[5] The late nineteenth century was an unstable and corrupt time in Spanish political life. After being overthrown in 1868, the Spanish monarchy was reinstated by a coup d'état in 1874, beginning a notorious period in national history known as the Restoration. Upon the death of King

Alfonso XII in 1885, the country fell under the regency of the child princess María Cristina of Austria, and was governed by the rule of *caciquismo*, which one scholar describes as "a system of scheming and manipulations which enabled the political bosses . . . in alliance with the wealthy land-owners, military leaders and government officials to rule the state for their own personal advantage."[6] Caught between a glorious past and its banal present, Spain fell under a "curious mood of self deception," in which any symbol of its self-ascribed national greatness, no matter how small or dubious, assumed high place in Spanish identity. Within this political universe, the colonies of Puerto Rico, the Philippines, and, most importantly, Cuba, played a special role as emblems of a yearning for national power and renown. They were said to be "living proof that God's blessing continued to shine on Spain's imperial status."[7] As living proof of God's blessings often do, this symbolic role belied actual conditions of exploitation—relations of extractive colonial rule that led some Cubans to rebel for independence in the late 1860s, beginning in the poor and underdeveloped province of Oriente. This revolt failed to spread across the island as a whole, and the fighting ended in 1878 with the signing of a truce brokered by Spanish General Arsenio Martínez Campos, who offered a variety of concessions to the rebels. These concessions were never fulfilled, however, and in the 1890s the independence movement resurfaced once more, this time under the leadership of José Martí, who established the Cuban Revolutionary Party in 1892 and launched a new fight for *Cuba libre* in 1895.

This renewed rebellion drew brutal resistance from the Spanish military. With the failure of the Cuban peace, Spain replaced General Campos with General Valeriano Weyler y Nicolau, a highly professional soldier of German descent who had developed a "reputation for ruthlessness" in earlier campaigns in Cuba and Catalonia.[8] With 200,000 troops against approximately 20,000 to 30,000 Cuban rebels, General Weyler undertook a variety of measures in his counterinsurgency campaign. Among the most prominent were, first, the use of specialized trenches approximately six hundred feet in width, filled with "trees, boulders, barbed wire and explosives" and guarded by "forts, towers and blockhouses," to surround Cuban towns and divide Cuban revolutionary forces from each other.[9] The second, more notorious action, for which Weyler still is remembered today, was the first widespread use of "reconcentration camps" as a pacification strategy. In his attempt to combat rebel forces, General Weyler "emptied the countryside of people, crops and livestock" and relocated Cuban civilians en masse to detention centers. By modern estimates, at least 100,000 Cubans died as a result of reconcentration, though assessments at the time put that number at 400,000. Characterized by its direct effect on civilians, General Weyler's campaign aroused international outrage and earned him the nickname "butcher." Neither trenches nor reconcentration, however, fulfilled Spanish hopes. As one military historian suggested recently, "Weyler should instead have taken the offensive, leaving the *trochas* behind and pursuing insurgents ruthlessly until they were pushed to the point of total exhaustion."[10] Whatever the moral merits of this proposed course of action, the rebels were gaining ground. While Spain attempted to concede a certain degree of home rule to Cuba in 1897, the die already had been cast. Spain was engaged in a total war with revolutionaries who made a reasonable claim that their opponents were engaged in systematic acts of lawlessness.

Many Americans were deeply moved by the struggle of Cubans for independence, and provided the rebels with financial and political support. There were a variety of reasons for American sympathy with the cause of Cuba libre. For one, Americans themselves were the symbolic descendants of a revolution and could claim as part of their republican heritage the cause of movements for national independence everywhere. The nation also was still torn by sectional strife between North and South, and it required a common cause that could provide a measure of reconciliation by helping to wash the "bloody shirt." Materially, some Americans feared what Cuban unrest might mean for the economic and political health of the United States. Still others, men like Josiah Strong, were animated by a Protestant sense of mission and a hatred of Catholic monarchy. One might say, in other words, that American investment in the Cuban Revolution was overdetermined. Within this emotional context, after repeated attempts by Presidents Grover Cleveland and William McKinley to escape direct military confrontation, the United States threw itself into war against Spain in 1898 after the well-known explosion of the *Maine,* driven forward by popular outcry against Spanish aggression. The stated purpose of the war was to free Cuba from Spanish domination, though the conflict had much further-reaching consequences. In a brief contest the United States quickly overtook Spain in Cuba, Puerto Rico, and the Philippines, finally bringing the fighting to an end with the Treaty of Paris, which ceded a variety of island colonies to the American nation. Congress soon began to reform the Spanish legal system with which the largely dark-skinned inhabitants of these islands had been governed, and to replace it with American law to impose social and economic order.

Senator Henry Cabot Lodge was one of the primary architects of American foreign policy during this period, and he was one of the most vociferous voices calling for the United States to enter the war with Spain.[11] Born in 1850, Lodge began his political career in the Massachusetts state legislature in the early 1880s, moving to the federal House of Representatives in 1887 and ultimately winning a seat in the United States Senate in 1893. Lodge, a Republican, had a special interest in foreign affairs and was a longtime member of the Senate Foreign Relations Committee. Like his friend Theodore Roosevelt, then Assistant Secretary of the Navy, he was a disciple of Alfred Thayer Mahan.[12] In his celebrated work *The Influence of Sea Power upon History,* Mahan argued that naval power was the central component of international political influence, and that the United States should look outward and develop an overseas empire like those of great European states.[13] As a member of Congress during the Republican McKinley administration, Lodge was able to put Mahan's teachings into practice as an outspoken advocate of American expansion. Lodge's imperial designs were bitterly opposed by his colleague Senator George Hoar of Massachusetts, as well as Senator Eugene Hale of Maine and other anti-imperialist Republicans. This diverse group of men, on the whole, considered overseas expansion to be fundamentally at odds with the spirit of the American nation, which itself had revolted against colonial domination; they believed that the development of an empire would undermine the very nature of American political identity.[14] Still, it was Lodge who ultimately won the ear of the president, helping persuade the more cautious McKinley to declare war on Spain even if the Spanish were willing to make concessions to Cuba or the United States. In this respect, one might describe Lodge as the individual subjective place from which the historical lever of Archimedes moved the geopolitical world.

Those who supported the Spanish-American War did so for a variety of reasons.[15] To understand what the hostilities meant for Lodge in particular, however—and to understand the place of ethno-juridical discourse within the drive toward conflict and the adjudication of the constitutional claims arising from its outcome—it is important to keep in mind a sense of historical periodization. Specifically, it is necessary to recall that the late nineteenth century in the United States was an era of economic and state modernization, similar to that undergone approximately thirty years earlier in western Europe and England, and that the war was a national event that materially advanced this historical movement. When I use the term *modernization,* I refer loosely to Max Weber's discussion of the development of formal, rational, bureaucratic state procedures under capitalism, the growth of a thoroughgoing concern for legal process and neutral administration.[16] But more importantly, I refer to a variety of phenomena that characterized what scholars once called the Progressive Era: the consolidation of national unity, the concentration of domestic wealth, the construction of a professional state apparatus, and the creation of new market outlets for surplus capital. Specifically, I refer to the militant assertion of an overarching American racial identity, the rise of the trusts, the construction of expert reform organizations and civil service bureaucracies, and the quest for foreign markets overseas. Studies of these phenomena reveal the many ways in which, in the late nineteenth and early twentieth centuries, the United States became a distinctively modern nation.[17]

The Spanish-American War was very much a part of this progressive shift. First, the war offered an occasion for national unity at home, healing sectional divisions across the Mason-Dixon, providing a common cause around which a shared national racial identity might be constructed from a fragmented sense of political self. Second, the war brought the United States onto the world stage, creating an overseas empire for a nation previously limited to its own continental territorial boundaries. It launched the United States on its career as a global power. Third, the war fueled industrial economic development and formed the basis for the further concentration of domestic capital through the expansion of global markets. By opening Cuba, Puerto Rico, the Philippines, and various Pacific regions to commercial exploitation—by providing coaling stations for ships on their way to Asian ports, particularly those of China—the war offered an outlet for surplus capital generated at home.[18] Finally, the war required the central administration of colonial peoples through the creation of a complex bureaucratic state apparatus. In the wake of the Treaty of Paris, a group of non-Anglo peoples came under the direct military and civil authority of the United States government, and the nation was forced to construct rational bureaucratic procedures and administrative agencies for maintaining an efficient peace. In these and other respects, the war not only was driven by the symbolic and emotional issues of national liberation, not only was a fight against monarchical Spain, but also participated in and was guided by the creation of a distinctly modern form of social and economic life. It was a war that brought the United States into the twentieth century, a conflict whose historical energies were directed forward, into the coming era.

The modernizing or "progressive" nature of the war is significant for understanding Lodge, because the senator from Massachusetts was hardly representative of the new nation America would become. He instead was a figure from the past, born into an old, distinguished line of Boston Brahmins, a class that had played an enormous role in national life in previous years but that was becoming increasingly marginal as a cultural and political force. Lodge was born in May of 1850, under the roof of a "granite mansion, in the best part of residential Boston." "No other infant who put in a first appearance that day," writes one Lodge biographer, "did so in more propitious circumstance." By the very pedigree of his familial heritage, Lodge was guaranteed "wealth, social position, intellectual stimulation, even a healthy body and reasonably good looks."[19] Lodge's father was a prominent Boston merchant with a stern and rigid cast of mind. His mother, Anna Cabot, who doted on him, sprang from an old and venerated New England family. Her grandfather, Federalist George Cabot, had been elected to the United States Senate and was a close associate of George Washington, Alexander Hamilton, and John Adams. The family itself lived within the highest ranks of Boston society, and its home was the site of visits by Charles Sumner, Henry Wadsworth Longfellow, Francis Parkman, William Prescott, John Motley, Charles Bancroft, and Louis Agassiz. Lodge's upbringing was typical of this elite social class. He attended grade school with the sons of the Bigelows, Cabots, and Parkmans, and later studied at a "private Latin school" with the Chadwicks and the Lymans. He came to know and love Shakespeare, watching Edwin Booth in *Julius Caesar* and *Hamlet;* he grew patriotic for the Union during the Civil War, though he did not become unduly rash or abolitionist in his sentiments; he traveled to Europe with servant and tutor in tow; he enrolled in Harvard College.

Lodge's relation to his family history was deeply reverent, and indeed verged on a form of ancestor worship.[20] After spending several years at Harvard as a self-described mediocre student, in 1871 Lodge launched a career as a scholar, critic, and essayist writing about the past in which his ancestors had played such an important role.[21] In addition to writing this ancestral hagiography, Lodge also served as an assistant editor at the prestigious *North American Review,* where he published numerous articles on topics of patriotic concern, also contributing to the *Nation* and the *Atlantic.* His book-length works during this period present a similar mien. Within only a few years, the prolific young Bostonian published *A Short History of the English Colonies in America,* a biography of Alexander Hamilton, a biography of Daniel Webster, an edited volume of *The Federalist,* a life of George Washington, and various collections of essays on civic themes (much later, in the early 1920s, he and Theodore Roosevelt would publish the equally representative work *Hero Tales from American History; or the*

Story of Some Americans Who Showed That They Knew How to Live and How to Die).[22]

Lodge was highly successful in this literary career, but in the late 1870s he left his life in letters for a life in politics, driven in part by a sense of aristocratic distaste with contemporary American social affairs. Although Lodge continued to write, beginning especially in the 1880s, he devoted himself increasingly to progressive political causes, moving from his home base in Massachusetts into the highest levels of the federal government. While it is common to hear Lodge spoken of with contempt in casual academic conversation today, it is important to recognize that he was also a reformer. Lodge advocated civil service professionalism, for example. Similarly, he supported the use of federal power to protect southern black voting rights, sponsoring the Federal Elections or "Force" bill as a matter of both principle and politics. And he advocated the use of the Sherman Antitrust Act, partly from a cultured opposition to the society of the industrial new rich and to what he meaningfully termed their "lawlessness."[23] Lodge's decision to enter politics—and his ultimate support of imperialist foreign policy—in this respect was a movement at once forward and back, an attempt to bring the past into the present. In the rapidly changing society of the Gilded Age, in an incorporating America, Lodge chose to forsake scholarship so as to rescue himself and his class from irrelevance, from being merely backward-looking men of breeding and history, merely writers and editors of the *North American Review*. While the United States was undergoing the structural changes shaping it into a modern nation, Lodge was attempting to modernize himself.

Significantly for the history of ethno-juridical discourse, in this process of self-modernization Lodge drew deeply on the lessons he learned in the backward-looking scholarly career he set aside—especially from his study of legal history. After graduating Harvard, Lodge remained in Cambridge to receive a degree in law and, in 1876, a Ph.D. in history. This was one of the early doctorates awarded in the discipline in the United States, where the social sciences were just beginning to become professionalized, and Lodge received it less for the study of the past per se than for the study of what has been called historico-politics.[24] Lodge's teacher, in fact, was Henry Adams, the antimodernist Boston Brahmin, an unruly blend of scholar and statesman who was an early enthusiast of the German historical method that became the foundation of much American scholarship in the early twentieth century. Adams led Lodge and two other graduate students through a doctoral seminar on medieval legal history or "Medieval Institutions," the term *institutions* often being used as a synonym for *law* during the period. Under Adams's direction, Lodge spent long hours carefully reading German, Anglo-Saxon, and Latin legal texts, drinking deeply from the highly retrospective and historical subject toward which his teacher had steered him, Anglo-Saxon land law.[25]

Lodge's work was published as "The Anglo-Saxon Land Law" in *Essays in Anglo-Saxon Law,* a volume to which Adams contributed an essay titled "The Anglo-Saxon Courts of Law" and Lodge's fellow students offered "The Anglo-Saxon Family Law" and "The Anglo-Saxon Legal Procedure." The volume makes for curious reading. Merely glancing through it, one notes immediately that it is exceptionally recondite in character, if not dusty and parched.[26] Lodge said as much himself many years later, partly in an effort to distance himself from the life of the mind with which he contrasted his later political career. "I doubt if I could have selected a drier subject," he noted ruefully. The process of writing a dissertation, he complained, "was not inspiriting, it was in fact inexpressibly dreary, and I passed a depressing winter so far as my own labors were concerned. I seemed to be going nowhere and to be achieving nothing. I led a solitary life, except for my immediate family, and I found it a doleful business struggling with the laws and customs of the Germanic tribes, without any prospect, so far as I could see, of either reward or result."[27] Still, despite such objections, Lodge's dissertation was deemed important enough to merit extended analysis by Frederick Pollock (he was deeply critical of Lodge's work, though he thought it showed "much ingenuity"), and the project indeed revealed ample and admirable evidence of the German methods of social science in which Adams had taken care to school his students.[28]

Anglo-Saxon land law was a relatively underdeveloped subject in Lodge's day, and the basic purpose of his project was therefore theoretically modest. He hoped simply to classify the various forms of landholding among ancient Anglo-Saxons and trace their changes over time. This was what one might call basic empirical work. Still, there also was a larger purpose behind Lodge's dissertation, one appropriate to a man deeply reverent of familial heritage and to a practitioner of a kind of family history. This was to bolster respect for the English common law and thereby strengthen the ideological foundations of the American political order. Encouraging reverence for American politics through a dry study of ancient German landholding may seem like a dubious proposition, but it is important to understand that the common law at the time was thought to have developed directly from the law of the Anglo-Saxons before the Norman invasion, and that its spirit in turn was said to find its highest expression in the political institutions of the United States. In this regard, Lodge's work took part in a larger debate among late-nineteenth-century legal scholars between those who revered the Romanized Normans and their way of life and those who favored Teutons. While Lodge was himself partly descendant from Huguenots and so appreciated the Norman position, he generally sided with the Teutonists. "Free from the injurious influence of the Roman and Celtic peoples," Lodge wrote in his dissertation, "the laws and institutions of the ancient German tribes flourished and waxed strong on the soil of England. . . . Strong enough to resist the power of the church in infancy, stronger still to resist the shock of Norman invasion, crushed then, but not destroyed, by foreign influence, the great principles of Anglo-Saxon law, ever changing and assimilating, have survived in the noblest work of the race,—the English common law."[29]

The idea that the greatest English and American political institutions derived from ancient Germany was highly popular in the late nineteenth century, forming the basis of what is known as the Teutonic origins thesis of American government.[30] Advanced by an array of writers and associated with John Burgess at Columbia and Herbert Baxter Adams at Johns Hopkins, the Teutonic origins thesis asserted that Americans were to play a unique role in world history because they were the spiritual and institutional descendants of the free and strong warrior peoples described in the writings of Tacitus, those hardy men and women who shunned gold, avoided pompous ostentation, and were steadfast in battle.[31] In particular, like the Teutons of the *Germania*, the English and Anglo-American people were understood to be specially endowed with a racial genius for law. They were thought to have the basic self-discipline necessary for political liberty and to have an innate capacity for state-building and the maintenance of legality. The Teutonic origins thesis held a dominant place in the social sciences in the years that Henry Adams taught "Medieval Institutions" and Henry Cabot Lodge pored over his Latin texts. Despite its prominence, however, contemporary scholarship on the theory tends to fall short in a critical respect. With the exception of Richard Cosgrove, historians have not done quite enough to stress the ways in which the Teutonic origins thesis formed a scholarly narrative not just about racial development but also about legal history, and that it was based firmly on the work of legal historians and anthropologists.[32] This professional class, from Coke to Maine to Vinogradoff to Maitland, the intellectual forebears of contemporary legal academics, were critical in helping generate the academic belief that white Anglo-Americans were a people especially capable of law and government.[33]

I use the terms *legal history* and *anthropology* somewhat interchangeably in describing the academic origins of the Teutonic thesis, and the conflation is deliberate. Around the time of the Spanish-American War, the social sciences generally were just beginning to become professionalized, and the boundaries between the disciplines were not so clear as they would become later in the twentieth century.[34] This was true of anthropology, which frequently produced works with historical ambitions, and also of history, which often referred to the anthropology of aboriginal peoples in its narrative and analysis. The link between these two seemingly distinct areas of knowledge was a central unifying idea: that of progressive social evolution. The link, that is, was the study of the laws that guided societies in their growth toward more complex and rule-bound forms of self-government—and in the case of the Teutonic thesis in particular, the evolution of the open-air councils, folk-moots, and early parliamentary capacities that fed into the creation of the ordered state. One need only think of the titles of two books of the preceding era to perceive the points at which the two disciplines overlapped: Henry Maine's *Ancient Law* of 1861 and Henry Morgan's *Ancient Society* of 1877, the first a classic work of legal history that relied heavily on anthropological data and analysis, the second a classic work of anthropology whose main focus was the law (and whose author was a New York corporations lawyer).[35] One also might think of Albert Kocourek and John Henry Wigmore's extraordinary edited series *Evolution of Law,* an important set of books published in the 1910s but that drew the majority of its scholarly material from the late nineteenth century, from the work of legal historians, such as Maine, and anthropologists and ethnological jurisprudents, such as John Wesley Powell and Joseph Kohler.[36]

One also might turn in this regard to the words of Lodge's teacher Henry Adams, writing in *Essays in Anglo-Saxon Law.* Himself an admirer of the Romanized Normans, Adams nevertheless advanced historical ideas essentially congruent to those of the Teutonic origins theory to which Lodge even more explicitly subscribed. Describing ancient Germanic society and the place of the modern legal historian in uncovering its present-day symbolic, ethno-juridical meaning, Adams mustered more than his usual eloquence. "The long and patient labors of German scholars," he writes in "The Anglo-Saxon Courts of Law," "seem to have now established beyond dispute the fundamental historical principle, that the entire Germanic family, in its earliest known stage of development, placed the administration of law, as it placed the political administration, in the hands of popular assemblies composed of the free, able-bodied members of the commonwealth." Adams continues:

> This great principle is, perhaps, from a political point of view, the most important which historical investigation has of late years established. It gives to the history of Germanic, and especially English, institutions a roundness and philosophic continuity, which add greatly to their interest, and even to their practical value. The student of history who now attempts to trace, through two thousand years of vicissitudes and dangers, the slender thread of political and legal thought, no longer loses it from sight in the confusion of feudalism . . . but follows it safely and firmly back until it leads him out upon the wide plains of northern Germany, and attaches itself at last to the primitive popular assembly, parliament, law-court, and army in one; which embraced every free man, rich or poor, and in theory at least allowed equal rights to all. Beyond this point it seems unnecessary to go. The State and Law may well have originated here.[37]

In the eyes of many, including Lodge the young doctoral candidate, America originated here as well. And from those wide plains of northern Germany, the United States received its special destiny, to bring to those peoples of the world sitting in darkness the law of a nation whose racial genius was jurisprudential—whose innate, Teutonic ethno-juridical abilities lay in the construction and administration of modern bureaucratic governance.[38]

Teutonic ethno-juridical discourse bears some similarity to other forms of ethno-juridical discourse, especially those used to characterize the racial abilities of Native Americans, but there are at least two ways in which Teutonic ethno-juridical rhetoric is historically unique.[39] The first concerns the nature of what dark-skinned peoples were said to lack. In the ethno-juridical characterization of Native Americans, for instance, Indians were described primarily as a race incapable of holding title to land, and the concept of fee simple absolute was described as peculiarly Euro-American in character. Conversely, the specific point of racial contrast in Teutonic ethno-juridical rhetoric is the state. In Teutonic ethno-juridical systems, Anglo-Saxon peoples are characterized ethno-juridically, above all, by their capacity for state-building. They are described as a people with a special genius for advancing efficient administration, and the state itself is seen as Anglo-Saxon in character. At the same time, dark-skinned others are described as incapable of living within an ordered society and thus existing in a status of essential criminality. The second significant difference between Teutonic ethno-juridical rhetoric and other forms of ethno-juridical discourse lies in its vision of racial intractability. In other forms of ethno-juridical discourse, those describing Native Americans, for instance, racial character is subject to change, sometimes indeed to rapid transformation (thus American Indians in the late nineteenth century were seen as potentially capable of assimilating into the larger white American legal community). In Teutonic ethno-juridical discourse, racial-legal character lacks all plasticity. Racial groups are understood to have ethno-juridical qualities anchored in the very depths of their individual and collective souls. While not explicitly genetic, Teutonic ethno-juridical discourse suggests that race is innate and cannot change over the course of a lifetime or even over the course of a century. In contrast to other ethno-juridical systems, Teutonic ethno-juridical discourse advances a vision of permanent racial-legal hierarchy.

In this respect, Teutonic ethno-juridical rhetoric is evident not only in those works of anthropological legal history that advanced the notion that Anglo-Saxon peoples were uniquely endowed with law—a positive assertion—but also in those works advancing the conjoint proposition, a negative corollary, that darker races were incapable of legal order, that they were slavish children living in earlier stages of evolutionary development. This was particularly the case with what were known as the Malay people of the Philippines, who were considered to be governed not so much by law as by opinion and caprice, who were thought to be racially incapable of the order necessary to live under the rule of a state, a view ultimately derived from Johann Friedrich Blumenbach's "On the Natural Variety of Mankind."[40] It is in this sense that the Teutonic origins thesis was not just racially self-aggrandizing but actively, destructively racist, an extreme form of what Robert Cover has called the jurispathic.[41] As Kocourek and Wigmore write in their *Evolution of Law,* "The greatest productive value of an inquiry into the juridical life of remote ages and of arrested developments lies in providing an indispensable standard by which the processes of human reason, so far as they enter the sphere of legal evolution, are *guided* and *corrected.*"[42] More dramatically, Daniel Brinton, president of the American Association for the Advancement of Science and a primary opponent of Franz Boas's theories of race and culture, in 1896 called on anthropology to become the handmaiden of government by proclaiming, "[T]here is in some stocks and some smaller ethnic groups a peculiar mental temperament, which has become hereditary and general, of a nature to disqualify them for the atmosphere of modern enlightenment . . . an inborn morbid tendency, constitutionally recreant to the codes of civilization, and therefore technically criminal."[43] For Brinton, in a very practical sense, peoples without law were peoples outside of America, a people to remain apart.

This was the intellectual atmosphere in which Lodge lived, and he brought varying shades of these ideas with him into the Senate, in his formulation of American imperialist policy, his discussion of the character and capability of the dark-skinned peoples the United States came to dominate, and in his analysis of the appropriate administrative measures to be taken by colonial rulers in insular governance. Examining Lodge's work in Congress, one finds him consistently expressing a Teutonic ethno-juridical vision—and one finds just how deeply his political concerns were driven by a Teutonic racial worldview. In an 1896 speech on immigration restriction, for instance, Lodge argued that race "is something deeper and more fundamental than anything which concerns the intellect." "When we speak of a race," he proclaimed, ". . . [w]e mean the moral and intellectual characters, which in their association make the soul of a race, and which represent the product of all its past, the inheritance of all its ancestors, and the motives of all its conduct. The men of each race possess an indestructible stock of ideas, traditions, sentiments, modes of thought, an unconscious inheritance from their ancestors, upon which argument has no effect."[44] The greatest race of all, of course, was the Anglo-Saxon, "descended from the Germanic tribes whom Caesar fought and Tacitus described."[45] Storming in waves across the channel into England, these various tribes, over centuries, "were welded together and had made a new speech and a new race, with strong and well-defined qualities, both mental and moral."[46] Lodge wished to restrict immigration, because it would degrade this Anglo-Saxon purity, would erode the racial "motives" of which the United States system of government indeed was just a single expression. "Mr. President," announced Lodge, "more precious even than forms of government are the mental and moral qualities which make what we call our race. While those stand unimpaired all is safe. When those decline all is imperiled."[47]

Lodge's discussion of Philippine policy followed a similar line of argument. When discussing the question of whether the United States should annex the Philippine islands and rule their inhabitants as a colonial power, for instance, Lodge turned to the fundamental racial motives animating Philippine society and to an ethno-juridical consideration of the nature of race itself. "The capacity of a people for free and representative government is not in the least a matter of guesswork," argued Lodge in 1900, two years after the Treaty of Paris had ended Spanish-American hostilities. "The forms of government to which nations or races naturally tend may easily be discovered from history." Echoing Adams's discussion in *Essays in Anglo-Saxon Law*, Lodge continued: "You can follow the story of political freedom and representative government among the English-speaking people back across the centuries until you reach the Teutonic tribes emerging from the forests of Germany and bringing with them forms of local self-government which are repeated today in the pure democracies of the New England town meeting." This historical perspective revealed not simply the permissibility but the need for American colonial power. "The tendencies and instincts of the Teutonic race which, running from the Arctic Circle to the Alps, swept down upon the Roman Empire, were clear at the outset," Lodge stated with blunt facticity. "Yet the individual freedom and the highly developed forms of government in which these tendencies and instincts have culminated in certain countries and under the most favorable conditions have been the slow growth of nearly fifteen hundred years." "You can not change race tendencies in a moment," Lodge warned. "[The] theory, that you could make a Hottentot into a European if you only took possession of him in infancy and gave him a European education among suitable surroundings, has been abandoned alike by science and history as grotesquely false. . . . We know what sort of government the Malay makes when he is left to himself."[48]

In this respect, Lodge's ethno-juridical views were common to other imperialists as well, for instance to his colleague Albert J. Beveridge, whom Theodore Roosevelt described as having "views on public matters [that] are almost exactly yours and mine."[49] Filipinos, proclaimed Beveridge, "are not yet capable of self-government. How could they be? They are not a self-governing race. . . . What alchemy will change the oriental quality of their blood, in a year, and set the self-governing currents of the American pouring through their malay veins?"[50] Anglo-Saxons, on the other hand, for Beveridge, were uniquely capable of state-building. The Anglo-Saxon people "is the most self-governing but also the most administrative of any race in history," he argued. "Our race is, distinctly, the exploring, the colonizing, the administrative force of the world." American imperialist policy, for Beveridge, thus arose "not from necessity, but from irresistible impulse, from instinct, from racial and unwritten laws inherited from our forefathers." "[W]herever our race has gone," he announced, "it has governed."[51] Indeed, even more so than Lodge, Beveridge believed that the U.S. Constitution was merely a single intellectual expression of Anglo-Saxon racial character. In arguing that the Constitution granted Congress extremely broad powers in the administration of colonial peoples, for instance, Beveridge asserted that the seemingly limiting provisions of the Bill of Rights should be read in light of what he called Anglo-Saxon "institutions," the fundamental ethno-juridical character of Americans as a race. "Institutional law is older, deeper, and as vital as constitutional law," argued Beveridge. He proclaimed:

> Our Constitution is one of the concrete manifestations of our institutions; our statutes are another; decisions of our courts are another; our habits, methods and customs as a people and a race are still another. . . . It is our institutional law which, flowing like our blood through the written Constitution, gives that instrument vitality and power of development. Our institutions were not established by the Constitution. Institutional law existed before the Constitution. . . . Partisanship shrieks "imperialism," and asks where we find words to prevent the development of a czar [in the Philippines]. . . . I find it in the speech of the people; in the maxims of liberty; in our blood; in our history; in the tendencies of our race.[52]

When reading ethno-juridical arguments such as those of Beveridge and Lodge, it is important to keep in mind that they represented anything but the strange, antiquated opinions of a passing time. They instead were the arguments of a people who considered themselves to be the forces of *progress,* opinions that were legitimated by one of the most modern groups of the early twentieth century, anthropological social scientists. For Lodge, it was the academic teachings of this new class, ensconced though it might have been in seemingly removed university life, that enabled his own personal modernization—a modernization that at the national, political level was based on a break with the civic tradition that Senators Hoar and Hale so admired: the notion that if the United States ever acquired an overseas colonial empire, it would forfeit its very identity.

Progressive Anglo-Saxon Interpretation in the Insular Cases

The United States, of course, did acquire that empire, and when it did, American jurists faced a series of pressing constitutional questions—questions that reenacted Lodge's own personal drama of modernization at the level of legal doctrine. Here I turn to the *Insular Cases,* and particularly to the case of *Downes v. Bidwell,* decided in 1901. With the conclusion of the Treaty of Paris on December 10, 1898, and the exchange of formally ratified agreements between Spain and the United States on April 11, 1899, the American national government found itself in a new geopolitical position. By the terms of the treaty, Spain had agreed to "relinquish" its sovereignty over Cuba, thus remaining accountable for prewar debts to the island while at the same time enabling the United States to establish a military protectorate in Havana; it had ceded its victors outright the islands of Puerto Rico and Guam; and for the sum of twenty million dollars, it had "sold" to the United States the islands of the Philippines. The American government took somewhat different approaches to each of its new acquisitions. Despite the desire of many imperialists, it did not annex Cuba directly but instead extended it a form of semisovereignty, first ruling it through military force, then through a form of economic colonialism following the transfer of power to a new government under President Tomás Estrada Palma. To Puerto Rico and Guam, the United States granted a liminal status still operative today. And in the Philippines, the source of the greatest geopolitical difficulty after 1898, the United States established itself as an ultimate sovereign power, incurring the resentment of many Filipinos, who began a protracted struggle against their American guardians. Despite this general diversity of approach, in each of its new possessions American actions shared one basic commonality: The United States instituted a series of wide-ranging reforms of social engineering, paying special attention to replacing the Spanish legal system with which the insular territories had been governed and replacing that system with American law.[53]

Until the Spanish-American War, the history of United States expansion had been a continuous one. In 1787, the nation grew to include the Northwest Territories. The Louisiana Purchase of 1803 extended the boundaries of the United States across the Mississippi. Texas became a part of the nation in 1845. Mexico ceded its lands in the West and Southwest in 1848 and 1853. Washington and Oregon joined the nation in 1853 and 1859 respectively. Alaska was purchased in 1866. According to one scholar, throughout this continuous expansion, the United States was guided by a "pattern of territorial development" outlined already in the Northwest Ordinance.[54] The ordinance outlined three basic steps in the acquisition of a territory. The first, which lasted from one to eight years, was that of federal plenary control, in which Congress appointed a governor, along with judiciary and other governmental officers, and assumed a strong hand in decision making for the region. The second period included the ability of territorial residents to elect their own legislature and form a constitution (the governor of the territory, however, was still appointed by Congress, with the ability to over-

turn the efforts of the legislative body). The final stage outlined by the Ordinance was statehood, the creation of an independent government within
the federal system. This pattern of territorial transformation, in which a
territory was acquired, briefly ruled under federal plenary control, and then
granted statehood, was definitively broken in 1898. Whereas the territories
of the western United States always had been conceived as being destined
for eventual membership in the Union, such was not the case with Guam,
Puerto Rico, and, especially, the Philippines. None of these insular possessions was considered a possible candidate for statehood in the foreseeable
future. With the Treaty of Paris, the United States thus broke a pattern of
republican territorial acquisition and entered into a truly imperial phase of
its national political development.

Among the many reasons the insular possessions were not perceived to
be destined for statehood, one played a central role: a sense of Anglo-Saxon
racial superiority. Shared by imperialists and anti-imperialists alike, the
belief in the racial inferiority of residents of the insular territories, especially
Filipinos, was common wisdom. There were exceptions to this general rule,
but for the most part, popular knowledge seems to have associated the
Philippines in particular with the basest forms of savagery, especially with
the head-hunting of the Ilongots, Igorots, and Ifugaos.[55] Significantly, this
perception of Filipinos as racially inferior was explicitly ethno-juridical in
character, focused on native inability for life within an ordered state. Indeed, in this regard, the society of traditional Filipino peoples aroused
much interest as a kind of ethno-juridical curio. "Every Igorot *barrio* has its
judicial body of old men, who dispose of all cases from petty theft to
murder," wrote one commentator, in a work whose staccato presentation
suggests its myopia. "Most penalties take the form of a fine payable in cattle,
or other property. Trial by ordeal is commonly practiced. The *podung*, or
bloody test, consists in boring holes in the scalps of the suspect and his
accuser. The verdict goes to the one who bleeds the least. When one of a
number of persons is believed to be a criminal, each of them is given a
mouthful of dry rice to chew. After mastication this is spat out upon the
hands of the judges and he whose mass exhibits the least saliva is deemed
convicted, in accordance with their proverb, which says, 'A guilty man has a
dry mouth.' "[56] In this respect, in accordance with the views of legal scholars
of the day, the natives of the Philippines were held to be in the very early
stages of the development of criminal law and in the construction of an
absolute legal sovereign, with its attendant willingness to submit to state
command.[57]

Such ethno-juridical assertions were present not only in popular writings but also in official government anthropology. When the United States began to govern the Philippines, it commissioned a series of studies to gather data that might be of use in insular administration, undertaking a general ethnographic survey of the islands.[58] The Taft Commission itself was headed by William Howard Taft, who met with the high praise of Theodore Roosevelt and Justice Henry Billings Brown, author of the opinion of the Court in *Downes*.[59] Among the products of the Commission's survey were Albert E. Jenks's "Bontoc Igorot," William A. Reed's "The Igorrotes of Zambales," Emerson Christie's study of native languages, Otto Scheerer's "Notes on the Nabaloi Dialect of Benguet," E. Y. Miller's "A Brief Report on the Bataks of Paragua," and a translation by N. M. Saleeby of "33 manuscripts, in part originals and in part copies" on the "History and Laws of the Moros" ("a knowledge of Moro law, customs, and ideas, such as these translations will afford," asserted the Commission, "should be very useful in dealing with the Moro tribes").[60] These studies deserve future detailed analysis, though that cannot be my purpose here.[61] Suffice it to say that, while many were strictly factual, revealing great scholarly care,[62] some included descriptions of native peoples, especially those living in small-scale tribes, that rested on the same vision of racial hierarchy that animated popular accounts of the region. "It is universally conceded," stated the Commission, for example, "that the Negritos of to-day are the disappearing remnants of a people which once populated the entire archipelago. They are, physically, weaklings of low stature, with black skin, closely-curling hair, flat noses, thick lips, and large, clumsy feet. In the matter of intelligence they stand at or near the bottom of the human series, and they are believed to be incapable of any considerable degree of civilization or advancement."[63]

It was in this ethno-juridical context that the Supreme Court heard the series of disputes that together would be known as the *Insular Cases*, especially the case of *Downes v. Bidwell*. The specific legal questions of the dispute in *Downes* revolved around the Uniformity Clause of Article I, section 8 of the U.S. Constitution, which requires that "all Duties, Imports and Excises shall be uniform throughout the United States."[64] While the case included a variety of legal and factual complexities not worth discussing here, the basic issue the Court faced was relatively straightforward: Was Puerto Rico part of the "United States" or not? If the Court held that the Foraker Act indeed made Puerto Rico part of the United States by establishing a civil government on the island, then Downes's oranges were exempt from the collector's tariff, because the imposition of duties on goods arriving from Puerto Rico would violate the Uniformity Clause. It would be an unconstitutional use of federal power to place duties on imports arriving from one part of the United States to another, analogous to the federal government today placing special duties on goods arriving from California to New York. On the other hand, if Puerto Rico were a "foreign country," despite the Foraker Act, then duties placed on goods arriving from Puerto Rico fell under the legitimate power of Congress, and the New York customs agent could have his way. In this interpretive reading, the Foraker Act could be understood as both establishing a civil government on the island of Puerto Rico under ultimate American control, yet at the same time imposing duties on the region as a territory that was not part of the United States itself.

At one level, then, *Downes* was a case about money. As always in great constitutional matters, however, the issue at stake was far more general than the financial, a question much broader than whether the Foraker Act imposed duties on merchandise imported to New York from San Juan, broader indeed than questions about the Uniformity Clause. As Justice Brown noted in the opinion of the Court, the primary query was whether the revenue clauses of the Constitution "extend of their own force to our newly acquired territories." In other words, the question was whether Congress could rule those regions America acquired in 1898 without regard to the revenue provisions of fundamental U.S. law unless it explicitly intended to be bound by that law when it established insular civil governments.[65] This was a significant issue, in fact even more significant than at first appears. For behind Justice Brown's question implicitly lay an even larger one: whether any, all, some, or none of the protections afforded by the Constitution extended to the new American territories, particularly to those that might never become states. If it were found that the Uniformity Clause did not apply as a matter of legal course to congressional legislation concerning Puerto Rico, for instance, then what of trial by jury? Could Congress create a system of justice for Puerto Rico, the Philippines, or Guam that failed to provide for this symbolically central right of the Anglo-American legal order? Just how free a hand could the United States take in the administration of its possessions? In fact, the issues in *Downes* were weightier still, for behind all these questions lay the most fundamental query of all, a question of civic identity: to what extent were the people of the insular territories members of the American nation, a community bound together by a shared commitment to live under liberal constitutional principles? Would these dark-skinned people automatically be entitled to the basic protections of the founding political document of the United States, or would they live, potentially forever, under the plenary power of Congress? Would they have a legal status one typically does not associate with American republican principles: the status not of citizens but of subjects?

In adjudicating *Downes,* the Court, which was intensely divided among various factions, broke along two basic constitutional lines: what one might call judicial traditionalists and judicial modernists.[66] The outspoken traditionalist on the Court was John Marshall Harlan of Kentucky, the great dissenter, author of the lone minority opinion in *Plessy v. Ferguson.*[67] The traditionalist position essentially asserted, in words of the day, that the Constitution "follows the flag," that all provisions of the Constitution extend by their own force, or *ex propio vigore,* into areas over which the United States exercises its civil control. For Harlan, the decision whether or not to acquire territories that included alien races could be made in any way Congress chose, but once those territories were acquired, the Constitution applied to them completely. No distinctions could be made between territories and states in this regard. "The idea that this country may acquire territories anywhere upon the earth, by conquest or treaty," wrote Justice Harlan, "and hold them as mere colonies or provinces,—the people inhabiting them to enjoy only such rights as Congress chooses to accord to them,— is wholly inconsistent with the spirit and genius, as well as with the words, of the Constitution."[68] After all, argued Justice Harlan, how could Congress not be bound by the Constitution in the administration of its new possessions, when it was the Constitution that created and granted those administrative powers, and in fact created the Congress itself? The threat feared most by the traditionalists in this regard was simple, and does not require extensive elaboration: It was the threat of tyranny. It was the threat that without the full force of the Constitution, Congress could maintain territories such as Puerto Rico and the Philippines indefinitely, and that it would maintain them, as described by another dissenter, Chief Justice Fuller, "like a disembodied shade, in an intermediate state of ambiguous existence for an indefinite period," subjected entirely to Congress's own will.[69]

The traditionalists relied on a number of arguments to advance their views, some of which were political in nature. Those who would become imperialists under the U.S. Constitution, they asserted, should consider the consequences before they acted, for the fundamental law of the United States would be interpreted strictly no matter what the changing geopolitical circumstances. "Whether a particular race will or will not assimilate with our people," wrote Justice Harlan, "and whether they can or cannot with safety to our institutions be brought within the operation of the Constitution, is a matter to be thought of when it is proposed to acquire their territory by treaty. A mistake in the acquisition of territory, although such acquisition seemed at the time to be necessary, cannot be made the ground for violating the Constitution or refusing to give full effect to its provisions."[70] Traditionalists also relied on a line of precedent suggesting that the term "United States" in the Constitution denotes both states and territories, rather than merely formal members of the Union. This position was suggested by Chief Justice Marshall in *Loughborough v. Blake.* There, in a case concerning an action of trespass to contest congressional ability to impose a direct tax on the District of Columbia, the Court upheld congressional authority, in dicta defining the "United States" broadly. "The power then to lay and collect duties, imposts, and excises," wrote Chief Justice Marshall, "may be exercised, and must be exercised throughout the United States. Does this term designate the whole, or any particular portion of the American empire?" "Certainly," he continued, "this question can admit of but one answer. It is the name given to our great republic, which is composed of both States and territories."[71] In the eyes of the traditionalists, Chief Justice Marshall's assertion that the term "United States" in the Constitution was wide and encompassing served as a general restraint on American power overseas.

For the judicial modernists, however, the traditionalist concern that Congress might maintain its insular possessions "like a disembodied shade" was precisely the point. The modernists included Justice Edward Douglass White and Justice Henry Billings Brown, author of the majority opinion in *Plessy* and a man whose autobiography begins, "I was born of a New England Puritan family in which there has been no admixture of alien blood for two hundred and fifty years."[72] Brown was born in 1836 in South Lee, Massachusetts, generally described as a small manufacturing village. Brown's father operated saw and flour mills there, and later moved to Stockbridge and, in 1849, to Ellington, Connecticut. Brown enrolled in Yale College in 1852, at the age of sixteen, and graduated in 1856, along with his eventual colleague on the Supreme Court, Justice David Brewer. After legal studies at Yale and Harvard, Brown moved to Detroit and embarked on a successful legal career, working as U.S. deputy marshal and U.S. attorney for the Eastern District of Michigan. He later entered private practice and developed a specialty in shipping and admiralty law. Brown was a staunchly Republican unionist, and in 1875 he was appointed to become a federal district judge by President Ulysses S. Grant. A nationally respected expert in the difficult field of admiralty law, and a successful professor at the University of Michigan, Brown was appointed to the U.S. Supreme Court by President Benjamin Harrison in 1890. He was known to be an agreeable jurist, well liked by his colleagues, and judicious in temperament. Assuming office upon the death of Justice Samuel Miller, known for his blend of liberal state-building and racial bigotry, Justice Brown in many respects maintained the views of his predecessor.

Looking forward into the coming century, both Justice Brown and his fellow modernists were concerned that too strict an adherence to the Constitution and too limited a reading of congressional powers would hinder the United States in its ability to act within a new world order. For modernists, the issue in the *Insular Cases* was not simply that of the revenue clauses, or even the Bill of Rights; it was the future expansion and progressive development of the United States itself. "Patriotic and intelligent men may differ widely as to the desireableness of this or that acquisition," asserted Justice Brown, "but this is solely a political question. We can only consider this aspect of the case so far as to say that no construction of the Constitution should be adopted which would prevent Congress from considering each case upon its merits." "A false step at this time," he continued, "might be fatal to the development of what Chief Justice Marshall called the American empire. Choice in some cases, the natural gravitation of small bodies toward large ones in others, the result of a successful war in still others, may bring about conditions which would render the annexation of distant possessions desirable."[73] "Take a case of discovery," wrote Justice White in his concurring opinion in *Downes*, offering an example of the negative potential consequences of the views advanced by Justice Harlan. "Citizens of the United States discover an unknown island, peopled with an uncivilized race, yet rich in soil, and valuable to the United States for commercial and strategic reasons. Clearly, by the law of nations, the right to ratify such acquisition and thus to acquire the territory would pertain to the government of the United States. Can it be denied that such right could not be practically exercised if the result would be . . . the immediate bestowal of citizenship on those absolutely unfit to receive it?"[74]

The judicial modernists, then, were caught in a contradiction. Like Lodge, they perceived the new world the United States was about to enter. On the other hand, like Lodge's enemies in the Senate, judicial traditionalists had raised the fear that departing from strict constitutional construction could lead to tyranny and so undermine national self-definition. Significantly, both Justice Brown's and Justice White's solutions to this conundrum strongly relied on Teutonic ethno-juridical discourse, the ethno-juridical vision of the Teutonic origins thesis. Indeed, for Justice Brown, the solution to the *Downes* case seemed almost simple: the residents of the insular territories, in effect, were not entitled to the guarantees of the Constitution because they were a racially alien people incapable of maintaining Anglo-Saxon notions of law—because they fell outside the bounds of the American ethno-juridical order. According to Justice Brown, there might be an extremely limited number of universally applicable personal rights, to which the people of Puerto Rico or the Philippines perhaps might be entitled. But on the whole, most guarantees of the Constitution, he believed, were simply "remedial rights which are peculiar to our own system of jurisprudence."[75] The greatest portion of American constitutional law, that is, applied only to a very limited group of people. When Congress legislated for dark-skinned others, therefore, it could not be bound by a document written for white Englishmen over one hundred years ago: the document applied only to a superior civilization that had reached a higher stage of social development. When the United States acquires new possessions "inhabited by alien races," Justice Brown wrote, "differing from us in religion, customs, laws, methods of taxation, and modes of thought, the administration of government and justice according to Anglo-Saxon principles may for a time be impossible."[76] This was the negative corollary to the Teutonic origins thesis.

Justice Brown disposed of Justice Harlan's concern that such a view could lead to tyranny in a similar manner, invoking the positive principles of the Teutonic origins thesis. Specifically, Justice Brown believed, as Lodge had noted in the Senate, that "more precious even than forms of government are the mental and moral qualities which make what we call our race."[77] And like Lodge and Beveridge, he argued that the Constitution ultimately was merely a single, non-necessary expression of the Anglo-Saxon racial genius for law—that beneath the Constitution lay the more fundamental racial principles of what Beveridge called "institutional law," the ethno-juridical spirit passed down to Anglo-Saxon peoples from Tacitus's Germanic tribes. In their administration of islands overseas, the American people in Justice Brown's view thus would be restricted by the innate ideals they carried in their blood, ideals that were foundational to and in fact superseded the Constitution itself. "Grave apprehensions of danger are felt by many eminent men," wrote Justice Brown in *Downes*, "a fear lest an unrestrained possession of power on the part of Congress may lead to unjust and oppressive legislation in which the natural rights of territories, or their inhabitants, may be engulfed in a centralized despotism. These fears, however, find no justification." "There are certain principles of natural justice inherent in the Anglo-Saxon character," he explained, "which need no expressions in constitutions or statutes to give them effect or to secure dependencies against legislation manifestly hostile to their real interests." This is to say that Justice Brown disposed of the concerns of the traditionalists, those who relied on a strict reading of the Constitution for their vision of national identity, by asserting that any action undertaken by an Anglo-Saxon American government overseas was ipso facto within the bounds of a transcendent, racially based legal order.[78]

Although Justice White's opinion differed in some respects from Justice Brown's, and was more sophisticated in its reasoning, it too found its basis in Teutonic ethno-juridical principles—and indeed, in this regard Justice White sought to grant Congress even greater control over its insular affairs than did his modernist colleague.[79] Making a distinction between "incorporated," "unincorporated," and foreign territories, Justice White argued along lines advanced by Abbott Lawrence Lowell in the *Harvard Law Review,* proclaiming that the Constitution applied only to those territories Congress explicitly had "incorporated" into the Union.[80] This became known as the "doctrine of territorial incorporation," a judicial principle first fully accepted by the Court in *Dorr v. United States* (1904).[81] The *Dorr* case involved the great Anglo-Saxon right of trial by jury in criminal cases, and posed the question of whether that right extended to the Philippine archipelago. The Court held that, because the Philippines had not been explicitly incorporated into the American constitutional order, trial by jury was not guaranteed. It held, in other words, that a right symbolically central to Anglo-Saxon claims of racial superiority did not apply to dark-skinned peoples, because those peoples were viewed as unfit by nature for participation in American civic life. Trial by jury was not guaranteed, because Filipinos as a race were thought to be incapable of law itself. Note, again, that for Justice White, as for Justice Brown, as for Henry Cabot Lodge, it was a seemingly antiquated racial worldview that allowed the constitutional contradictions of twentieth-century imperial expansion to be overcome. If the Spanish-American War and the desire for territories overseas created a gap between state ambition and fundamental principles, between modernizing, progressive will and traditional constitutional standards, that gap was bridged at the level of jurisprudence by the social scientific notion of Teutonic legality. It was bridged by what one might call *Teutonic constitutionalism,* a method of ethno-juridical legal decision making that was as modern as the world it helped to bring about.

Conclusion: Death, Law, and the Philippines

I wish to conclude this chapter by briefly exploring one aspect of the ideological significance of Teutonic constitutionalism, moving forward a short period of time to the immediate aftermath of the Spanish-American War, to the Philippines.[82] After ratifying the Treaty of Paris, the United States began to face a long, protracted struggle with the native inhabitants of those islands, who previously had been engaged in a movement for national independence against Spain. This was an independence movement the United States chose to resist as well, and it endured the consequences of that choice by undergoing the very ideological reversal feared by so many anti-imperialists. That is, the United States switched places with Spain and became a power working against forces of national political liberation. Ideology, like dreams in Freudian psychoanalysis, also operates through a process of reversal, positing the very negation of the social world it conceals, and this was evident in the relation between the ethno-juridical language and the military reality of the Philippine conflict. Because for all the references to the Anglo-Saxon genius for law made during the Spanish-American and Philippine-American wars—whether in the formation of imperialist policy, in the adjudication of claims arising from imperial expansion, or in the writings of men in the armed forces[83]—American soldiers in the Philippines, in fact, came to shed many of the restraints of the civilization to which they so often referred and engaged with "surprising alacrity" in what historian Stuart Miller calls a "penchant for lawlessness."[84] This was especially the case on the island of Samar, the "most vicious, and certainly the most controversial, campaign of the Philippine War," the site of Magellan's landing in 1521 and of Douglas MacArthur's in 1944.[85] Over the course of 1902, Americans at home were treated to repeated news reports of the terrible cruelty inflicted on Filipinos by the American military: rape, the burning of villages, the indiscriminate murder of civilians, the killing of the wounded, the use of the water cure as a form of torture. These were *crimes* of war, and indeed the Philippine conflict came to a conclusion through what most agreed was an illegal act, in which high-ranking American military officers dressed in enemy uniform and daringly infiltrated enemy headquarters, capturing the commander of the Philippine forces, General Aguinaldo.[86] In the Philippines, Americans often seemed very much like their own worst image of the Malay savage: a people without law.[87]

Naturally, against the harsh words from critics such as Moorfield Storey, there were a variety of attempts to justify or explain away such behavior. For instance, the Roosevelt Administration asked for assistance from Yale University's distinguished professor Theodore S. Woolsey, son of the illustrious Theodore Dwight Woolsey, for whom the university named Woolsey Hall (one can still walk through Woolsey Hall today and gaze upon moving plaques commemorating men who died in the Philippine Insurrection, including on the island of Samar). Woolsey was a central academic defender of the Philippine-American War and an expert in international law. In regard to the capture of General Aguinaldo, Woolsey counseled the Administration that the United States was not at war with "a civilized power," and that because Aguinaldo "was not a signatory of the Hague Convention . . . there was no obligation on the part of the United States Army to refrain from using the enemy's uniforms for the enemy's deception." On the other hand, noted Woolsey, Filipinos were bound to follow the rules of the Hague Convention since they were fighting a civilized power and a signatory of that agreement. The strategy used by Americans in capturing Aguinaldo, in other words, was illegal "only with a lawful belligerent."[88]

The task of justifying military illegalities similarly fell to Henry Cabot Lodge, who managed to become chair of a controversial Senate committee investigating U.S. war atrocities.[89] Lodge stacked the hearings with witnesses friendly to the Administration, but in the context of repeated reports of brutality from American soldiers who had seen it firsthand, even these witnesses seemed to undermine the very position they were brought to support through the wide gaps they displayed between rhetoric and reality. For instance, beginning his testimony with what he called his "ethnological premises," a close variant of the Teutonic origins thesis, the notorious General Arthur MacArthur gave this characterization of the conflict. "Many thousands of years ago," proclaimed MacArthur, "our Aryan ancestors raised cattle, made a language, multiplied in numbers, and overflowed. By due process of expansion to the west they occupied Europe, developed arts and sciences, and created a great civilization, which, separating into innumerable currents, inundated and fertilized the globe with blood and ideas, the primary basis of human progress, incidentally crossing the Atlantic and thereby reclaiming, populating, and civilizing a hemisphere." "The broad actuating laws which underlie all these wonderful phenomena," continued MacArthur, "are still operating with relentless vigor and have recently forced one of the currents of this magnificent Aryan people across the Pacific—that is to say, back almost to the cradle of its race—thus initiating a [new] stage of progressive social evolution. . . . [T]he human race, from time immemorial, has been propagating its higher ideals by a succession of intellectual waves, one of which is now passing, through our mediumship, beyond the Pacific, and carrying therewith everything that is implied by the beautiful flag which is a symbol of our nationality." "We are now living," glorified MacArthur, "in a heroic age of human history."[90] The grim statistics of the war, and the thousands of Filipino dead, suggested very much the opposite.

Soon after General MacArthur gave his testimony, Albert Beveridge, instructed by Lodge, closed the Senate investigation over a storm of protest,[91] but not before Lodge's witnesses thus revealed in retrospect one of the central functions of Teutonic ethno-juridical discourse in an age of modernization: the rhetorical elision of violence and the concealment of death. This was a concealment in which the academic forebears from whom contemporary legal academics descend—J.D.-Ph.D. candidates at Harvard, professors of international law at Yale, the variety of legal historians and anthropologists writing and teaching during this brutal period of state development—played a terribly unfortunate role.

Notes

1 For an approach to law and rhetoric that has influenced this analysis, see Peter Goodrich, *Legal Discourse: Studies in Linguistics, Rhetoric, and Legal Analysis* (1987).

2 I develop the concept of ethno-juridical discourse in greater detail in "Race, Citizenship, and Culture in American Law, 1883–1954: Ethno-Juridical Discourse from *Crow Dog* to *Brown v. Board of Education*" (Ph.D. diss., Yale University, 1998). In my analysis, I am centrally guided by Rogers M. Smith, *Civic Ideals: Conflicting Visions of Citizenship in U.S. History* (1997). According to Smith, throughout American history political leaders of varying ideological stripes have employed "engaging, reassuring, inspiriting, often intoxicating" stories or "civic myths" to explain and justify racial, ethnic, and sex-based ascriptive limits to American national belonging. Political leaders have used these myths "to explain why persons form a people, usually indicating how a political community originated, who is eligible for membership, who is not and why, and what the community's values and aims are." Ibid. at 33. Ethno-juridical discourse can be understood as one type of civic myth.

3 In this respect, the role of ethno-juridical discourse in debates concerning national identity has been similar to that of what Fredric Jameson calls an "ideologeme," the smallest unit of class ideology in culture, or what Claude Lévi-Strauss, in his classic structuralist analysis of myth, more prominently called "mythemes." See Fredric Jameson, *The Political Unconscious: Narrative as a Socially Symbolic Act* (1981), at 87. On mythemes, see Claude Lévi-Strauss, *The View from Afar*, trans. Joachim Neugroschel and Phoebe Hoss (1985), at 144–47.

4 *Downes v. Bidwell*, 182 U.S. 244 (1901).

5 For a concise factual treatment, see Joseph Smith, *The Spanish-American War: Conflict in the Caribbean and the Pacific, 1895–1902*, Modern Wars in Perspective, ed. B. W. Collins and H. M. Scott (1994).

6   Ibid. at 1.

7   Ibid.

8   Ibid. at 19.

9   Ibid. at 11.

10   David F. Trask, *The War with Spain in 1898,* The Macmillan Wars of the United States, ed. Louis Morton (1981), at 9.

11   For a discussion of Lodge's place in the history of American foreign policy, see William C. Widenor, *Henry Cabot Lodge and the Search for an American Foreign Policy* (1980).

12   For Lodge on Roosevelt, see Henry Cabot Lodge, "Theodore Roosevelt," in *The Senate of the United States and Other Essays and Addresses Historical and Literary* (1921).

13   Alfred Thayer Mahan, *The Influence of Sea Power upon History* (1960 [1890]).

14   On anti-imperialism, see Robert L. Beisner, *Twelve Against Empire: The Anti-Imperialists, 1898–1900* (1968). On the complexities of immigrant responses to the Spanish-American War in this regard, see Matthew Frye Jacobson, *Special Sorrows: The Diasporic Imagination of Irish, Polish, and Jewish Immigrants in the United States* (1995), at 177–216. "While the patricians of the Anti-Imperialist League decried imperialism for the threat it posed to American institutions," notes Jacobson, ibid. at 181, "and while commentators on the left worried over the threat which Philippine 'coolie' labor posed to American workers, immigrant nationalists forged a damning critique of American empire-building based upon a rare empathy with the Filipinos themselves." Such empathy, however, continues Jacobson, "did not preclude Eurocentric, racialist conceptions of 'civilization' and 'savagery' which comfortably cast the Filipinos as the 'other.' Through the prism of race, an unthinkable sympathy with the conquering nation became thinkable for many."

15   For an overview of motivations, see David Healy, *U.S. Expansionism: The Imperialist Urge in the 1890s* (1970).

16   See Anthony T. Kronman, *Max Weber* (1983).

17   On the legal aspects of this modernizing transformation, see Martin J. Sklar, *The Corporate Reconstruction of American Capitalism, 1890–1916: The Market, the Law, and Politics* (1988). On its cultural components, see Alan Trachtenberg, *The Incorporation of America: Culture and Society in the Gilded Age* (1982).

18   For an early estimate of Philippine market opportunities, see Philippine Commission [Taft Commission], "Market for American Products," in *Reports of the Taft Philippine Commission* (Washington: GPO, 1901), at 57–62.

19   John A. Garraty, *Henry Cabot Lodge: A Biography* (1965), at 3. For other biographical material on Lodge, see Widenor, supra note 11. Much useful and important material on Lodge's history can be drawn from his autobiography, *Early Memories* (1913).

20   One historian describes Lodge's vision as that of "filiopietism." Edward N. Saveth, *American Historians and European Immigrants, 1875–1925* (1965), at 30, 201–3.

21   His first major work concerned George Cabot. See Henry Cabot Lodge, *Life and Letters of George Cabot* (1877), at v, 578.

22   Henry Cabot Lodge, *A Short History of the English Colonies in America* (1882), *Alexander Hamilton* (1882), *Daniel Webster* (1883); Henry Cabot Lodge, ed., *The Federalist* (1888); Henry Cabot Lodge, *George Washington* (1889); Theodore Roosevelt and Henry Cabot Lodge, *Hero Tales from American History; or the Story of Some Americans Who Showed That They Knew How to Live and How to Die* (1921).

23   Lodge (1913), supra note 19, at 211. "The other fact in regard to them which seems to me

obvious is their lawlessness," writes Lodge, "their disregard of the rights of others, especially of others about whom they are not informed, and as they know only money, their information is limited. I do not mean by this to say merely that they are arrogant; that is an old characteristic of the type. I use the word 'lawless' in its exact sense. They pay no regard to the laws of the land or the laws and customs of society if the laws are in their way."

24 See Dorothy Ross, *The Origins of American Social Science* (1992).

25 For Adams's approach to the seminar, see Ernest Samuels, *The Young Henry Adams* (1948), at 247–58.

26 [Henry Adams], ed., *Essays in Anglo-Saxon Law* (1905).

27 Lodge, supra note 19, at 239.

28 Frederick Pollock, *The Land Laws, the English Citizen* (1883), at 190–96. Lodge dodges Pollock's rather stern criticism of his scholarly presentism in *Early Memories,* ibid. at 263: "Years after Sir Frederick Pollock sent me his book on 'Land Laws,' and I found in it a note discussing some opinion which I had expressed in my essay on 'The Anglo-Saxon Land Law.' So completely had I been drawn to other subjects and other interests that every vestige of knowledge of what I had myself written had been swept away, and I stared in blank ignorance at my own statement."

29 Lodge, "The Anglo-Saxon Land Law," in Adams, supra note 26, at 56.

30 For the best general contemporary treatment of the Teutonic origins thesis, see Reginald Horsman, *Race and Manifest Destiny: The Origins of American Racial Anglo-Saxonism* (1981). For a thorough and readable treatment focusing on historians, see Saveth, supra note 20. See also Ross, supra note 24.

31 For a translation, see P. Cornelius Tacitus, *Tacitus on Britain and Germany: A Translation of the "Agricola" and the "Germania,"* trans. H. Mattingly (1964).

32 See the discussion of James Bryce in Richard A. Cosgrove, " 'One Ancient Root': James Bryce and the Legal Dimension of Anglo-Saxonism," in *Our Lady the Common Law: An Anglo-American Legal Community, 1870–1930* (1987), at 59–94.

33 Among other scholarly studies of the period, see George Laurence Gomme, *Primitive Folk-Moots; or, Open-Air Assemblies in Britain* (1880); Frederic Seebohm, *Tribal Custom in Anglo-Saxon Law* (1911 [1902]); and John M. Stearns, ed., *The Germans and Developments of the Laws of England, Embracing the Anglo-Saxon Laws Extant . . .* (1889). See also Henry Sumner Maine, *Lectures on the Early History of Institutions,* 6th ed. (1893 [1874]), 225–305.

34 See Ross, supra note 24.

35 Henry Sumner Maine, *Village-Communities of the East and West,* 2d ed. (1872); Lewis Henry Morgan, *Ancient Society, Classics of Anthropology,* ed. Ashley Morgan, intro. Elisabeth Tooker (1985 [1877]).

36 Albert Kocourek and John H. Wigmore, eds., *Sources of Ancient and Primitive Law,* vol. 1 of *Evolution of Law: Select Readings on the Origin and Development of Legal Institutions* (1915); *Primitive and Ancient Legal Institutions,* vol. 2 of *Evolution of Law* (1915); *Formative Influences of Legal Development,* vol. 3 of *Evolution of Law* (1918). For an excellent survey that places such ideas in broad historical intellectual context, see Peter Stein, *Legal Evolution: The Story of an Idea* (1980).

37 Henry Adams, "The Anglo-Saxon Courts of Law," in Adams, supra note 26, at 1.

38 On the transformation of the Teutonic origins thesis between 1815 and 1850, from a descriptive statement of the nature of Anglo-Saxon life to a prescriptive theory advocating Anglo-Saxon world domination, see Horsman, supra note 30, at 62–77.

39 I examine the ethno-juridical characterization of Native Americans in Weiner, supra note 2, at
    72–126.

40 See Thomas Bendysshe, ed. and trans., *The Anthropological Treatises of Johann Friedrich
    Blumenbach* (1865).

41 Robert Cover, "Nomos and Narrative," in *Narrative, Violence, and the Law: The Essays of
    Robert Cover,* ed. Martha Minow et al. (1992), at 95.

42 Kocourek and Wigmore, supra note 36, vol. 2, "Preface," at v–vi, v (emphasis added).

43 Daniel G. Brinton, "The Aims of Anthropology," *Proceedings of the American Association for
    the Advancement of Science* 44 (1895): 1, at 12. On Brinton, see Regna Darnell, *Daniel Garrison
    Brinton: The "Fearless Critic" of Philadelphia,* University of Pennsylvania Publications in
    Anthropology 3 (1988). For Boas's response, see Franz Boas, "Human Faculty and Determined
    by Race," *Proceedings of the American Association for the Advancement of Science* 43 (1895): 301,
    and "The Limitations of the Comparative Method of Anthropology," *Science* (December 18,
    1896): 901.

44 *Cong. Rec.,* 54th Cong., 1st sess. (March 16, 1896): 2817, at 2819.

45 Ibid. at 2819.

46 Ibid. at 2818. For Lodge, these descendants included not only successive waves of Germans and
    Danes, but Normans as well, who in Lodge's view were Germanic people who spoke French.

47 Ibid. at 2820.

48 *Cong. Rec.,* 56th Cong., 1st sess. (March 7, 1900): 2621.

49 Theodore Roosevelt to Henry Cabot Lodge, September 11, 1899, in *Selections from the Corre-
    spondence of Theodore Roosevelt and Henry Cabot Lodge, 1884–1918,* vol. 1 (1925), at 421.

50 Albert J. Beveridge, "Our Philippine Policy," *The Meaning of the Times, and Other Speeches*
    (1968 [1908]), at 71. For another expression of this position, written after the decision in the
    primary *Insular Cases,* see Albert J. Beveridge, "The Development of a Colonial Policy for the
    United States," *The Annals of the American Academy of Political and Social Science,* ed. Emory
    R. Johnson, vol. 30 (1907): 3. See also Louis Livingston Seaman, "The Problem of the Philip-
    pines," *The Annals of the American Academy of Political and Social Science* 30 (1907): 130–34,
    which, like Beveridge's essays and speeches, also makes comparisons, at 134, between Filipino
    inferiority and the recent national "attempted elevation of the blacks."

51 Beveridge (1968), ibid., "Institutional Law," at 113–14. On Beveridge, see John Braeman, *Albert
    J. Beveridge: American Nationalist* (1971); see also Claude G. Bowers, *Beveridge and the Progres-
    sive Era* (1932).

52 Beveridge, ibid. at 106–7.

53 See generally a fascinating study which has influenced my own analysis, Winfred Lee
    Thompson, *The Introduction of American Law in the Philippines and Puerto Rico, 1898–1905*
    (1989). For a study of social engineering in the Philippines paying special attention to educa-
    tional issues, see Glenn Anthony May, *Social Engineering in the Philippines: The Aims, Execu-
    tion, and Impact of American Colonial Policy, 1900–1913* (1980). See also Peter W. Stanley, *A
    Nation in the Making: The Philippines and the United States, 1899–1921* (1974), at 81–138. For a
    contemporary description of activities, see, e.g., United States Philippine Commission
    [Schurman Commission], *Report* (December 1901) (Washington: GPO, 1901), at 76–91. See
    also Philippine Commission, *Report* (January 1900) (Washington: GPO, 1900), at 122–26, 137–
    41. "And so it has come to pass," stated James T. Young at the eleventh annual meeting of the
    American Academy of Political and Social Science, "that we Americans went into the Spanish
    tropics as the political champions of oppressed peoples, with the Declaration in one hand, the

United States Constitution in the other and something of a halo round our heads, but we have folded up the Declaration for possible future use and laid aside our halo to settle down to the business task of building railroads, introducing law and order, putting up telegraph poles, settling people on the farms, studying the possibilities of the soil, developing new crops, digging harbors, paving streets, suppressing disease and building school houses. We went to the tropics to preach political liberty and remained to work." James T. Young, remarks at the eleventh annual meeting of the American Academy of Political and Social Science, in *The Annals of the American Academy of Political and Social Science,* 30 (1907): 138.

54 Arnold H. Leibowitz, *Defining Status: A Comprehensive Analysis of United States Territorial Relations* (1989), at 6. See also Earl S. Pomeroy, *The Territories and the United States, 1861–1890: Studies in Colonial Administration,* 2d ed. (1947).

55 On the exceptions, see, e.g., the work of Ferdinand Blumentritt, or the more popular Homer C. Stuntz, *The Philippines and the Far East* (1904), which takes a comparatively judicious approach to the question, "Who are the Filipinos?" On the Ifugao, see the classic R. F. Barton, *Ifugao Law,* University of California Publications in American Archaelogy and Ethnology, vol. 15 (1919). On the perceptions of the Igorots by the West, see John Henry Scott, *The Discovery of the Igorots: Spanish Contacts with the Pagans of Northern Luzon* (1974). On the Ilongot, see Renato Rosaldo, *Ilongot Headhunting, 1883–1974* (1980) and Michelle Z. Rosaldo, *Knowledge and Passion: Ilongot Notions of Self and Social Life* (1980). For an early ethnographic study of the main Philippine island of Luzon, see Alfred Marche, *Luzon and Palawan,* trans. Carmen Ojeda and Jovita Castro (1970 [1887]).

56 C. H. Forbes-Lindsay, *The Philippines under Spanish and American Rule* (1906), at 102. Significantly, *The Philippines under Spanish and American Rule* is dedicated to William Howard Taft, first civil governor of the Philippines. The work of Forbes-Lindsay, observed one contemporary reviewer, " 'stands pat' with the present American administration." Carl C. Phlehn, review, *The Annals of the American Academy of Political and Social Science,* 30 (1907): 179, at 180. For a European counterpart of some traditional Filipino practices, see Robert Bartlett, *Trial by Fire and Water: The Medieval Judicial Ordeal* (1986).

57 For an important view on the development of criminal law at the time, see Richard R. Cherry, *Lectures on the Growth of Criminal Law in Ancient Communities* (1890).

58 These surveys also formed the basis for a large exhibition about the Philippines at the Louisiana Purchase Exposition of 1904. See Philippine Commission, *Report of the Philippine Exposition Board* (Washington: Bureau of Insular Affairs, War Department, 1905). See especially Albert E. Jenks, "Ethnological Exhibit," ibid., at 19–20, and photographs, passim.

59 On the great respect held by Justice Brown for Taft, see H. B. Brown to Theodore Roosevelt (January 6, 1903), Theodore Roosevelt Papers, Library of Congress, Washington, D.C. Taft would later serve on the Supreme Court as its Chief Justice and would later author the opinion of the Court in *Balzac v. Porto Rico,* 258 U.S. 298 (1922).

60 Philippine Commission, *Fifth Annual Report of the Philippine Commission,* part 2 (Washington: GPO, 1905), at 79.

61 It would be particularly important in such a study to consider the relation of U.S. ethnographic surveys to the expansion of American commercial interests. One anthropologist working for the Commission asserted that Secretary of the Interior Dean Conant Worcester had "given a large amount of valuable and accurate information to inquiring manufacturers and explorers relative to the lines of goods suitable for the Philippines." Ibid. at 79. On Worcester, see Arthur S. Pier, *American Apostles to the Philippines* (1950), at 69–84.

62   See, e.g., Otto Scheerer, "The Igorrotes of Benguet," in Taft Commission, supra note 18, at 149–61. And see generally Philippine Commission [Schurman Commission], *Report*, vol. 3 (Washington: GPO, 1901).

63   Philippine Commission [Schurman Commission], *Report*, vol. 1 (Washington: GPO, 1900), at 11.

64   *United States Constitution*, art. I, sec. 8, cl. 1.

65   *Downes*, 182 U.S. at 249.

66   For a related classification of the Court, see Frederic R. Coudert, "The Evolution of the Doctrine of Territorial Incorporation," *Columbia Law Review* 26 (1926): 823, at 825–26, which divides the body into "fundamentalists and modernists," as well as "strict constructionists" and "opportunists" or "latitudinarians."

67   *Plessy*, 163 U.S. (1896).

68   *Downes*, 182 U.S. at 380 (Harlan, J., dissenting).

69   Ibid. at 372 (Fuller, C. J., dissenting).

70   Ibid. at 384 (Harlan, J., dissenting).

71   *Loughborough v. Blake*, 18 U.S. (5 Wheat.) 317, 319 (1820).

72   Justice Brown's views on his familial origins, in this respect, were similar to those of Henry Cabot Lodge. On Justice Brown, see Joel Goldfarb, "Henry Billings Brown," in *The Justices of the Supreme Court, 1789–1978: Their Lives and Major Opinions*, vol. 2, ed. Leon Friedman and Fred L. Israel (1980), at 1553–76, and Charles A. Kent, *Memoir of Henry Billings Brown* (1915). See also Robert J. Glennon Jr., "Justice Henry Billings Brown: Values in Tension," *University of Colorado Law Review* 44 (1973): 553. Few of Brown's personal papers survive.

73   *Downes*, 182 U.S. at 286.

74   Ibid. at 306 (White, J., concurring). According to Coudert, based on a conversation after the conclusion of the case, Justice White "was much preoccupied by the danger of racial and social questions" in his decision-making process. Coudert, supra note 66, at 832.

75   *Downes*, 182 U.S. at 282.

76   Ibid. at 287.

77   *Cong. Rec.*, 56th Cong., 1st sess. (March 16, 1896): 2820.

78   *Downes*, 182 U.S. at 280. Responding to this Teutonic ethno-juridical assertion, Justice Harlan wrote, in ibid. at 381: "The wise men who framed the Constitution, and the patriotic people who adopted it, were unwilling to depend for their safety upon what, in the opinion referred to, is described as 'certain principles of natural justice inherent in Anglo-Saxon character, which need no expression in constitutions or statutes to give them effect or to secure dependencies against legislation manifestly hostile to their real interests.' They proceeded upon the theory—the wisdom of which experience has vindicated—that the only safe guarantee against governmental oppression was to withhold or restrict the power to oppress. They well remembered that Anglo-Saxons across the ocean had attempted, in defiance of law and justice, to trample upon the rights of Anglo-Saxons on this continent, and had sought, by military force, to establish a government that could at will destroy the privileges that inhere in liberty."

79   Not surprisingly, therefore, Theodore Roosevelt and Justice White held each other in high political regard. On the close policy relationship between Theodore Roosevelt and Justice White, see Theodore Roosevelt to E. D. White (October 19, 1903) and E. D. White to Theodore Roosevelt (1907), Theodore Roosevelt Papers, supra note 59.

80   Abbott Lawrence Lowell, "The Status of Our New Possessions—A Third View," *Harvard Law Review* 13 (1899): 155.

81   *Dorr v. United States*, 195 U.S. 138 (1904). Similar and related holdings were later expressed in

the remainder of the *Insular Cases*, including *Rassmussen v. United States*, 197 U.S. 516 (1905) and *Dowdell v. United States*, 221 U.S. 325 (1911).

82   For an overview of the Philippines in the wake of the Treaty of Paris, see Smith, supra note 5, at 216–31. For an introduction to American history in the Philippines, extending through World War II and to the present, see Stanley Karnow, *In Our Image: America's Empire in the Philippines* (1989). For a radical history of the Philippines, see Renato Constantino, *A History of the Philippines: From the Spanish Colonization to the Second World War* (1975). For an intriguing account blending historical and first-person contemporary perspectives, see David Bain, *Sitting in Darkness: Americans in the Philippines* (1984).

83   See, e.g., *The Story of Our Wonderful Victories Told by Dewey, Schelley, Wheeler, and Other Heroes: A True History of Our War with Spain by the Officers and Men of Our Army and Navy* (1899), at 509–608. For one soldier's less than patriotic view, see the anonymous "For Future Reference," ibid. at 531–32. See also William R. Wood, "The Saxons," ibid. at 554, for a more patriotic exemplar.

84   Stuart Creighton Miller, *"Benevolent Assimilation": The American Conquest of the Philippines, 1899–1903* (1982), at 187. I have been especially influenced by Miller's work in my analysis.

85   Brian M. Linn, "The Struggle for Samar," in *Crucible of Empire: The Spanish-American War and Its Aftermath*, ed. James C. Bradford (1993), at 158. For discussions of the notorious Samar campaign, see Joseph L. Schott, *The Ordeal of Samar* (1965). Samar assumed particular importance during the Philippine Insurrection because it was a critical supplier of commercial hemp. For an analysis that suggests the variety of military responses to the conflict in the Philippines, and suggests that military men acted with more than simple racist brutality, see Brian McAllister Lin, *The U.S. Counterinsurgency in the Philippine War, 1899–1902* (1989).

86   On the raid and the man who led it, see Pier, supra note 61, at 13–28.

87   For an analysis of anti-imperialist opinion in this regard, see Daniel B. Schirmer, *Republic or Empire: American Resistance to the Philippine War* (1972), and Richard E. Welch Jr., *Response to Imperialism: The United States and the Philippine-American War, 1899–1902* (1979). For a well-known anti-imperialist critique, see Jim Zwick, ed., *Mark Twain's Weapons of Satire: Anti-Imperialist Writings on the Philippine-American War* (1992).

88   Miller, supra note 84, at 169–70.

89   Ibid. at 212–18, 239–45.

90   Arthur MacArthur, "Testimony of Arthur MacArthur," in *American Imperialism and the Philippine Insurrection: Testimony taken from Hearings on Affairs in the Philippine Islands before the Senate Committee on the Philippines—1902*, ed. Henry F. Graff (1969), at 136.

91   Miller, supra note 84, at 245.

A Constitution Led by the Flag: The *Insular Cases* and the Metaphor of Incorporation

Brook Thomas

In an 1899 *Harvard Law Review* essay James Bradley Thayer set out to prove that the Constitution allowed "acquiring, holding, and permanently governing territory of any sort and situated anywhere."[1] He also proclaimed that, in wake of events in 1898, "We must face and take up the new and unavoidable duties of the new colonial administration, however unwelcome they may be, handsomely and firmly. There is no question now of any choice as to whether we will have a colonial policy." A foundation of that policy had to be this: "We should never admit any extracontinental State into the Union; it is an intolerable suggestion." Indeed, according to Thayer, "The remark attributed to a judge of the Supreme Court of the United States in presiding, lately, over a popular meeting in Washington, that we have no power to hold colonies except for the purpose of preparing them to come in as States, has no judicial quality whatever. It is simply . . . a political theory entertained by some persons, but resting upon no ground of constitutional law."[2] Exactly what status the Constitution had in the territories was "[a] difficult question, and very fit to be deliberately and fully considered by Congress and by the Supreme Court: a question never yet satisfactorily disposed of; perhaps one not to be answered finally by a court."[3]

A major figure at the Harvard Law School in the last part of the nineteenth century, Thayer was a member of the law firm that first employed Oliver Wendell Holmes Jr. when Holmes came to the Massachusetts bar. He was also a close friend of Chauncey Wright, the philosopher who had an important influence on members of the "Metaphysical Club," including Holmes, William James, and Charles S. Peirce, as they formulated the tenets of pragmatism. His knowledge of Greek, Latin, the classics, and literature in general prompted President Eliot of Harvard, a relative of T. S. Eliot, to offer him a professorship of English in 1872. Thayer refused, but then accepted a professorship of law in 1874. Nonetheless, he kept up his literary efforts, publishing *Western Journey with Mr. Emerson* (1884), which describes their travels together in 1871. He is remembered today, however, for his influence as a scholar and as a teacher advocating the doctrine of judicial restraint. That doctrine explains his reservations about having constitutional authority in the new territories resolved by a court, even the Supreme Court. He proposed instead "amending the Constitution and limiting the States of the Union to the continent." "Guarded by such an amendment," he concludes, "we might enter upon the new and inevitable career which this Spanish war has marked out for us, with a good hope of advancing the honor and prosperity of our country and the welfare of mankind."[4]

Thayer's proposed amendment never materialized, and the constitutional issues identified as in doubt were resolved by the Supreme Court in the *Insular Cases*. Nonetheless, it is worth pondering how our sense of the events of 1898 might be different if an amendment of the sort he imagined had been enacted. For instance, teachers of constitutional law courses would presumably be forced to pay more attention to the legal issues raised by the events of 1898, since it would be hard to ignore an amendment to the body one is studying.

In literary and cultural studies focusing on issues of United States imperialism, the effect would most likely be different. In these realms the events of 1898 get lots of attention. But one irony of the attention paid to them in their centennial year is the growing consensus that the Spanish-American War and its aftermath were are not all that unique after all. According to this consensus, these events were the logical result of an imperial spirit animating United States history from the start. Beginning with the colonial wars waged against Native Americans, that spirit transformed into a policy of Manifest Destiny, leading to the Louisiana Purchase, then to the Mexican-American War, and fifty years later, to the Spanish-American War. Indeed, a number of 100th anniversary conferences on the Spanish-American War coupled 1898 with 1848, the 150th anniversary of the Mexican-American War. That link makes it tempting to treat the 1848 Treaty of Guadaloupe Hidalgo as a precursor to the 1898 Treaty of Paris.[5]

If an amendment had been passed, it would be more difficult to buy into this teleological narrative by which the events of 1898 were simply a logical extension of the United States's history of imperialism. An amendment would have called attention to the unique challenges that the results of the Spanish-American War posed to the Constitution. Indeed, that war sparked a major constitutional crisis, one addressed in serious periodical essays by former presidents Benjamin Harrison and Grover Cleveland, by future presidents of Harvard and the University of Chicago, by the heads of the Harvard and Yale law schools, and by many of the best legal minds of the day. Resolution of that crisis did not result from the logical extension of an imperial spirit animating United States history from the start but, on the contrary, from a reinterpretation of history—especially constitutional history—to accommodate the past to felt political needs in the present.

To assume a teleological narrative about the imperial movement of United States history is to adopt the historical perspective of pro-imperialists, like Abbott Lawrence Lowell, who, looking at "the past and the future," asserted that "the question is, not whether we shall enter upon a career of colonization or not, but whether we shall shift into other channels the colonization which has lasted as long as our national existence."[6] For Lowell and many of today's students of the "cultures of United States imperialism" the events of 1898 marked a continuity with the country's history, but for anti-imperialists—including a number of Justices on the Supreme Court in 1901—these events threatened a radical break with the past unless checked by longstanding constitutional principles. If an amendment had resolved this constitutional crisis at the start of the twentieth century, we might be more likely today to recognize the rupture in constitutional doctrine that took place. In contrast, the Supreme Court's rulings in the *Insular Cases* helped to create the illusion that no rupture occurred.

In this essay, I emphasize—perhaps for polemical purposes a bit too strongly—an important change in the relation between the Constitution and the nation brought about by the *Insular Cases*. Specifically, I argue that they document how the country—or at least the Supreme Court speaking for the country—moved from a model of the United States held together as a compact of contracting entities to a corporate model of the nation-state. To state my point slightly differently, what was at stake was how the United States thought of itself—or themselves—as a nation. (The fact that we are no longer accustomed to hearing the United States referred to in the plural supports my argument.) As one of Chief Justice Fuller's friends wrote him, "In my judgment no more important question has ever come before the Court, for it involves shaping the future policy and destiny of the *Nation*—I begin to like the last word in speaking of this country and people."[7] Or as Justice White, who became the architect of the doctrine that would eventually prevail in the *Insular Cases,* put it later in his life, "Why, sir, if we had not decided [the cases] as we did, this country would have been less than a nation."[8]

This change in the constitutional definition of the nation brings me to a second point, concerning the role of metaphors in bringing about legal transformations. It has long been recognized that the metaphoric nature of poetic language allows poets to adhere to past conventions while generating new meaning. Metaphors can do so because their meanings are more suggestive than fixed, allowing for a slippage between what they seem to refer to and what they can potentially mean.[9] This suggestiveness carries over into the law, allowing judges to use metaphors creatively to give new meaning to precedent while seeming to honor it. White succeeded in bringing about a change in constitutional doctrine that Thayer thought necessitated a constitutional amendment in part because of his strategic use of the metaphor of "incorporation."

White's success should remind us that, whereas the meanings of metaphors are suggestive, the meanings that any one metaphor can suggest are limited. White's metaphor of incorporation was effective because it suggested possibilities that other metaphors could not. Metaphors of mechanization, for example, would not have suggested the same possibilities for the nation. As we will see, possibilities available for the metaphor of incorporation arose in part because of prior meanings that the metaphor had acquired in the realm of business. Changing attitudes about the constitution of business corporations opened up new possibilities for imagining the corporate status of the nation.

The constitutional issue eventually resolved by White's metaphor was whether or not the Constitution follows the flag. That question echoes an often-repeated aphorism encouraging imperialism: Trade follows the flag. But William Jennings Bryan raised the question about the relation between the Constitution and the flag in the 1900 presidential campaign to challenge the imperial policies of the McKinley administration. For Bryan the Constitution should indeed follow the flag and apply fully to the new possessions. In contrast, the administration insisted that the nation had the power to treat the new possessions as colonies that did not have the same constitutional protection as the existing United States and territories.

The 1900 election returned McKinley to power, and Congress passed a law imposing tariffs on goods from Puerto Rico despite the constitutional guarantee that "all duties, imposts and excises shall be uniform throughout the United States." In the 1901 case of *Downes v. Bidwell* the Supreme Court affirmed Congress's power to do so, causing the fictional Mr. Dooley of Finley Peter Dunne's newspaper column to remark, "No matter whether th' Constitution follows th' flag or not, th' Supreme Coort follows th' iliction returns."[10] This famous comment on the Court's politics was, however, a bit misleading. More accurate was Secretary of War Elihu Root's quip, "As near as I can make out the Constitution follows the flag—but doesn't quite catch up with it."[11]

Root's witty remark played on a double meaning of which Bryan was unaware. Bryan clearly intended his question to imply that constitutional rule should coincide with the territory over which the flag of the United States flew. But the phrase can also imply that the Constitution is not coincident with but follows *behind* the flag. This meaning generates an image that is the opposite of what anti-imperialists like Bryan wanted to convey. They argued that the Constitution should be supreme, and that the nation and all of its possessions should be bound by its provisions. But insofar as the flag stands symbolically for the nation, Bryan's phrase also generated an image of the nation leading the Constitution rather than vice versa. As we will see, White's metaphor of incorporation effectively let the flag lead the Constitution while maintaining the appearance that the two were coincident. That appearance could not have been maintained by a different metaphor used by Justice Brown, who delivered the opinion of the Court in *Downes*.

Much more explicitly than White's concurring opinion, Brown's gave the administration the imperial power it wanted. Adopting arguments similar to those made by prestigious figures like C. C. Langdell of Harvard Law School, Simeon E. Baldwin of Yale Law School, and the soon-to-be-named president of the University of Chicago, Brown asserted that full constitutional protection was guaranteed to only the United States, which he defined as the states alone, not territories. Not a part of the United States, territories were, Brown claimed, "appurtenant" to it.[12] They were, in other words, appended to the United States but in a relation of subordination. Congress could, he admitted, extend full constitutional protection to various territories. But until it did, Congress could rule as it saw fit, constrained only by "certain principles of natural justice inherent in the Anglo-Saxon character which need no expression in constitutions or statutes to give them effect."[13]

Brown was, however, alone in the reasoning, if not the result, of his opinion. Four Justices dissented, insisting that "the United States" meant both states and territories and that the Constitution did indeed apply in full to the new territories. Their anti-imperialist sentiments were clearly expressed by Chief Justice Fuller when he refused to endorse a decision assuming that "the Constitution created a government empowered to acquire countries throughout the world, to be governed by different rules than those obtaining in the original States and territories," one substituting "for the present system of republican government, a system of domination over distant provinces in the exercise of unrestricted power."[14] As Justice Harlan put it, "The idea that this country may acquire territories anywhere upon the earth, by conquest or treaty, and hold them as mere colonies or provinces—the people inhabiting them to enjoy only such rights as Congress chooses to accord to them—is wholly inconsistent with the spirit and genius as well as with the words of the Constitution."[15] In fact, Brown's views never did gain a majority. The doctrine that prevailed and eventually won unanimous support was articulated in *Downes* by White.[16]

White and three other Justices agreed with the result of Brown's opinion, but they disagreed with his reasoning.[17] If Brown argued that territories were "appurtenant" to the United States and that the Constitution applied only when it was extended to them, White argued that the Constitution did apply to them, but that all of its explicit provisions did not apply until territories were "incorporated" into the United States, which for him, like the dissenters, meant states and territories. White's theory of incorporation drew on a *Harvard Law Review* essay by Lowell, who was the brother of the poet Amy Lowell and who would become the president of Harvard. It also drew on White's knowledge of the Napoleonic Code from his upbringing in Louisiana. The Napoleonic Code in turn is indebted to Roman law and its tradition of dealing with questions of empire. White's knowledge of both and his Catholicism led McKinley to select him as one of the representatives to negotiate the Treaty of Paris—a job that he declined. Nonetheless, White took *the* major role in formulating constitutional doctrine for governing the new United States empire.

White's doctrine of incorporation allowed him to carve out what seemed to be a middle position between Brown's extension theory and the dissenters' insistence on fundamental republican principles embodied in the Constitution. Unlike Brown, he insisted that the Constitution did follow the flag, but, like him, he allowed the country to treat the new possessions as colonies with a separate status. White never precisely defined what he meant by *incorporation*, causing Fuller to protest that he gave the word an "occult" meaning[18] and put each insular possession in the position of being governed "like a disembodied shade."[19] Harlan complained, "[T]his idea of 'incorporation' has some occult meaning which my mind does not apprehend. It is enveloped in some mystery which I am unable to unravel."[20] Nonetheless, the mysteriousness of White's metaphor actually helped his doctrine's triumph, since it allowed the Court to claim that the Constitution applied to unincorporated territories when in fact important parts of it did not.

The doctrine of incorporation created a new relation between the Constitution and the country it constituted. The *Downes* dissenters adhered to the traditional view that a government could not exert powers without explicit constitutional sanction. For White, however, it was inconsistent for the Constitution to establish the United States as a nation and then to strip it of "those powers which are absolutely inherent in and essential to national existence."[21] Those powers must, he reasoned, be implied by the document, even if not explicitly stated in it. To be a modern nation, for White, meant to have the power to acquire and to hold colonies just as the imperial powers of Europe did, even if that power had no sanction from the literal wording of the Constitution. To interpret the Constitution this way it was necessary, as Thayer put it, to abandon "the childish literalness which has crept into our notions of the principles of government, as if all men, however savage and however unfit to govern themselves, were oppressed when other people governed them; as if self-government were not often a curse,"[22] and to read the Constitution instead contextually "in the atmosphere of the common law and of the law of nations."[23] White, however, outdid Thayer. By abandoning "childish literalness" in his reading of the Constitution and strategically using his metaphor of incorporation, he was able to transform the nation into a modern imperialist state without reverting to the constitutional amendment urged by Thayer.

The metaphor of incorporation aided this transformation by casting the United States in corporate rather than contractual terms. For instance, comparing the sense of a nation endorsed by the Articles of Confederation with that endorsed by the Constitution, Lowell claimed, "The Constitution brought about a new relation between the States and the federal government, and the expressions suitable for articles of partnership gave way before those adapted to the charter of a corporation."[24] There is, of course, nothing new about comparing the relationship between states and the federal government under the Articles and the Constitution. But to define that difference in terms of a partnership (which is contractually based) and a corporation is telling, if not completely surprising in an age described by Alan Trachtenberg as "the incorporation of America."[25] What Trachtenberg does not note, however, is that the incorporation involved not only the organization of businesses and capital along corporate lines but also reconception of the nation in corporate terms. The most important consequence of this model is that, rather than constituting a nation whose component parts remain strictly accountable to its explicit provisions, the Constitution brought into existence a corporate entity with a life or spirit of its own that, by the terms of its charter, could legitimately do what was necessary for its survival and development.

To have a better sense of what was at stake in this transformed sense of the nation, we can compare the constitutional issues raised by the events of 1898 with those raised at the very beginning of the nineteenth century by the Louisiana Purchase. The Louisiana Purchase was the centerpiece of Jefferson's vision of an "empire for liberty."[26] Jefferson's vision proved so powerful that today a number of histories of the United States evoke his phrase in their title. An "empire for liberty" is subtly different from his earlier formulation of an "empire of liberty."[27] If an "empire of liberty" is one in which liberty exists, an "empire for liberty" is one in the service of liberty.

In celebratory accounts of United States history, the idea of an empire in the service of liberty is laudatory and distinguishes the American empire from others. For instance, in a textbook written in the height of the Cold War, the authors assert that "with occasional exceptions, an 'Empire for Liberty' comprises the ambition that Americans have had for their expanding society." They go on: "The word 'empire,' as used by Thomas Jefferson in the quotation on our title-page, connotes no exploitation of subject regions on this continent or anywhere else. Its meaning has been newly illustrated by the admission of Alaska and Hawaii as full-bodied members of the Union of self-governing states."[28]

If Jefferson's phrase evokes this vision of American exceptionalism, it also contains elements of its own critique. For instance, in a book on Melville that uses Jefferson's phrase as its title, Wai-Chee Dimock remarks on the "not altogether oxymoronic" conjunction of "empire" and "liberty." "Far from being antagonistic, 'empire' and 'liberty' are instrumentally conjoined. If the former stands to safeguard the latter, the latter, in turn, serves to justify the former. Indeed, the conjunction of the two, of freedom and dominion, gives America its sovereign place in history—its Manifest Destiny, as its advocates so aptly called it."[29] For Dimock, therefore, Jefferson's phrase tellingly reveals how the seeds of American imperialism were planted early and continued to grow throughout the country's history.

There is certainly truth to this view. We can see it in debates over the Constitution. For instance, though both Jefferson and fellow Virginian Patrick Henry were lovers of liberty, Jefferson's expansionist vision of the country was at odds with Henry's vision. Henry opposed the Constitution because he feared the effect its "ropes and chains of consolidation" would have on liberty. Playing on the difference between the subjects of empires and the citizens of republics, he declared, "If you make the citizens of this country agree to become the subjects of one great consolidated empire of America, your government will not have sufficient energy to keep them together. Such a government is incompatible with the genius of republicanism."[30] In contrast, Jefferson, although like Henry an advocate of states' rights, felt that republican liberty for the United States could be preserved only through a federal government that allowed for expansion. Expansion would remove the presence of potentially dangerous neighbors and thus the threat of war and the need of a standing army, which would have given undue power to the federal government and would have led to burdensome taxes. Expansion would also provide land to sustain a republic of self-supporting yeoman farmers even with an increase in population.

Nonetheless, in purchasing Louisiana to bring about an "empire for liberty" Jefferson in his own mind worried about constitutional issues similar to those raised at the end of the century. For instance, Jefferson felt, just as Thayer felt, that a constitutional amendment might be necessary for proper governance of newly acquired territory. Indeed, although he had engineered the treaty of purchase, he worried that the purchase itself might not be covered by the Constitution. Fearing opposition to the treaty by his foes in Congress, Jefferson wrote a friend about "a difficulty in this acquisition which presents a handle to the malcontents among us, though they have not yet discovered it. Our confederation is certainly confined to the limits established by the revolution. The general government has no powers but such as the constitution has given it; and it has not given it a power of holding foreign territory, and still less of incorporating it into the Union. An amendment of the Constitution seems necessary for this."[31]

Jefferson felt the need for an amendment because he was a strict constructionist. Since the Constitution granted no explicit power either to hold foreign territory or to incorporate it into the Union, he felt that an amendment would be necessary to grant those powers. In a letter to his Secretary of the Treasury, Albert Gallatin, he even composed a draft of an amendment. Gallatin, however, felt that no amendment was necessary. His reasoning is very similar to that used almost a century later by Justice White. According to Gallatin, the United States "as a nation have an *inherent* right to acquire territory" (my emphasis).[32] Furthermore, "Congress have the power either of admitting into the Union as a new state, or of annexing to a State with the consent of that state, or of making regulations for the government of such territory." In his response to Gallatin, Jefferson sounds very much like Thayer when he declares, "I think it will be safer not to permit the enlargement of the Union but by amendment of the Constitution."[33] Nonetheless, as was the case a century later, no amendment materialized.

Why Jefferson dropped his plan is not completely clear. He might simply have been convinced by trusted advisers, including Gallatin, that an amendment was not necessary. He was almost certainly guided by pragmatic considerations. Worried that Napoleon might back out of the agreement if the treaty were not ratified quickly, Jefferson did not want to risk giving the congressional opposition the advantage of his own expression of doubt about the treaty's constitutionality. According to Dumas Malone, Jefferson "was characteristically undogmatic about means." Having determined that the purchase was necessary for the welfare of the country, Jefferson most likely concluded that, in Malone's words, "[t]o have expressed his constitutional scruples publicly would have endangered an agreement that he deemed essential to national security, while putting weapons into the hands of his political enemies; but he wanted his intimate friends to know that these scruples were still present in his mind."[34] In any case, the Senate ratified the treaty without its constitutionality becoming an issue.

This lack of public controversy over the constitutionality of the purchase points to a crucial difference between events that otherwise seem so similar. The constitutional debate concerning the Louisiana Purchase took place almost exclusively in private correspondence and within the conscience of Jefferson himself; the debate surrounding the *Insular Cases* was very public. That debate was public because in the interim the Court had resolved the constitutional issues that had raised doubts in Jefferson's mind. In 1898 precedent suggested that holding colonies on the European model was unconstitutional, so much so that the strict constitutionalist Thayer recommended passage of a new amendment in order to ensure its constitutionality.

When the issue of whether or not Congress had the power to acquire and govern territories came to the Supreme Court in the antebellum period, Justice Taney ruled that it did. Nonetheless, he derived that power from an explicit provision in the Constitution that granted Congress the power to admit new states. Under this ruling there was no imperial power in the nation itself nor was there any power to hold territories as colonies. Instead, all territory acquired should eventually become a state of the Union. In short, Taney's ruling was much closer to the spirit of Jefferson than to that of Gallatin. In fact, although he clearly had scruples about the constitutionality of the Louisiana Purchase, Jefferson seems to have dropped them by 1809. The very sentence to Madison celebrating an "empire for liberty" ends: "I am persuaded no constitution was ever before so well calculated as ours for extensive empire and self-government."[35] Since Jefferson remained a strict constitutionalist his entire life, this declaration indicates that by 1809 he felt that a strict reading of the Constitution sanctioned the empire he had worked to acquire.

Constitutionally sanctioned, but imperialist nonetheless, especially in its treatment of Indian tribes. That treatment has caused Priscilla Wald and others to claim that Supreme Court rulings on Indians are precedents for the *Insular Cases.* For instance, Wald compares Chief Justice Marshall's declaration that tribes are "domestic, dependent nations" to *Downes*'s sanction of the "nation's right to own territory and legislate over subjects that it does not incorporate."[36] But similarities should not cause us to neglect important differences. In fact, to establish a continuity between the Indian and *Insular Cases,* as Wald does, is to adopt a logic similar to that of the pro-imperialist Thayer, who cited the status of Indian tribes to support his argument that people in the new possessions "do not necessarily hold the same relation to the nation which the occupants of the territories hold."[37] To adopt Wald's logic is to risk overlooking the uniqueness of both the constitutional status of Indians and of people affected by the *Insular Cases.*

Thayer himself unwittingly suggests one difference by claiming that the status of Indians supported the imperialist position that "[i]t is for the political department of the government, that is, Congress or the treaty-making power, to determine what the political relation of the new people shall be."[38] What Thayer did not note is that the relation between the nation and Indian tribes in terms of treaties is quite different from the relation between the nation and the insular possessions. Whereas Congress endorsed treaties made directly with the tribes, in the case of the insular territories it endorsed a treaty with Spain, a treaty that transferred colonies to the United States. To be sure, in the Louisiana Purchase and others, the United States made a treaty with a separate country that ceded to the United States territory containing Indian tribes. Nonetheless, the government acknowledged the special status of Indian nations by recognizing the need to make separate treaties with them. No separate treaty was ever made with peoples of the insular possessions.

Furthermore, Thayer, detailing Congress's authority, cited its power to regulate "commerce with the Indian tribes," which is enumerated in Article I, section 8 of the Constitution, the same section whose guarantee of uniform duties, imposts, and excises was at issue in *Downes.* Thayer's detail should remind us that, if Congress's power to regulate commerce with tribes derives from a specific provision of the Constitution (one giving special status to tribes), no provision was made for Congress to impose a duty on products from a territory like Puerto Rico.

Not to recognize these important Constitutional distinctions would be to give credence to Thayer's claim that Congress "can reduce [tribes] at any moment to full subjection."[39] Despite the horrendous treatment that Indians received from the United States and despite the injustice of many of the Supreme Court's rulings on Indian affairs, constitutional doctrine does make for very circumscribed tribal independence, a fact brought into focus through a comparison with (until very recently) the total lack of legal recognition given to the prior existence of Aborigines on the Australian continent. My point is not to deny abuses to Indians; it is simply to focus on the special circumstances of the *Insular Cases.*

Indeed, there is no need to deny the exploitation of Indians and others brought about in the name of Jefferson's "empire for liberty" to note that prior to the *Insular Cases* what Chief Justice Marshall referred to as the "American empire" had two significant differences from the British empire from which the United States had broken. First, it was presided over in its entirety by the Constitution and all of its provisions. Second, by guaranteeing that all territory held should eventually become states, it stressed, as Jefferson claimed it did, the principle of self-government. The *Insular Cases* changed that situation. If in 1798 Jefferson, even with imperial designs, was intent on distinguishing the United States's republican form of government from European examples, in 1898 imperialists insisted that nostalgic sentiment about a republican form of government distinguishing the United States from European powers must give way to the practical necessity of competing with those powers on terms set by the "law of nations." Thus, in his famous "The March of the Flag" speech, ardent imperialist Albert J. Beveridge declared, "Fate has written our policy for us; the trade of the world must and shall be ours. And we will get it as our mother [England] has told us how."[40] Similarly, Lowell and Thayer adopted England as their model, Lowell for the colonial administrative apparatus it developed to rule its empire, Thayer for not "letting in her colonies to share the responsibility of governing the home country and all the rest of the empire."[41] Ironically, then, it was by abandoning its claims to constitutional exceptionalism and embracing a more "cosmopolitan" view that the United States legitimated its new empire.[42]

In doing so, it changed the relation between the Constitution and the nation. Since that change was accomplished without a constitutional amendment, it necessitated a revisionist interpretation of earlier cases. White's metaphor of incorporation served his revisionist efforts well. Take, for instance, his interpretation of the Louisiana Purchase. The treaty of purchase stated: "The inhabitants of the ceded territory shall be incorporated into the Union of the United States as soon as possible according to the principles of the federal Constitution." This sentence seems to promise statehood to the newly acquired territory as soon as possible. White, however, used it to support his contention that there was an intermediary stage for a territory between acquisition and statehood: the stage of being "incorporated" without achieving statehood. Thus, for him, there could be incorporated and unincorporated territories, and Puerto Rico, Hawaii, and the Philippines were unincorporated until incorporated by Congress.[43]

To be sure, there was some sleight of hand involved. Soon after *Downes* former Secretary of the Treasury George S. Boutwell assumed that White's opinion was closer to the dissenters' anti-imperialist logic than to Brown's pro-imperialist logic. The only difference between the dissenters and White, he felt, was that the dissenters "were of the opinion that the Constitution applies to the new possessions of the United States as soon as such possessions are transferred by treaty with the former sovereign, followed by the proclamation of the President that the treaty had been duly ratified," whereas White and those joining him "maintained, as a doctrine, that, whenever a possession had been organized as a Territory, it became at once and thenceforth a part of the United States and subject to the jurisdiction of the Constitution, without any special declaration by Congress to that effect." Thus, he assumed, it was only a matter of time till the new possessions were properly "organized" in order to meet White's standard of "incorporation." "This being the case," he assumed, "the practical conclusion must be that which has been demanded by the Anti-imperialists of the country, namely: that the entire possessions of the United States that have been acquired in conformity to the law of nations, will be under the jurisdiction of the Constitution, and that to them as to the States the clause which requires that 'all duties, imposts and excises shall be uniform throughout the United States' will be applicable."[44]

Boutwell, along with others, was misled by the slipperiness of White's metaphor of incorporation. For White incorporation meant more than organization. One reason it did was that for him and others more was at stake than the issue of uniform duties. There was also a racial question. Fully to incorporate the new territories might well have meant giving their residents citizenship with full constitutional guarantees. Many at the time were reluctant to do so. Lowell articulated reasons why. According to him, the belief that all men are created equal had become an unexamined political axiom in the United States. As far as civil rights were concerned, Lowell fully agreed with the axiom. But when it came to equal political rights that would be guaranteed by full citizenship, Lowell disagreed. Here the theory of equality could be applied only "where the inequalities are not too great," only "where the population is tolerably homogeneous and political education is widely diffused."[45] The Jeffersonian ideal of universal self-government was flawed because the "art of self-government is one of the most difficult to learn." It "requires a perpetual self-restraint on the part of the whole people, which is not really attained until it has become unconscious."[46] If "centuries of discipline under the supremacy of law"[47] had prepared the Anglo-Saxon race for it, those living in the new possessions were not ready for it. As a result, "[o]ne element of our success in the management of the [continental] territories—their treatment as infant states, with institutions like our own and prospective equality of rights—cannot . . . be applied to our new possessions."[48] Instead, Lowell urged adoption of the British model of colonial rule.

The British organized their territorial possessions, but they did not incorporate them into the United Kingdom. And here we can see how effective the metaphor of incorporation was for those, like White, who shared Lowell's belief that the racial makeup of the insular possessions made their inhabitants incapable of self-government. A bodily metaphor, incorporation made it possible to imagine the new possessions within the United States at the same time that they were foreign to it, just as something can be lodged in a body but not be part of its organic functioning. This possibility was extremely attractive to those who opposed the idea that the insular possessions were automatically incorporated into the political body of the United States as fervently as they opposed the idea that those of non-European races could be naturally assimilated into the body of the American people.

The racial aspect of the *Insular Cases* makes it very tempting to see the imperial racism of 1898 as a logical extension of domestic racism so prevalent in the era of Jim Crow. This view is bolstered by the fact that Lowell supported his argument about the folly of allowing the new possessions self-government by pointing out that within the United States the "theory of universal political equality does not apply to tribal Indians, to Chinese, or to negroes under all conditions."[49] It is also supported by the fact that five years before he wrote the controlling opinion in *Downes,* Justice Brown wrote the majority opinion in *Plessy v. Ferguson,* while *Plessy's* lone dissenter, Justice Harlan, also dissented in *Downes.* Nonetheless, whereas there was much overlap between racism at home and abroad, the situation was once again complicated.

What, for instance, are we to do with Chief Justice Fuller, who dissented with Harlan in *Downes* but supported the *Plessy* decision? Even more telling, what are we to do with the fact that in the 1898 case of *United States v. Wong Kim Ark* Fuller and Harlan were the lone dissenters when the rest of the Court guaranteed citizenship to anyone—no matter of what racial descent—born in the United States?[50] Those protesting against racism in one case seem to support it in another and vice versa. Indeed, *Wong Kim Ark* was more important for the *Insular Cases* than is normally acknowledged. By declaring that anyone born within the territorial limits of the United States was a United States citizen, *Wong Kim Ark* forced any Justice intent on denying citizenship to residents of the insular territories to restrict the definition of what comes within the territorial limits of the United States.[51] The metaphor of incorporation allowed White and others who had upheld the birthright citizenship of Wong Kim Ark to include the insular territories as unincorporated entities within the United States while still denying their residents citizenship. This relation between *Wong Kim Ark* and the *Insular Cases* is not, I hasten to point out, an example of the logic of domestic racism being extended through the practice of imperialism. On the contrary, it is an example of the complicated process by which a positive decision on the nonracial makeup of citizenship affected how the Court dealt with racial attitudes underlying the country's new form of imperialism.

Of course, it could be argued that in the long run the question of whether or not a United States possession could be left unincorporated is not all that important for an understanding of United States imperialism in the twentieth century. According to Owen Fiss, "[b]y 1905 the real question was not whether the Constitution would follow the flag, but whether it would follow the United Fruit Company."[52] Fiss's comment suggests that in order to understand the forces of United States imperialism at this time, we need to look not only at the *Insular Cases* but also at legal decisions making way for the rise of what Martin Sklar has called "corporate liberalism."[53] Indeed, White's metaphor of incorporation in the former suggests the need to explore possible connections between these two areas of law. For instance, the fact that White also formulated the famous "rule of reason" that helped to undercut the regulatory power of the Sherman Anti-Trust Act is a tantalizing bit of evidence. I do, however, caution against the impulse to construct a conspiracy theory from such evidence, just as I have cautioned against succumbing to teleological narratives about United States history. What we find, instead, is a loose parallel between the transformation in how the corporate body of the United States related to the Constitution and a transformation in how business corporations related to their charters of incorporation.

In both cases there was a general movement away from the primacy of contract.[54] Traditionally, Anglo-American law considered corporations fictional persons that owed their existence to the state. Orthodox legal doctrine concerning corporations in the United States was formulated in *Dartmouth College v. Woodward* (1819) when Chief Justice John Marshall drew on common law tradition to define a corporation as "an artificial being, invisible, intangible, and existing only in contemplation of law. Being the mere creature of law, it possesses only those properties which the charter of its creation confers upon it, either expressly, or as incidental to its very existence."[55] If Marshall's definition granted a corporation a legal status different from the people who comprise it, by calling a corporation an artificial creation of the state he continues to assume that its real basis is contracting individuals. Marshall's decision also furthered the primacy of contract by holding that legislative charters creating corporations are themselves contracts that cannot be impaired. Furthermore, although *Dartmouth College* protected corporations from state legislatures altering the terms of their charter, it also confirmed a state's sovereignty over them.

Nonetheless, Marshall's doctrine was gradually altered when, with limited success, corporate advocates put forth arguments granting corporations an existence independent of the state.[56] For instance, in the antebellum period most states replaced special legislative charters of incorporation with laws that made incorporation available to anyone following proper procedures. After the Civil War pro-corporate forces also won certain Fourteenth-Amendment protections in *Santa Clara v. Southern Pacific Railroad Company* (1886) when a unanimous Court ruled that both its equal protection and due process clauses applied to all "persons," including the legal fiction of corporate personalities.[57]

This movement in corporate law from the view that corporations are contractually bound by the terms of their charter to one in which they have an independent existence with a "personality" that is greater than the sum of the contracting individuals is similar to the movement in the notion of the nation as strictly bound by the terms of its "charter"—the Constitution—which creates a compact of individual states, to one in which the nation is a corporate body with certain powers inherent in its very existence. The corporate sense of the nation sanctioned by White in the *Insular Cases* was most likely more palatable to people in the early part of the twentieth century because of the changing views on the constitution of a business corporation.[58]

Indeed, the role that corporations played in the United States's economic imperialism helped to create an unconscious alliance between advocates of political imperialism and some of their anti-imperialist opponents. Although anti-imperialists resisted the move toward a corporate sense of the nation endorsed by White, many, if not all, endorsed a world in which business corporations played a more and more important role in the life of the nation and its citizens. I offer two examples, one from the world of literature the other from the world of education.

William Dean Howells was a prominent anti-imperialist; Frank Norris, an imperialist. Norris's imperial vision is dramatized at the end of *The Octopus,* which was published the same year as the first of the *Insular Cases.* Although Norris seems to criticize the practices of "the octopus," a huge railroad corporation that controls the lives of independent farmers by monopolizing the wheat market, he also sees it as the vehicle of an inevitable and "mighty world-force" that will help the United States control the global economy. Thus in the last chapter "the octopus" has extended its reach through a "new venture—the organizing of a line of clipper wheat ships for Pacific and Oriental trade." As the corporate spokesman tells one of the characters, "We'll carry our wheat into Asia yet. The Anglo-Saxon started from there at the beginning of everything and it's manifest destiny that he must circle the globe and fetch where he began his march. You are up with the procession, Pres, going to India this way in a wheat ship that flies the American colours."[59] Howells opposed such imperialist sentiments. Nonetheless, in *The Rise of Silas Lapham,* published sixteen years earlier, Silas's individually owned business is taken over by a corporation that employs Silas's new son-in-law, who represents possibilities for the next generation. The son-in-law's job is to open up new markets in South America for the corporation. Although Howells does not see this corporate expansion overseas linked to imperialism, its end effect is similar to the expansion imagined by Norris.

An even more telling comparison is between two presidents of Harvard. If Lowell was pro-imperialist, his predecessor Eliot was an important anti-imperialist. However, Eliot saw large, jointly owned corporations as the best way to unite the interests of a diverse American society. For instance, he called "incorporation with limited liability . . . the greatest business invention of the nineteenth century," because it responded to the conflict between "collectivism" and "individualism" by providing for structures that "are great diffusers of property among the frugal people of the country."[60] Eliot's support of corporations also addressed Lowell's heightened concern: that diminished economic expansion brought about by closing of the western frontier would jeopardize the social position of well-educated "native-born Americans," who hitherto had "found plenty of room higher up the economic ladder" as "the captains, and . . . non-commissioned officers of labor."[61] Development of a colonial empire along the British model, he felt, would address that threat. Proper administration of that empire would require "a permanent and highly paid colonial administrative service, which shall offer an honorable and attractive career for young men of ability."[62] "In fact"—and we can hear the future president of Harvard speaking—"the rapid growth in America of schools for educating lawyers, doctors, and engineers shows that experts, with a highly specialized training, are quite as much in demand—and hence quite as much needed—in democracy as anywhere else."[63] As it would turn out, jobs for many of these experts would be provided, not by the government's colonial bureaucracy, which never developed on the British scale, but by private corporations of the sort that employed Silas Lapham's son-in-law to expand markets overseas. Even so, the corporate model of a government with its own "brain trust" of specially trained experts gained more and more force.

The "incorporation" of United States imperialism eventually brought about an important change in governmental policy on trade that was the explicit issue in the first of the *Insular Cases.* One reason White, a former prosperous planter, upheld the constitutionality of imposing duties on goods from Puerto Rico in *Downes* was that he wanted to protect vested interests against an influx of duty-free sugar and tobacco. As corporations expanded their markets overseas during the twentieth century, vested interests eventually would be better served by a policy of free trade. In this new world order, we have come perilously close to a situation in which both the flag and the Constitution follow the imperatives of trade rather than vice versa. The process by which this transformation occurred is, of course, far too complicated for me to develop in this essay. Nonetheless, I do hope that I have drawn attention to the important change in constitutional doctrine brought about by the *Insular Cases,* a change that is illuminated through careful attention to White's metaphor of incorporation in its historical context.

Notes

1   James Bradley Thayer, "Our New Possessions," *Harvard Law Review* 12 (1899): 464, at 478.

2   Ibid. at 484–85.

3   Ibid. at 478.

4   Ibid. at 485.

5   This consensus grows out of a challenge to what Amy Kaplan calls "a long historical tradition of explaining away U.S. imperialism as an aberration, or a fleeting episode in the brief period following the Spanish-American War." Kaplan, " 'Left Alone with America,' " in *Cultures of United States Imperialism,* ed. Amy Kaplan and Donald E. Pease (1993), at 13. In order to do so Kaplan and other contributors to *Cultures of United States Imperialism* accept the revisionism of William Appleman Williams. Williams explains the events of 1898 as the result of a "self-legitimatizing dynamism" of imperial expansion "*rooted* in Jeffersonian universalism . . . implicit in the Monroe Doctrine . . . blantant in the *spirit* (and practice) of Manifest Destiny." Williams, *Empire as a Way of Life: An Essay on the Causes and Character of America's Present Predicament along with a Few Thoughts about an Alternative* (1980), at 113 (my emphasis). See also Williams's "The Frontier Thesis and American Foreign Policy," *Pacific Historical Review* 24 (1955): 379. Williams, however, focuses on diplomatic history, whereas those in literary and cultural studies are intent on showing how U.S. imperialism is served by the country's cultural production. Kaplan, for instance, notes that the essays in *Cultures of United States Imperialism* "explore in varied contexts how the United States, as Richard Drinnon has claimed, exports its past 'metaphysics of Indian-hating' and Indian fighting into new frontiers abroad and across new borders." Kaplan, ibid. at 17. The corrective work that these essays do is important, and I in no way want to return to the view of history that they challenge. I do, nonetheless, question their somewhat uncritical adoption of the teleological sense of U.S. history assumed by people like Williams and Drinnon, especially insofar as it keeps us from seeing the unique features of the constitutional crisis that arose as the result of the Spanish-American War. See Richard Drinnon, *Facing West: The Metaphysics of Indian-Hating and Empire-Building* (1980).

6   Abbott Lawrence Lowell, "The Colonial Expansion of the United States," *Atlantic Monthly* 83 (1899): 145, at 147. Lowell relied on the work of historian Albert Bushnell Hart, who claimed that the United States "for more than a hundred years has been a great colonial power without suspecting it." Hart, "Brother Jonathan's Colonies: A Historical Account," *Harper's New Monthly Magazine* 98 (1899): 319, at 319.

7   Quoted in Willard L. King, *Melville Weston Fuller: Chief Justice of the United States, 1888–1910* (1950), at 268.

8   Quoted in Frederic R. Coudert, "The Evolution of the Doctrine of Territorial Incorporation," *Columbia Law Review* 26 (1926): 823, at 834. In a New York district court decision leading to the first of the *Insular Cases,* Judge Townsend declared that the framers intended to make the United States "an unfettered sovereign in foreign affairs," not "a cripple among nations." *Goetze v. United States,* 103 F. 72, 85–86 (1900).

9   See Owen Barfield, "Poetic Diction and Legal Fiction," *Essays Presented to Charles Williams* (1947), at 106.

10 Finley Peter Dunne, *Mr. Dooley at His Best* (1938), at 77.

11 Quoted in Philip C. Jessup, *Elihu Root,* vol. 1 (1938), at 348.

12 *Downes v. Bidwell,* 182 U.S. 244, 287 (1901).

13 Ibid. at 280.

14   Ibid. at 373.

15   Ibid. at 380.

16   Unanimous support came in *Balzac v. Porto Rico,* 258 U.S. 298 (1922).

17   Justice Gray wrote his own opinion that in substance agreed with White's. He, however, argued that the issues in *Downes* did not touch on the authority of the United States over territories, but only over regions gained by war or treaty from a foreign state. For such possessions, he reasoned, there must be a period of transition, even after a treaty, and Puerto Rico was in that period. See *Downes,* 182 U.S. at 344 (Gray, J., concurring).

18   Ibid. at 373.

19   Ibid. at 372.

20   Ibid. at 391.

21   Ibid. at 311.

22   Thayer, supra note 1, at 475.

23   Ibid. at 483.

24   Abbott Lawrence Lowell, "The Status of Our New Possessions—A Third View," *Harvard Law Review* 13 (1899): 155, at 158.

25   Alan Trachtenberg, *The Incorporation of America: Culture and Society in the Gilded Age* (1982).

26   *The Republic of Letters: The Correspondence between Thomas Jefferson and James Madison 1804–1836,* vol. 3, ed. James Morton Smith (1995), at 1586 (letter to Madison, April 27, 1809).

27   Letter from Thomas Jefferson to George Rogers Clark, December 25, 1779. Quoted in Julian P. Boyd, "Thomas Jefferson's 'Empire of Liberty,'" *Virginia Quarterly Review* 24 (1948): 538, at 550.

28   Dumas Malone and Basil Rauch, *Empire for Liberty: The Genesis and Growth of the United States of America,* vol. 2 (1960), at vii. The metaphor of incorporation is implied by the phrase "full-bodied members of the Union."

29   Wai-Chee Dimock, *Empire for Liberty: Melville and the Poetics of Individualism* (1989), at 9.

30   *Patrick Henry, the Orator,* ed. David A. McCants (1990), at 135.

31   Quoted in Robert W. Tucker and David Hendrickson, *Empire of Liberty: The Statecraft of Thomas Jefferson* (1990), at 164.

32   Gallatin's use of the plural to speak of the nation implies the sovereignty of individual states.

33   Tucker and Hendrickson, supra note 31, at 164.

34   Dumas Malone, *Jefferson and His Time,* vol. 4 (1948), at 319.

35   Smith, supra note 26, vol. 3, at 1586. Williams uses Jefferson's passage as an epigram to the preface of *Empire as a Way of Life.* For him the distinctions made between the United States's mode of empire and that of European powers are "formally correct and yet seriously misleading." Williams, supra note 5, at 129. I argue instead, as did anti-imperialists in 1898, that they have serious consequences.

36   Priscilla Wald, "Terms of Assimilation: Legislating Subjectivity in the Emerging Nation," in Kaplan and Pease, supra note 5, at 79. Wald mistakenly has *Downes* governed by White's metaphor of incorporation, not by Brown's theory of extension.

37   Thayer, supra note 1, at 471.

38   Ibid.

39   Ibid. at 472.

40   Quoted in Malone and Rauch, supra note 28, vol. 2, at 205.

41   Thayer, supra note 1, at 484.

42   In "The United States as a World Power: A Chapter of National Experience," *Harper's New*

Monthly Magazine 98 (1899): 485, at 485, the historian Albert Bushnell Hart explicitly challenges "talk of 'Old World' and 'New World' " and argues that "from the earliest colonial times the international forces which have moved Europe have affected the Western hemisphere."

43   In a subtle, retrospective construction of constitutional history Chief Justice Taft in *Balzac v. Porto Rico,* 258 U.S. at 306, wrote, "Before the question became acute at the close of the Spanish War, the distinction between acquisition and incorporation was not regarded as important, or at least it was not fully understood and had not aroused great controversy."

44   George S. Boutwell, "The Supreme Court and the Dependencies," *North American Review* 173 (1901): 154, at 156, 159–60 See also Boutwell's *The President's Policy: War and Conquest Abroad, Degradation of Labor at Home* (1900).

45   Lowell, supra note 6, at 150.

46   Ibid. at 152.

47   Ibid.

48   Ibid. at 153.

49   Ibid. at 152.

50   See Charles J. McClain, "Tortuous Path Elusive Goal: The Asian Quest for American Citizenship," *Asian Law Journal* 2 (1995): 33. In contrast, Rogers Smith claims that the majority's point of view in *Wong Kim Ark* "fit the ascriptive, nationalistic, and often mystical spirit" of nineteenth-century ideas of racial homogenization. He prefers instead the "rationalistic, consensual account of citizenship" that Fuller presented with Harlan in dissent. But Smith misreads the significance of both the majority and minority decisions as indicated by a footnote admitting that evidence about both Fuller and Harlan does not support his argument. *Civic Ideals: Conflicting Visions of Citizenship in U.S. History* (1997), at 441, 625 n. 89. For Smith's earlier view of the case, see Peter H. Schuck and Rogers M. Smith, *Citizens without Consent* (1985), at 78, 103, 157 n. 39. For my account of the case, see "China Men, *United States v. Wong Kim Ark,* and the Question of Citizenship," *American Quarterly* 50 (1998): 689.

51   C. C. Langdell, for instance, clearly alludes to *Wong Kim Ark* when he notes: "What is the true meaning of 'United States' in the [citizenship clause of the Fourteenth Amendment] is certainly a question of great moment, for on its answer depends the question whether all persons hereafter born in any of our recently acquired islands will be by birth citizens of the United States." Langdell, "The Status of Our New Territories," *Harvard Law Review* 12 (1899): 365, at 376. Lowell explicitly mentions *Wong Kim Ark* when he argues, "It may also be objected that in *United States v. Wong Kim Ark* the court based citizenship upon birth within the allegiance; but the question whether the nation could hold possessions which were not a part of the United States, so that persons born in them would not be citizens within the meaning of the Fourteenth Amendment, was not before the court, and there is nothing in the opinion to suggest that it was present in the minds of the judges." Lowell, supra note 24, at 175 (footnote omitted); see also 168.

52   Owen M. Fiss, *Troubled Beginnings of the Modern State,* vol. 8 in *History of the Supreme Court of the United States* (1993), at 252.

53   Martin Sklar, *The Corporate Reconstruction of American Capitalism: 1890–1916* (1988).

54   A staunch advocate of "freedom of contract," the social Darwinist William Graham Sumner was an ardent opponent of colonial expansion and its paternal attitude toward the new possessions. See "The Conquest of the United States by Spain," *Yale Law Journal* 8 (1899): 168.

55   *Dartmouth College v. Woodward,* 17 U.S. (4 Wheat.) 518, 636 (1819).

56   See Morton Horwitz, "*Santa Clara* Revisited: The Development of Corporate Theory," *West Virginia Law Review* 88 (1985): 173, at 180–82.

57   Charles and Mary Beard subscribed to a conspiracy theory in which Republican framers of the Fourteenth Amendment intentionally used "person" in order to expand corporate rights. *The Rise of American Civilization,* vol. 2 (1927), at 111–14. Horwitz, ibid., makes a convincing argument that in *Santa Clara* the Court was still intent on protecting the individual people making up the corporation, not the corporate personality itself. For confirmation of Horwitz's argument, see my discussion of *In re Tiburcio Parrott* in *American Literary Realism and the Failed Promise of Contract* (1997), at 236–39.

58   I can reinforce my point through an example that would seem to challenge it. In a *Yale Law Journal* article that supported the Spanish-American War for liberating people oppressed by Spain's feudal yoke, Talcott H. Russell argued against the notion that a nation is "a sort of corporation limited." "The nation is not a mere machine or business organization," he asserted. It is instead a "personality." Russell denied the corporate nature of the nation, but did so by adhering to an earlier notion of the corporation as simply a mechanical business organization. The newer model stressed the organic nature of a corporation and insisted that it had precisely what Russell granted to a nation: a personality. Russell, "The National Ideal," *Yale Law Journal* 7 (1898): 346, at 347.

59   Frank Norris, *The Octopus* (1994 [1901]), at 647–48.

60   Charles W. Eliot, *The Conflict between Individualism and Collectivism in a Democracy* (1910), at 15.

61   Lowell, supra note 6, at 148.

62   Ibid. at 154.

63   Ibid. See also Francis Newton Thorpe, "The Civil Service and Colonization," *Harper's New Monthly Magazine* 98 (1899): 858. Thorpe associated colonial administration with "modern monarchial" forms of government. He was confident that "we, as a people, will not hesitate to adapt our republicanism to monarchial methods whenever necessary." "Our written constitution," he predicted, "will not be suffered to stand in the way." Ibid. at 862.

Deconstructing Colonialism: The "Unincorporated Territory" as a Category of Domination

Efrén Rivera Ramos

The United States entered the twentieth century as a colonial power.[1] The question now is whether it will continue to be one as the twenty-first century dawns. The problem, however, is not only whether the United States will keep holding whole populations in a condition of political subordination but whether it will decide to abandon a particular attitude, a certain perspective, a set of legal and political categories and concepts, a whole discourse that—regardless of good or bad intentions—is ultimately imperial in nature.

The acquisition of new territories by the United States at the end of the nineteenth century opened up an intense debate regarding the status of those territories and their populations within the American political system. The discussion took place at the highest levels of the nation's political and legal establishment.[2] It is evident from the interventions of many of the players in this domestic drama that there was a heightened awareness that the resolution of the question would signify a turning point in the development of the United States as a political community, for in determining the status of the new territories and the nation's approach to those "foreign" populations, the United States would also be shaping its own identity within the international community. With good reason, American intellectuals and decision-makers viewed the issue as one of paramount importance. The future of the United States as a world player, its image of itself, and the world's perception of the newcomer in the international arena were in the process of being defined. The author of a recent review of the events surrounding this period does not exaggerate when he tersely comments: "In 1898, America's role in the world changed forever."[3]

The national controversy over the question of the status of the newly acquired territories eventually led to a resolution that was both expressed and, to a certain extent, fashioned by the Supreme Court of the United

States. The "solution" was recorded in the series of decisions known as the *Insular Cases*.[4] Responding to suggestions advanced by congressional, executive, and academic leaders, in those decisions the Supreme Court devised a new theory and a new legal and political category in American constitutional discourse: the theory of incorporation and the category of the "unincorporated territory." According to the Court, "unincorporated territories" belong to, but are not a part of, the United States.[5] Congress, said the Court, enjoys "plenary powers" over such territories, subject only to certain restrictions relating to some then-undetermined "fundamental rights."

The term "plenary powers" is, of course, riddled with ambiguity. It may be taken to mean "absolute," in the sense of unbridled or even arbitrary power. Yet, inasmuch as the Court itself expressed in 1901 that such power was restricted by "fundamental limitations in favor of personal rights,"[6] it may be concluded that the phrase was intended to carry a different meaning. The majority opinion written by Justice Harlan in *Grafton v. United States*[7] seems to provide some clarification. Referring to the relationship between the Philippines—then considered an unincorporated territory— and the United States, Harlan explained that the relation was not the same as that between a state and the United States government. The government of a state does not derive its powers from the United States, while the government of a territory owes its existence wholly to the United States. Thus, Harlan stated: "The jurisdiction and authority of the United States over the territory and its inhabitants, for all legitimate purposes of government is paramount."[8] This reading seems to equate "plenary" with "exclusive." In other words, whereas in the case of the states, the powers of government over their populations are deemed to have a dual origin—some derive from the people of the state and others from the will of the people of the United States as a whole—in the case of the territories, all governmental power derives not from the will of their peoples but from the powers conferred upon the federal government by the people of the United States.[9] The conclusion, per force, is that the peoples of the territories are not governed by effect of their consent but as a result of the powers that the United States enjoys as a sovereign nation. This power to govern territories was read by the different majorities in the *Insular Cases* as emanating from the nation's inherent rights to acquire territory, the Territorial Clause of the United States Constitution,[10] the treaty-making power, and the power to conduct and declare war.[11] In short, the Supreme Court subscribed to the proposition that the United States, like other sovereign powers of the times, had the right to acquire territories and govern their populations without their consent. This was decidedly an imperialistic conception of power.

As the Court itself explained, the restrictions of that power of governance arose from "fundamental" principles inherent in the American system of government that prevented the arbitrary treatment of persons subjected to its jurisdiction. In fact, it was the extension, or rather the narrowness, of those limitations, as interpreted by the majority of the Court, that Justice Harlan was most concerned with in his famous opinions.[12] The 1901 decisions left those restraints open to determination on a case-by-case basis by the judiciary. Most of the cases decided after that date dealt with this issue.[13]

Regarding the situation of specific territories, the Court eventually concluded that Alaska and Hawaii had been "incorporated" into the Union,[14] while Puerto Rico and the Philippines had not. Thus the latter should be treated as unincorporated territories. In fact, today Guam and the Virgin Islands are also included in that category.

To fashion the doctrine of "unincorporation," the majority of the Court adopted a strategy of interpretation characterized by a pronounced pragmatism and an overt instrumentalism that looked at the potential domestic and international effects of the decisions on the current and future situation of the United States.[15] This instrumental approach to legal interpretation was predicated on three principal substantive considerations: (1) the acute awareness that the Republic was entering a new stage in its historical development; (2) the perceived need to accord to the nation's political leaders the maximum flexibility possible, allowing for experimentation, in dealing with the new territories; and (3) the clearly articulated belief that the country and its political and constitutional systems were confronting a situation characterized by important differences from previous historical experiences, thus calling for new legal and constitutional solutions. Those differences were principally associated with the ethnic, racial, and cultural configuration of the populations of the recently acquired territories and the degree of effective control that white Anglo-Saxon settlers could eventually exercise in those new spaces of operation. In all these senses, the Court's approach reflected the political and cultural concerns permeating the wider national debate.[16]

With the constitutional doctrine adopted in the *Insular Cases*, the Court not only adapted to what was perceived as a new situation; it actually created a new legal and political reality. If before those cases were decided there were no such things as "unincorporated territories," after their rendition, the American political and constitutional world would include such entities. Through this doctrine, the United States was also constituting itself, officially, as an imperial world power. This, to my mind, is one of the most perfect examples of the law's "power of naming"[17] and of the capacity of law to generate new understandings and, therefore, new realities.

Categorizing Puerto Rico and other lands as "unincorporated territories" would have significant long-term normative and political effects. I will briefly examine those which, in my judgment, have been the most important ones.

First, the Court in effect legitimated the exercise of power by the United States over other peoples in much the same way as had been the practice among the European imperial powers. A new understanding, a new common sense, emerged within the dominant legal and political circles in the United States: an understanding that propounded as justified, natural, appropriate, and morally correct the acquisition of lands inhabited by people who, as in the case of Puerto Rico, viewed themselves as distinct nations; holding the lands as territorial possessions; and governing them as colonial dependencies.

Second, in conjunction with the legislation that they interpreted and upheld, those decisions constituted a new legal and political subject: the inhabitant of the unincorporated territory. Clearly, those subjects were legitimated to make certain claims on the United States government. At the same time, they became "subject," in another sense, to the "plenary powers" of the government that had recognized them as legal subjects. The extension of American citizenship to Puerto Ricans by the Jones Act in 1917 redefined, in some measure, the relationship between individual Puerto Ricans and the American political community.[18] But as the Court made clear in 1922 in *Balzac v. Porto Rico,* that action was not understood to go as far as altering in any fundamental way the political status of Puerto Rico, nor the conclusion that the rights of its inhabitants would still be conditioned by the fact that they resided in an "unincorporated territory."[19] In fact, a derived symbolic effect of the interaction between the Jones Act and the *Balzac* case was yet another transmutation of the meaning of citizenship in the American political system.[20] Before 1917, Puerto Ricans, like Filipinos, were considered "nationals," not citizens, of the United States. Their conversion into citizens was seen by many as an indication that the situation of Puerto Rico within the American constitutional structure had changed. However, the Court in *Balzac* dispelled that notion. Puerto Rican jurist and legal historian José A. Cabranes has made the point that as the nineteenth century came to an end "the exaltation of American citizenship—by impe-

rialist and anti-imperialist alike—was a notable and not surprising characteristic of the expansive and optimistic period during which the United
States embarked upon its colonial enterprise."[21] The touting of the privileges of citizenship, according to Cabranes, became a way of reinforcing
"the sense of permanent inclusion in the American political community in
a non-subordinate condition, in contrast to the position of aliens, subjects
or even nationals."[22] The use of the legal construct "national" in opposition
to "citizen" would allow governing the peoples of the recently acquired
territories while holding them in a position of political subordination. At
that point it seemed that being a "citizen" did make a difference. However,
after the Jones Act and *Balzac,* the concept of citizenship was divested again
of any special, homogeneous meaning denoting full membership in the
political community, a connotation that appeared to have developed during
the course of the debate regarding the future of the new possessions. In the
new "legal situation," after *Balzac,* to be a full member of the political
community a person had to be a citizen, but being a citizen was not of itself
a sufficient condition to be considered a full member of the political community—especially if the person was a resident of one of the territories. As
Rogers M. Smith has commented, Puerto Ricans were in fact placed in a
category that was somewhat like "the second-class citizenship of blacks and
Native Americans, as well as women."[23]

Detaching citizenship from the right of political participation, as in the
case of the residents of Puerto Rico, the Commonwealth of the Northern
Mariana Islands, Guam, and the Virgin Islands, has become a central feature of the legal framework of the American colonial enterprise. This re-
creation of citizenship in a redefined hierarchical mold allowed for a new
construction of the "other": the former "aliens" residing in the territories,
who later had become "nationals" of the United States (different from its
"citizens"), now were transformed into "citizens," but still of a different
kind. The prevailing perception and feeling that Puerto Ricans are only
"second-class citizens" and the debate regarding the "nature" of that citizenship[24] may be understood as a manifestation—in the realm of experience—of that differentiated representational construction.

A third important effect of the theory of unincorporation was the enormous flexibility which it accorded the political branches of the federal
government. In fact, that was the main purpose of the doctrine. In the end,
it authorized the United States to exert direct rule over other lands and
other peoples without the difficulties inherent in dealing with formally
sovereign states and unencumbered by the complications of admitting
those "distant and different peoples" into the American federation.

Congress has used that flexibility in many ways. In the case of Puerto Rico, for example, it has provided for various forms of internal government, beginning with a two-year period of military rule and gradually allowing for the popular election of local officials; it authorized Puerto Ricans to draft our own internal constitution, within the limitations imposed by Congress;[25] it has extended United States citizenship, without purporting to incorporate the islands; it has experimented with a variety of fiscal measures, including granting and dismantling tax exemption schemes; it has made available to the population some of the social and economic programs provided for residents of the states (of course, it has also placed caps on the access that those residing in Puerto Rico may have to such programs);[26] and, as in the case of the other remaining territories, it has withheld from its residents full participation in the adoption of legislation that directly affects them.[27] Moreover, a distinction made early on between the political condition of the territories and the civil rights of its inhabitants has allowed for the development of a political system that may be described as a partial democracy, based on the liberal ideology of the rule of law and the discourse of individual rights, but coexisting with a situation of collective political subordination.[28] In effect, what has emerged, at least in the case of Puerto Rico, is a new type of colonial society, which I have characterized elsewhere as a "modern colonial welfare state."[29] Though different in many important respects from other forms of colonialism, this type of arrangement is nonetheless colonial. And it is so because it entails the direct, formal, material, legal, and political control of one country over another in an undeniable situation of subordination.

Some may argue that these developments have benefited Puerto Rico and the other territories. Others will contend that they have been detrimental. This is explained by the fact that, regarding specific policies and programs, congressional flexibility to govern Puerto Rico may have cut both ways. Colonialism, after all, like many other social and political phenomena, has never been unidimensional. It may have had both progressive and regressive effects over the course of history. However, the crucial issue is that it is still colonialism. From the perspective of anyone concerned with democratic ideals and the values that inform the principle of self-determination, the relevant consideration, in this context, is that the United States government understands that it may exercise largely unlimited power over the peoples of the territories, as long as they remain "unincorporated," and that it persists to act in accordance with that belief.

This brings me to the last effect of the doctrine of incorporation. The legal and constitutional doctrine originated by the events that commenced shortly before the Spanish-American War and ended with the decision in the *Balzac* case in 1922 has produced a certain discourse of power. By that I mean a set of concepts, categories, notions, and meanings, and a series of related practices, which have defined the framework within which the political reality emerging from that period has come to be understood. That discourse has become a conceptual cage that has significantly constrained the discussion of the political condition of the territories and of the claims that their peoples may legitimately make.

Of course, that framework has not determined everything in Puerto Rico. Within it, during the past one hundred years, the country has undergone significant demographic, economic, social, political, and cultural changes. The Puerto Rican nation has been transformed from a community of scarcely one million people, living for the most part within the confines of its territory, to a people comprising more than six million souls extending well beyond its territorial borders.[30] From being a fundamentally rural and agricultural society, largely looking inward, it has become a relatively modern, urban, industrial, almost postindustrial society linked to the outer world by advanced means of communication. From constituting a political community that in 1898 exhibited relatively feeble state institutional arrangements, it has evolved to live within the structure of a modern welfare state that seems to penetrate the most recondite spaces of social life. Also within the legal framework established by the *Insular Cases,* a renewed awareness of the cultural particularity of the Puerto Rican people has seemed to emerge with force. In fact, the different sectors of Puerto Rican society have been creative both in their accommodation and in their resistance to the enormous power of Congress. In our daily lives many of us have appropriated the categories imposed upon us, trying to make the best of them; some have struggled to give them new meanings; and others have even attempted to create new ways of naming ourselves. We have reaffirmed our sense that, as a people, we possess an identity, a distinct subjectivity— many sided, plural, differentiated, complex, but still identifiable. Yet, regardless of all these developments, which demonstrate that the relative flexibility exercised by Congress has worked in multiple, complex forms, the fact still is that the legal and ideological framework produced to govern us at the beginning of the twentieth century continues to constrain our possibilities.

Almost one hundred years after the creation of the doctrine of incorporation and of the category of the "unincorporated territory," as a category of domination and as a justification for the exercise of colonial power, the United States Congress, the executive branch, and the federal courts continue acting under the understanding that that is a proper way of visualizing the relationship between the American Republic and millions of people who have come under its political control. To confirm this conclusion one would only need to review several relatively recent federal court decisions and the documents that have emerged from the United States Congress on the issue. Thus, in 1978 and 1980 respectively, the United States Supreme Court relied on the rationale of the *Insular Cases* to hold that Congress could constitutionally exclude Puerto Rico from the applicability of social security and welfare programs or place limits not applicable to the several states on the amounts of assistance extended to residents of the islands.[31] In 1993 a federal circuit court of appeals concluded that, as pertains to Puerto Rico, "Congress continues to be the *ultimate source of power* pursuant to the Territory Clause of the Constitution."[32] Relying on these and other judicial and legislative materials, on October 13, 1998, a Puerto Rican judge sitting on the federal District Court for the District of Puerto Rico concluded that whatever limited powers of self-government Puerto Rico enjoys have been delegated by Congress pursuant to the Territorial Clause. Therefore, he added, "under the Supremacy Clause, the constitution and laws of Puerto Rico cannot limit the plenary power of Congress under the Territorial Clause, so as to provide for a relationship with the United States distinct to that provided by federal law."[33] In the congressional sphere similar pronouncements have been frequent. On March 4, 1998, the United States House of Representatives passed legislation to provide for a federally sanctioned plebiscite for Puerto Rico.[34] The measure, known as the Young bill after its main proponent, Representative Don Young, a Republican from Alaska, contained an extensive list of "findings." In their relevant parts, the findings adopted the theory established in the *Insular Cases,* reaffirming the notion that Puerto Rico is still subject to the plenary powers of Congress under the Territorial Clause of the United States Constitution.[35] On September 17, 1998, a Senate resolution stated straightforwardly: "The political status of Puerto Rico can be determined only by the Congress of the United States."[36] Executive officials in charge of coordinating territorial affairs have subscribed to this assessment of Congress's current power under the Constitution.[37] There is no doubt that the principal players in the United States government, acting as representatives of the United States as a metropolitan power, share the view that the legal framework established in that group of early-twentieth-century decisions is still the law of the land regarding territorial affairs and that they are compelled to act according to its dictates.

Yet those categories, and the meanings assigned to them, derive from a particular vision of power. When applied to the relationship with the newly acquired territories, that vision assumed a concrete form, taking shape in a particular legal and constitutional doctrine. But this operated only as a corollary of a wider discourse that was part of the image that the United States forged of itself as an actor in the international arena. It is not surprising, then, that even today the consequences of that discourse of power extend well beyond the sphere of United States territorial relations. In fact, the very doctrine of the *Insular Cases* itself has been harnessed to buttress the legitimacy of actions conducted outside this field of United States policy. Thus, for example, its basic rationale has been used to justify extraterritorial actions of the United States government on foreign sovereign soil. As recently as 1990, the United States Supreme Court called upon the doctrine of the *Insular Cases* to sustain actions of United States federal agents in Mexico which were deemed by some to contravene the United States Constitution and basic principles of international law.

The situation arose in the context of the prosecution of a Mexican citizen in United States federal courts for crimes allegedly committed on Mexican soil. The defendant had been apprehended in Mexico by Mexican authorities and delivered to federal agents in California. After his arrest, U.S. Drug Enforcement Administration agents conducted a search of the defendant's residence in Mexico without securing a warrant. The defendant's lawyer, as well as the American Civil Liberties Union, argued that the search had violated his client's rights under the Fourth Amendment of the United States Constitution. Both the federal District Court and the Court of Appeals for the Ninth Circuit agreed with the defendant's contention. However, eventually, the Supreme Court rejected his argument.[38] What is interesting for our purposes is that, among several grounds for its decision, the majority of the Court included the legal doctrine established by the *Insular Cases.* Writing for the Court, Chief Justice William Rehnquist cited *Balzac, Ocampo, Dorr, Mankichi,* and *Downes.*[39] The Chief Justice wrote:

> The global view taken by the Court of Appeals of the application of the Constitution is also contrary to this Court's decision in the *Insular Cases,* which held that not every constitutional provision applies to governmental activity even where the United States has sovereign power. . . . If that is true with respect to territories ultimately governed by Congress, respondent's claim that the protections of the Fourth Amendment extend to aliens in foreign nations is even weaker. And certainly, it is not open to us in light of the *Insular Cases* to endorse the view that every constitutional provision applies wherever the United States Government exercises its power.[40]

This way of expressing the matter certainly constitutes a certain view of the nature of governmental power. It comprises a particular notion of the legitimacy of its exercise over people who either have not given their consent to such power or who are deemed to fall outside the protections of the constitutional norms that should govern those who govern.[41] The discourse of the *Insular Cases*, those twenty-three decisions rendered at the beginning of the twentieth century, seems thus to be alive and well as we enter the twenty-first. Its juridical implications have been extended beyond United States-territorial relations, and it has been endowed with a new vitality respecting the latter.

This discourse continues to be used, particularly in relation to the peoples of the territories, despite the fact that the vision of power in which it rested, dominant at the turn of the last century, can no longer hold. The discourse of the *Insular Cases* was undeniably racist; it was built upon conceptions related to long-discredited theories, such as Manifest Destiny and Social Darwinism; it was premised on the legitimacy of treating other countries and peoples as if they were property; it sought justification on now abandoned principles of international law; it ended up constructing an "other" considered inferior and incapable of self-government; and it explicitly adhered to a conception of democracy as a privilege of the Anglo-Saxon "race," and not as a right of those whose lives are affected by collective decisions in a given political community.[42] Despite this ideological lineage, the doctrine of incorporation and the category of the "unincorporated territory" are still referred to as if they were merely technical legal terms, untarnished by the imprint of their historical, political, and cultural origin. It seems to be forgotten that the concept itself is tinted with an imperial vision of power and a political justification that should be held untenable in the supposed age of postcolonialism, of respect for self-determination and the generalized appreciation for democratic values.

The category of the "unincorporated territory," when used to justify the exercise of so-called "plenary power" upon other peoples, is contrary to the concept of self-determination itself. As we have seen, the power held over the peoples of the territories is understood to emanate not from their will but from the powers inherent in, or accorded to, the United States as a sovereign nation. Yet however ambiguous it may be, at a minimum the concept of self-determination implies the notion that a people or community (no matter how it is defined) has the legal or moral right to determine for itself its associations with others and the principles, rules, and organization that should govern its collective life.[43] To insist that Congress has plenary power—and will continue to exercise that power—over other peoples, in the sense sanctioned by the *Insular Cases,* is to persist in the denial of the right to self-determination of the peoples over which it is exercised, as the latter concept has come to be understood at the end of the twentieth century.

In this regard, however much one may applaud any attempt to move the discussion of the decolonization process forward, it is still rather perplexing to see the United States Congress, regardless of the good intentions of its members, trying to put in motion a process for self-determination for Puerto Rico while, at the same time, reproducing the very discourse that reaffirms its colonial power and making sure that, in all stages of the game, Congress will have the upper hand, retaining the trump card of the Territorial Clause as interpreted by the *Insular Cases.*[44]

I propose that it is time for the United States to abandon the notion that it may keep other peoples in conditions of political subordination. That a new understanding of its relationships to those peoples must emerge. That a new common sense must replace the old and still current one. That it should not continue applying categories born of another age in a world whose moral ambiance is decidedly contrary to the idea of the legitimacy of colonialism, no matter in what terms it is cast.

One way to achieve those objectives would be through a judicial reassessment of the incorporation doctrine. However, absent an indication from Congress and the executive branch in that direction, the probabilities of such a development are minimal. A more feasible approach would be through congressional action. That would entail a clear expression from Congress of its commitment to end as soon as possible all relationships of political subordination with its territorial dependencies.

In the case of Puerto Rico, I would argue for a declaration from Congress that it recognizes the people of Puerto Rico as a fully self-governing community and that it is willing to initiate immediately a process to reshape the current relationship, exploring different alternatives, including, of course, national independence. All of the alternatives, however, would be based on the premise of full self-government.

Other considerations would also have to be addressed. For example, the people of Puerto Rico have understandable concerns, not only about their political empowerment but also about the possibilities of their economic survival and the preservation of a cherished and distinct national and cultural identity. These are preoccupations that the United States government should address imaginatively and creatively, unrestrained by concepts that may no longer speak to the realities we live in. It should do so taking into

account the long-term relationship between both communities, acknowl-
edging its obligations under current international law, and recognizing that
many of the predicaments in which we find ourselves have been, to a large
extent, the result of federal action and inaction. Such an approach would
probably require a willingness to make accommodations regarding the traditional political status solutions as well as any other arrangement that may
substantially address the three fundamental concerns mentioned above:
political empowerment, economic viability, and respect for cultural differences. In any event, the new attitude would have to involve shedding the
particular discourse of power that so far has underlined the relationship
between the United States and the peoples of the territories.

I am quite sure that if Congress were to take the initiative, in the name of
the American people, of divesting itself of its imperial and colonial powers,
the federal courts, just as they did at the beginning of the last century, would
gladly follow the congressional flag.

Notes

1   On July 7, 1898, the United States annexed Hawaii. On December of that year, as a result of the
     Spanish-American War, it acquired the islands of Puerto Rico, in the Caribbean, and Guam
     and the Philippines in the Pacific, and managed to secure effective political control over Cuba.
     In 1917, the United States purchased the Danish Virgin Islands.
2   See, e.g., Carman F. Randolph, "Constitutional Aspects of Annexation," *Harvard Law Review*
     12 (1898): 291; Simeon E. Baldwin, "The Constitutional Questions Incident to the Acquisition
     and Government by the United States of Island Territory," *Harvard Law Review* 12 (1899): 393;
     C. C. Langdell, "The Status of Our New Territories," *Harvard Law Review* 12 (1899): 365; James
     Bradley Thayer, "Our New Possessions," *Harvard Law Review* 12 (1899): 464; Abbott Lawrence
     Lowell, "The Status of Our New Possessions—A Third View," *Harvard Law Review* 13 (1899):
     155. For a review of the positions of some of the leading public figures who intervened in
     territorial affairs, see Warren Zimmerman, "Jingoes, Goo-Goos, and the Rise of America's
     Empire," *Wilson Quarterly* (Spring 1998): 42.
3   Zimmerman, ibid. at 42.
4   The name *Insular Cases* was originally given to a group of nine decisions rendered in 1901: *De
     Lima v. Bidwell,* 182 U.S. 1 (1901); *Goetze v. United States,* 182 U.S. 221 (1901); *Crossman v. United
     States,* 182 U.S. 221 (1901); *Dooley v. United States,* 182 U.S. 222 (1901) (*Dooley I*); *Armstrong v.
     United States,* 182 U.S. 243 (1901); *Downes v. Bidwell,* 182 U.S. 244 (1901); *Huus v. New York and
     Porto Rico Steamship Company,* 182 U.S. 392 (1901); *Dooley v. United States,* 183 U.S. 151 (1901)
     (*Dooley II*); and *Fourteen Diamond Rings v. United States,* 183 U.S. 176 (1901). The designation
     has been extended to another set of cases decided from 1903 to 1914 and to a decision handed
     down in 1922, dealing with the same or related issues. The decisions included in this second
     group are: *Hawaii v. Mankichi,* 190 U.S. 197 (1903); *Gonzales v. Williams,* 192 U.S. 1 (1904);
     Kepner v. United States, 195 U.S. 100 (1904); *Dorr v. United States,* 195 U.S. 138 (1904); *Men-*

dezona v. United States, 195 U.S. 158 (1904); *Rassmussen v. United States,* 197 U.S. 516 (1905); *Trono v. United States,* 199 U.S. 521 (1905); *Grafton v. United States,* 206 U.S. 333 (1907); *Kent v. Porto Rico,* 207 U.S. 113 (1907); *Kopel v. Bingham,* 211 U.S. 468 (1909); *Dowdell v. United States,* 221 U.S. 325 (1911); *Ochoa v. Hernandez,* 230 U.S. 139 (1913); *Ocampo v. United States,* 234 U.S. 91 (1914); and *Balzac v. Porto Rico,* 258 U.S. 298 (1922).

5   Strictly speaking, the Court did not adopt the doctrine of incorporation in *Downes* or any other of the cases decided in 1901. However, in that case, Justice Brown, writing for the majority, did describe Puerto Rico as "a territory *appurtenant* and *belonging to* the United States, but not a *part* of the United States within the revenue clauses of the Constitution." *Downes,* 182 U.S. at 287 (emphasis added). It was Justice White, in what proved to be a highly influential concurring opinion in that case, who used the term *incorporation* to refer to the same idea expressed by Justice Brown. In subsequent cases, the concept would be utilized, both in arguments before the Court and in several concurring and dissenting opinions, until in 1904 a majority of the Court expressly adopted the "incorporation" doctrine as expounded by Justice White in his concurring opinion in *Downes.* See *Dorr,* 195 U.S. 138.

6   *Downes,* 182 U.S. at 268.

7   *Grafton,* 206 U.S. 333.

8   Ibid. at 354.

9   In one of the early cases Justice Brown commented: "There is a wide difference between the full and paramount power of Congress in legislating for a territory in the condition of Porto Rico and its power with respect to the States, which is merely incidental to its right to regulate interstate commerce." *Dooley II,* 183 U.S. at 157.

10   *United States Constitution,* art. IV, sec. 3, cl. 2.

11   See, e.g., *Downes,* 182 U.S. at 268.

12   See ibid. at 380; *Rassmussen,* 197 U.S. at 530 (Harlan, J., concurring); *Mankichi,* 190 U.S. at 239–40 (Harlan, J., dissenting).

13   See supra note 4.

14   See *Rassmussen,* 197 U.S. 516; *Mankichi,* 190 U.S. 197.

15   See Efrén Rivera Ramos, "The Legal Construction of American Colonialism: The Insular Cases (1901–1922)," *Revista Jurídica Universidad de Puerto Rico* 65 (1996): 225, at 272–83.

16   See ibid. at 284–300.

17   Pierre Bourdieu, "The Force of Law: Toward a Sociology of the Juridical Field," *Hastings Law Journal* 38 (1987): 805, at 838.

18   American citizenship was collectively extended to Puerto Ricans by virtue of the *Jones Act, U.S. Statutes at Large* 39 (1917): 951.

19   *Balzac,* 258 U.S. 298.

20   For a recent study of the changing meanings of citizenship in American history, see Rogers M. Smith, *Civic Ideals: Conflicting Visions of Citizenship in U.S. History* (1997).

21   José A. Cabranes, *Citizenship and the American Empire: Notes on the Legislative History of the United States Citizenship of Puerto Ricans* (1979), at 5 n.12.

22   Ibid.

23   Smith, supra note 20, at 430.

24   See, e.g., Johnny H. Killian, Congressional Research Service, *Discretion of Congress Respecting Citizenship Status of Puerto Ricans* (1989); José Julián Álvarez González, "The Empire Strikes Out: Congressional Ruminations on the Citizenship Status of Puerto Ricans," *Harvard Journal on Legislation* 27 (1990): 309; Johnny H. Killian, Congressional Research Service, *Questions in re Citizenship Status of Puerto Ricans* (1990).

25   See Act of July 3, 1950, *U.S. Statutes at Large* 64 (1950): 319.

26   See *Harris v. Rosario*, 446 U.S. 651 (1980) (per curiam) (holding that pursuant to its powers under the Territorial Clause, Congress can determine that Puerto Rico receives less financial assistance for families with needy dependent children than the states).

27   Puerto Rico's representation in Congress is limited to a Resident Commissioner, who sits in the House of Representatives. The Resident Commissioner can vote in congressional committees (see Rules of the House of Representatives, Rule 12) but cannot cast a final vote on legislation proposed in the House. There is no representation in the Senate. Yet, federal legislation applies in Puerto Rico, except when otherwise indicated by Congress.

28   For a fuller discussion of this aspect, see Efrén Rivera Ramos, *The Legal Construction of Identity: The Judicial and Social Legacy of American Colonialism in Puerto Rico* (2001).

29   Efrén Rivera-Ramos, "Self-determination and Decolonisation in the Society of the Modern Colonial Welfare State," in *Issues in Self-Determination,* ed. William Twining (1991), at 115.

30   Puerto Rico has a population of nearly 3.8 million. Approximately 3 million persons of Puerto Rican origin live in the continental United States. See 2000 Census; 1999 Census.

31   See *Califano v. Torres*, 435 U.S. 1 (1978) (per curiam); *Harris v. Rosario,* 446 U.S. 651.

32   *United States v. Sanchez,* 992 F.2d 1143, 1152 (11th Cir. 1993) (emphasis in the original).

33   *Partido Popular Democrático v. Estado Libre Asociado de Puerto Rico,* 24 F. Supp. 2d 184 (D.P.R. 1998).

34   *United States-Puerto Rico Political Status Act,* H.R. 856, 105th Cong., 2d sess. (1998).

35   See ibid., "Findings." See also House Committee on Resources, *Report together with Dissenting and Additional Views to Accompany H.R. 3024,* 104th Cong., 2d sess. (1996).

36   S.R. 279, 105th Cong., 2d sess. (1998).

37   See, e.g., Committee on Energy and Natural Resources, *Hearing to Receive Testimony on H.R. 856, to Provide a Process Leading to Full Self-Government for Puerto Rico and S. 472, to Provide for Referenda in Which the Residents of Puerto Rico May Express Democratically Their Preferences Regarding the Political Status of the Territory, and for Other Purposes, before the Senate Committee on Energy and Natural Resources,* 105th Cong., 2d sess. (July 15, 1998) (statement of Jeffrey L. Farrow).

38   See *United States v. Verdugo-Urquidez,* 494 U.S. 259 (1990).

39   See supra note 4.

40   *Verdugo-Urquidez,* 494 U.S. at 268–69 (citations omitted). As Justice Brennan suggested in his dissent, the Court's decision created a situation in which foreign nationals would be subject to U.S. criminal laws but would be deprived of some of the most fundamental protections that the U.S. Constitution provides against the actions of government agents that enforce such laws. Ibid. at 282.

41   See ibid. at 282-91 (Brennan, J., dissenting). Regarding the majority's use of the rationale of the *Insular Cases* to justify its decision, Justice Brennan repeated the admonishment contained in Justice Black's plurality opinion in *Reid v. Covert,* 354 U.S. 1, 14 (1956), to the effect that "neither the cases nor their reasoning should be given any further expansion." Ibid. at 291.

42   See Rivera Ramos, supra note 15, at 284–96.

43   For more detailed arguments on this issue, see Rivera Ramos, supra note 29, at 122–27; Rivera Ramos, supra note 15 at 298–300.

44   See, e.g., H.R. 856, supra note 34.

II. Expansion and Constitution

Installing the *Insular Cases* into the Canon of Constitutional Law

Sanford Levinson

.

All disciplines are constituted by their canons—that series of "set texts" that comprise the core materials of any given academic area. As Jack Balkin and I have written elsewhere, debates about the canon are rife in many contemporary disciplines, most notably, perhaps (at least in terms of public attention), in English and American literature, but certainly in legal studies as well.[1] One can ask very generally what legal materials all law students should be exposed to, or one can ask the more limited question as to what students studying constitutional law should be expected to read. That is, what should constitute the canon of constitutional law?

Even this way of putting the question may be too broad, though, for we argue that one cannot begin constructing a set of canonical materials without first addressing the purpose of the proposed canon. Is it, for example, to teach students within the legal academy those cases (and other materials) most likely to structure their own practice of constitutional law, assuming, contrary to fact, of course, that many—let alone most—students will ever find themselves litigating a constitutional issue? Still, one could begin with the "legal fiction" that students must be aware of the most lively issues currently before courts and of the various doctrines likely to prove interesting (or at least useful) to adjudicators called upon to decide cases involving those issues. Or, again focusing on the specific needs of students preparing to become practicing lawyers, should we pick materials that are especially useful in teaching the arts of lawyering, namely, those cases that offer especially useful examples of legal reasoning that can serve as models of lawyers' rhetorical arts? Even cases involving no-longer-live issues could, nonetheless, serve as paradigms of such reasoning.[2] Both of these criteria, whatever their differences, identify candidates for what we call the "pedagogical canon,"[3] that is, the preparation of students for their professional lives as practicing lawyers.

But one might have aims other than preparing persons, even those persons called "law students," for the actual practice of constitutional law. After all, many undergraduate and graduate students take courses in constitutional law without intending to become lawyers. Indeed, some law students even attend law school without envisioning themselves as future legal practitioners. Yet all may well view some familiarity with the materials of American constitutional development as part of what constitutes their being educated citizens, and their teachers are thus charged with the task of identifying the canon of such materials. We label this the "cultural literacy canon."[4]

Finally, there is what we denominate the "academic theory canon,"[5] by which we identify those crucial episodes within American constitutional history that must be confronted by legal academics who wish to be taken seriously within the community of constitutional scholars. Here, one is not at all concerned with what is best for one's students, treated either as pre-professionals or future citizens, but, rather, what is best for oneself as someone who wishes to establish his or her presence within an ongoing conversation among trained academics.

My argument in this essay is that the *Insular Cases*[6] deserve an important place within each of these canons, though, as one might expect, the reasons are different depending on the canon to which one is referring. I should confess, though, that I speak a bit with the zeal of a convert, for prior to the Yale Law School conference on Puerto Rico at which most of the papers in this volume were originally given, I had never read the cases. Neither in my graduate studies at Harvard prior to writing a dissertation on Justices Holmes and Frankfurter nor at the Stanford Law School, where I received my J.D., were they ever assigned; I have also managed to teach constitutional law for almost two decades at the University of Texas (and co-edit what I immodestly believe is a first-rate casebook in the field)[7] without filling in this blank. One factor encouraging this public confession is that conversation with other adepts in constitutional law, including editors of competing casebooks, leads me to believe that my story is not in the least unusual.

At the present time, few cases can be said to be *less* canonical, regardless of criterion, than *Downes* (or any of the other *Insular Cases*).[8] Indeed, Balkin and I present a practical test of what is, or is not, a canonical case: Just play the wonderful game, "Humiliation," invented by the British novelist David Lodge as part of his academic novel *Changing Places,* in which one wins points by naming, in a group of presumably sophisticated fellow academics, books that one has *not* read that have, in fact, been read by the rest of the group. The "winner" of the game, in the novel, was a hapless, overly competitive, untenured professor of English who could not resist using *Hamlet* as his trump.[9] The constitutional law equivalent would presumably be the admission that one had never read McCulloch v. Maryland.[10] Somewhere there may be a legal academic who has never pored through this most important of all constitutional law opinions, but one would truly risk one's reputation (and one's job) by admitting it. *That* is the operational test of a case's being canonical. The *Insular Cases,* on the other hand, might be taken, at least at the present time, as exemplifying the "anticanon" (just as matter is complemented by antimatter) insofar as no ostensible constitutional scholar risks blotting his or her reputation, save, presumably, in Puerto Rico itself, by admitting to one's ignorance.

Evidence of this proposition can be found not only in personal anecdote. Just look at contemporary constitutional law casebooks or treatises, where one will find almost no mention at all of the cases. No casebook that I have examined has even the briefest reference to the cases and to the issues raised by them. One will search in vain for index entries to, say, "Puerto Rico," "territories," or "expansion." In addition to the "standard" constitutional law casebooks, I searched as well Derrick Bell's *Race, Racism, and American Law,*[11] inasmuch as one might well view the *Insular Cases* as central documents in the history of American racism. They were absent there as well. Indeed, the only reason for my "almost" in the sentence above is a two-page discussion, in John Nowak and Ronald Rotunda's hornbook on constitutional law, of "To What Extent Does the Constitution Follow the Flag; Does the Constitution Apply to the Territories?"[12] Professor Laurence Tribe also cites *Downes v. Bidwell* in the second edition of his magisterial *American Constitutional Law,* at the conclusion of a single footnote concerning congressional power over aliens.[13] There was, as implied, no mention at all in the first edition, as is the case in the competing treatise authored by Erwin Chemerinsky.[14] The cases would never constitute an intelligent play in "Humiliation," assuming there is nothing truly unusual about the group within which one is playing (such as their being Puerto Ricans).

It is time to change this situation. I have played my own part by including in the most recent edition of *Processes of Constitutional Decisionmaking,* as I promised Judge José Cabranes at the Yale symposium, substantial material from *Downes.* The inclusion, though, was not at all motivated merely by a feeling of obligation to keep one's promises (even to a federal judge). I hope that the inclusion of *Downes* will, in short order, no longer be regarded as yet another idiosyncrasy of our book and that it will be found as well in our competitors' casebooks. I think it is worth mentioning that I included, obviously for the first time, *Downes* in the 1998 version of my first-year introductory constitutional law course, and it sparked a good discussion among students.[15] Thinking about the issues raised in that case has also led me to offer, again for the first time, a seminar on "The Constitution and American Expansion," a topic that is remarkably understudied by constitutional scholars, much to our detriment.

So let me now try to answer the central question: What justifies imposing upon students, especially first-year law students, even an edited version of a very, very long case dealing, at a formal level, with the meaning of Article I, section 8, clause 1 and its requirement that "all duties, imposts, and excises shall be uniform throughout the United States"? The answer surely doesn't lie in what undergirds the first version of the pedagogical canon, namely, the high probability that students will be faced with "uniformity clause" issues; indeed, if truth be known, even though the field of taxation of interstate commerce, especially by states, continues to generate significant cases,[16] the general subject has disappeared from almost all contemporary casebooks, including *Processes of Constitutional Decisionmaking*. Nor am I really concerned to prepare students for possible cases concerning the particular (and perhaps peculiar) constitutional status of Puerto Rico, Guam, and the Virgin Islands, though, to be sure, there is certainly opportunity for some lawyers to litigate such issues.[17] Still, if prediction of litigation is at all relevant, one should note that it is far more likely that students will address in their practice the First Amendment implications of regulating cigarette advertising than whether, for example, Puerto Ricans are properly regarded as Fourteenth Amendment birthright citizens rather than citizens only because of congressional grace as manifested in a 1917 statute conferring that status.[18]

One could easily justify assigning *Downes* in terms of the second notion of the pedagogical canon, for the debates among the contending Justices are indeed carried on at a high level of professional ability, and students can certainly learn a lot about legal rhetoric from the close study of the various opinions. For someone like me, who emphasizes learning the "modalities" of legal argument,[19] the case is almost a treasure trove. After all, the formal question before the Court is whether Puerto Rico, ceded to the United States by Spain in the aftermath of the Spanish-American War of 1898 and thus fully subject to American sovereignty, is within "the United States" for purposes of the Uniformity Clause. One might think this would be an easy question, but students (and their teachers) are consistently surprised by the fundamental questions that the Constitution leaves unanswered. Presidents must be "natural born citizens,"[20] but the constitutional text gives nary a clue as to how one discovers who is, with certainty, within that status. Similarly, one might think that the question as to what constitutes "the United States" that is, after all, presumptively structured by the Constitution would have a clear constitutional answer, but that, just as obviously, is untrue. If Puerto Rico is not part of "the United States," then what (or where) is it, and how does one derive the answer? One answer, of course, is that offered by the plurality opinion authored by Justice White. It is an "unincorporated territory," a term that, of course, appears nowhere in the constitutional text or anywhere in the various debates surrounding the formation of the Constitution. So where does it come from? Perhaps from prior case law, as suggested in the plurality opinion. Perhaps also, and even more importantly, from the perceived exigencies of the moment, which made Puerto Rico and the Philippines at once highly desirable as possessions of the United States yet, it was thought, unsuitable for genuine membership in the American Union. I shall return to this theme presently.

Of course, even if Puerto Rico had been treated as a full-fledged, first-class "territory" of the United States, that would still invite further discussion of the implications of the distinction drawn in the Constitution between states and territories. Some of the ramifications are obvious and unproblematic. Only states can have voting representatives in Congress or representation in the electoral college.[21] But what about, for example, the Privileges and Immunities Clause of Article IV,[22] specifically limited in its language to "the Citizens of each State"? Would, then, a state be free to discriminate against citizens of the United States who were not, however, citizens of any particular state, meaning those citizens of the United States living in territories, at least in the absence of Equal Protection limitations? And section 4 of Article IV guarantees "a Republican Form of Government" only to "every State in this Union,"[23] just as the United States apparently must protect only "each *of them* against Invasion."[24] Can the United States blithely govern, indefinitely, *any* territory in a decidedly nonrepublican manner and cite the text of Article IV as licensing such governance? This is, of course, no idle question, not only in regard to territories like Puerto Rico and Guam but also, as Mark Tushnet points out elsewhere in this volume, with regard to the District of Columbia, which continues in basic ways to be under the iron fist of a Congress in which it has no voting representation.[25] Surely one task of any first-year constitutional law course is to teach the techniques of close textual analysis, including the importance of reading the Constitution in its entirety and discerning from the language used in one part implications for the analysis of other parts.[26]

All of these pedagogical goals are amply furthered by *Downes*. Yet, in all candor, my own interest in adding it to the syllabus and my zeal in urging that other teachers do likewise comes less from its potential utility as part of the pedagogical canon than from its importance for those interested in constructing the best cultural-literacy canon in order to create citizens who are well informed about key episodes in American constitutional development or, indeed, for the value it would have within the academic theory canon in directing constitutional scholars toward important questions that have tended to be ignored within contemporary scholarship.

The culturally literate citizen should be aware of the particularities of American expansionism found in the late nineteenth century, on which the *Insular Cases* throw immense light. Earlier moments of expansionism—the move westward, in the name of what would be denominated "Manifest Destiny,"[27] toward the Pacific as evoked so powerfully in Marshall's opinion in *McCulloch*[28]—involved lands that were clearly meant to become, after settlement and development by whites, full members of the United States of America, with concomitant full rights of participation in the House, Senate, and electoral college. Permanent colonization was not viewed as "the American way," save, of course, for American Indians, whose story—also, one might note, excluded from the current canon of constitutional law—is vital to any narrative of American expansionism and whose legal history is linked in important ways to that of the Puerto Ricans whose fate is ultimately at issue in *Downes.*

What I now realize, in a way that was simply not part of my consciousness prior to my immersion in *Downes,* is how much the entire story of American expansionism has been ignored within the currently operative canon(s) of constitutional law. The central narratives of American constitutional history tend to be those sketched out in Robert McCloskey's classic work *The American Supreme Court,*[29] which features three organizing story-lines. The first describes the complex (and, of course, ultimately violent) grappling with the implications of federalism, a story that began with the 1787 drafting of the Constitution and lasts at least until Appomattox. At that point, although the issue of federalism obviously does not disappear, it moves to the background, to be replaced in the starring role by the constitutional issues generated by the development of industrial capitalism and a national economy. To what extent would government, both at the state and national levels, be deemed to have the power to regulate the new forms of business enterprise that had developed? This legal struggle, of course, culminated in the New Deal revolution that removed the doctrinal obstacles that had been created by the "Old Court" in the earlier half-century. Again, issues of economic regulation have not entirely disappeared, but they, too, have moved substantially into the shadows, as the central story shifts to the Constitution's role as guarantor of the civil rights and liberties of vulnerable minorities, what might be termed the "footnote 4" narrative featuring the Court as vigorous protector of the politically and socially downtrodden.[30] Or, as I have suggested in my own revisions to McCloskey's text, the post–Great Society Court has taken on the task of monitoring the operation of the significantly enlarged welfare state that emerged in the 1960s.[31] What is notably absent from McCloskey's account—and, of course, the point is that he is not in the least unique—is the epic story of American expansionism that pervades our entire nineteenth-century history.

The *Insular Cases,* of course, deal with one important episode in the history of expansionism, the aftermath of the Spanish-American War of 1898, which represented, among other things, the forthright decision by American ruling elites—and the electorate in the 1900 presidential contest between William McKinley and William Jennings Bryan—to join European countries in becoming a frankly imperialist power. This meant, among other things, the capture and subsequent politico-legal control by the United States of hitherto foreign territory that would not, in any way, be viewed as a potential member of the organic entity known as the United States of America. But one of the marvelous things about *Downes,* pedagogically speaking, is that it contains within it a capsule history of some other crucial chapters in the expansionist saga.

The most important example surely involves the Louisiana Purchase. Students can learn from *Downes* of Thomas Jefferson's belief that the Louisiana Purchase was unconstitutional. At one level, this basic fact is probably known to most reasonably well-informed students of American history. But most people, I dare say, assume that the only problem involved presidential authority to commit the United States to the purchase of foreign territory prior to congressional authorization. That, to be sure, was no small issue, but the far more profound problem, at the heart of Jefferson's concerns, involved the radical transformation generated by the Purchase in the very nature of the United States as a sociopolitical entity. Most obviously, it greatly increased the size of the United States, more than doubling it. This could be no small point for anyone at all committed to the classical republican belief that republican government could not be successfully achieved in an "extended" territory.

This was, of course, the subject of a classic essay by James Madison in *The Federalist,*[32] which displayed little patience for the small-area theory of republicanism espoused by many anti-Federalists. But Madison's argument was written to justify what from our own perspective is a remarkably modest extended republic of thirteen states (and attached territories that would be ceded to the new United States as the seedbed for expansion west of the Alleghenies) consisting of approximately three million people, of whom the majority (or, more to the point, the overwhelming majority of the people permitted to participate in the polity) were white, Protestant, and English-speaking. It requires a substantial leap of faith to assume that even Madisonians, let alone Jeffersonians fearful of potential tyranny from an impersonal government far removed from local networks, would necessarily applaud a vastly larger country, the most important city of which, New Orleans, was dominated by French-speaking Catholics and legally organized under that most basic rejection of the wisdom of the common law, the Napoleonic Code. And, of course, it could readily be predicted that many of the new lands would be conducive to the expansion of slavery and, just as importantly, the creation of new states committed to maintaining (and expanding) chattel slavery; the explicit terms of the Purchase seemed to guarantee the eventual (but not too-long deferred) admission as full-fledged, and equal, states of the territories that would be carved out of the Purchase.

It is little wonder that Jefferson believed that a constitutional amendment was necessary to justify the expansion instantiated in the Louisiana Purchase. "Our Confederation is certainly confined to the limits established by the revolution. The general government has no powers but such as the constitution has given it; and it has not given it a power of holding foreign territory, and still less of incorporating it into the Union. An amendment of the constitution seems necessary for this."[33] Ironically enough, his Federalist opponents professed to share such constitutional doubts, presumably because of the obvious increase in Southern power presaged by the Purchase. Obviously, Jefferson changed his mind, not least because of what Holmes would well label "the felt necessities of the times." If the United States appeared to tarry in taking advantage of Napoleon's remarkable offer, there was a danger that Spain would attempt to undo the deal, to the severe detriment of American national interests.[34] There is, therefore, no amendment licensing the purchase, and executive-congressional power under the Treaty Clause was expanded in a coup d'main. I shall have more to say about this presently, but for now I will limit myself to declaring how useful as an intellectual challenge it is to try to recapture the mind-set that initially convinced Jefferson of the constitutional irregularities presented by the

Purchase and then the political realities that persuaded him that there were more important things than sheer fidelity to abstract constitutional norms. As he wrote at the time, "[T]he less that is said about my constitutional difficulty, the better; and . . . it will be desirable for Congress to do what is necessary *in silence.*"[35] Or, as he put it in 1810, upon further reflection, "A strict observance of the written law is doubtless one of the high duties of a good citizen but it is not the highest. The laws of necessity, of self-preservation, of saving our country when in danger, are of higher obligation."[36] Even if one agrees with Jefferson, it remains well worth asking how this justifies the Purchase (or the other expansionist acts that would be carried out with questionable constitutional provenance).

Finally, it is worth noting Jefferson's deviation from republican principles of governance, as he chose to impose on the new territory what his most recent biographer calls "a blatantly nonrepublican territorial government"[37] that denied the residents participatory rights in their new government. Jefferson argued in private correspondence that "our new fellow citizens are as yet incapable of self-government as children, yet some cannot bring themselves to suspend [republican] principles for a single moment."[38] Indeed Joseph Ellis seems to sympathize, arguing that "both the sheer size of the region and the ethnic diversity of the Creole population posed governance problems that justified a firmer hand at the start."[39] At least the whites, though, *were* deemed to be "fellow citizens," and the operative assumption was that various territories to be carved out of the Purchase would indeed become states of the Union in due time. As we shall see, many of the same arguments were revived at the time of the *Insular Cases,* and this time the fears of diversity led to quite different results.

A major reality of the new Louisiana territories, of course, was their "suitability" for slavery, a subject raising the most tortuous constitutional issues. It can, therefore, occasion little surprise that the discussion in *Downes* segues from consideration of Jefferson's constitutional doubts about the Purchase to an extensive treatment of Chief Justice Taney's opinion in *Dred Scott,*[40] which, after all, centrally concerned Congress's power to regulate the vast new territories brought within the United States by Jefferson's action. For understandable reasons, the case is usually treated, when it is found at all in canonical materials,[41] as a case only about slavery and, even more so, about the status of blacks, deemed by Taney to have "no rights that the white man was bound to respect."[42] With the demise of slavery—and the solution to the problem of citizenship provided by the first sentence of the Fourteenth Amendment—*Dred Scott* is thought to be a case with little enduring importance for post-Reconstruction constitutional analysis. This is false. The meta-issue, as it were, of *Dred Scott,* is whether Congress possesses truly "plenary," that is, unconstrained, power in regard to the territories of the United States. No issue was more relevant at the turn of the twentieth century, given the turn toward expansion by the United States.

Taney's conclusion that Congress did not enjoy plenary power rendered unconstitutional the Missouri Compromise of 1820, with its prohibition of slavery in the northern regions of the Louisiana Purchase. Although Article IV gives Congress the power to make "all *needful* rules" (emphasis added), it takes only minimal acquaintance with the issues surrounding the exegesis of the "necessary and proper" clause to realize that this can easily be read as considerably less than an assignment of plenary power to Congress to do whatever it thinks desirable concerning the territories. To speak somewhat anachronistically, Taney was a "premature anti-imperialist," who rejected the notion of the United States as a country that could conquer territory and govern it at the unfettered behest of Congress. Instead, for Taney, all territory was in effect held in trust for those Americans who would settle it and then establish full and equal states within the American polity. And, while in the territory, they maintained a full set of constitutional rights. To be anachronistic once more, Taney would presumably have answered yes to the question surrounding the *Insular Cases:* Does the Constitution follow the flag? It is a useful exercise to ask whether Taney was wrong in his entire theory of the case, or "only" in the absolutely disastrous application of his theory to protect the purported property rights of slaveowners.

To be sure, *Downes* does not present a comprehensive overview of American expansionism. There is, for example, no discussion of the significant constitutional issues surrounding the annexation of Texas[43] (perhaps because the Lone Star Republic was never a "territory" of the United States). Anyone interested, though, in the meaning of the Treaty Clause as a significant procedural hurdle to foreign entanglements should certainly be interested in the rather remarkable process surrounding Texas's entry into the Union. The annexation of Texas was first presented to the Senate in the form of a treaty between two sovereigns, requiring ratification by two-thirds of the Senate. However, upon the realization of the impossibility of securing such support, given the antagonism of antislavery northerners to this boon to slaveowners, the admission of Texas as a state was transformed into ordinary legislation admitting a new state, which requires only the approval of a majority of each house of Congress. The fact that all prior states were carved out of territory belonging to the United States was deemed constitutionally irrelevant. *Downes* is also silent on the particular history of the United States in relation to conquered tribes of American Indians. All of these are parts of the expansionist epic, and all deserve placement that is now lacking in the canon.

The *Insular Cases* should be placed not only in the context of American expansionism but also within the sadly rich history of American racism or, perhaps more to the point, the history of American "ascriptivism," the view that to be a "true American" one had to share certain racial, religious, or ethnic characteristics.[44] No one can read *Downes* without realizing the extent to which the "un-Americanness" of the people in the new American territories is fundamental to the outcome. Thus Justice Brown, denying that Puerto Rico is within the United States, notes the implications of a contrary decision for "what Chief Justice Marshall termed the 'American empire.' There seems to be no middle ground between [Brown's] position and the doctrine that if their inhabitants do not become, immediately upon annexation, citizens of the United States, [then at least] their children thereafter born, *whether savages or civilized,* are such, and entitled to all the rights, privileges and immunities of citizens."[45] This was, apparently, unthinkable. Yet there was no doubt in Brown's mind that annexation of what he termed "outlying and distant"[46] lands might serve American national (and imperial) interests.

> If those possessions are inhabited by alien races, differing from us in religion, customs, laws, methods of taxation and modes of thought, the administration of government and justice, according to Anglo-Saxon principles [presumably instantiated in the Constitution], may for a time be impossible; and the question at once arises whether large concessions ought not to be made for a time, that, ultimately, our own theories may be carried out, and the blessings of a free government under the Constitution extended to them.[47]

It is almost needless to add that Justice Brown authored the egregious opinion in *Plessy v. Ferguson,*[48] which can be understood only against a background assumption that it was entirely reasonable for racially superior whites to wish to avoid the prospect of association as presumptive social equals with African Americans. Students should realize that these cases arise out of a common intellectual milieu. Similarly, cases at the time involving American Indians featured the same assumptions. Thus the Court in *Elk v. Wilkins*[49] had refused to recognize American Indians as birthright citizens.

For certain purposes, then, Indian lands were also viewed as not being within the United States, though of course this had no effect on the extent of the governing authority Congress would claim vis-à-vis the Indian nations.[50] And, in a 1913 decision, a unanimous Court described the Pueblo Indians of New Mexico as "adhering to primitive modes of life . . . and chiefly governed according to the crude customs inherited from their ancestors[;] they are essentially a simple, uninformed and inferior people," thus much in need of "special consideration and protection, like other Indian communities."[51]

One ought, of course, not treat the Court as some kind of deviation from an otherwise more enlightened universalism found in the other branches, for that was surely not the case. Congress was, during this era, passing laws excluding the immigration of Asians.[52] Indeed, Justice Harlan, in his famous dissent in *Plessy v. Ferguson,* after arguing that "the destinies of the two races, in this country, are indissolubly linked together," went on to note, alluding to "the Chinese race," that "[t]here is a race so different from our own that we do not permit those belonging to it to become citizens of the United States."[53] Even more telling—and shocking to those for whom Harlan has become an icon of antiracist sensibility—is his joining in Chief Justice Fuller's dissent in *United States v. Wong Kim Ark.*[54] The majority had held that persons of Chinese descent born in the United States were indeed birthright citizens under the Fourteenth Amendment. Fuller and Harlan, on the other hand, accepted the argument made by the United States that "[t]here should be some honor and dignity in American citizenship that would be sacred from the foul and corrupting taint of a debasing alienage."[55] Fuller, joined by Harlan, agreed and denounced "the presence within our territory of large numbers of Chinese laborers, of a distinct race and religion, remaining strangers in the land, residing apart by themselves, tenaciously adhering to the customs and usages of their own country, unfamiliar with our institutions, and apparently incapable of assimilating with our people."[56] It can, then, occasion no surprise that they were not willing to admit "that the children of persons so situated become citizens by the accident of birth."[57]

It is also worth paying some attention to the politics of statehood in regard to the New Mexico and Arizona territories, which were very much affected by concerns about the prevalence of Spanish-speaking Mexican Americans in the former. An initial proposal that New Mexico and Arizona be admitted together as one state was rejected in a "Protest" by the Arizona territorial legislature, which referred to "the decided racial difference between the people of New Mexico, who are not only different in race and largely in language, but have entirely different customs, laws, and ideals and would have but little prospect of successful amalgamation." Describing the people of Arizona, the "Protest" stated that "95 percent . . . are Americans," which suggests an unwillingness to treat most of their fellow American citizens in New Mexico as "real" Americans because of these differences.[58] The good news, of course, is that New Mexico was in fact admitted to the Union in 1912, with Arizona as a separate state, but the concern about difference, especially of language, has certainly not disappeared. Indeed, any discussion of the prospects of Puerto Rican statehood today quickly turns to the fact that most Puerto Ricans speak only (or, certainly, principally) Spanish and that Puerto Rico, if a state, might take advantage of the "equal footing doctrine"[59] to emulate other states who have declared an "official" language,[60] though in Puerto Rico's case the official language would presumably be Spanish.

Nor, if one is to be honest, can one simply dismiss as irrelevant the questions asked by Justice Brown, even if they are phrased in a decidedly odious manner. Only the most naive, and indeed chauvinistic, American could believe that our particular Constitution is a one-size-fits-all model of how *all* societies, whatever their particular histories, social structures, traditions, or state of economic development, should be governed. One must recognize that to this day Puerto Ricans are scarcely undivided in regard to the basic issue underlying the *Insular Cases,* namely, the complete absorption of the island into "the United States." A (slim) majority of Puerto Ricans, after all, reject statehood in favor of alternatives, either retention of commonwealth status or independence, that presuppose a certain lack of "fit," as it were, between full membership in the Union, with all attendant constitutional obligations, and the particular interests of Puerto Rico. Moreover, to this day the Constitution does not truly follow the flag in regard to Indian nations within the territorial United States. The Bill of Rights has never been formally "incorporated" against Indian nations, and even the Indian Civil Rights Act extending most of the protections of the Bill of Rights to members of Indian tribes nonetheless omits the Establishment Clause of the First Amendment.[61] Indian nations are thus allowed to be theocracies in a way that would be wholly impermissible in any other institution of American governance.

Few cases, then, offer so much as *Downes* in learning about the interplay of general American political ideologies and the development of constitutional doctrine. Moreover, insofar as the lessons are sometimes unpleasant,

Downes can serve as an important corrective against some of the more cheerleading views of constitutional history (and the Supreme Court) as necessarily progressive in its thrust.

There is also the third canon, which consists of cases (or episodes) raising fundamental questions for the academic constitutional theorist. Here, too, the *Insular Cases* amply pay their way, especially if one agrees with such leading figures as Bruce Ackerman[62] and Stephen Griffin[63] that the duty of the constitutional theorist is to explain the actual mechanisms of constitutional change that have undoubtedly occurred in the American polity. Both sharply reject the altogether naïve—indeed, literally incredible—notion that the Constitution over the past two hundred years can be understood in terms of a canonical text drafted in 1787 plus those written textual additions we call "amendments" and "interpretations" of these canonical texts proffered by the Supreme Court. Both argue, and I strongly agree, that significant "amendment" has taken place outside the confines of Article V.[64]

Ackerman, of course, is famous for his notion of "constitutional moments," whereby an aroused American public, confronting issues of great import, makes a conscious decision to strike out on transformative constitutional paths. Although his initial writings suggested that there were only three such moments—the founding in 1787, Reconstruction immediately after 1865, and then the New Deal—his more recent work has acknowledged the possibility of additional such moments. Indeed, Ackerman has recognized that his own earlier work was too much focused on domestic events; a book co-authored with David Golove, on the other hand, argues that an important lesson of World War II was the inutility of the Treaty Clause as a constraint on foreign agreements, so that broad notions of "executive agreement," coupled with majority approval of both houses of Congress, in effect substituted for the far more onerous requirement of the Treaty Clause (shades of Texas annexation!).[65]

It is, I think, easy to view the *Insular Cases* as the product of just such an Ackermanian "moment." Although historians differ on the extent to which the election of 1900 was a referendum on American imperialism,[66] it is clear that the 1898 war and its aftermath constituted one of the central issues placed before the public. The two sides could hardly have been more clear in their views, the Republican McKinley embracing the duty to "educate the Filipinos [and, presumably, Puerto Ricans], and uplift and civilize and Christianize them,"[67] while William Jennings Bryan pressed the anti-imperialist cause. McKinley obviously won, and the *Insular Cases* were decided accordingly. It was, indeed, these cases that generated Finley Peter Dunne's immortal aphorism, "No matther whether th' constitution follows th' flag or not, th' Supreme Coort follows th' iliction returns."[68] For many, this is a cynical observation. For Ackerman, though, following the election returns, at least when the electorate has been properly primed by political leaders as to what is at stake, is precisely what the Supreme Court should do in order to recognize the successful culmination of a constitutional moment. The importance of Ackerman's argument, relative to the *Insular Cases,* is this: Even if one concedes the validity of the dissenters' analysis that the distinction between "incorporated" and "unincorporated" territories is made up of whole cloth and that Taney was basically correct in his anti-imperialist (albeit, in this instance, proslavery) reading of the initial Constitution, the Constitution had in effect been amended as the result of the events of 1898 and the ratifying election that took place two years later. Thus the majority was perhaps right on the merits, though not for the reasons they gave.

Conclusion

In some ways, this essay should be regarded as a "brief," making the case for inclusion of *Downes v. Bidwell* into the various canons of American constitutional law. Its intended audience is by no means the already well-informed scholar who will, no doubt, profit far more from the other essays in this collection than from this one. Instead, I am writing for those readers like myself, sadly underinformed about the case and about the profound issues it involved. I hope that I have said enough to whet their own appetites and to encourage them to offer their own welcome to *Downes* and its companion cases within the various canons of American constitutional inquiry.

Notes

I am grateful to Scot Powe and Fred Schauer for their comments on an earlier draft of this essay.

1 See J. M. Balkin and Sanford Levinson, "The Canons of Constitutional Law," *Harvard Law Review* 111 (1998): 963.

2 I should note that "useful" does not necessarily mean "admirable." See the discussion of *Downes v. Bidwell,* 182 U.S. 244 (1901), below, at notes 44–47 and accompanying text. One might, of course, select canonical cases on the basis of their admirability as exercises in legal reasoning. This is one rationale, for example, for teaching *Youngstown Sheet and Tube Co. v. Sawyer,* 343 U.S. 579 (1952), which includes what I regard as the greatest single opinion ever written by a Supreme Court justice, Robert Jackson's concurrence in that case, ibid. at 634. See

Sanford Levinson, Introduction [to Favorite Case Symposium]: "Why Select a Favorite Case?," *Texas Law Review* 74 (1996): 1195, at 1197–1200. Obviously, the issue of "inherent" presidential power could arise again in our own time, but, just as obviously, this is not at the forefront of contemporary constitutional controversy, and the rationale for including it within the canon would be something other than preparing students for the most likely subjects of litigation.

3   Balkin and Levinson, supra note 1, at 975. Apropos of current events (at least as of December 1998), it might be useful if the ordinary lawyer knew more about presidential impeachment than is likely to be the case, not, obviously, because of the likelihood of representing the president or his adversaries, but, rather, because of the propensity of nonlawyers to ask lawyers about the legal merits of impeachment and because of the propensity of lawyers to answer such questions, whether or not they are truly knowledgeable about the matter.

4   Ibid. at 976.

5   Ibid.

6   See *Downes v. Bidwell,* 182 U.S. 244 (1901). This is, obviously, only one of the many cases that, taken together, comprise the *Insular Cases.* See "A Note on the *Insular Cases*" in this volume. Most discussants of the cases seem to agree that *Downes* is the most significant single case. As shall be seen below, it certainly contains a treasure trove of issues for those interested in constitutional law and theory. A comprehensive treatment of the issues is Juan R. Torruella, *The Supreme Court and Puerto Rico: The Doctrine of Separate and Unequal* (1985).

7   Paul Brest and Sanford Levinson, *Processes of Constitutional Decisionmaking,* 3d ed. (1992).

8   Obviously, there are many obscure cases that would be equally uncanonical. The difference between them and *Downes* is that it, and the other *Insular Cases,* were once at the center of American constitutional debate, whereas many cases are deservedly obscure insofar as no one really cared about them at the time (other than the particular litigants) or afterward. What has to be explained in regard to *Downes* and its companion cases is why an issue that was once deemed so vital to American constitutionalism has almost entirely disappeared from view. One cannot even take refuge in the answer that is sometimes given in regard to, say, the disappearance of many slavery cases from the canon—"we don't have slavery anymore"— because we most certainly *do* continue to have Puerto Rico as a live issue of American politics and constitutional inquiry.

9   See David Lodge, *Changing Places: A Tale of Two Campuses* (1992), at 136. He "won" the game, though he subsequently was not awarded tenure.

10   17 U.S. (4 Wheat.) 316 (1819).

11   Derrick Bell, *Race, Racism, and American Law,* 3d ed. (1992).

12   See John E. Nowak and Ronald D. Rotunda, *Constitutional Law,* 5th ed. (1995), at 210–11.

13   See Laurence Tribe, *American Constitutional Law,* 2d ed. (1988), at 361 n. 41.

14   See Erwin Chemerinsky, *Constitutional Law: Principles and Politics* (1997).

15   I also note, for what it is worth, I do *not* assign *Marbury v. Madison,* 5 U.S. (1 Cranch) 137 (1803), even though it is regarded by many as the most important of all constitutional law cases. Teaching *Marbury* well requires the expenditure of several class hours, and I believe that it simply isn't worth taking that much time in a course in which many issues and cases compete with one another for scarce time in a course that meets only forty-two times the entire semester. It is also the case that the substantive issue raised by *Marbury*—the power of Congress to add to the original jurisdiction of the Supreme Court—is really quite trivial. In contrast, the substantive issues raised by the *Insular Cases* are far more important, and I think that students can grasp the basic constitutional problems in a single, albeit intense, class hour.

16 See Nowak and Rotunda, supra note 12, §8.11, at 311–14, for a recent overview of the case law.

17 See generally, Arnold H. Leibowitz, *Defining Status: A Comprehensive Analysis of United States Territorial Relations* (1989).

18 See *Jones Act, U.S. Statutes at Large* 39 (1917): 353, discussed in Leibowitz, ibid. at 144–46.

19 The term comes from Philip Bobbitt's seminal work. See Bobbitt, *Constitutional Fate: Theory of the Constitution* (1982), and *Constitutional Interpretation* (1991). For Bobbitt there are six "modalities," i.e., constitutive rhetorics of constitutional analysis: textualism, historical analysis, structuralism, doctrinalism, prudentialism, and what he calls "ethical" analysis, by which he means attention to the underlying assumptions of the American "ethos" captured in the overall nature of the constitutional enterprise. For further analysis (and critique), see J. M. Balkin and Sanford Levinson, "Constitutional Grammar," *Texas Law Review* 72 (1994): 1771. See also T. Alexander Aleinikoff, "Puerto Rico and the Constitution: Conundrums and Prospects," *Constitutional Commentary* 11 (1994): 15.

20 *United States Constitution,* art. II, sec. 1, cl. 5.

21 The District of Columbia, which is not a state, does have representation in the electoral college (and, like Puerto Rico, non-voting representation in the House of Representatives), but it took a constitutional amendment (see *United States Constitution,* Twenty-third Amendment) to gain the electoral votes enjoyed by the District.

22 "The Citizens of each State shall be entitled to all Privileges and Immunities of citizens in the several States."

23 Art. IV, sec. 4: "The United States shall guarantee to every State in this Union a Republican Form of government, and shall protect each of them against Invasion; and on Application of the Legislature, or of the Executive (when the Legislature cannot be convened) against domestic Violence."

24 Ibid. (emphasis added).

25 See, e.g., Francis X. Clines, "$1.64 May Block Medical Use of Marijuana in Capital," *New York Times,* Nov. 13, 1998, at A22, detailing the inability of the District government to compute (and inform the public of the result of) the vote regarding the medical use of marijuana because of a statute passed in the waning days of the congressional session forbidding the District to spend any funds at all tabulating the vote.

26 This methodology is probably most identified these days with Akhil Reed Amar. Indeed, Amar discusses the issues raised by the *Insular Cases* in his recent article "Intratextualism," *Harvard Law Review* 112 (1999): 747, at 782–87 (discussing varying approaches of C. C. Langdell and A. Lawrence Lowell in their articles on the constitutional status of Puerto Rico).

27 See, e.g., Frederick Merk, *Manifest Destiny and Mission in American History* (1963).

28 "Throughout this vast republic, from the St. Croix to the Gulf of Mexico, from the Atlantic to the Pacific, revenue is to be collected and expended, armies are to be marched and supported. . . . Is that construction of the constitution to be preferred, which would render these operations difficult, hazardous, and expensive?" 17 U.S. (4 Wheat.) at 408.

29 Robert McCloskey, *The American Supreme Court* (1960). I have prepared updated versions of this book, published in 1994 (2d ed.) and 2000 (3d ed.). I did not, however, revise any of McCloskey's original analysis.

30 See *United States v. Carolene Products Co.,* 304 U.S. 144, 152–53 n. 4 (1938) (setting out the circumstances in which the Court would refuse simply to defer to legislative judgment and would, instead, engage in significant monitoring of statutes). An especially interesting account of the jurisprudence of footnote 4 is J. M. Balkin, "The Footnote," *Northwestern University*

Law Review 83 (1989): 275. I do not want to be read as necessarily endorsing the descriptive accuracy of the standard narrative and its tendency to praise the Court as a fearless protector of the downtrodden. My colleague Lucas Powe challenges this conventional wisdom in *The Warren Court and American Politics* (2000), which argues that even this Court most esteemed by political liberals scarcely proved particularly protective of truly vulnerable minorities (i.e., those minorities who did not enjoy significant support from the wider polity).

31   See McCloskey (3d ed.), supra note 29, at 184.

32   See The Federalist No. 14, in *The Federalist,* ed. Benjamin F. Wright (1961), at 150.

33   Thomas Jefferson to John Dickinson, quoted in David N. Mayer, *The Constitutional Thought of Thomas Jefferson* (1994), at 247. See generally Everett Somerville Brown, *The Constitutional History of the Louisiana Purchase, 1803–1812* (1920).

34   See ibid. at 250.

35   Thomas Jefferson to Levi Lincoln, August 30, 1803, quoted in Joseph Ellis, *American Sphinx: The Character of Thomas Jefferson* (1996), at 210.

36   Quoted in Gerald Stourzh, *Alexander Hamilton and the Idea of a Republican Government* (1970), at 34.

37   Ellis, supra note 35, at 210.

38   Quoted in ibid. at 211.

39   Ibid.

40   *Scott v. Sandford,* 60 U.S. (19 How.) 393 (1857).

41   As a matter of fact, *Dred Scott* just barely hangs on to canonical status. See Sanford Levinson, "Slavery in the Canon of Constitutional Law," *Chicago-Kent Law Review* 68 (1993): 1087, at 1090–91.

42   *Dred Scott,* 60 U.S. (19 How.) at 407.

43   See Frederick Merk, *Slavery and the Annexation of Texas* (1972): 121–51.

44   See, generally, Rogers Smith, *Civic Ideals: Conflicting Visions of Citizenship in U.S. History* (1997). Smith notes, for example, the presence of an influential ideology, especially prevalent during the period of the *Insular Cases,* that "America was by rights a white nation, a Protestant nation, a nation in which true Americans were native-born men with Anglo-Saxon ancestors." Ibid. at 3. Smith specifically discusses the treatment of Puerto Rico (and Puerto Ricans) at 438–39.

45   *Downes,* 182 U.S. at 279 (emphasis added).

46   Ibid. at 282.

47   Ibid. at 287.

48   163 U.S. 537 (1896).

49   112 U.S. 94 (1884).

50   See *United States v. Kagama,* 118 U.S. 375 (1886) (enunciation of the plenary power doctrine in regard to congressional power to regulate tribes).

51   *United States v. Sandoval,* 231 U.S. 28, 39 (1913).

52   Upheld in *Chae Chan Ping v. United States* (the *Chinese Exclusion Case*), 130 U.S. 581 (1889).

53   163 U.S. at 561.

54   169 U.S. 649, 705 (1898) (Fuller, C. J., joined by Harlan, J., dissenting). See, generally, Gabriel J. Chin, "The *Plessy* Myth: Justice Harlan and the Chinese Cases," *Iowa Law Review* 82 (1996): 151.

55   Brief for the United States, reprinted in *Landmark Briefs and Arguments of the Supreme Court of the United States: Constitutional Law,* vol. 14, ed. Philip Kurland and Gerhard Casper (1975), at 37.

56   169 U.S. at 731 (quoting *Fong Yue Ting v. United States,* 149 U.S. 698, 717 (1893)).

57   Ibid.

58   The "Protest" is quoted in "Language Rights and New Mexico Statehood," in *Language Loyalties: A Source Book on the Official English Controversy,* ed. James Crawford (1992), at 59.

59   On "equal footing," see *Ward v. Race Horse,* 163 U.S. 504, 514–15 (1896).

60   See, e.g., Crawford, supra note 58, at 132–35, for the texts of nine such declarations from various states.

61   See *U.S. Code* 25 (1994) § 1301.

62   See Bruce Ackerman, *We the People: Foundations* (1991); *We the People: Transformations* (1998).

63   See Stephen Griffin, *American Constitutionalism* (1996).

64   See Sanford Levinson, "How Many Times Has the United States Constitution Been Amended? (A) < 26; (B) 26; (C) 27; (D) > 27: Accounting for Constitutional Change," in *Responding to Imperfection: The Theory and Practice of Constitutional Amendment,* ed. Sanford Levinson (1995), at 13.

65   See Bruce Ackerman and David Golove, "Is NAFTA Constitutional?" *Harvard Law Review* 108 (1995): 801.

66   See Thomas A. Bailey, "Was the Presidential Election of 1900 a Mandate on Imperialism?" *Mississippi Valley Historical Review* 24 (1937): 43, discussed in Owen M. Fiss, *Troubled Beginnings of the Modern State, 1888–1910,* in *History of the Supreme Court of the United States,* vol. 8 (1993), at 229. Fiss has an excellent chapter focusing on the *Insular Cases,* at 225–56.

67   Quoted in Fiss, ibid. at 227 n. 5 (quoting James F. Rhodes, *The McKinley and Roosevelt Administrations, 1897–1909* [1922], at 106–7).

68   Quoted in Fiss, ibid. at 229.

Fulfilling Manifest Destiny:
Conquest, Race, and the *Insular Cases*

Juan F. Perea

Race and racism have always played central roles in the ideology of United States conquest and United States citizenship. Racial difference or, more specifically, the racial inferiority attributed to the people targeted by American conquest has been offered as the justification for this conquest. According to Albert Memmi, racism is a necessary justification for the fundamental aggression and oppression of a conquest:

> The fact remains that *we have discovered a fundamental mechanism,* common to all racist reactions: *the injustice of an oppressor toward the oppressed,* the former's permanent *aggression* or the aggressive act he is getting ready to commit, *must be justified.* And isn't privilege one of the forms of permanent aggression, inflicted on a dominated man or group by a dominating man or group? How can any excuse be found for such disorder (source of so many advantages), if not by overwhelming the victim? Underneath its masks, *racism is the racist's way of giving himself absolution.*[1]

Memmi defines racism in a way that is particularly apt for considering its role in conquest: "Racism is the generalized and final assigning of values to real or imaginary differences, to the accuser's benefit and at his victim's expense, in order to justify the former's own privileges or aggression."[2] The question is how racism, so defined, has been deployed to justify United States conquests—to deliver the desired absolution—beginning with the conquest of the Indians and ending with the conquest of Puerto Rico.

The proximity, the resources, the economic opportunities, the wealth, and the strategic value of lands makes them desirable. But the darker skin of the inhabitants of those desirable lands has led to conquest. American conquests have targeted principally lands occupied by nonwhite peoples.

The English settlement (or occupation) of the mainland United States required the conquest of Indians deemed uncivilized savages by the English. The conquest of Mexico during the United States's war against Mexico of 1846–48 required the conquest of lands owned and occupied mostly by brown-skinned mestizos, the racially mixed descendants of Spaniards, Indians, and blacks. The presumed racial inferiority of mixed-race Mexicans underlay the doctrine of Manifest Destiny and justified and provided absolution for the conquest of Mexico.[3] The conquest of Puerto Rico during the Spanish-American War of 1898 involved conquering a land occupied by some Spaniards and the mixed-race descendants of Spaniards and Africans. In contrast, during the era of the war with Mexico, the United States refrained from the military conquest of the desirable Oregon territory, over which the British asserted dominion. Although war was considered, the idea was abandoned with respect to that territory in part because it was populated and controlled by fellow Anglo-Saxons. Such a war could not be justified by racism.[4]

Successful American conquests—the conquest of the Indians, the conquest of Mexico, and the conquest of Puerto Rico—have posed serious questions about what to do with the presumed racially inferior people inhabiting the conquered areas. The resolution of these questions, by treaty, by statute, and by Supreme Court decision, reveals the enormous reluctance in majoritarian institutions to admit to full and equal citizenship the non-white inhabitants of conquered areas. The very importance and attention given to the status of nonwhite inhabitants, and the reluctance to grant them full and immediate citizenship, demonstrates the importance of race and racism in defining American citizenship.

Racism as an ideological strand in conquest and in decisions about citizenship can be traced in several arenas.[5] The Supreme Court, from its earliest days, espoused an ideology of conquest that asserted, and depended upon, the alleged superiority of white Europeans over native peoples. Racism later played an important role in justifying the conquest of Mexico and in the drafting and ratification of the treaty that settled the war with Mexico. Similarly, racism provided absolution to the United States from responsibility for the Spanish-American War and the ensuing conquest of Puerto Rico. The language of the Treaties of Guadalupe Hidalgo and Paris, respectively, shows the reluctance of Congress to grant full, participatory citizenship to nonwhite persons. Against the background of this legal history, it is not surprising that Puerto Ricans were (originally for racial reasons) and remain only partial citizens without representation.

Racism and the Initial Conquest of the Indians

Europeans first crossed the ocean armed with the ideology that lands inhabited by "heathens and infidels" should be possessed by Europeans for religious, "civilizing" purposes. The Spanish justification for conquest was the spread of Christianity everywhere through the conversion of native, heathen peoples.[6] The Spanish demanded that Indians accept the Requerimiento, obligating them to submit peacefully to the Spanish and to accept the Catholic faith. According to Robert Williams Jr., the Requerimiento "informed the Indians in the simplest terms that they could either accept Christian missionaries and Spanish imperial hegemony or be annihilated."[7]

The English had their own, equally effective version of this doctrine. In *Calvin's Case,* decided in 1608, Lord Coke stated that upon conquest by a Christian king, "the laws of the infidel are abrogated, for that they be not only against Christianity, but against the law of God and of nature."[8] Furthermore, according to Lord Coke, "all infidels are in law . . . perpetual enemies."[9] Both Spanish and English legal authority, then, supplied racist justifications for their respective conquests over native Indian peoples deemed by Europeans to be heathen and inferior.

This racial ideology provided the intellectual foundation for the doctrine of discovery described by Chief Justice Marshall in *Johnson v. M'Intosh,* in which the Supreme Court decided that conquest justified the conqueror's assertion of dominion and title to lands formerly possessed by Indians. Chief Justice Marshall wrote:

> On the discovery of this immense continent, the great nations of Europe were eager to appropriate to themselves so much of it as they could respectively acquire . . . and the character and religion of its inhabitants afforded an apology for considering them as a people over whom the superior genius of Europe might claim an ascendancy. . . . [D]iscovery gave title to the government by whose subjects, or by whose authority, it was made, against all other European governments, which title might be consummated by possession.[10]

The prior possession of desirable lands by Indians, according to Justice Story, "was not treated as a right of property and dominion, but as a mere right of occupancy. As infidels, heathens, and savages, they were not allowed to possess the prerogatives belonging to absolute, sovereign, and independent nations."[11] As Chief Justice Marshall explained, "[T]heir rights to complete sovereignty, as independent nations, were necessarily diminished, and their power to dispose of the soil at their own will, to whomsoever they pleased, was denied by the original fundamental principle, that discovery gave exclusive title to those who made it."[12] But the doctrine of discovery itself was built upon a foundation of racism, the belief in the inherent superiority of white Europeans compared to the "fierce savages," the ungovernable Indians: "[T]he character and religion [of the Indians] . . . afforded an apology for considering them as a people over whom the superior genius of Europe might claim an ascendancy."[13] Marshall's language sounds the theme of racism as absolution in the idea that the attributed inferiority and savagery of the Indian character and religion affords an apology, a justification for acts of conquest.

The Court's early expression of white European racism as a justification for the deprivation of the lands and the sovereignty of others reflected widely held beliefs that later provided justification for the subsequent conquests of Mexico and Puerto Rico.

Racism and the Conquest of Mexico

In the case of Mexico, Manifest Destiny provided the ideology of Anglo-Saxon superiority which justified the conquest of Mexico and the seizure of its desirable northern lands. The earliest sustained contacts between Anglos and Mexicans occurred in the first quarter of the nineteenth century. As reports from early travelers to Mexico became more widely known, Americans began to realize that Mexicans were not Spanish (read: European) but mostly mestizos, mixed-race people of Spanish, Indian, and black parentage. Mestizaje, racial mixture, became one of the defining characteristics of the Mexican and Mexican American populations. The first census of Los Angeles, taken in 1781, demonstrates the predominantly mixed-race character of the Mexican population of the time. Only two of forty-six persons counted were identified as Spaniards; the rest were Indians, mestizos, mulattos, and blacks.[14]

The response of white Anglos to their first encounters with mixed-race, brown-skinned Mexicans was overwhelmingly negative. As historian David Weber has written, "American visitors to the Mexican frontier were nearly unanimous in commenting on the dark skin of Mexican mestizos who, it was generally agreed, had inherited the worst qualities of Spaniards and Indians to produce a 'race' still more despicable than that of either parent."[15] Given the strong American prohibitions against racial mixture and intermarriage, forged in the crucible of white-black relations during the seventeenth century, the stage was set for American revulsion at the sight and presence of the brown, mixed-race Mexican.[16] "Inhabitants of a catholic country, living under Spanish rule, displaying by their dark complexions the consequences of racial intermixture, Mexicans were an almost complete antithesis to the ideals Americans held concerning culture, race and color."[17] The antithetical nature of Mexicans in the eyes of white Americans both justified the United States conquest of Mexico and generated great revulsion at the thought of actually incorporating Mexicans within the political borders and structures of the United States.

Like the European theories of conquest, the American theory of Anglo-Saxon racial supremacy and its "manifest destiny" led directly to the war with Mexico and to the annexation of northern Mexico. The English had justified the conquest of Indian lands by reference to the inferior uses that the Indians had for the land. Richard Henry Dana described compellingly the American wish for Mexican land in *Two Years before the Mast:*

> [Mexicans in California] inhabit a country embracing four or five hundred miles of sea-coast with several good harbours, with fine forests in the north, the waters filled with fish, and the plains covered with thousands of herds of cattle; blessed with a climate than which there can be no better in the world; free from all manner of diseases, whether epidemic or endemic; and with a soil in which corn yields from seventy to eighty-fold. In the hands of an enterprising people, what a country this might be![18]

White Americans felt justified in "forcibly taking the northern provinces of Mexico, for Mexicans, like Indians, were unable to make proper use of the land. The Mexicans had failed because they were a mixed, inferior race with considerable Indian and some black blood. The world would benefit if a superior race shaped the future of the Southwest."[19]

Long before the war, commentators wrote of this race-based incapacity. T. J. Farnham described Mexican Californians as "an imbecile, pusillanimous, race of men, and unfit to control the destinies of that beautiful country."[20] It was up to Anglo-Saxons, wrote Farnham, to "stride the continent," and control California.[21] Writers described Mexicans as ineffective "semi-barbarians," comparable to Indians. Since they were barbarians, it was the duty of Anglo-Saxons to take their lands and to make them productive.[22]

Comparisons between the fate of Mexicans and the fate suffered by American Indians were frequent. Lansford Hastings wrote that, "as most of the lower order of Mexicans, are Indians in fact, whatever is said in reference to the one, will also be applicable to the other."[23] Senator Waddy Thompson commented on the inevitable spread of Anglo-Saxon language and culture: "That the Indian race of Mexico must recede before us is quite as certain as that that is the destiny of our own Indians."[24] Or as Sam Houston asserted, "They will, like the Indian race yield to the advance of the North American population."[25]

The racist character of the war with Mexico is made evident by the reluctance of Americans to go to war with Britain over the disputed Oregon territory.[26] While a war with Mexico would be a war against an inferior people for the purpose of conquest and fulfillment of the white man's self-proclaimed manifest destiny, a war with Britain would pit Anglo-Saxons against Anglo-Saxons. The former situation resulted in a war of conquest in which Americans could revel and claim racial dominion; the latter resulted in an affirmation of Anglo-Saxon brotherhood. As Reginald Horsman describes the situation:

> In discussing Texas and Mexican rule Congressmen drew few distinctions between Mexicans and their government. It was argued that the instability and ineffectiveness of the Mexican government stemmed from the inadequacies of an inferior population. In discussing great Britain and Oregon, even those Congressmen who were most critical of the British government usually made a clear distinction between the British government and the English race. The English were respected as fellow Anglo-Saxons who were not to be swept out of Oregon as an inferior breed; and those who opposed war with England frequently discussed the diastrous effects of a clash between the two great branches of the Anglo-Saxon race. The sense of Anglo-Saxon racial community, combined with a respect for British power and ability, helped mute the most strident demands for war. While the Texas issue had provided an opportunity for accentuating the differences between superior Americans and inferior Mexicans, the Oregon crisis stimulated a public avowal of the common roots of the American and English peoples.[27]

Racism against the Mexican People: American Statesmen Speak Out

The Mexican War and the Treaty of Guadalupe Hidalgo posed a fascinating dilemma for United States politicians. Given the commitment of many, if not most, politicians to notions of white supremacy, victory over Mexico and President Polk's plan to annex Mexican land as indemnification posed a severe threat to the cherished white purity and presumed "racial integrity" of the United States. Adding desirable Mexican lands to the United States meant adding undesirable Mexicans to the American people.

Important politicians voiced the grave concerns of white Americans who feared incorporating brown Mexicans into the United States. Senator John C. Calhoun did not want to conquer Mexico, and objected to Polk's war, because the United States would have to deal "with eight or nine millions of Mexicans, without a government, on our hands, not knowing what to do with them."[28] According to Calhoun, an American conquest and annexation of Mexico would wreak unprecedented havoc with white racial purity and political control:

> We have conquered many of the neighboring tribes of Indians, but we never thought of holding them in subjection—never of incorporating them into our Union. . . .
>
> I know further, sir, that we have never dreamt of incorporating into our Union any but the Caucasian race—the free white race. To incorporate Mexico, would be the very first instance of incorporating an Indian race; for more than half of all the Mexicans are Indians, and the other is composed chiefly of mixed tribes. I protest against such a union as that! Ours, sir, is the Government of a white race. The greatest misfortunes of Spanish America are to be traced to the fatal error of placing these colored races on an equality with the white race. That error destroyed the social arrangement which formed the basis of society. . . .
>
> Are we to associate with ourselves as equal, companions, and fellow citizens, the Indians and mixed race of Mexico?[29]

Calhoun, unable to countenance the prospect, argued for ending the intrusion into Mexico and keeping only the sparsely populated lands already won.

The subsequent annexation of Mexican territory inflamed concerns about granting citizenship to Mexican people. Senator James D. Westcott of Florida objected to the inclusion of "not merely the white citizens of California and New Mexico, but the peons, negroes, and Indians of all sorts, the wild tribe of Camanches, the bug-and-lizard-eating 'Diggers,' and other half-monkey savages in those countries, as *equal citizens of the United States.*"[30] Ultimately, the concerns of Calhoun and Westcott, and others like them, were resolved by the annexation of only the northernmost, sparsely populated parts of Mexico and by the changes made to the original draft of the Treaty of Guadalupe Hidalgo.

Racism and the Treaty of Guadalupe Hidalgo

Congress and the Supreme Court facilitated major transfers of Mexican-owned lands in the territories newly conquered and acquired from Mexico. President Polk recommended that the Senate delete Article X of the Treaty of Guadalupe Hidalgo, which stated that Mexican land grants would be respected as valid if they were valid under Mexican law. Once the Senate deleted Article X, Mexican land grants could be, and would soon be, attacked as invalid under standards applied by American tribunals. Congress established tribunals that placed into question all lands claimed under Mexican and Spanish grants preceding the war. Two tribunals and a surveyor general's office resolved previously undisputed land grants that were put into dispute after the war.[31] The Supreme Court played an essential role in facilitating land transfers by approving the exercise of congressional discretion in structuring the creation and resolution of land disputes. The Supreme Court approved Congress's creation of the California land commission, even if it conflicted with the Treaty of Guadalupe Hidalgo, in *Botiller v. Dominguez*.[32] The Court reasoned that "if the treaty was violated by this general statute . . . it was a matter of international concern, which [Mexico and the United States] must determine by treaty, or by such other means as enables one state to enforce upon another the obligations of treaty." In other words, the Supreme Court would not enforce the provisions of the treaty contrary to the will of Congress. It would be up to Mexico to attempt to enforce what it might perceive as a departure from the treaty. Congress could therefore handle questions of land ownership as it saw fit without concern about consistency or inconsistency with the treaty.

Under Article VIII of the treaty, both as drafted and as ratified, Mexicans in formerly Mexican territories now possessed by the United States had the right to remain in the United States and, either by election within one year or by continued residence within the United States, they "shall be considered to have elected to become citizens of the United States."[33] Article IX of the draft treaty, and subsequent modifications of the article, however, are instructive about the limited meaning of federal citizenship and the intentions of the United States government. Under the original draft of Article IX, those Mexicans who became United States citizens "shall be incorporated into the Union of the United States, *and admitted as soon as possible, according to the principles of the Federal Constitution, to the enjoyment of all the rights of citizens of the United States.* In the meantime, they shall be maintained and protected in the enjoyment of their liberty, their property, and the civil rights now vested in them according to the Mexican laws."[34] This language was modified by the Senate so that the final ratified version read: "The Mexicans . . . shall be incorporated into the Union of the United States and be admitted, *at the proper time (to be judged of by the Congress of the United States) to the enjoyment of all the rights of citizens of the United States according to the principles of the Constitution.*"[35] Thus, rather than be admitted into the Union "as soon as possible," the Senate substituted incorporation "at the proper time" to be judged by Congress.

One can infer from these changes the Senate's desire not to incorporate Mexicans "as soon as possible" because of their mestizo racial character, deemed so threatening to the United States. The revised language proved sufficient for approval by the Senate. It was supported even by Senator Calhoun, who had strenuously voiced his concerns over the Mexican threat to white rule in the United States.[36] The revised language also eased public concerns over the prospects of equality between whites and Mexicans. As the *New Orleans Picayune* reported:

> In the annexation of New Mexico and California the United States will incur none of the danger which have been predicted of admitting a race of men, differing from us in language, religion, descent, laws, manners, and social condition to an equal participation in the benefits and responsibilities of free government. The country thus acquired is comparatively unsettled, and by the time it has a population enough to send a member of Congress, will be thoroughly Americanized. So all of the forebodings concerning the appearance in the Senate or House of Representatives of a thorough-bred Mexican or half-breed Mexican will be dissipated.[37]

Racism, Unequal Citizenship, and the Denial of Political Participation for Nonwhite Mexicans

The changes made in the Treaty of Guadalupe Hidalgo before ratification suggest that, despite its citizenship-granting and property-protecting provisions, Mexicans were not seen as equal to white Americans nor were they intended to be treated as such. The manifest concerns over the racially mixed character of most Mexicans precluded their treatment as equals.

Subsequent evidence confirms that whatever the nature of federal citizenship that Mexicans received in the treaty, it was not citizenship equal to that enjoyed by most white Americans. As a result of the changes to Article IX of the treaty, New Mexico became a territory, unable to represent itself but still subject to congressional rules and regulations until Congress deemed it the proper time to do otherwise.

One can reasonably wonder why, if Mexicans were not intended ever to be full citizens, did the Senate ratify a treaty granting them federal citizenship? The answer to this question lies in the very limited scope and meaning of federal citizenship at this time. Prior to the enactment of the Civil War–era amendments, the states, and not the federal government, were seen as the primary grantors of citizenship and the primary guarantors of civil rights. The states were understood to be powerful and largely independent of federal limitations. Thus, for example, the Supreme Court early on easily rejected the argument that the federal Bill of Rights restrained the legislative or constitutional power of a state.[38] Even in the post–Civil War era, the Supreme Court's early interpretation of the Fourteenth Amendment described the "privileges and immunities" of federal citizenship in very limited terms calculated not to upset the traditional primary role of the states in the areas of citizenship and civil rights.[39]

The federal Constitution originally left all voting rights, in both federal and state elections, to be determined by the states.[40] State citizenship was the primary vehicle for suffrage, eligibility for which varied as each state dictated. Although alien suffrage was permitted in some territories, it was not permitted in the territories acquired in the Mexican war.[41] The grant of federal citizenship in the Treaty of Guadalupe Hidalgo, then, did not mean voting rights and representation in Congress. There is little doubt that this fact eased the minds of opponents of the annexation of the territories ceded in the treaty.

The power of states to allocate suffrage according to race prior to the Reconstruction Amendments is well illustrated by California. The question of voting privilege was a major subject of debate at the California constitutional convention of 1849.[42] Indeed, Article II of the California state constitution of 1849, enacted after the Treaty of Guadalupe Hidalgo, allocated the right to vote on explicitly racial terms. The debates over suffrage during the constitutional convention made clear that Indians, particularly "savage" Indians, and blacks were to be kept from voting:

> The delegates at Monterey in 1849 remained firm in their convictions that no persons other than whites should play any part in the govern-

ing of the state and proceeded to disenfranchise many of those individuals who had originally cast their ballots in the special election that put these very same delegates in their convention seats. Even an amendment that proposed to grant the right to vote to those Indians who had been citizens of Mexico and were taxed as owners of real estate, and expressly excepted all Negroes, was defeated by a vote of 22 to 21.[43]

Pablo de la Guerra, an influential Mexican Californian and a delegate to the 1849 constitutional convention, objected to the disfranchisement of Mexicans of Indian ancestry. When the proposal was made to limit suffrage to white males, "[d]e la Guerra arose to argue that many Californios were dark-skinned, and that to disenfranchise them would be tantamount to denying them a part of their citizenship as granted by the Treaty of Guadalupe Hidalgo."[44]

The convention ultimately agreed upon the following provision regarding suffrage:

> Every white male citizen of the United States, *and every white male citizen of Mexico,* who shall have elected to become a citizen of the United States, under the treaty of [Guadalupe Hidalgo], of the age of twenty-one years who shall have been a resident of the state six months next preceding the election . . . shall be entitled to vote at all elections which are now or hereafter may be authorized by law: Provided, That nothing herein contained, shall be construed to prevent the Legislature, by a two-thirds concurrent vote, from admitting to the right of suffrage, Indians or the descendants of Indians, in such special cases as such a proportion of the legislative body may deem just and proper.[45]

Predictably, Article II of the California constitution raised provocative questions about who was a "white Mexican male" and entitled to vote. Who would decide?

Congress also played a major role in determining the political participation of citizens by granting or withholding statehood. The roles of congressional discretion and congressional fears of a mixed-raced population were apparent in determining the "proper time" for admission of New Mexico as a state. From the time of its achievement of territorial status in 1850, and despite fairly continuous attempts to petition for statehood, New Mexico was not admitted as a state until 1912. This sixty-two-year delay remains the longest in United States history, with the exception of Puerto Rico.[46] Among the principal reasons for denying statehood to New Mexico were that racially mixed, dark-skinned Mexicans lived there and that they spoke Spanish.

Senator Albert Beveridge, chairman of the Senate Committee on Territories, was one of the strongest and most effective opponents of statehood for New Mexico between 1902 and 1912. Although writers have posited reasons for Beveridge's opposition, including partisan politics,[47] the grave import of the creation of new states, and ethnic incompatibility between the populations of New Mexico and Arizona, it is apparent that the race and language of Mexicans were of great concern to him and his colleagues. When Beveridge led a subcommittee to the territory including New Mexico to conduct hearings on the question, the principal themes of his questions concerned the racial composition of New Mexicans and the extent of their use of the Spanish language in all aspects of private and public life.[48] Beveridge's first question during these hearings was a request for a description of "the differences in the races, and the relative proportions of each."[49] In the understanding of many witnesses, as well as of Beveridge, "American" meant English-speaking white person, and did not include Mexicans.[50] Beveridge asked many questions regarding the need for Spanish- and English-language interpretation in courtrooms and Spanish-language instruction in classrooms in New Mexico. He clearly felt that a Mexican population was incompatible with statehood. Concluding the report on his investigation of the New Mexico territory, Beveridge wrote:

> On the whole, the committee feel that in the course of time, when education . . . shall have accomplished its work; when the masses of the people or even a majority of them shall in the usages and employment of their daily life have become identical in language and customs with . . . the American people; when the immigration of English-speaking people who have been citizens of other States does its modifying work with the "Mexican" element—when all these things have come to pass, the committee hopes and believes that this mass of people, unlike us in race, language, and social customs, will finally come to form a creditable portion of American citizenship.[51]

Subsequently, in a letter written on February 18, 1903, Beveridge identified the Mexican "preponderance in population, whose solidity fifty years of American influence has not changed, is the chief reason against the admission of that Territory."[52] Other members of Congress shared Beveridge's opinion of Mexicans as unfit for full citizenship in the United States. Senator Nelson, for example, stated that "it is for our interest to be, and it is one of the glories of this country that we are, a homogeneous, Anglo-Saxon nation, speaking the English language. We do not want any other language to usurp and maintain a foothold in this country; we do not want a Spain . . . in this country; we want the whole of it a homogeneous, Anglo-Saxon, English-speaking people; and so long as any portion of our country is in that un-American condition. . . . I submit that [New Mexico] ought to remain in a state of pupilage."[53]

Thus, despite the grant of federal citizenship to Mexicans in the Treaty of Guadalupe Hidalgo, it was within Congress's discretion to decide the "proper time" for full membership, reserved in Article IX, that enabled race discrimination against Mexicans to play out in the denial of statehood to New Mexico. Beveridge and his colleagues, like the advocates of Manifest Destiny, saw Americans as a "conquering race" of "nobler and more virile types of men" whose destiny it was to eliminate "debased civilizations and decaying race" whom he deemed incapable of democratic self-governance.[54] Thus they were loathe to support the admission of a state populated by Mexicans.

In sum, several essential legal interventions facilitated the conquest of Mexico and the subsequent unequal citizenship of Mexicans-now-Americans. Treaty provisions granted discretion to Congress to decide the "proper time" for admission of the acquired territories to statehood. The Supreme Court's decisions supported the exercise of congressional discretion, regardless of the abrogation of other provisions of the Treaty of Guadalupe Hidalgo. Through these means, majoritarian racism dictated the exclusion of Mexicans from their lands and from meaningful citizenship in the states. Many of these same legal absolutions, laws founded upon racism, were to dictate the outcomes of the later conquest of Puerto Rico.

The Supreme Court and Race Prior to the Insular Cases

As demonstrated in *Johnson v. M'Intosh,* white European racism had already provided important justification, the apology, for the conquest of Indian lands. Subsequent Supreme Court decisions contained ample expressions both of the Court's belief that United States citizenship was properly and principally limited to white Anglo-Saxons and that decisions about the racial composition of the United States were properly left to Congress. In the infamous *Dred Scott* decision, the Court held that Dred Scott, a former slave, was not a citizen of Missouri under the Constitution for purposes of suing in federal court. Chief Justice Taney described the views that the framers of the Constitution had of blacks: "They had for more than a century before been regarded as beings of an inferior order, and altogether unfit to associate with the white race, either in social or political relations; and so far inferior, that they had no rights which the white man was bound to respect; and that the negro might justly and lawfully be reduced to slavery for his benefit."[55]

Despite ratification of the Fourteenth Amendment, which effectively reversed the *Dred Scott* decision and created birthright citizenship for all persons born in the United States and subject to its jurisdiction, the Court continued to support a white supremacist view of American citizenship. When it upheld the exclusion of Chinese laborers in 1889, the opinion focused on racial differences between whites and the Chinese and the difficulties these differences posed for whites.[56] Justice Field described the motivations underlying the Chinese exclusion acts:

> The competition steadily increased as the laborers came in crowds on each steamer that arrived from China, or Hong Kong, an adjacent English port. They were generally industrious and frugal. Not being accompanied by families, except in rare instances, their expenses were small; and they were content with the simplest fare, such as would not suffice for our laborers and artisans. The competition between them and our people was for this reason altogether in their favor, and the consequent irritation, proportionately deep and bitter, was followed, in many cases, by open conflicts, to the great disturbance of the public peace. The differences of race added greatly to the difficulties of the situation. . . . [T]hey remained strangers in the land residing apart by themselves, and adhering to the customs and usages of their own country. It seemed impossible for them to assimilate with our people, or to make any change in their habits or modes of living. As they grew in numbers each year the people of the coast saw, or believed they saw, in the facility of immigration, and in the crowded millions of China, where population presses upon the means of subsistence, great danger that at no distant day that portion of our country would be overrun by them, unless prompt action was taken to restrict their immigration. The people there accordingly petitioned earnestly for protective legislation.[57]

Field concluded that "[i]f, therefore, the government of the United States, through its legislative department, considers the presence of foreigners of a different race in this country, who will not assimilate with us, to be dangerous to its peace and security, their exclusion is not to be stayed because at the time there are no actual hostilities with the nation of which the foreigners are subjects."[58]

Accordingly, the Supreme Court acquiesced in Congress's racist decision to exclude the Chinese from the United States, and the Court deferred to congressional determinations regarding the presence or absence of racially different foreigners within the United States. More generally, the Court's affirmation of Congress's plenary power in the immigration and naturalization field, and the Court's many decisions denying naturalization to non-white persons, solidified the principle that Congress could accept or deny people based on their race.[59]

The racial context of imperialism and United States expansion was an extension of the racial context inside the United States, well described by David Healy:

> The truth was that the American public of the early twentieth century expected to find inferior qualities in nonwhite peoples from tropical societies. Racism in the United States was older than the nation itself; Indians and blacks had suffered from the stigma of inequality since early colonial times. The legacies of the frontier and slavery had long since hardened into fixed attitudes, only superficially changed by the passing of Indian resistance or the episodes of the Civil War and Reconstruction. By the late nineteenth century the South was resubmerging its black population under grandfather clauses, Jim Crow legislation, and lynch law, while Indians were consigned to segregated "reservations" and forgotten. Even the newer European immigrants, flocking in from Southern and Eastern Europe and bringing different cultural backgrounds into the mainstream, were received with deep suspicion and scarcely concealed intimations of inferiority. The inequality of peoples was a pervasive idea in turn-of-the-century America; the Indians, mestizos, and blacks of the Caribbean could hope for little from United States public opinion.[60]

The Supreme Court facilitated the effective resubjugation of the black population by supporting the Jim Crow regime that reestablished inequality after Reconstruction. Just prior to the *Insular Cases*, the Court had decided *Plessy v. Ferguson,* sanctioning a regime of blatant racial inequality for blacks under the deceptive rationale of "separate but equal."[61] Even Justice Harlan, author of the celebrated dissent in Plessy, could not countenance the presence of Chinese in the United States: "There is a race so different from our own that we do not permit those belonging to it to become citizens of the United States. Persons belonging to it are, with few exceptions, absolutely excluded from our country. I allude to the Chinese race."[62]

By the time the United States conquered Puerto Rico, then, the Court had supported the congressional determination that the Chinese were properly excluded from the United States solely because of their race. In addition, the Court had reinforced domestic white supremacy by giving constitutional sanction to state decisions to segregate by race. The Court's deference to Congress in determining citizenship on the basis of race, and to the states in allowing racial segregation, allowed majoritarian racism to control the outcomes in determinations of citizenship and participation in social and political life.

As Rubin Weston describes, the internal racism prevalent in the United States was exported through U.S. colonialism:

> Those who advocated overseas expansion faced this dilemma: What kind of relationship would the new peoples have to the body politic? Was it to be the relationship of the Reconstruction period, an attempt at political equality for dissimilar races, or was it to be the Southern "counterrevolutionary" point of view which denied the basic American constitutional rights to people of color? The actions of the federal government during the imperial period and the relegation of the Negro to a status of second-class citizenship indicated that the Southern point of view would prevail. The racism which caused the relegation of the Negro to a status of inferiority was to be applied to the overseas possessions of the United States.[63]

Racism and the Conquest of Puerto Rico

The experience of Puerto Rico was shaped by mechanisms similar to those used in the conquest of Mexico. When the Spanish-American War was settled by the Treaty of Paris in 1898, no Puerto Ricans participated in the negotiation and the language of the treaty left the civil and political rights of Puerto Ricans to the discretion of Congress. This treaty language was supported by Supreme Court decisions that allowed Congress to determine the specific rights that Puerto Ricans would enjoy. As in the case of conquered Mexicans and their subsequent struggles for full citizenship and representation, the racial mixture of blacks and Spaniards and the racism of the conquering United States played a profound role in determining the ultimate status of Puerto Ricans at every stage of the United States's relationship with the island.

Article IX of the Treaty of Paris provides that:

> Spanish subjects, natives of the Peninsula, residing in the territory over which Spain by the present treaty relinquishes or cedes her sovereignty, may remain in such territory or may remove therefrom. . . . In case they remain in the territory they may preserve their allegiance to the Crown of Spain by making, before a court of record, within a year from the date of the exchange of ratifications of this treaty, a declaration of their decision to preserve such allegiance; in default of which declaration they shall be held to have renounced it and to have adopted the nationality of the territory in which they may reside.
>
> The civil rights and political status of the native inhabitants of the territories hereby ceded to the United States shall be determined by the Congress.[64]

Article IX distinguishes between "Spanish subjects, natives of the [Iberian] Peninsula," and "native inhabitants of the territories." Only the Spanish, not the predominantly mixed-race criollos (creoles), who were citizens under the former Spanish rule, could elect to retain their Spanish citizenship. Thus the "native inhabitants" lost their Spanish citizenship and became subject to the will of Congress in defining their "civil rights and political status."

As in the Treaty of Guadalupe Hidalgo, although perhaps more directly, the civil and political rights and the citizenship of Puerto Rican natives were to be determined by Congress. It has been observed that this was the first time in American history that "in a treaty acquiring territory for the United States, there was no promise of citizenship . . . [nor any] promise, actual or implied, of statehood. The United States thereby acquired not 'territories' but possessions or 'dependencies' and became, in that sense, an 'imperial' power."[65] As in the case of conquered Mexico and the New Mexico territory, Puerto Rico's population, "composed of a mixture of Negro, Indian, and Spanish ancestry . . . rendered the island incapable of independent self-government" in the eyes of Americans.[66] Nonwhite racial characteristics were, once again, seen as utterly inconsistent with democratic self-governance. This attitude, held by many Americans and by the United States government, is evident in Article IX of the Treaty of Paris, in the determination that native Puerto Ricans would have only the civil and political rights that Congress might grant.

The Supreme Court also played a key role in defining the territorial status of Puerto Rico and the very wide scope of congressional discretion in dealing with Puerto Ricans. In *Downes v. Bidwell,* the Court decided that Puerto Rico was a territory subject to the power of Congress and one to which the full protections of the Constitution did not apply.[67] The Court's opinion expresses concerns about the implications for self-governance of incorporating into the United States people racially different from Anglo-Saxon Americans:

> We are also of opinion that the power to acquire territory by treaty implies not only the power to govern such territory, but to prescribe upon what terms the United States will receive its inhabitants, and what their *status* shall be in what Chief Justice Marshall termed the "American Empire." There seems to be no middle ground between this position and the doctrine that if their inhabitants do not become, immediately upon annexation, citizens of the United States, their children thereafter born, whether savages or civilized, are such, and entitled to all the rights privileges and immunities of citizens. If such be their *status,* the consequences will be extremely serious. Indeed, it is doubtful if Congress would ever assent to the annexation of territory upon the condition that its inhabitants, however foreign they may be to our habits, traditions and modes of life, shall become at once citizens of the United States.[68]

The Court viewed citizenship as reserved for "civilized" people like Anglo Americans, and not for others. It feared "extremely serious" consequences if citizenship were conferred upon "savages." These statements suggest the degree of threat the Court felt at the prospect of full citizenship for Puerto Ricans.

The Court invokes its earlier ideology of conquest by quoting *Johnson v. M'Intosh* at some length in the *Downes* opinion:

> The title by conquest is acquired and maintained by force. The conqueror prescribes its limits. Humanity, however, acting on public opinion, has established, as a general rule, that the conquered shall not be wantonly oppressed, and that their condition shall remain as eligible as is compatible with the objects of the conquest. Most usually, they are incorporated with the victorious nation, and become subjects or citizens of the government with which they are connected. The new and old members of the society mingle with each other; the distinction

between them is gradually lost, and they make one people. Where this incorporation is practicable, humanity demands, and a wise policy requires, that the rights of the conquered to property should remain unimpaired; that the new subjects should be governed as equitably as the old, and that confidence in their security should gradually banish the painful sense of being separated from their ancient connections, and united by force to strangers.

When the conquest is complete, and the conquered inhabitants can be blended with the conquerors, *or safely governed as a distinct people,* public opinion, which not even the conqueror can disregard, imposes these restraints upon him; and he cannot neglect them without injury to his fame, and hazard to his power.[69]

Chief Justice Marshall's quoted language recognizes the violence of conquest, and the oppressive prerogatives of conquerors, who shall "prescribe the limits" of the conquest, dependent upon public opinion. Marshall also recognizes two options for dealing with the vanquished, who will either "be blended with the conquerors, or safely governed as a distinct people." This language, describing directly the demographic and societal problem of disposing of the vanquished by majority will, supports the ultimate conclusion that emerges from *Downes,* that Congress, and public opinion, shall dictate the political and civil rights of conquered Puerto Ricans.

The *Downes* Court's concerns with the human results of conquest—the potential threat to white governance posed by the annexation of racially different others—are evident throughout the opinion: "It is obvious that in the annexation of outlying and distant possessions grave questions will arise from differences of race, habits, laws and customs of the people, and from differences of soil, climate and production, which may require action on the part of Congress that would be quite unnecessary in the annexation of contiguous territory inhabited only by people of the same race, or by scattered bodies of native Indians."[70] The Court's concern with the threat posed to self-governance within the United States by the incorporation of "alien races" is also evident in the closing paragraphs of the opinion:

We can only consider this aspect of the case so far as to say that no construction of the Constitution should be adopted which would prevent Congress from considering each case upon its merits, unless the language of the instrument imperatively demand it. *A false step at this time might be fatal to the development of what Chief Justice Marshall called the American Empire. . . .* If those possessions are inhabited by alien races, differing from us in religion, customs, laws, methods of taxation, and modes of thought, the administration of government and justice, according to Anglo-Saxon principles, may for a time be impossible; and the question at once arises whether large concessions ought not to be made for a time, that, ultimately, our own theories may be carried out, and the blessings of a free government under the Constitution extended to them. We decline to hold that there is anything in the Constitution to forbid such action.[71]

Thus the "alien races" of Puerto Rico and the Philippines were thought to present a serious threat to United States governance, a threat that could only be handled by buying time for decision by conferring discretion upon Congress to decide the political fate of these vanquished peoples.

Justice White's concurring opinion, which ultimately became the controlling view, expresses similar concerns about the proper races for citizenship and political participation, and offers a stronger solution, placing greater discretion in Congress to decide the rights of Puerto Ricans. If conquest were to lead to full incorporation within the United States, then this would "strip [the United States] of all power to protect the birthright of its own citizens."[72] Furthermore, "although the House of Representatives might be unwilling to agree to the incorporation of alien races, it would be impotent to prevent its accomplishment. . . . And the consequent result—incorporation—would be beyond all future control of or remedy by the American people, since, at once and without hope of redress or power of change, incorporation by the treaty would have been brought about."[73] Placing the political fate and identity of Puerto Ricans in the discretion of Congress guaranteed that racism would play a major role in shaping that fate.

In *Downes,* the Court demonstrates its ideological commitment to an Anglo-Saxon conception of United States citizenship. The Court fears that incorporation of non-Anglo-Saxons, presumed racial inferiors, within United States citizenship could be "fatal to the development of what Chief Justice Marshall called the American Empire." The Court resolves the tension produced by the conquest and possession of lands populated by racially alien, undesirable people by placing largely unfettered discretion in Congress to determine if and when such people should become citizens and when, if at all, conquered territories should become states. In addition, Congress also had discretion to determine the civil and political rights of Puerto Ricans under Article IX of the Treaty of Paris. The Court's decision to defer to congressional discretion in matters concerning the racial composition of the citizenry guaranteed that racism, as felt and practiced according to majoritarian beliefs, would play a prominent role in subsequent determinations regarding the citizenship of Puerto Ricans.

Racism and Puerto Rican Citizenship

It should come as no surprise, then, that concerns about the nonwhite race of Puerto Ricans also played an important role in congressional debates about whether or not Puerto Ricans would become United States citizens. A principal objection to granting citizenship to Puerto Ricans was their objectionable racial composition and, therefore, their presumed incapacity for self-government. Throughout the years of debate regarding Puerto Ricans' capacity for self-government, concern focused on the effects of climate and racial mixture. Representative Slayton attributed the incapacity for self-government to "the character of the people and the climate. The Tropics seem to heat the blood while enervating the people who inhabit them." He continued:

> Many people in this country who want to sever the tie that binds us to tropical and alien people take that position, because they see in it danger for us. . . . [P]eople who "live within 20 degrees of the equator" can neither comprehend nor support representative government constructed on the Anglo-Saxon plan.
>
> They also see the physical degeneracy that will come from personal contact. Intimate personal association will result, as it nearly always has resulted, in a race of hybrids, who will, if experience may guide us to a conclusion, inherit the vices of both parents and the virtues of neither.
>
> That danger has been recognized by England and Germany, and steps have been taken to avoid it. Of the two, England has made the greater effort to preserve the purity of the blood of her people, but Germany is not far behind in the struggle to keep an undefiled racial standard.[74]

Four years later, while debating the Jones Act, Representative Cannon's remarks reflected similar racism:

> Now, when you talk about a people competent for self-government, certain things are to be taken into consideration. One is the racial ques-

tion. Another is the climatic conditions. Now we boast and say that the Caucasian race, a term the German, the Scandinavian, the Irishman, the Englishman, the Scotchman, the Frenchman, and others—we say that they are competent for self government, and that is substantially correct. . . . Now, in the fortune or misfortune of the Spanish War— whether it was fortune or misfortune God knows, and it will take the future to tell—we got the Phillippines; we became responsible for Cuba; we got Porto Rico. . . .

. . . The people of Porto Rico have not the slightest conception of self-government. . . .

Porto Rico is populated by a mixed race. About 30 percent are pure African. I was informed by Army officers when I was down there that when the census was taken every man that was a pure African was listed and counted as such, but that there was really 75 to 80 per cent of the population that was pure African or had an African strain in their blood. Now, gentlemen, will anybody say that I am abusing the African? I am not any more than I am abusing the Filipinos or the Moros; and I am certainly not abusing the Africans in the United States. The race has made great advance since servile labor was abolished, attributable to its association with the Caucasian race, being one-tenth of our population and living in the north temperate zone.[75]

These comments support Memmi's observation that racism provides absolution. If, as these congressmen believed, Puerto Ricans were racially inferior and unfit for self-governance, then the oppression of a regime under which Puerto Ricans exercised no equal voice in national governance was justified.

Although the Jones Act was ultimately enacted, granting United States citizenship to Puerto Ricans in 1917, this grant of citizenship was never intended to be a grant of full citizenship as non–Puerto Rican United States citizens know it. When Senator Foraker had first introduced legislation granting United States citizenship to Puerto Ricans in 1900, he described their federal citizenship not as any recognition of individual rights they might have but rather to "recognize that Puerto Rico belongs to the United States of America."[76] Foraker had also commented,

We considered very carefully what status in a political sense we would give to the people of [Puerto Rico], and we reported that provision not thoughtlessly. . . . We concluded . . . that the inhabitants of that island must be either citizens or subjects or aliens. We did not want to treat our own as aliens, and we do not propose to have any subjects. Therefore, we adopted the term "citizens." In adopting the term "citizens" we did not understand, however, that we were giving to those people any rights that the American people do not want them to have. "Citizens" is a word that indicates, according to Story's work on the Constitution of the United States, allegiance on the one hand and protection on the other.[77]

Foraker ultimately amended his legislation in 1900 to omit United States citizenship for Puerto Ricans, opting instead to consider them "citizens of Puerto Rico, and as such entitled to the protection of the United States."[78] Again, Congress's ability to define the civil and political rights of Puerto Ricans, the quality of their citizenship and political participation, allowed racism to shape less-than-equal citizenship for the Puerto Rican people. As Rubin Weston has written: "Americans in positions to influence or to establish policy were not very generous in giving to the Puerto Ricans rights usually given to Americans. For the first third of the twentieth century they rationalized the inconsistency of their treatment of the Puerto Ricans on the basis of cultural differences. In the final analysis, race emerged as the determining factor in establishing policy. That policy assumed that the Puerto Ricans were radically different from the Anglo-Saxons and were unassimilable into the American body politic."[79]

Conclusion

Racism serves as the ideological absolution for the aggressions and oppressions of conquest. Racism is the apology provided by the "character and religion," the racial distinction, of vanquished peoples. Racism has played a key role in the United States's ideology of justification for its conquests and the ongoing legacy of those conquests. This legacy lives on in the isolated, subordinate status of American Indian nations and their diminished sovereignty. The legacy of conquest lives on in the Spanish-language place names of the Southwest, skeletal remains of former Mexican land ownership. And the legacy lives on in the subordinate commonwealth status of Puerto Rico, whose citizens continue to lack representation and voice in our national affairs. Majoritarian racism, expressed through neutral-sounding treaty language and federal legislation, supported by the Supreme Court, sought to justify the perpetuation of such unequal treatment. As long as fundamental civil and political rights of conquered peoples remain subject to majoritarian resolution, such bitter legacies shall continue.

Within the historical context, Puerto Rico's unconvincing common-wealth status, and the persistent, unequal United States citizenship legislated for Puerto Ricans can come as no surprise, for equal citizenship and equal participation in governance were never meant to be for Puerto Rico. Unlike the lands of Indians and Mexicans, which were coveted for expansion, settlement by whites, and ultimate incorporation, Puerto Rico was coveted by the government largely for strategic military and commercial purposes. Such tropical lands as Puerto Rico, thickly populated with mixed-race peoples, were not well suited to what was seen as the warrior temperament of the Anglo-Saxon and could lead only to his moral and physical degeneration. Congressmen said as much. Since the lands were thought to be unfit for whites, unlike the lands of other conquests, there would be no migration of whites to make the lands palatable, no assimilation to make them Anglo enough for statehood. Unlike the discretionary inclusion of Mexicans "at the proper time" in the Treaty of Guadalupe Hidalgo, stronger language in the Treaty of Paris allowed Congress unfettered discretion to determine all of the civil and political rights of native inhabitants of Puerto Rico. It appears that the absolution of racism, yearned for so long, yields only the greater paradoxes of inequality and contradiction of the national creed.

Notes

1   Albert Memmi, *Dominated Man: Notes toward a Portrait* (1968), at 194 (italics in original).

2   Ibid.

3   For a detailed history of the annexation of Mexico and the settlement of the dispute over the Oregon territory, see David M. Pletcher, *The Diplomacy of Annexation: Texas, Oregon, and the Mexican War* (1975).

4   Reginald Horsman, *Race and Manifest Destiny: The Origins of American Racial Anglo-Saxonism* (1981), at 220–25.

5   Rogers Smith has also argued for, and provided, "an alternative account that gives full weight to America's pervasive ideologies of ascriptive inequality, as well as to liberalism and democratic republicanism, and explains why each has been centrally constitutive of American life." Rogers M. Smith, *Civic Ideals: Conflicting Visions of Citizenship in U.S. History* (1997), at 30.

6   J. H. Parry, *The Spanish Theory of Empire in the Sixteenth Century* (1940), at 5; Tzvetan Todorov, *The Conquest of America* (1984), at 10. (Columbus stated: "I hope in Our Lord to be able to propagate His holy name and His Gospel throughout the Universe.")

7   Robert A. Williams Jr., *The American Indian in Western Legal Thought* (1990), at 88–93; see also Robert A. Williams Jr., "Columbus's Legacy: The Rehnquist Court's Perpetuation of European Cultural Racism against American Indian Tribes," *Federal Bar News & Journal* 39 (1992): 358.

8   *Calvin's Case*, 77 Eng. Rep. 377 (K.B. 1608).

9   Williams (1990), supra note 7, at 300.

10 21 U.S. (8 Wheat) 543, 572–73 (1823).

11 Joseph Story, *Commentaries,* section 152, quoted in Williams (1990), supra note 7, at 316.

12 *Johnson,* 21 U.S. (8 Wheat) at 573–74.

13 Ibid. at 572–73.

14 First Census of Los Angeles (trans. Thomas W. Temple II, 1781), in *Historical Society of Southern California Annual Publications* 15.2 (1931): 148–49, excerpted from "New Spain's Far Northern Frontier," in *Foreigners in Their Native Land: Historical Roots of the Mexican Americans,* ed. David J. Weber (1973), at 34–35.

15 Weber, ibid., at 59–60.

16 See Philip Anthony Hernandez, "The Other North Americans: The American Image of Mexico and Mexicans, 1550–1850" (Ph.D. diss., U. Cal. Berkeley, 1974), at 34–57.

17 Ibid. at 56.

18 Richard Henry Dana Jr., *Two Years before the Mast: A Personal Narrative of Life at Sea* (1986 [1840]), at 237.

19 Horsman, supra note 4, at 210.

20 Ibid.

21 Ibid.

22 Ibid. at 211.

23 Ibid.

24 Ibid. at 212.

25 Ibid. at 214.

26 See Pletcher, supra note 3.

27 Horsman, supra note 4, at 220-1; see also Pletcher, ibid. at 224–25.

28 *Cong. Globe,* 30th Cong., 1st sess. (1848): 53.

29 Ibid. at 96–98.

30 Horsman, supra note 4, at 276 (quoting *Cong. Globe,* 30th Cong., 1st sess. (July 25, 1848): appendix, at 48–49).

31 The California Land Claim Act of 1851 established a commission, consisting of three appointed commissioners, whose purpose it was to ascertain the validity of private land claims in California. *U.S. Statutes at Large* 9 (1851): 631. Congress then established the office of surveyor general of New Mexico, Kansas, and Nebraska. *U.S. Statutes at Large* 10 (1854): 308. Finally, because of the burdensome procedures of the surveyor general, in 1891 Congress created the Court of Private Land Claims, which eventually had jurisdiction to resolve land claims in the entire region acquired from Mexico during the war. See *U.S. Statutes at Large* 26 (1891): 854; *U.S. Statutes at Large* 27 (1893): 470.

32 130 U.S. 238, 247 (1889).

33 *Treaty of Guadalupe Hidalgo,* art. VIII, *U.S. Statutes at Large* 9 (1848): 922.

34 *Treaty of Guadalupe Hidalgo,* art. IX (original draft treaty language), reprinted in Hunter Miller, ed., *Treaties and Other International Acts of the United States,* vol. 5 (1937), at 241.

35 *Treaty of Guadalupe Hidalgo,* supra note 33, art. IX.

36 *Senate Executive Documents,* 30th Cong., 1st sess. (1848): no. 52:27.

37 *New Orleans Picayune,* February 15, 1848, quoted in Hernandez, supra note 16, at 268–69.

38 *Barron v. Mayor & City Council of Baltimore,* 32 U.S. (7 Pet.) 243 (1833).

39 See, e.g., *Slaughter-House Cases,* 83 U.S. (16 Wall.) 36 (1873).

40 Gerald L. Neuman, *Strangers to the Constitution: Immigrants, Borders, and Fundamental Law* (1996), at 63.

41   Ibid. at 64–66.

42   See Robert F. Heizer and Alan F. Almquist, *The Other Californians* (1977), at 92–119.

43   Ibid. at 96; see also Horsman, supra note 4, at 277–78.

44   Leonard Pitt, *Decline of the Californios* (1970), at 45.

45   *California Constitution* (1849), art. 2, sec. 1 (emphasis added).

46   Although there is an ongoing debate in Puerto Rico regarding whether or not to petition for statehood, Puerto Rico has never formally done so. Puerto Rico, therefore, presents a different case from New Mexico, since the New Mexico territory requested and demanded statehood for sixty-two years before winning such status. If Puerto Rico were to petition formally for statehood, I believe that many of the same arguments used to deny statehood to New Mexico would resurface, though perhaps in disguised form.

47   See John Braeman, "Albert J. Beveridge and Statehood for the Southwest, 1902–1912," *Arizona and the West* 10 (1968): 313.

48   See *Hearings before the Subcommittee of the Committee on Territories on House Bill 12543,* 57th Cong., 2d sess., Sen. Doc. No. 36 (1902).

49   Ibid. at 2.

50   See, e.g., ibid. at 2, 20–21.

51   Quoted in Jesse de la Cruz, "Rejection Because of Race: Albert J. Beveridge and Nuevo Mexico's Struggle for Statehood, 1902–1903," *Aztlan* 7 (1976): 79, at 84.

52   Braeman, supra note 47, at 318.

53   de la Cruz, supra note 51, at 88.

54   Ibid.

55   *Scott v. Sanford,* 60 U.S. (19 How.) 393, 407 (1857).

56   *Chae Chan Ping v. United States,* 130 U.S. 581 (1889).

57   Ibid. at 594–95.

58   Ibid. at 606.

59   See generally Ian F. Haney López, *White by Law* (1996); Gabriel J. Chin, "Segregation's Last Stronghold: Race Discrimination and the Constitutional Law of Immigration," *U.C.L.A. Law Review* 46 (1998): 1 (discussing flaws in racial foundations of the plenary power doctrine, and criticizing the Supreme Court's adherence to the doctrine).

60   David Healy, *Drive to Hegemony: The United States in the Caribbean 1898–1917* (1988), at 65.

61   163 U.S. 537 (1896).

62   Ibid. at 561.

63   Rubin Francis Weston, *Racism in U.S. Imperialism* (1972), at 15.

64   *Treaty of Peace between the United States and the Kingdom of Spain,* reprinted in Charles I. Bevans, *Eleven Treaties and Other International Agreements of the United States of America 1776–1949* (1974), at 615–19.

65   J. Pratt, *America's Colonial Experiment* (1950), at 68.

66   Weston, supra note 63, at 184.

67   182 U.S. 244 (1901).

68   Ibid. at 279–80.

69   Ibid. at 281–82 (quoting *Johnson v. M'Intosh,* 21 U.S. [8 Wheat.] 543, 589); see also *Downes,* 182 U.S. at 306 (White, J., concurring) (relying on *Johnson v. M'Intosh*).

70   *Downes,* 182 U.S. at 282.

71   Ibid. at 286–87 (emphasis added).

72   Ibid. at 306 (White, J., concurring).

73   Ibid. at 313.

74   *Cong. Rec.,* 62d Cong., 2d sess. (March 4, 1912): 2798 (remarks of Rep. Slayton).

75   *Cong. Rec.,* 64th Cong., 1st sess. (May 5, 1916): 1036 (remarks of Rep. Cannon).

76   Juan R. Torruella, *The Supreme Court and Puerto Rico: The Doctrine of Separate and Unequal* (1985), at 36.

77   Quoted in José A. Cabranes, *Citizenship and the American Empire: Notes on the Legislative History of the United States Citizenship of Puerto Ricans* (1979), at 37.

78   Torruella, supra note 76, at 36.

79   Weston, supra note 63, at 204.

U.S. Territorial Expansion: Extended Republicanism versus Hyperextended Expansionism

E. Robert Statham Jr.

There are no great men without virtue; and there are no great nations—it may almost be added, there would be no society—without respect for right; for what is a union of rational and intelligent beings who are held together by the bond of force?—Alexis de Tocqueville, *Democracy in America*

[T]he power over the territories is vested in Congress without limitation, and . . . this power has been considered the foundation upon which the territorial governments rest.—Justice Henry Billings Brown, *Downes v. Bidwell*

Constitutional justice is essential to the safety, perpetuation, and well-being of American democracy. All too often, its safeguards—government by consent, the rule of law, the separation of powers, checks and balances, federalism, and republican representation—have been discarded. Nowhere is the neglect of the animating principles of constitutionalism more evident than in United States territorial policy and relations. The relationship between the United States and its offshore territories poses one of the most pressing problems that America has had to face since the Civil War, in that the issues involved hinge upon the nation's public philosophy. The contemporary disregard for the tenets of the rule of constitutional law in the United States is rooted in a crisis of reason, of public philosophy, of the role of reason in American political life.[1] The seemingly foreign problem concerning the U.S. off-shore territories in fact points toward a more insidious domestic one. The United States has lost its way; it has deviated from its core animating principles. This is evident in the way in which the nation deals with its territories.

Whereas America was, like most other regimes, created by particular acts of violence, unlike most other regimes, it was at the same time created through a claim to justice.[2] This claim to justice, which was widely understood by the founding generation and which was boldly expressed in the Declaration of Independence and eloquently reinvigorated in the words of Abraham Lincoln at Gettysburg, was founded upon the proposition of certain natural, self-evident, permanent truths which apply to all men without exception in all times: that all men are created equal, and that they are as human beings in possession of certain basic and unalienable natural rights which government is expressly intended to secure.[3] This is the principled foundation of American constitutional democracy. And yet the question arises, in the words of a twentieth-century political philosopher: "Does this nation in its maturity still cherish the faith in which it was conceived and raised? Does it still hold those 'truths to be self-evident'?"[4] That government must be by consent of the governed, that the purpose of government is the security of the basic natural rights of the people, and that the people must be treated equally before the government are essential conditions of U.S. constitutionalism and American citizenship. Unfortunately, the United States has failed to apply these principles in its territories. Puerto Rico, Guam, the Commonwealth of the Northern Mariana Islands, American Samoa, and the Virgin Islands have been held as possessions, or property, by the United States, in some cases for over a century. In the cases of Puerto Rico and Guam, the civil rights and political status of the native inhabitants have not been fully determined by the Congress in accordance with the Treaty of Paris. American citizenship has been granted, but territorial incorporation and the full application of the U.S. Constitution and its animating principles have been withheld.[5]

The nation dedicated to equality and natural rights has quite clearly deviated from its public philosophy and from the Constitution, which is intended to perpetuate this philosophy. The annexation of the offshore territories without the concomitant resolution of the issue of the political status of territorial inhabitants has "established the United States as a colonial power."[6] The worst fears expressed by President George Washington in his "Farewell Address" have been realized as America has succumbed to "the usual current of the passions" which has marked the destiny of nations, to "the mischiefs of foreign intrigue."[7]

I

George Washington used the classical platonic conception of the soul in his articulation of American foreign policy. He considered that the soul consists of both the passions and reason, and that justice is obtained when the latter regulates and properly controls the former.[8] To the extent that the passions dominate over reason, in either individuals or the state, the soul is enslaved:

> Observe good faith and justice towards all nations. . . . In the execution of such a plan nothing is more essential than that permanent, inveterate antipathies against particular nations and passionate attachments for others should be excluded and that in place of them just and amicable feelings toward all should be cultivated. The nation which indulges toward another an habitual hatred or an habitual fondness is in some degree a slave. It is a slave to its animosity or to its affection, either of which is sufficient to lead it astray from its duty and its interest. . . . The government sometimes participates in national propensity, and adopts, through passions, what reason would reject.[9]

President Washington held that the "great rule of conduct" for the United States, in regard to foreign nations, should be one of extending commercial relations with as little political connection as possible.[10] He therefore recommended that America "steer clear of permanent alliances with any portion of the foreign world," so that even U.S. commercial policy "should hold an equal and impartial hand, neither seeking nor granting exclusive favors or preferences; consulting the natural course of things; diffusing and diversifying by gentle means the streams of commerce but forcing nothing."[11]

As is now evident, the United States has not followed the advice of President Washington. Perhaps his advice has lost much of its force in an increasingly globalized, interdependent world. America now enters the twenty-first century as a superpower that considers itself largely responsible for policing the world through the internationalization of U.S. national policy. It is worthwhile, therefore, to examine the extent to which the implementation of U.S. policy internationally is directly associated with American imperialism.

America has progressively evolved from a dysfunctional, confederal, decentralized polity in the mid-1700s to a profoundly centralized, bureaucratized, and expansive nation at present. At the midpoint of its development from a confederacy to a centralized nation, America decided to become an imperial power. Its explicit imperialist designs were short-lived, but its empire lives on, in the form of its territories and possessions.

It has been said of empires that: (1) they are despotic and tyrannical, and (2) they eventually fall apart from the inside out.[12] Imperialist nations often go through distinct phases of a syndrome which eventually transforms the ultimate source of all value and law in the society from either divine or natural transcendental standards such as those found, for example, in the Mayflower Compact and the Declaration of Independence, to utilitarianism, pragmatism, and positive law, or the law of the state.[13] Once a regime reaches the final stage of positive law and statism, the rational justification for political and governmental action is lowered to the level of instrumentalism so that politics becomes the art of the possible and principle is lost sight of. When power and instrumental state action become the core of a regime's political life, might (power) is assumed to make right (justice). Politicization and the hyperextension of empire, therefore, mark this final stage in the syndrome of imperialism.[14]

Great empires require an external or foreign enemy of some kind in order to establish their identities and maintain themselves, since they are poorly ordered internally.[15] Yet the real enemy often proves to be internal. Abraham Lincoln feared that America would become such a powerful nation that, although it could not be conquered by a foreign enemy, it might disintegrate from the inside out due to the deterioration of the rule of law, of the public philosophy of constitutionalism.[16] Lincoln feared that a great increase in national power might be inversely related to the principles of constitutional justice.

Even before Lincoln's time, a blatant disregard for constitutional principles was evident in the nation's westward expansion. James Madison was particularly concerned with governmental extraconstitutionalism in the western territories when he wrote: "Congress have assumed the administration of this stock. They have begun to render it productive. Congress have undertaken to do more: they have proceeded to form new States; to erect temporary governments; to appoint officers for them; and to prescribe the conditions on which such States shall be admitted into the confederacy. All this has been done; and done without the least colour of constitutional authority."[17] Madison was referring to the Congress's governing of territorial inhabitants in direct conflict with the basic tenets of constitutionalism: republican representation, the separation of powers, checks and balances, and federalism. Constitutional government must be limited (as constitutionalism limits and qualifies democracy), and it is limited in part by the direct representation of the people following their consent to be governed. The basic principles and practices of constitutional democracy had been discarded in the westward expansion of Madison's time. Disregard for law and the constitutional process were again evident in William McKinley's handling of the Cuban Revolution, the coming of the war with Spain, and the intervention in the Philippines in the late 1890s.[18] Then, the American federal government's extraconstitutionalism became institutionalized in an expansive off-shore empire.

II

The expansion of the American republic, in and of itself, is neither just nor unjust. James Madison himself understood that the United States would inevitably grow when he said, "It is now no longer a point of speculation and hope, that the Western territory is a mine of vast wealth to the United States" and stated that he did not intend to "throw censure on the measures which had been pursued by Congress" because "they could not have done otherwise."[19] Madison's concern was with the need to attach the actions of the government to the Constitution and the principles that animate it.

Whether the Constitution that Madison and the other framers instituted is sufficient for the tasks they set forth is, however, open to question. The explanation for the deficiencies of the Constitution of 1789 is a complicated one, but one which can, to a considerable degree, be reduced to an over-emphasis upon Enlightenment-based rationality and an underemphasis upon classical political-philosophical directives.[20] In attempting to devise an institutional mechanism based upon a skeptical generalization regarding human nature which would effectively prevent majoritarian tyranny, Madison developed the concepts of republican representation and of an extended republic. These mechanisms were designed to operate in quasi-automatic fashion in regulating human nature. The federal constitution would qualify or limit democracy in two ways: (1) government would be delegated to a small number of citizens elected by the rest, and (2) the sphere or size of the country, and therefore the number of citizens, would be extended and increased.[21] Madison emphasized external-institutional remedies for the deleterious effects of human nature in a democratic polity as opposed to focusing upon civic education and the inculcation of public virtue.[22]

He approached the problem of majoritarian tyranny empirically, quantitatively, and in terms of size: "The smaller the society, the fewer probably will be the distinct parties and interests composing it. . . . Extend the sphere, and you take in a greater variety of parties and interests; you make it less probable that a majority of the whole will have a common motive to invade the rights of other citizens."[23] This Madisonian conception of an extended republic, along with the accompanying application of a republican scheme of representation, serves to "not only guard the society against the oppression of its rulers" but "to guard one part of the society against the injustice of the other part."[24] Inasmuch as "society itself will be broken into so many parts, interests and classes of citizens," the "rights of individuals, or of the minority, will be in little danger from interested combinations of the majority."[25]

While Madison's institutional mechanisms were a great advance in the science of politics, they are not without certain specific flaws. Extending the range and sphere of a republic does indeed diversify the number and variety of interests and classes of citizens. However, that is all that it does. Madison's extended republic effectively prevents majoritarian tyranny within the United States through the diversification of interests and classes, but this instrument does not provide for the effective limitation of extension, and it therefore does not take account of the very real possibility of hyperextension. Hyperextension of the American republic occurs as a result of the extraconstitutional use of federal power in territorial expansion. Hyperextension entails the acquisition of territory by way of and in terms of sheer power, and it often results in an excessive diversification of the polity and a crisis of public philosophy and political culture. In this way it works against the original objectives of the Madisonian plan.

The Anti-Federalists were, for example, quite apprehensive about adopting Madison's project, as they believed that "only a small republic can secure a genuine responsibility of government to the people," and only a "small republic can form the kind of citizens who will maintain republican government."[26] The Anti-Federalists were particularly concerned about the citizenship of a free people and they believed that the relationship between citizenship and the law had been dangerously ignored in the framing of the Constitution. Their contention was ultimately rooted in the understanding that "a republican citizenry must be free and independent-minded, but it must also be homogeneous," and they "saw, although sometimes only dimly, the insufficiency of a community of mere interest. They saw that the American polity had to be a moral community if it was to be anything, and they saw that the seat of that community must be the hearts of the people."[27]

Unfortunately, the lack of a constitutional limitation upon expansion has indeed resulted in the hyperextension of the American federal republic. The federal acquisition of Puerto Rico, Guam, the Northern Mariana Islands, American Samoa, and the U.S. Virgin Islands provides pertinent examples of U.S. territorial extraconstitutionalism, one in which mechanisms for expansion were actually utilized in contravention of the principles of constitutionalism. After a century, these culturally diverse and distinct entities have yet to be fully integrated into the American Union. They have been held as possessions, without the formal consent of their inhabitants.

III

In order to examine U.S. territorial hyperextension it is necessary to consult the Constitution. The Constitution addresses the issue of territorial expansion in Article IV. Section 3 reads: "New States may be admitted by the Congress into this Union; but no new State shall be formed or erected within the Jurisdiction of any State; nor any State be formed by the Junction of two or more States, or Parts of States, without the Consent of the Legislature of the States Concerned as well as of the Congress." Section 3, clause 2 provides: "The Congress shall have Power to dispose of and make all needful Rules and Regulations respecting the Territory or other Property belonging to the United States; and nothing in this Constitution shall be so construed as to Prejudice any Claims of the United States, or of any Particular State."[28]

The main cause of U.S. territorial hyperextension is the misinterpretation of Article IV, section 3. As the nation expanded westward on the North American continent, it was expected that new territory would be acquired and new states admitted into the Union. Article IV, section 3 therefore provides for the admission of new states by the Congress (with certain consent-based stipulations) and for the resolution of U.S. concerns regarding this territory and property. A careful reading of this section of the Constitution makes clear the distinction between "states" of the Union and U.S. "territory." States are created by people and are subsequently admitted into the Union. Territory is property, and is, therefore, distinct from people and citizenship. For this reason, the Constitution always addresses citizenship within the context of the political status of statehood. This is because individuals possess certain basic natural rights which government is expressly intended to protect, and the governmental protection of these rights requires appropriate representation in the government. The Declaration of Independence articulates these constitutional principles of natural law, which form the basis for government by consent. Government of, by, and for the people (government by consent) assumes that human beings are equal before the law and government simply by virtue of the fact that they are human: "The equal protection of the laws is a central tenet of constitutional government. . . . [A]s a constitutional precept, equal protection derives its dignity from the fact that it is the conventional reflection of principles that flow directly from natural human equality."[29] In other words, there is a direct relationship between the equal protection of the laws and the equal protection of natural rights. The Constitution embodies the idea that precisely because human beings are by nature equal insofar as government is concerned, all governmental authority or power derives from the People, who in turn derive their power and authority from Nature.

The United States Supreme Court misinterpreted Article IV, section 3 in *Downes v. Bidwell* (1901). The Court pragmatically severed the interpretation of the Constitution from the principles of constitutionalism (i.e., government by consent of the governed, equality before the law, republican representation) in the determination of whether Puerto Rico (and the other off-shore territories by implication) was a part of the "United States." Justice White's concurring opinion deserves particular attention, as it demonstrates well the pragmatic tendency to treat the actions of Congress differently in foreign and domestic affairs, whereas the Constitution makes no such distinction with respect to territories:

> The Constitution has undoubtedly conferred on Congress the right to create such municipal organizations as it may deem best for all the territories of the United States whether they have been incorporated or not, to give to the inhabitants as respects the local governments such degree of representation as may be conducive to the public well-being, to deprive such territory of representative government if it is considered just to do so, and to change such local governments at discretion.[30]

The imperialistic premises of the contention above are evident. Justice White discards the fundamental principles of constitutional government that all men are created equal and that government derives its ultimate authority from the consent of the governed. Madison's concern that Congress had expanded west extraconstitutionally is worth recalling in this regard.[31] Here the Court simply reinforces U.S. federal imperialism by maintaining that Congress has the right to: (1) create local governments; (2) give those governments degrees of representation as opposed to equal representation; and (3) retain the right to deprive territories of representative government. These contentions contradict the letter and spirit of the rule of law and lead to the conclusion that Congress may treat territorial inhabitants differently from U.S. citizens. Justice White in this way selectively applies the Constitution and its principles by making a distinction between congressional power in foreign as opposed to domestic affairs. He applies the limitations of power which the Constitution requires in the latter instance, but grants great, if not unlimited (i.e., unconstitutional) power in the former.

White's pragmatic distinction between foreign and domestic spheres derives from two underlying motivations, the desire to apply the principles of constitutionalism selectively, and the accompanying desire to make power the foundation for U.S. foreign expansion and constitutional law the foundation for domestic growth: "It may not be doubted that by the general principles of the law of nations every government which is sovereign within its sphere of action possesses as an inherent attribute the power to acquire territory by discovery, by agreement or treaty, and by conquest."[32] In other words, in order to justify taking sovereignty over new territories while disregarding the connection between this acquisition and the ultimate equality implied by statehood, White had to turn to the law of nations and the powers inherent in sovereignty. The basis for expansion thus became extraconstitutional power, where it had previously been constitutional growth.

IV

Why would the Court attempt to treat the offshore territories differently from those of the mainland? Why the interest in distinguishing between foreign and domestic affairs in territorial concerns? The answer to these questions lies in a resistance to diversity of a particular kind: racial and cultural. Although the Constitution created a large, extended, and diverse republic, the offshore territorial acquisitions of the turn of the century and after seemingly threatened a nation of excessive diversity, of more diversity than the American public (and their Supreme Court) could accept. Justice White wrote:

> Take a case of discovery. Citizens of the United States discover an unknown island, peopled with an uncivilized race, yet rich in soil, and valuable to the United States for commercial and strategic reasons. Clearly, by the law of nations, the right to ratify such acquisition and thus to acquire the territory would pertain to the government of the United States. Can it be denied that such right could not be practically exercised if the result would be to endow the inhabitants with citizenship of the United States and to subject them not only to local but also

to an equal proportion of national taxes, even although the consequence would be to entail ruin on the discovered territory and to
inflict grave detriment on the United States to arise both from the
dislocation of its fiscal system and the immediate bestowal of citizenship on those absolutely unfit to receive it?[33]

White's concern here was that the treaty-making power could, "without the
consent of Congress, incorporate territory," leading to the possibility that
"millions of inhabitants of alien territory, if acquired by treaty" could "be
immediately and irrevocably incorporated into the United States."[34] Immediate incorporation upon the ratification of a treaty would permanently
bind the Congress and the American people to these "alien races," something White feared. Justice White was opposed to the application of the
principles of constitutionalism universally; he presumed that they were
culturally and racially specific.

Justice Brown raised similar doubts regarding the incorporation of alien
peoples: "We are also of opinion that the power to acquire territory by
treaty implies not only the power to govern such territory, but to prescribe
upon what terms the United States will receive its inhabitants."[35] Similarly
concerned with excessive diversity, he affirmed the "denial of the right of
the inhabitants [of territories] to American citizenship until Congress by
further action shall signify its assent thereto."[36] Against charges that Congress might use unrestrained power leading to the oppression of territorial
inhabitants, Brown disclosed his partiality in stating that "[t]here are certain principles of natural justice inherent in the Anglo-Saxon character
which need no expression in constitutions or statutes to give them effect."[37]
These principles of natural justice seem to have implied an inability to
conceive of territorial inhabitants as equal:

> It is obvious that in the annexation of outlying and distant possessions
> grave questions will arise from differences of race, habits, laws and cus-
> toms of the people, and from differences of soil, climate and produc-
> tion, which may require action on the part of Congress that would be
> quite unnecessary in the annexation of contiguous territory inhabited
> only by people of the same race, or by scattered bodies of Native
> Indians.[38]

Brown made a pragmatic distinction between "natural rights enforced in
the Constitution" and "artificial or remedial rights" which are peculiar to
"Anglo-Saxon jurisprudence," separating the basic protection of the natural
rights of territorial inhabitants from those of American citizenship.[39]

The pragmatic distinctions between foreign and domestic affairs, between power and constitutional law as the basic source of congressional action, between unincorporated and incorporated territory, and between natural rights and American citizenship are ultimately rooted in the distinction between Anglo-Saxon Americans and other human beings. The decision of the Court in *Downes v. Bidwell* is the product of an attempt to make a distinction between human beings which by nature and by right does not exist. The Court wanted to affirm the power of the federal government to acquire territory, but to deny the inhabitants of that territory natural human rights, which the U.S. Constitution is intended to secure. In sum, the Court held that territories and their inhabitants could be annexed and held by the Congress for an indefinite period of time as a result of cultural and racial differences. The Constitution, however, does not make a distinction between human beings on the basis of culture or race.

In Article IV, section 3, clause 2, the term *territory* is synonymous with the term *property.* Territory or property is held to "belong to" the United States, and the Congress is given by law power to "dispose of" U.S. territory or property. The United States is implicitly given power to *claim* territory or property. Property refers to ownership, especially with respect to real estate. To "dispose of" refers to settlement, or the giving away or selling of something owned. And *claim* refers to a demand upon something that rightfully belongs to one, or a right to something. Clearly, if the principles of constitutionalism (particularly the ones articulated in the Declaration of Independence) are to be rightly understood, the United States has the right as a sovereign, independent nation to acquire territory or property. But territory refers to land, or real estate, or other belongings. The United States does not, however, possess the right to acquire, purchase, own, claim, or dispose of human beings living on that land or real estate. Human beings possess certain natural rights, which no government can rightfully give or take away. And the U.S. government is expressly intended constitutionally (legally) to secure the basic rights of individuals within its territorial limits.

To contend that the Constitution (and the Territorial Clause in particular) gives complete power over and ownership of territorial acquisitions and their inhabitants is to treat inhabitants as property to be disposed of at the pleasure of Congress, a single branch of the national government. This is by definition tyrannical, whereas the Constitution was instituted to prevent the rule of will. The government, which was created to secure human rights, cannot possibly be authorized to infringe upon them. Whereas the United States has the right to acquire territory, it has no right whatsoever to acquire people.

The Constitution contemplates the circumstance of inhabited territory becoming part of the Union in allowing for new states to be admitted by the Congress. There is no provision for the admission of territories, since admission refers to the consent (deliberation and voluntary choice) of the governed. Property or territory, unlike human beings, does not reflect upon and make choices regarding questions of justice and right of great magnitude. The U.S. Constitution was created out of human deliberation (reason) and choice (decision). Alexander Hamilton, therefore, began *The Federalist* by stating: "It has been frequently remarked that it seems to have been reserved to the people of this country, by their conduct and example, to decide the important question, whether societies of men are really capable or not of establishing good government from reflection and choice, or whether they are forever destined to depend for their political constitutions on accident and force."[40] Accident and force replaced deliberation and choice more than once, not least in 1898.

V

This analysis began with the assertion that America is in crisis and that that crisis is one of public philosophy, of the role of reason in American political life. As is evident from the foregoing examination, the crisis of American constitutionalism, which is in no small part a crisis of Western civilization, "lies precisely in the denial that there are any such principles or truths" which are "applicable to all men and all times" such as those found in the Declaration of Independence.[41]

The American nation has lost sight of its own animating principles in the area of territorial relations, proceeding upon the basis of positive state right and power. Even the Constitution, which created and is intended to regulate and limit the government, has in many ways been effectively discarded and replaced by statism and interest-group pluralism.[42] The American republic has been overextended, and this is a symptom of an overcentralized, overbureaucratized, politicized government which operates in terms of power as opposed to right. America is experiencing a crisis of public philosophy: Americans and their government have neglected the ultimate principled reason for their polity and way of life.[43] They have forgotten who they are and from whence they came.

The people and government of the United States must ultimately come to recognize the equality and natural rights of territorial inhabitants. This requires that the inhabitants of the U.S. territories be allowed to determine, through deliberation and choice, whether they desire to be Americans in the fullest sense of that term (i.e., domestic), or independent in the fullest sense of that term (i.e., foreign). This is not to say that territorial inhabitants are obligated in any way to become Americans, or that the American people and their government are obligated fully to include the territories in the Union. It is to say that territorial inhabitants are not "foreign in a domestic sense." They are human beings who are in possession of certain natural rights which no government can give or take away, and which have yet to be exercised in the determination of political status. The political status of the inhabitants of the territories remains to be determined, not exclusively by Congress, nor by the Supreme Court, but by the territorial inhabitants themselves in concert with the people of the United States through their elected representatives in Congress. This determination of the political status of territorial inhabitants should have occurred in conjunction with the process of territorial acquisition.[44] Are the American people and their elected representatives capable of assisting the territories in this most crucial endeavor? How this question is answered in practice will most certainly contribute to either the freedom or bondage of the territories, and of America itself, as the United States is a regime which stands or falls upon the principle of securing human rights by law in freedom and equality.

Notes

1   E. Robert Statham Jr., *The Constitution of Public Philosophy: Toward a Synthesis of Freedom and Responsibility in Postmodern America* (1998), at 1–16. See also Walter Lippmann, *The Public Philosophy* (1956), at 11–54.

2   Fred Baumann, "Historicism and the Constitution," in *Confronting the Constitution,* ed. Allan Bloom (1990), at 284.

3   Ibid. at 284. See also "The Declaration of Independence" in *Soul of America: Documenting Our Past, 1492–1974,* ed. Robert C. Baron (1989), at 45–49.

4   Leo Strauss, *Natural Right and History* (1953), at 1.

5   *Treaty of Peace between the United States and Spain, Hale'-ta* (Agana, Guam: Produced and Published by the Political Status Education Coordinating Commission as Mandated by Public Law 20–99, 1993), at 19. Unification occurs constitutionally through the admission of new states into the Union by Congress. See *United States Constitution,* art. IV, sec. 3, cl. 1.

6   Felix Morely, *Freedom and Federalism* (1981), at 118.

7   George Washington, "Farewell Address," in Baron, supra note 3, at 132.

8   See, e.g., Plato, *The Republic* (1984), bk. 1; Aristotle, *The Politics* (1987), bks. 1, 5.

9   George Washington, "Farewell Address," in Baron, supra note 3, at 129.

10   Ibid. at 130.

11   Ibid. at 131.

12   William Marina, "Egalitarianism and Empire," in *The Politicization of Society,* ed. Kenneth S. Templeton Jr. (1979), at 134–35.

13   Ibid. at 139. See also "The Mayflower Compact" and the "Declaration of Independence," in Baron, supra note 7, at 8–9, 45–49.

14   See Marina, supra note 12.

15   Samuel P. Huntington, "The Erosion of American National Interests," *Foreign Affairs* 76 (1997): 28–34.

16   Abraham Lincoln, "The Perpetuation of Our Political Institutions," in *On Civil Disobedience: American Essays, Old and New,* ed. Robert A. Goldwin (1968), at 2.

17   The Federalist No. 38, in *The Federalist,* ed. Jacob E. Cooke (1961), at 248.

18   See Marina, supra note 12, at 160–61. See also William Marina, "Opponents of Empire: An Interpretation of American Anti-Imperialism, 1898–1921" (Ph.D. diss., University of Denver, 1968).

19   See, e.g., The Federalist No. 38, in *The Federalist,* supra note 17, at 239.

20   See E. Robert Statham Jr., supra note 1, chaps. 2–3. The modern approach focuses upon the development of institutions and structures, whereas the classical approach emphasizes the formation of character and citizenship.

21   The Federalist No. 10, in *The Federalist,* supra note 17, at 56.

22   George W. Carey, *In Defense of the Constitution* (1995), at 50–51.

23   The Federalist No. 10, in *The Federalist,* supra note 17, at 63–64.

24   The Federalist No. 51, in ibid. at 351.

25   Ibid.

26   Herbert J. Storing, *What the Anti-Federalists Were For: The Political Thought of the Opponents of the Constitution* (1981), at 16.

27   Ibid. at 19, 76.

28   *United States Constitution,* art. IV, sec. 3, cl. 2.

29   Edward J. Erler, *The American Polity: Essays on the Theory and Practice of Constitutional Government* (1991), at 9.

30   *Downes v. Bidwell,* 182 U.S. 244, 289–90 (1901) (White, J., concurring).

31   The Federalist No. 38, in *The Federalist,* supra note 17, at 239.

32   *Downes,* 182 U.S. at 300.

33   Ibid. at 306 (citations omitted).

34   Ibid. at 312–13.

35   Ibid. at 279.

36   Ibid. at 280.

37   Ibid.

38   Ibid. at 282.

39   Gordon Silverstein, *Imbalance of Powers: Constitutional Interpretation and the Making of American Foreign Policy* (1997), at 36.

40   The Federalist No. 1, in *The Federalist,* supra note 17, at 3.

41   Harry V. Jaffa, *Original Intent and the Framers of the Constitution: A Disputed Question* (1994), at 42.

42   See Theodore J. Lowi, *The End of Liberalism: The Second Republic of the United States* (1979), at 22.

43   See Edward B. McLean, "Introduction," in *Derailing the Constitution: The Undermining of American Federalism,* ed. Edward B. McLean (1995), at 7.

44   Since the United States possesses the right and power as a sovereign independent nation to

acquire territory (i.e., property or real estate) by treaty, but has no right to acquire territorial inhabitants (i.e., human beings), it follows that the political status of the inhabitants of the U.S. territories must be determined via treaty or social contract in conjunction with the resolution of territorial acquisition. If the territorial inhabitants, as a matter of popular sovereignty, refuse to covenant with the American people, the territory itself must, by right, be set free (as occurred in the Philippines) absent extraordinary circumstances of national interest which are temporary in nature. If the Congress refuses to covenant with the inhabitants of the territories in a reasonable period of time through the admission of new states into the Union, it must set the territories free or it acts against the purposes and principles of a free, constitutional order. The following provisional distinction and definition of terms is in this respect applicable: Under the U.S. Constitution, "territory," which is to be governed and controlled by Congress under Article IV, section 3, clause 2, is either uninhabited, or in the process of being settled. The congressional power to make all needful rules and regulations with respect to unincorporated territory in this way specifically refers to the drawing of boundaries and the eventual admittance of new states. Inhabited U.S. territory must be eventually either incorporated into the Union through the granting of statehood (as "incorporation" is the process and end result of the admission of new states [see *United States Constitution,* art. IV, sec. 3, cl. 1]) or released. Incorporated U.S. territories are by this definition states, and unincorporated U.S. territories are U.S. property or land (the language of treaties notwithstanding). In this regard, see Article VI of the Constitution and the dissenting opinion of Justice Harlan in *Downes,* 182 U.S. at 375–91. Justice Harlan understood that the principle of equality secured by the Constitution is binding in territories following their annexation when he stated that "whether a particular race will or will not assimilate with our people, and whether they can or cannot with safety to our institutions be brought within the operation of the Constitution, is a matter to be thought of when it is proposed to acquire their territory by treaty." Ibid. at 384.

Constitutionalism and Individual Rights
in the Territories

Gerald L. Neuman

In federal constitutional law, it is usual to speak of "the Constitution" as a unity. In textual terms, we may speak of the Constitution as composed of the original 1787 text and its subsequent amendments. In a broader sense, we may speak of the Constitution as a normative system embracing both the amended text and its currently operative interpretations. We may recognize, of course, that the Constitution has changed over time, both textually and in its interpretations, and therefore distinguish between the antebellum Constitution and the Reconstruction Constitution, or the pre- and post-1937 Constitutions. But at any particular moment in history, we imagine the Constitution as single, and permit ourselves to draw structural inferences from the relations of its various parts, and to reason by analogy from one area of constitutional law to another.

To view the Constitution as a unity does not mean viewing it as simple, or denying its capacity to tolerate distinctions. The Constitution may be interpreted as applying differently in different areas of regulation or of life, and we may speak of aspects of the constitutional system, such as the constitution of the military, or the constitution of the welfare system. Still, we do not really view these as separate and unrelated constitutions, but rather as particularized aspects of a common system. Precedents from one subfield of constitutional law may not straightforwardly guide the reasoning in another subfield, but neither are they wholly without normative force, as precedents from a foreign constitutional system would be. The Constitution is not separable into a series of mutually autonomous normative systems.

Or does the constitutional history of the territories demonstrate that the Constitution is not unified at all? The territories are excluded from certain basic structural features of the Constitution. Unlike the states, they do not elect voting members of Congress; unlike the states (and, since 1961, the District of Columbia), they do not participate in the electoral college; unlike the states, they lack guarantees of independence for their federal judges; and unlike the states, they are not guaranteed a republican form of government. And, as a result of judicial interpretation, not all individual rights provisions of the Constitution apply to the federal government's actions in the territories.[1]

At the same time, the Constitution of the territories is not as separate as it could have been, and as some have advocated in the past that it should be. The territories might have been placed, as for example Daniel Webster argued, wholly outside the constitutional system.[2] This could have been accomplished in either of two ways. The governance of the territories might have been conceptualized as literally extraconstitutional, to be governed without reference to the Constitution at all; they might then have been subject to unsupervised dictatorial powers of the president, or legislation by the Senate acting alone. Or, more likely, the Territorial Clause of Article IV might have been viewed as giving Congress absolute power, unconstrained by any notions of separation of powers or individual rights, but minimally structured by a few provisions of Articles I and II and the Territorial Clause itself.

The foregoing were possible strategies of constitutional *interpretation;* one should also consider alternative strategies of constitutional *drafting,* which could have specified in separate documents or in distinct articles of the same document parallel constitutions and insulated them from mutual influence. In fact, some Enlightenment writers of the natural law school had expressed approval of sovereigns who continue to rule an acquired territory under its prior form of government.[3]

If one included under the rubric of "territory" the relationship between the United States and the Freely Associated States of the former Pacific Trust Territory, then they would illustrate the strategy of parallel constitutions: the Freely Associated States have delegated certain functions normally associated with sovereignty to the United States, while maintaining their own sovereignty and exercising most sovereign powers exclusively themselves, under a treaty arrangement that is subject to unilateral termination by either party.[4] Their domestic governance arrangements are not addressed by the U.S. Constitution at all.

To the contrary, I will focus here on the relationship between the United States and territories over which it is sovereign. The five current examples of territories with resident populations are American Samoa, Guam, the Northern Mariana Islands, Puerto Rico, and the Virgin Islands.[5] Each has its distinctive history, and their political institutions have different configurations. At the risk of oversimplification, I will try to address them at a level of generality in this short essay. It should also be observed that referring to the Commonwealth of Puerto Rico and the Commonwealth of the Northern Mariana Islands as territories is itself controversial; I will use the term here in a generic sense, without implying a particular stance on the legal consequences of commonwealth status.

The Evolution of Territorial Doctrine

The relation of the territories to the U.S. Constitution has evolved over two centuries, but not in a consistent direction.[6] The salient political issues of territorial governance have varied, and basic principles of constitutional doctrine have been contested and sometimes reversed. Both the source and nature of the federal government's power over the territories and the applicability of express constitutional limitations to that power have been at issue.

As far as power is concerned, the Supreme Court has never held that federal authority to acquire and govern territories derives from a source outside the Constitution. President Jefferson initially doubted his authority to acquire Louisiana, but Federalist methods of broad construction prevailed.[7] Territorial powers have been attributed, for various reasons and from various motives, to the Territorial Clause of Article IV, to the war power, to the treaty power, to the power of Congress to admit new states, and to implied powers of national sovereignty.

Supreme Court precedent on the applicability of constitutional limitations has been more varied. It is possible to distinguish four phases in the historical development of understandings concerning the geographical scope of constitutional limitations.[8] In the first phase, extending from 1789 through the first decades of the nineteenth century, the issue was highly unsettled; politicians took various positions, sometimes dictated by their immediate interests, but no consistent resolution had been made. In the second phase, extending from the middle until the end of the nineteenth century, courts routinely held that generally phrased constitutional limitations applied in the District of Columbia and the territories as well as the states. At the turn of the last century, however, this settled understanding was overthrown by the *Insular Cases,* which adopted a new distinction between "incorporated territories" and "unincorporated territories" for the explicit purpose of facilitating colonial expansion. The doctrine of the *Insular Cases* decreed that "nonfundamental" constitutional limitations do not apply in unincorporated territories, although truly "fundamental" constitutional limitations do. This new regime inaugurated a third phase of confident colonialism, which lasted until the mid–twentieth century. In the fourth phase, from the 1950s to the present, the courts have recognized that constitutional limitations may apply even outside the boundaries of the United States. At the same time, the postwar rejection of colonialism has caused a reevaluation of the purposes for which territories may legitimately be governed. Thus far, despite continuing criticism of the *Insular Cases* doctrine, its approach has been subtly transformed rather than overruled.

In broader context, the normative debate that structured these shifting regimes has involved competition between two different kinds of approaches to determining the personal and geographic scope of constitutional rights and limitations.[9] The first kind, *membership* approaches, treat certain individuals or locales as participating in a privileged relationship with the constitutional project, and entitled to the benefit of constitutional provisions as a result of that relationship. The second kind, approaches based in *mutuality of obligation,* treat constitutional rights and limitations as necessary to justify the exercise of governing power, and therefore extend those rights and limitations to persons or places that become subject to the governing power of the United States.[10] The difference may be illustrated by the debates over the Alien Act of 1798, in which some Federalist defenders of the Act argued that the Bill of Rights did not protect foreign residents, because only U.S. citizens were parties to the Constitution, while the Jeffersonian critics of the Act maintained that foreigners who were subject to U.S. laws were correspondingly entitled to the protection of U.S. constitutional rights.[11] Similar strategies of argumentation have also been employed in determining the geographic scope of constitutional rights.[12]

When employed as methodologies of constitutional interpretation, membership and mutuality approaches necessarily interact with the constitutional text. In some instances, the text contains explicit references to its personal or geographic scope. For example, the Privileges and Immunities Clause of Article IV by its terms addresses the rights of citizens of states, in states. More often, constitutional provisions do not specify their personal or geographic extension, or use general terms like "the accused," making interpretation dependent on background assumptions like the membership and mutuality approaches.

The Constitution exhibits definite features of the membership approach in its distribution of opportunities for political participation. Despite the framers' professed dedication to the republican principle of self-government, they structured the federal government in a manner that accorded actual representation only to the residents of the states. The Constitution subjected both the District of Columbia and the territories to direct governance by Congress, while denying the District and the territories participation in the election of Congress and the president.[13] The Constitution contained no guarantee that subordinate institutions of local self-governance would be established in the District or the territories, although such institutions were contemplated and have sometimes been provided. In contrast, the Constitution not only gives the states representation in Congress and in the electoral college but also requires the federal government to guarantee to each *state* a republican form of government.

These deviations from republican principle originally received separate justifications based on the circumstances of the District and the territories. As regards the District, the framers believed, partly from experience, that the safety and autonomy of the federal government required that it have a capital city subject to its own rule and independent of the states.[14] Moreover, the disenfranchisement would be consensual to the extent that future residents of the District had chosen for economic reasons to move to the new city rather than retain their political rights in the states. As regards the territories, the Northwest Ordinance provided a model of governance of underpopulated frontier regions in successive stages.[15] As population increased and self-government became more feasible, republican institutions would be progressively strengthened, culminating in admission of the territory as a state. The temporary character of territorial status, and its basis in practical necessity, made it possible to reconcile the denial of representation with the republican *spirit* of the Constitution.[16] But no comparable effort was needed to reconcile this denial with the letter of the Constitution, which contained no positive provision guaranteeing voting rights to residents of the territories.[17]

In the early nineteenth century, some advocates used the absence of constitutional guarantees of self-government in the District and the territories to support a thoroughgoing membership approach to the applicability of other constitutional limitations.[18] They contended that the Constitution was created by the people of the states and for the states, and therefore its restrictions did not apply outside the states. Opponents argued that the Constitution was the law of the land, and that its restrictions applied according to their terms wherever the United States was sovereign.[19] This version of a mutuality approach was later expressed in the slogan stating that the Constitution "follows the flag."

To summarize briefly the first two phases of the doctrinal development, the text of the Constitution left its intended geographic scope uncertain,[20] and both state-centered membership approaches and mutuality approaches received support in the era of westward expansion on the North American continent. The issues at stake involved structures of governance for newly acquired territory, procedural aspects of civil and criminal justice, and the highly divisive question of the status of slavery in the territories. Chief Justice Marshall's nationalist opinions expressed the view that the Constitution applied throughout the whole of the "American empire," including states, territories, and the District of Columbia.[21] A series of Supreme Court decisions in the 1850s confirmed the applicability of constitutional rights in the territories.[22] Ironically, the most important of these precedents was the *Dred Scott* decision, in which Chief Justice Taney employed the Due Process Clause of the Fifth Amendment to protect slaveholders against congressional prohibition of slavery in the territories.[23] The dissenting Justices in that case agreed that the Bill of Rights bound Congress in all territories governed by the United States.[24] Although some critics of the decision rejected this aspect as well,[25] courts continued to affirm the force of the Bill of Rights in the territories during the Civil War and thereafter.[26] Perhaps the best evidence of the solidity of the mutuality approach after the Civil War lies in its consistent application in the Mormon polygamy cases, the most politically charged territorial controversies of the period.[27]

The second phase thus achieved a partial constitutional unification of the states and the territories. Territories were in preparation for eventual statehood (although the Constitution did not expressly require this). Their systems of civil and criminal procedure were governed by the Bill of Rights, like federal procedure in the states. Birth in the territories conferred U.S. citizenship. Territorial legislatures were, however, subordinate to Congress, which could legislate on local matters over local opposition—as the antipolygamy laws also illustrate. And the very existence of territorial legislatures resulted from political tradition, not constitutional mandate.

The third phase reflected the events of the turn of the last century—the Spanish-American War, the acquisition of distant insular territories, and the determination of the United States to become a great colonial power on the European model.[28] Imperialists sought a free hand to rule newly acquired subjects without constitutional constraint, without admitting them to privileges of citizenship, and without including them in a customs union with the mainland. The Supreme Court accommodated the imperialists by a bare majority in *Downes v. Bidwell,* the most important of the *Insular*

Cases of 1901.[29] The most extreme membership vision was expressed in portions of Justice Brown's opinion announcing the judgment—he maintained that the Constitution does not apply of its own force to an acquired territory, but may be voluntarily extended to such a territory by Congress.[30] The four dissenters asserted the orthodox position of mutuality, affirming that the Constitution and its limitations on government power extend over all territory acquired by the United States.[31] In the words of the first Justice Harlan's individual dissent: "The Constitution speaks not simply to the States in their organized capacities, but to all peoples, whether of States or territories, who are subject to the authority of the United States."[32]

The intermediate position, which soon became established doctrine, was articulated in the concurring opinion of Justice Edward Douglass White.[33] White insisted that the federal government must have the same sovereign right to determine the status of newly acquired territories that other sovereigns (viz. European colonial powers) enjoyed under international law.[34] That mode of argument echoed other post–Civil War assertions of federal powers implied from national sovereignty, like the power to regulate immigration and the power to issue paper money as legal tender.[35] He also invoked the nation's right to protect the birthright of its own citizens by withholding citizenship from acquired populations that might belong to "an uncivilized race" and be "absolutely unfit to receive it."[36]

Nonetheless, White did not relegate colonial subjects to extraconstitutional status and absolute government power. He rejected Brown's notion that Congress had discretion as to whether or not to extend the Constitution.[37] White emphasized that the Constitution itself was applicable everywhere and at all times—though, on the other hand, particular constitutional provisions limiting government power were not necessarily applicable everywhere.[38] White contended that the Court could determine on an objective basis whether a particular territory had been "incorporated" into the United States, or left as an unincorporated territory appurtenant to the United States.[39] He distinguished the nineteenth-century precedents as confirming the full applicability of constitutional limitations to incorporated territories, but as not addressing the limits on congressional power in unincorporated territories.[40] Even in unincorporated territories, congressional power was not absolute, but rather was limited by "inherent, although unexpressed, principles which are the basis of all free government . . . restrictions of so fundamental a nature that they cannot be transgressed."[41]

As thus expressed, White's theory might threaten to create two parallel systems of constitutionalism for the states and incorporated territories on the one hand and for the unincorporated territories on the other.[42] The former would be entitled by their membership to the benefit of the written, positive Constitution, while the latter would be entitled by mutuality to be governed in a manner consistent with natural law—but judicially enforceable natural law, hierarchically superior to statute.[43] As White gained a majority for his position, the *Insular Cases* doctrine came to involve the categorization of positive constitutional rights and limitations as "fundamental" or nonfundamental, with only the fundamental rights and limitations being binding in unincorporated territories.[44] The criteria for distinguishing between fundamental and nonfundamental provisions remained uncertain, and were certainly not provided by the text of the Constitution. Unincorporated territories were not guaranteed U.S. citizenship under the Fourteenth Amendment for persons born therein; criminal and civil jury guarantees did not apply; the Article I requirement of uniformity in taxation did not apply.[45]

The regime established in the third phase is apparently still controlling, but its significance and context changed sufficiently in the latter half of the twentieth century to require recognition of a fourth phase. After the Second World War, both international and domestic developments called the regime into question.

First, the frank racism and enthusiastic colonialism that formed part of the explicit justification of the *Insular Cases* could no longer be maintained in the postwar environment. Where nineteenth-century international law had recognized the sovereign prerogative of European powers to dominate weaker populations, modern international law recognized the right of all peoples to self-determination and the mandate for decolonization.[46] Modern international law—as well as modern constitutional principles and modern science—also repudiates the racist assumptions of the *Downes* majority.

Second, the mobility of the Constitution and the flag have increased in the twentieth century, requiring new analyses of the extraterritorial applicability of constitutional limitations.[47] Extraterritorial federal regulation has expanded with the abandonment of nineteenth-century territorial conceptions of legislative jurisdiction. As the United States progressed from great power to superpower, its overseas official and military presence vastly increased. The United States also took on governance responsibilities for territories over which it was not sovereign, including United Nations Trust Territories created after the war, in addition to older nonsovereign territories like the Panama Canal Zone.[48]

These developments formed part of the background of *Reid v. Covert*, a 1957 watershed holding that the Constitution prohibited the trial by court-martial of U.S. citizen civilians on foreign soil.[49] Justice Black's plurality opinion refashioned and revived the mutuality of obligation approach, taking into fuller account the exercise of legislative jurisdiction over American citizens worldwide. Black not only held that *some* constitutional rights were binding extraterritorially, he insisted that extraterritorial government action must comply "with all the limitations imposed by the Constitution."[50] Black's rejection of judicial discretion to identify a narrower category of "fundamental" rights applicable extraterritorially mirrored his contemporary attack on judicial discretion to decide which rights applied against the states under the Fourteenth Amendment.[51] Black halfheartedly distinguished the *Insular Cases,* and then severely criticized their doctrine:

> [N]either the cases nor their reasoning should be given any further expansion. The concept that the Bill of Rights and other constitutional protections against arbitrary government are inoperative when they become inconvenient or when expediency dictates otherwise is a very dangerous doctrine and if allowed to flourish would destroy the benefit of a written Constitution and undermine the basis of our Government.[52]

As I have written elsewhere, I find Black's critique of the *Insular Cases* wholly persuasive.[53]

Black was writing, however, only for a plurality of four, and the concurring opinions of Justice Frankfurter and the second Justice Harlan—both adherents of discretionary due process methodologies in the Fourteenth Amendment context—expressed greater sympathy for the *Insular Cases* approach.[54] They were willing to determine on a case-by-case basis whether particular constitutional rights could practicably be extended to U.S. citizens in particular locations in particular contexts.

Juxtaposing *Reid v. Covert* with the *Insular Cases* produces bizarre results. For example, a U.S. citizen prosecuted by the federal government has a constitutional right to jury trial in Japan, but not in Puerto Rico. For a while, it appeared as if the overruling of the *Insular Cases* was in prospect. But Justices critical of the doctrine never mustered a majority to reject it. Chief Justice Burger restated the doctrine in *Torres v. Puerto Rico,* advertently or inadvertently describing the applicability of a constitutional right as a matter that may vary from one unincorporated territory to another.[55] This is potentially a very significant change in the methodology.

More recently, the Rehnquist Court has retreated from *Reid v. Covert* rather than retreating from the *Insular Cases*. In *United States v. Verdugo-Urquidez*, the Court confronted the problem of extraterritorial constitutional rights of nonresident aliens, and held that they were not protected extraterritorially by the Fourth Amendment.[56] Both Chief Justice Rehnquist's opinion and Justice Kennedy's crucial concurrence maintained the continuing validity of the *Insular Cases,* and emphasized the concurring opinions in *Reid v. Covert* at the expense of Black's plurality opinion.[57] Kennedy's concurrence endorses a "global due process" approach to determining the applicability of constitutional limitations to exotic locations outside the states.[58] Flexibility, adaptation to local conditions, attention to practical constraints that already diminish federal power, and a normative hierarchy of fundamentality must all be considered, instead of relying solely on the constitutional text and on precedents applicable in the states.

Meanwhile, the character of the United States's relationship with its unincorporated territories has also changed. In the atmosphere of postwar decolonization, the political rights of territorial populations have received greater respect. Puerto Rico pioneered the model of commonwealth status based on mutual consent in 1952,[59] followed by the Commonwealth of the Northern Mariana Islands between 1975 and 1986 (when the status finally took effect).[60] American Samoa also adopted its own local constitution in 1960.[61] Constitution-making processes in Guam and the Virgin Islands have been under way, but have been more protracted.[62]

The "fitness" of territorial inhabitants for U.S. citizenship is no longer questioned. Citizenship was extended to Guam in 1950; Puerto Rico and the Virgin Islands had already received it before the Second World War.[63] The only territory where citizenship has not been conferred is American Samoa, apparently due to concern that abolishing the distinction between citizen and noncitizen national would threaten local arrangements that *disadvantage* non-Samoans.[64]

The *Insular Cases* doctrine was emphatically not designed for the purpose of accommodating the self-determination of the people of the territories; it was designed to facilitate ruling over them. But the flexibility it creates can also be used to modify constitutional structures in response to local customs and preferences. In the fourth phase, some disputes over the application of constitutional provisions have resulted from the *territory's* omission of jury trial guarantees in the territorial constitution, rather than Congress's refusal to submit criminal cases to juries of territorial inhabitants.[65] Another important class of disputes, to which I will return, has

involved the applicability of mainland equal protection doctrine to ethnically based rules in the Pacific island territories, intended to protect the
interests of the earlier inhabitants against later arrivals. These include provisions restricting alienation of land,[66] preference in government employment,[67] and the reservation of a right to self-determination in the proposed
Guam Commonwealth Act.[68] Although arguably these provisions might be
sustainable under federal equal protection doctrine by analogy with federal
preferences for members of Native American tribes,[69] some courts have
supported their approval of such provisions by denying the full applicability of equal protection principles in unincorporated territories.[70]

A Relatively Unified Constitution

As matters currently stand, even a critic of the *Insular Cases* might conclude
that the constitutional regime for the territories is recognizably part of the
same Constitution, rather than a separate normative system. This is visible
both in how the Constitution applies to the territories and in how the
territories have influenced the rest of the Constitution.

First, the Court has been careful to maintain that federal power over the
territories is based in the Constitution, not extraconstitutional in nature.
That insistence preserves the Court's own role in defining the boundaries of
federal power, even if the Court performs that role infrequently and defer-
entially.

Second, although the *Insular Cases* doctrine radically revised the prior
approach to territorial governance, it had methodological affinities to other
constitutional doctrines of the period. *Downes v. Bidwell* was decided in
what we now call the Lochner era, in which the Supreme Court was engaged
in enforcing unwritten natural law under the rubric of due process as part
of the written Constitution in the states. The selective application of the Bill
of Rights to the territories was also methodologically similar to the hesitant
partial application of Bill of Rights provisions against state action under the
Fourteenth Amendment. (The continuing inapplicability of criminal jury
trial rights, however, and the inapplicability of the Citizenship Clause of the
Fourteenth Amendment, illustrate that the notion of fundamentality employed in the unincorporated territories has not always coincided with the
notion of fundamentality employed for Fourteenth Amendment purposes.
Moreover, the nonapplication of nonfundamental rights to federal action
in the territories lacks even the slender textual basis that the Fourteenth
Amendment provides for the nonapplication of nonfundamental rights to
state action.) The positions taken by Justices prominent in the debates on

the *Insular Cases* have often paralleled their positions on the relation between the Bill of Rights and the Fourteenth Amendment.

Third, the usual consequence of finding an individual right applicable in
the territories has been to interpret that right as it is interpreted in the states.
Concepts that enjoy internationally widespread support, such as freedom of
speech, are nevertheless understood differently in different cultures and
legal traditions. Territories, like states, are entitled to develop their own
conceptions of freedom of speech under their own local constitutions, but
they will, like states, be bound by the national conception when federal
constitutional challenges are brought. Furthermore, the Supreme Court
applies not only the same conception of the right but also the same legal
standards for implementing the right. For example, in *Examining Board of
Engineers v. Flores de Otero,* the Court proceeded swiftly from recognizing
the applicability of the equal protection principle in the unincorporated
territories to measuring Puerto Rico's discrimination against alien residents
by the standard of strict scrutiny that had been developed in cases involving
discrimination by the states.[71] In its per curiam decision in *El Vocero de
Puerto Rico v. Puerto Rico,*[72] the Court specifically rejected the Puerto Rico
Supreme Court's reliance on "the unique history and traditions of the
Commonwealth," including a "special concern for the honor and reputation of the citizenry," as irrelevant to the established nationwide standard
for evaluating the media's First Amendment right of access to preliminary
proceedings in criminal cases.

Conversely, decisions involving constitutional rights applicable to the
unincorporated territories become precedents available for construing
those rights as they apply elsewhere. Citizens in the states thus have a greater
stake in the constitutional jurisprudence of the territories than they may
suspect, because their own rights at home are implicated by disputes in the
territories.

Moreover, the *in*applicability of constitutional rights under the *Insular
Cases* doctrine has been relied upon as an argument for denying the extraterritorial applicability of the full Bill of Rights to citizens of the states. After
United States v. Verdugo-Urquidez—to my regret[73]—the *Insular Cases* doctrine can be seen as embedded in a more general "global due process"
approach to the rights of both citizens and aliens in "overseas" locales.[74]

Beyond the Insular Cases

The harm done by the *Insular Cases* doctrine in the twentieth century is
undeniable. In its direct legal effects and in the political attitudes that it

ratified and fostered, the doctrine was a vehicle of injustice. The opinions of Justices Brown and White are classic documents of the racism of their period, comparable to Brown's opinion in *Plessy v. Ferguson* and Justice Field's opinions on Chinese exclusion, and their presence in the United States Reports is painful to citizens of both the territories and the states.

As we enter the twenty-first century, what direction should U.S. constitutionalism take? The Supreme Court could reinstate the method of interpreting constitutional rights in light of the mutual relation of power and rights and restore greater unity to the Constitution by overruling the *Insular Cases*. At present, however, this course is unlikely. Congress could render the doctrine irrelevant on its own terms, by "incorporating" the remaining territories, or admitting them to statehood. The dichotomy of incorporated and unincorporated territories might be transcended by recognizing newer status alternatives as outside the scope of the doctrine. Or, the territories might embrace the membership approach and try to turn it to other uses, accepting that states and territories have different kinds of membership in the constitutional compact, but seeking a way to exploit their flexibility so that their membership is different, but not inferior.

THE TURN TO STRUCTURES

Today, the direct legal effects of continuing adherence to the doctrine are fewer. Putting aside the question of what the Constitution *requires,* most of the rights of citizens of the states are available, at least on a statutory basis, to the citizens of the territories. Although the *Insular Cases* delayed the grant of citizenship to residents of the territories, birth in every territory except American Samoa entailed citizenship by the 1950s. There are no restrictions on the freedom of territorial residents, including the Samoans, who are technically noncitizen nationals, to move to the mainland if they wish. All the territories have institutions of local self-government.

As an essential part of the decolonization process, Puerto Rico assumed the status of a commonwealth with local autonomy in 1952, on the basis of a series of reciprocal acts of local constitution making and congressional legislation "in the nature of a compact."[75] The Northern Mariana Islands, which were previously independent of the United States, although governed as a Trust Territory, came under United States sovereignty by means of the negotiated Covenant to Establish a Commonwealth, approved by plebiscite on the one side and enacted into legislation by the other.[76] The Covenant specifically provides that certain fundamental provisions may be modified only by the joint consent of both governments.[77]

Nonetheless, the legal effect of these organic documents remains unclear, for two reasons. First, as a matter of interpretation, the degree to which Congress has acted to bind itself is disputed.[78] Second, as a matter of constitutional law, it is uncertain whether Congress *can* commit itself in a binding fashion not to exercise legislative powers that it would otherwise have over a territory, assuming that a commonwealth *is* a species of territory.[79] Undoubtedly, Congress can assume solemn obligations to a territory, and pledge the faith of the United States in ways that could create political impediments to future inconsistent action.[80] But the extent of Congress's ability to adopt a political instrument that legally precludes future legislation is unclear, as is the possibly separable question of the judicial enforceability of such limitations on future legislation.[81]

Disputes over the degree of autonomy guaranteed by existing commonwealth statuses have led to explorations of enhanced commonwealth statuses that would afford stronger safeguards of autonomy.[82] But the pursuit of enhanced commonwealth meets obstacles both in the federal government's unwillingness to make such commitments and in the uncertainty over whether the federal government has power to do so.

The possible vulnerability of commonwealths to continued federal interference with local issues is an extremely sore point in U.S. territorial relations. It supplies one of the major bases for the diagnosis that commonwealth status has failed to accomplish decolonization. In his recent eloquent summation of the status dilemma of Puerto Rico, Chief Justice José Trías Monge offers a list of twelve reasons leading to the conclusion that Puerto Rico is still a colony, which I will partly quote and partly paraphrase:

1. "United States laws apply to the Puerto Rican people without their consent."

2. "United States laws can override provisions of the Commonwealth Constitution."

3. "The President of the United States and executive appointees negotiate treaties and take other actions which affect Puerto Rico without consulting it."

4. "Through the unilateral grant by Congress of diversity jurisdiction, United States courts decide cases involving strictly local matters of law."

5. "There is no equality or comparability of rights between United States citizens residing in Puerto Rico and those domiciled in the States."

6. "Congress assumes that it can unilaterally exercise plenary powers over Puerto Rico under the territorial clause of the United States Constitution."

7. "The United States government contends that sovereignty over Puerto Rico resides solely in the United States and not in the people of Puerto Rico."

8. Both Congress and the executive branch deny that federal power is limited, or could be limited, by a compact with Puerto Rico.

9. Even if the 1952 compact is binding, the consent it expressed to future federal regulation is too broad, and still results in colonial status.

10. "Puerto Rico plays no role in the life of the international community, either directly or indirectly as a participant in the decisions taken by the United States."

11. "Commonwealth status as it is at present does not meet the decolonization standards established by the United Nations."

12. "There is no known noncolonial relationship in the present world where one people exercises such vast, almost unbounded power over the government of another."[83]

Without quarreling with this indictment, it is striking that none of its counts, with the possible or partial exception of the fifth, depends on the continuation of the *Insular Cases* doctrine. If *Downes v. Bidwell* were overruled, or if Puerto Rico were made an incorporated territory, all these criticisms would remain.[84]

It is true that statehood would cure some of these objections, but the *Insular Cases* doctrine in its current form has little to do with statehood. Even though incorporated territories were likely candidates for future statehood, the Supreme Court has never interfered with Congress's discretion as to whether and when to admit a state. The dissenters in the *Insular Cases* did not maintain that Congress was obliged to admit eventually as a state every territory that the United States acquired; they insisted only that Congress was obliged to govern acquired territories in accordance with the written Constitution, which contains no such provision. Nor, of course, is Congress precluded in any way from admitting an unincorporated territory as a state.

Thus the central thrust of the indictment of territorial colonialism today is not that the Constitution took a wrong turn in 1901 but that the Constitution has *never* contained sufficient barriers against colonialism. The fundamental republican defect, that the Constitution restricts national representation to the states while giving the national organs governing power over the territories, provides the focus. Even establishing subordinate republican institutions of local government does not suffice, if their autonomy is not shielded from interference by national organs in which the territories are not represented.

From one perspective, the formal solution to the problem is statehood. Statehood would cure the formal absence of representation, although risks remain concerning how actually responsive the national political process would be to the distinctive needs of one or a few states. But statehood in the U.S. federal system has some consequences that may make territorial residents who are conscious of colonial grievances pause, even if Congress were willing to grant it. The United States is an "indestructible Union, composed of indestructible States."[85] The Civil War was a central constitutional experience, fought in explicit opposition to the theory that states have sovereign peoples entitled to achieve self-determination by leaving the Union. The unity of the nation emerged reinforced after the Civil War, with a strengthened federal government and an emphasis on national citizenship. The Fourteenth Amendment subordinates state citizenship to national citizenship by requiring states to treat all national citizens resident within their borders as citizens of the state. Case law decided under the rubrics of equal protection and the right to travel precludes states from differentiating between earlier residents and newer arrivals. Equal protection principles preclude the states from viewing themselves as vehicles for the self-determination of some privileged subgroup of their citizens. If statehood entails these consequences, and permanently, then some territorial residents would prefer a status that does not.[86]

APPROPRIATING THE *INSULAR CASES*?
For some territorial residents and advocates, then, *Downes v. Bidwell* and its colonial legacy should be repudiated, but the opportunity it created should be seized. They would not wish the unified vision of the dissenters to prevail. Justice Harlan, for example, warned in his dissent, "[w]hether a particular race will or will not assimilate with our people, and whether they can or cannot with safety to our institutions be brought within the operation of the Constitution, is a matter to be thought of when it is proposed to acquire their territory by treaty."[87] His vision was assimilationist, not multicultural. He was not seeking to foster the self-determination of territorial inhabitants as separate peoples but rather their inclusion in the one American people.

The degree to which territorial and commonwealth statuses would permit a group that views itself as a territorial people to achieve self-determination within the U.S. constitutional system, while maintaining its distinctiveness as a people on a permanent basis, is uncertain, both as to efficacy and as to legitimacy. The efficacy of such a project depends on securing the federal government's noninterference, either through an enforceable binding commitment (which may not be possible), or through federal self-restraint (which may not be likely in the long term).

The legitimacy of the project depends on whether the constitutional system can admit the permanent coexistence of separate peoples of (some or all) territories, with geographically defined political units, within or alongside the American people. This problem might be viewed in terms of equal protection, or in terms of the character of American citizenship. It is one thing to say that the United States has colonized peoples of insular territories against their will, and must afford them the opportunity to exercise self-determination in order to choose between converting their union with the United States into a voluntary one, and achieving independence. It is something quite different to say that they can choose union while maintaining their separate identity as a people and embodying that identity in governmental form. By saying that the second proposition is different from the first, I do not mean to assert that it is necessarily wrong. But it raises harder questions for the United States.

The United States is, by aspiration, a nonethnic nation. That vision has been achieved by struggle, and progress toward it has not been consistent. The overruling of the *Dred Scott* decision by the Fourteenth Amendment repudiated Chief Justice Taney's ideal of white nationhood, but that amendment was betrayed after Reconstruction. The majority opinions in the *Insular Cases* reveal the ascendancy of an ideal of so-called Anglo-Saxon nationhood, whose pretensions were nicely punctured in Justice Harlan's dissent. More lasting implementation of the vision of nonracialized citizenship occurred after the Second World War. The equal protection norm—which applies to persons, and not only citizens—is now a central pillar of that vision, and one of the defining values of the Constitution. I do not mean to offer an opinion on whether the various territorial proposals and laws comport with or violate the norm of equal protection. But I do want to suggest that tampering with the *applicability* of that norm would be a serious inroad on the unity of the Constitution.

Such tampering was nonetheless the strategy employed by the Ninth Circuit in upholding the ethnically defined restrictions on alienation of land in the Northern Mariana Islands, in *Wabol v. Villacrusis*.[88] The Ninth Circuit did not articulate and defend an analogy between the indigenous people of the Commonwealth and Native American tribes on the mainland that would justify transference of the Supreme Court's approach to preferential treatment of Native Americans in *Morton v. Mancari*.[89] Nor did it subject the land restrictions to strict scrutiny and find them necessary to the achievement of a compelling interest. Instead, the Ninth Circuit decomposed the equal protection norm into separate strands, and held that the right at stake was not applicable to the Commonwealth. It defined the right as "equal protection of the laws regarding access to long-term interests in real property."[90] It concluded that this right was not fundamental "in the international sense," a standard that would "incorporate the shared beliefs of diverse cultures."[91] And (in what could be considered a methodologically inconsistent move), the court concluded that the application of this aspect of equal protection would be "impractical and anomalous" in the particular circumstances of the Northern Mariana Islands.[92]

From an alternative perspective, entrenching the separateness of territorial peoples creates challenges for the concept of U.S. citizenship. Common citizenship has operated in the United States as a unifying institution, undermining rather than reinforcing ethnic differences. One of the great wrongs of the *Insular Cases* was their manipulation of the geographical content of the term "United States" in the first sentence of the Fourteenth Amendment, in order to avoid a guarantee of citizenship for children born in the territories. Congress, however, has explicitly extended citizenship in all existing territories except American Samoa.[93] To be sure, territorial citizenship has been characterized as "statutory" rather than "constitutional," a status shared by children born in foreign countries to citizens of the states, and by most Native Americans. The distinction rarely has legal relevance.[94]

These statutory corrections of the territorial exclusions bring U.S. nationality law into greater harmony with the understanding of the United States as a political union. The "people of the United States" is an aggregate of individuals defined by their political relation to the United States, and not the kind of prepolitical organic unity assumed by European romantic nationalism.

Claims for the recognition of separate peoples within the American citizenry challenge that understanding. Concededly, the dual status of members of Native American tribes demonstrates that the United States already recognizes one form of group-differentiated citizenship, defined by descent, within the population of the states. To the extent that indigenous inhabitants of the territories can articulate their situations as analogous to those of tribes, accommodating their claims might not change the character of U.S. citizenship. But accepting linguistic and cultural differences as the basis for recognizing separate peoples within a permanent political union would pose greater challenges.[95]

Conclusion

From the perspective of constitutional theory, one consequence of the unity of the Constitution is that stateside constitutional scholars cannot afford to ignore territorial issues. So long as the United States maintains territories, the citizens of the states have a stake in how the territories are governed, not only because they are morally responsible for how power is exercised in their name, but also because rights in the territories are ultimately linked to rights in the states.

The legacy of the *Insular Cases* doctrine weighs heavily on the constitutional system, and some of its wrongs are obvious. The citizens of the states have no monopoly on civic virtue or political wisdom, and they cannot presume to decide what is best for the citizens of the territories. All the voices must contribute to the dialogue that will determine the next phase of constitutional development. Whether there are separable elements of that doctrine that are worth preserving is a question that we must decide together.

Notes

1   See *Downes v. Bidwell*, 182 U.S. 244 (1901); Arnold H. Leibowitz, *Defining Status: A Comprehensive Analysis of United States Territorial Relations* (1989), at 26–28.

2   See Gerald L. Neuman, *Strangers to the Constitution: Immigrants, Borders, and Fundamental Law* (1996), at 78–79.

3   See ibid. at 13 (discussing views of Burlamaqui and Vattel on governance of acquired territory).

4   See Leibowitz, supra note 1, at 595–96; Jon M. Van Dyke, "The Evolving Legal Relationships between the United States and Its Affiliated U.S.-Flag Islands," *University of Hawaii Law Review* 14 (1992): 445, at 502–3.

5   See, e.g., Van Dyke, ibid. at 447. The United States also maintains sovereignty over various islands without permanent populations, including Baker, Howland, Kingman Reef, Jarvis, Johnston, Midway, Palmyra, and Wake Islands. See id. The District of Columbia raises some of the same issues as do the territories, but it has a distinct constitutional status, and I will refer to it separately.

6   See, e.g., Leibowitz supra note 1, at 6–32; Neuman, supra note 2, at 72–94.

7   See Leibowitz, ibid. at 11–12; Neuman, ibid. at 73–74.

8 See generally Neuman, ibid. at 72–94, 104–8 (tracing these developments, but not dividing them into four phases).

9 See ibid. at 6–8 (describing membership and mutuality of obligation approaches to the scope of constitutional rights).

10 In the context of Puerto Rico, I should emphasize that the principle of mutuality of obligation—that a government that seeks to impose obligations on individuals should also be subject to obligations to them that could justify its exercise of power—must be distinguished from mutuality of *actual consent* as the historical basis for the acquisition of governing power.

Perhaps I should also mention that the designation "mutuality of obligation" for an approach to the scope of constitutional rights replaces the terminology "municipal law approach" that I used in my first investigation of this subject—see Gerald L. Neuman, "Whose Constitution?" *Yale Law Journal* 100 (1991): 909—but without changing its content. See Neuman, supra note 2, at 7, n.a.

11 See Neuman, supra note 2, at 54–59.

12 See ibid. at 72–74.

13 *United States Constitution,* art. I, sec. 8, cl. 17 (Seat of Government Clause) and art. IV, sec. 3, cl. 2 (Territorial Clause). The Twenty-third Amendment gave the District a voice in election of the president.

14 See, e.g., Gerald L. Neuman, "Anomalous Zones," *Stanford Law Review* 48 (1996): 1197, at 1215–16.

15 See Leibowitz, supra note 1, at 6–8; Francis S. Philbrick, ed., *Laws of Illinois Territory, 1809–1818* (1950).

16 See, e.g., *Loughborough v. Blake,* 18 U.S. (5 Wheat.) 317, 324 (1820) (Marshall, C. J.).

17 In the *Dred Scott* decision, however, Chief Justice Taney expounded in dictum the view that Congress's power to govern territories was derived from its power to admit new states:

[N]o power is given to acquire a Territory to be held and governed permanently in that character.

. . . the power to expand the territory of the United States by the admission of new States is plainly given; and in the construction of this power by all the departments of the Government, it has been held to authorize the acquisition of territory, not fit for admission at the time, but to be admitted as soon as its population and situation would entitle it to admission. It is acquired to become a State, and not to be held as a colony and governed by Congress with absolute authority. . . .

Scott v. Sandford, 60 U.S. (19 How.) 393, 446–47 (1857). This explanation was part of Taney's complicated strategy for evading the force of the Northwest Ordinance as a precedent for Congress's power to ban slavery in the territories; Taney contended that the Territorial Clause authorized Congress to govern only those territories already possessed in 1787, and that power to govern after-acquired territories was implied and subject to greater limitations.

18 See Neuman, supra note 2, at 78–79.

19 See ibid. at 74–78.

20 Gouverneur Morris later asserted in a letter to Henry W. Livingston that he had deliberately drafted the Territorial Clause of Article IV in an ambiguous way and had sought to avoid debate. See *Dred Scott,* 60 U.S. at 507 (Campbell, J., concurring) (quoting Morris's letter). The letter was written on December 4, 1803, during the controversy over the Louisiana Purchase. It appears in volume 18, folio 159 of Gouverneur Morris, Papers (Library of Congress 1965) (microfilm).

21   *Loughborough,* 18 U.S. (5 Wheat.) at 319.

22   See *Dred Scott,* 60 U.S. 393 (due process clause of Fifth Amendment); *United States v. Dawson,* 56 U.S. (15 How.) 467 (1853) (venue requirements of Article III, sec. 2); *Webster v. Reid,* 52 U.S. (11 How.) 437 (1850) (Seventh Amendment).

23   See *Dred Scott,* 60 U.S. at 450–52.

24   See ibid. at 544 (McLean, J., dissenting); ibid. at 614 (Curtis, J., dissenting).

25   See Neuman, supra note 2, at 242 n. 64 (citing tract by Thomas Hart Benson).

26   See ibid. at 81.

27   See ibid. at 81–82.

28   See, e.g., Leibowitz, supra note 1, at 17–26; Neuman, supra note 2, at 83–89; José Trías Monge, *Puerto Rico: The Trials of the Oldest Colony in the World* (1997), at 21–51; Juan R. Torruella, *The Supreme Court and Puerto Rico: The Doctrine of Separate and Unequal* (1985); Efrén Rivera Ramos, "The Legal Construction of American Colonialism: The Insular Cases (1901–1922)," *Revista Jurídica Universidad de Puerto Rico* 65 (1996): 225.

29   *Downes,* 182 U.S. 244.

30   See ibid. at 278–79 (opinion of Brown, J.).

31   See ibid. at 347 (Fuller, C. J., joined by Harlan, Brewer, and Peckham, JJ., dissenting); ibid. at 375 (Harlan, J., dissenting).

32   Ibid. at 378.

33   See ibid. at 287 (White, J., joined by Shiras and McKenna, JJ., concurring in the judgment).

34   See ibid. at 300–2.

35   See *Chae Chan Ping v. United States,* 130 U.S. 581 (1889) (the *Chinese Exclusion Case*); *Knox v. Lee* 79 U.S. (12 Wall.) 457 (1870) (the *Legal Tender Cases*).

36   *Downes,* 182 U.S. at 306.

37   See ibid. at 287–89.

38   See ibid. at 288–89, 292.

39   See ibid. at 299, 341–42.

40   See ibid. at 293–94.

41   Ibid. at 291.

42   It may be worth reiterating that the doctrine makes location rather than personal status decisive; not only colonial subjects but also citizens of the states lose the benefit of nonfundamental rights while present in an unincorporated territory.

43   See Neuman, supra note 2, at 87.

44   See ibid.; Leibowitz, supra note 1, at 26–29.

45   See Leibowitz, ibid. Apparently the Nineteenth Amendment, forbidding discrimination among U.S. citizens in voting rights on the basis of sex, was not understood as applying in Puerto Rico in the 1920s. See Gladys M. Jiménez-Muñoz, " 'So We Decided to Come and Ask You Ourselves': The 1928 U.S. Congressional Hearings on Women's Suffrage in Puerto Rico," in *Puerto Rican Jam: Rethinking Colonialism and Nationalism,* ed. Frances Negrón-Muntaner and Ramón Grosfoguel (1997); Linda K. Kerber, "The Meanings of Citizenship," *Journal of American History* 83 (1997): 833, at 840. The Nineteenth Amendment raises interesting variations on the issue of interpreting constitutional rights in the territories, because it was adopted *after* the first *Insular Cases* and after the extension of (statutory) U.S. citizenship to Puerto Rico, though before the Supreme Court's confirmation that the grant of citizenship did not make Puerto Rico an incorporated territory, see *Balzac v. Porto Rico,* 258 U.S. 298 (1922). Under current doctrine, presumably those questions are moot because the later prohibition of sex

discrimination in voting rights would be doubly condemned by equal protection principles that *are* fundamental. Cf. *Rodriguez v. Popular Democratic Party*, 457 U.S. 1, 8 (1982) ("the voting rights of Puerto Rico citizens are constitutionally protected to the same extent as those of all other citizens of the United States").

46   See Leibowitz, supra note 1, at 56–68; Trías Monge, supra note 28, at 121–24, 136–40.

47   See Neuman, supra note 2, at 89–90.

48   For lower court cases protecting fundamental rights of *alien* residents in regions where the United States was not sovereign but exercised governmental powers, see, e.g., *Ralpho v. Bell*, 569 F.2d 607 (D.C. Cir. 1977) (Trust Territory of the Pacific Islands); *Canal Zone v. Scott*, 502 F.2d 566 (5th Cir. 1974); *United States v. Tiede*, 86 F.R.D. 227 (U.S. Ct. for Berlin 1979).

49   *Reid v. Covert*, 354 U.S. 1 (1957). The holding was originally restricted to capital cases, because of limitations in the concurrences; it was extended to noncapital cases in *Kinsella v. United States ex rel. Singleton*, 361 U.S. 234 (1960), and *McElroy v. United States ex. rel. Guagliardo*, 361 U.S. 281 (1960).

50   *Reid*, 354 U.S. at 5–6 (plurality opinion).

51   See Neuman, supra note 2, at 91.

52   *Reid*, 354 U.S. at 14 (plurality opinion).

53   See Neuman, supra note 2, at 100–101.

54   See *Reid*, 354 U.S., at 53–54 (Frankfurter, J., concurring); *Reid*, 354 U.S., at 74–75 (Harlan, J., concurring).

55   *Torres v. Puerto Rico*, 442 U.S. 465, 470–71 (1979).

56   *United States v. Verdugo-Urquidez*, 494 U.S. 259 (1990).

57   See *Verdugo-Urquidez*, 494 U.S. at 268–70 (Rehnquist, C. J.); *Verdugo-Urquidez*, 494 U.S. at 277–78 (Kennedy, J., concurring). The Justices did not take note of the fact that the plurality approach was endorsed by a majority in later cases. See *Kinsella v. Singleton*, 361 U.S. 234; *Grisham v. Hagan*, 361 U.S. 278 (1960); *McElroy v. Guagliardo*, 361 U.S. 281.

58   See Neuman, supra note 2, at 8, 107–8.

59   See Leibowitz, supra note 1, at 162–78; Trías Monge, supra note 28, at 107–18.

60   See Leibowitz, ibid. at 530–39; Trías Monge, ibid. at 148–54.

61   See Leibowitz, ibid. at 453.

62   See ibid. at 266, 311 (Virgin Islands), 336–38 (Guam).

63   See ibid. at 329 (Guam), 254 (Virgin Islands, 1927), 145 (Puerto Rico, 1917). The absence of citizenship for residents of the Northern Mariana Islands in the first decades of their relationship with the United States reflected the fact that the United States had not yet become sovereign in the Islands, which were governed as part of a Trust Territory. See ibid. at 559.

64   See ibid. at 460–61.

65   See *Commonwealth of Northern Mariana Islands v. Atalig*, 723 F.2d 682 (9th Cir. 1984) (applying *Insular Cases* doctrine to approve denial of jury trial; territorial procedure was challenged by a citizen of a Trust Territory); *Commonwealth of Northern Mariana Islands v. Peters*, 1991 WL 70078 (CNMI 1991) (following *Atalig* after accession of Northern Mariana Islands to United States); *King v. Andrus*, 452 F. Supp. 11 (D.D.C. 1977) (extending constitutional right of jury trial to American Samoa on the ground that it would not be impracticable or anomalous; territorial procedure was challenged by non-Samoan).

66   See, e.g., *Wabol v. Villacrusis*, 958 F.2d 1450 (9th Cir. 1992), cert. denied, 506 U.S. 1027 (1992) (upholding transitional restrictions on alienation of land in the Northern Mariana Islands); Leibowitz at 362–63, 423–40 (discussing land restrictions in Guam and American Samoa);

Marybeth Herald, "Does the Constitution Follow the Flag into United States Territories or Can it be Separately Purchased and Sold?" *Hastings Constitutional Law Quarterly* 22 (1995): 707 (critique of *Wabol* decision by counsel on appeal).

67   See *Banks v. American Samoa Government*, 4 Am. Samoa 2d 113 (H.C.T.D. 1987) (upholding employment preference in American Samoa).

68   See *Guam Draft Commonwealth Act*, H.R. 1056, 104th Cong., 1st Sess. (1995): sec. 102(a); Ignacio Cruz Aguigui, "The Emerging Contours of Equal Protection under the Territory Clause: Implications for Guam's Political Status Development" (1995) (unpublished paper on file with author).

69   See Leibowitz, supra note 1, at 433–35; cf. *Morton v. Mancari*, 417 U.S. 535 (1974). On the other hand, in 1980 the High Court of American Samoa concluded that the restrictions on aliena-tion of land *survived* strict scrutiny under equal protection analysis. *Craddick v. Territorial Registrar of American Samoa*, 1 Am. Samoa 2d 10 (App. Div. High Ct. of Amer. Samoa 1980).

70   See *Wabol*, supra note 66; *Banks*, supra note 67.

71   See *Examining Board v. Flores de Otero*, 426 U.S. 572, 599–606 (1976). Given Justice Rehnquist's dissent, which questioned both the applicability of the equal protection guarantee to the Commonwealth of Puerto Rico and the Court's choice of the standard of review for state rather than federal action, see *Flores de Otero*, 426 U.S. at 608 (Rehnquist, J., dissenting), it is interesting that the Court found it unnecessary to explain at greater length its choice of precedent. But this merely underlines the practice of applying mainland precedents.

　　Califano v. Torres, 435 U.S. 1 (1978) (per curiam), sometimes cited as a counterexample, was expressly based on reasoning that addressed travel from state to state. The constraints on federal discrimination against particular states are primarily political, not constitutional. See generally Gerald L. Neuman, "Territorial Discrimination, Equal Protection, and Self-Determination," *University of Pennsylvania Law Review* 135 (1987): 261 (discussing equal pro-tection analysis of geographical discrimination with regard to states and the District of Columbia).

72   508 U.S. 147, 149–50 (1993).

73   See Neuman, supra note 2, at 104–17.

74   As regards our own insular territories, one might well wonder why such credibility is given to puns on the word *overseas*.

75   Act of July 3, 1950, preamble, *U.S. Statutes at Large*, 64 (1950): 319; see Leibowitz, supra note 1, at 162–78; Trías Monge, supra note 28, at 107–18.

76   See Leibowitz, supra note 1, at 530–36.

77   Covenant, sec. 105, *U.S. Code* 48 § 801 note.

78   See Leibowitz, supra note 1, at 543–44; Van Dyke, supra note 4, at 483–85.

79   See, e.g., Leibowitz, supra note 1, at 63–66; T. Alexander Aleinikoff, "Puerto Rico and the Constitution: Conundrums and Prospects," *Constitutional Commentary* 11 (1994): 15, at 34–40. In stating this as an assumption, I do not intend to take a position on the question of whether a commonwealth is necessarily a territory within the meaning of the Territorial Clause; if it were not, the authority of Congress over a commonwealth might derive from some other sources such as the treaty power or the foreign affairs power and might be subject to somewhat different constraints.

80   See David M. Helfeld, "How Much of the United States Constitution and Statutes are Applica-ble to the Commonwealth of Puerto Rico?," *Federal Rules Decisions* 110 (1985): 452, at 465.

81   But see *United States ex rel. Richards v. Guerrero*, 4 F.3d 749, 754–55 (9th Cir. 1993) (concluding

that Congress's power over the Commonwealth of the Northern Mariana Islands is limited by the Covenant in a judicially cognizable manner).

82 See Trías Monge, supra note 28, at 125–35, 189–91; Aleinikoff, supra note 79, at 33–35; Van Dyke, supra note 4, at 499–502.

83 Trías Monge, supra note 28, at 162–63. Some of the listed criticisms, taken separately, would not be cured even by statehood. I assume that these criticisms are meant to be taken in conjunction with Puerto Rico's lack of national representation.

84 Cf. José A. Cabranes, "Puerto Rico: Colonialism as Constitutional Doctrine," *Harvard Law Review* 100 (1986): 450, at 463 ("It is unlikely, however, that a judicial rejection of the doctrine of territorial incorporation would have much practical effect on the lives of most Puerto Ricans.").

85 *Texas v. White*, 74 U.S. 700, 725 (1868).

86 See, e.g., Leibowitz, supra note 1, at 447–48 (describing American Samoan legislation that controls residence by U.S. citizens); Trías Monge, supra note 28, at 184–86, 188–89 (describing feelings of separate nationhood in Puerto Rico as obstacle to statehood).

87 *Downes*, 182 U.S. at 384.

88 *Wabol*, 958 F.2d 1450. Given the Ninth Circuit's jurisdiction over cases arising from the Pacific territories, this is a very significant precedent.

89 *Morton v. Mancari*, 417 U.S. 535.

90 *Wabol*, 958 F.2d at 1460.

91 Ibid. at 1460, 1462. Such an inquiry would be likely to lead to the conclusion that various aspects of First Amendment law were not fundamental in the international sense, such as the restrictions on the law of libel, or the U.S. tolerance for hate speech. See, e.g., International Covenant on Civil and Political Rights, art. 20(2), December 16, 1966, 999 U.N.T.S. 171.

92 *Wabol*, 958 F.2d at 1461–62.

93 I will not try to explore the status of noncitizen national here.

94 But see *Miller v. Albright*, 523 U.S. 420 (1998) (debating standard of review applicable to gender distinctions in the grant of statutory citizenship); *Rogers v. Bellei*, 401 U.S. 815 (1971) (holding that a reasonable condition subsequent of residence in the United States can be attached to statutory citizenship derived from overseas birth to a citizen parent). For discussions of whether Congress has power to divest statutory citizenship if a territory becomes independent, see José Julián Álvarez González, "The Empire Strikes Out: Congressional Ruminations on the Citizenship Status of Puerto Ricans," *Harvard Journal on Legislation* 27 (1990): 309; John L. A. de Passalacqua, "The Involuntary Loss of United States Citizenship of Puerto Ricans upon Accession to Independence by Puerto Rico," *Denver Journal of International Law and Policy* 19 (1990): 139.

95 While this chapter was in press, the U.S. Supreme Court issued two decisions particularly relevant to the analysis. In *Rice v. Cayetano*, 528 U.S. 495 (2000), the Court invalidated a Hawai'i statute that reserved voting rights for particular state offices to persons defined by ancestry as either Hawai'ians or native Hawai'ians. In *Torres v. Sablan*, 528 U.S. 1110 (2000), the Court affirmed without opinion a decision that had rejected an equal protection challenge to the unequal apportionment of the legislature of the Commonwealth of the Northern Mariana Islands. The lower court opinion, *Rayphand v. Sablan*, 95 F. Supp. 2d 1133 (D.N.M.I. 1999), was consistent with the Ninth Circuit trend criticized in this chapter.

III. Constitution and Membership

Partial Membership and Liberal Political Theory

Mark Tushnet

May a liberal state have partial members, or must all citizens in such a state be equal?[1] In general, liberal principles of state organization are universalist. But the world is divided into territorial nation-states, and people are citizens of one state and not another. What principles does liberal political theory recommend when the issue of membership itself is placed on the table? The important question of Puerto Rico's status provides an opportunity to examine this puzzle in liberal political theory. The status question shows that membership issues raise problems along several dimensions. First, there is the problem of full or partial *membership.* In the status debate proponents of statehood and independence seek full membership, in different forms of state organization, whereas proponents of commonwealth or enhanced commonwealth status seek forms of partial membership.[2] Second, there is the problem of defining the *goods* associated with full and partial membership—matters such as the right to vote, to obtain public assistance of various types, to obtain police protection, and the like. Next there is the problem of *choice,* which arises in the status debate but is posed more sharply by the situation of a nation's resident aliens who are eligible for citizenship (and therefore for full membership in the nation) but choose to remain noncitizens. And finally there is the problem of *individual* or *collective* choice. However the status debate is resolved, at least in the short run some people who would prefer that Puerto Rico have one particular status will be disappointed by a collective choice for an alternative.[3]

We can begin by noting a few features that make the question of partial membership quite difficult. Liberal political theorists develop principles for regulating a society of free and equal people; liberal activists invoke the Declaration of Independence for the proposition that all men are created equal.[4] Liberal universalism makes questions about citizenship themselves quite troublesome. Such questions arise only because the world is divided into nation-states. And yet, in Martha Nussbaum's words, "[A]ny human being might have been born in any nation."[5] In a world divided into nation-states, however, even liberal states will make one particularist distinction, that between members and nonmembers, between citizens and noncitizens.[6] Defending this distinction is itself difficult within liberal political theory.[7] Are any further distinctions, within the class of members, permissible in liberal states?[8]

The category of *partial membership* is difficult to define as well. In light of liberalism's concern to ensure that principles of political organization respect the different choices individuals make in light of their diverse values, we might think that full or partial membership might depend on the values people have. Any other principle of allocating membership, we might think, would deny the individualist commitments of liberal political theory. But consider two reasonably cosmopolitan people, one a citizen of the United States and one a citizen of the United Kingdom. Their values are likely to overlap a great deal: They may admire the dynamic thrust of the U.S. economic system, they may be a bit nervous about what they view as the degraded nature of political and cultural discourse in both nations, and so on. They may share more common values than the cosmopolitan U.S. citizen shares with many other U.S. citizens. Yet the citizen of the United Kingdom is not a partial member of the United States; she is a nonmember. This example shows that some sort of rough territorial association between the nation-state and the putative partial member seems necessary even to get the question of partial membership going.[9] And this signals why the questions of membership and, even more, partial membership are hard ones for liberal political theory. Individual values and choices matter in liberal political theory, but nothing in it makes territory as such at all relevant to the relation between a person and her government.[10]

The fact that partial membership is problematic is signaled as well by the observation that the term *second-class citizenship* almost never functions simply as a description but is almost always a term of criticism. And yet liberal states do seem to put up with a fair amount of partial membership. Long-term resident aliens, citizens of Puerto Rico and the District of Columbia, some members of Indian nations—all have less-than-complete membership in the United States. How, if at all, can these statuses be understood and justified?

This essay explores the question of partial membership by examining the dimensions identified earlier: the goods associated with full and partial membership, and the various forms of choice. Although we will see that these two dimensions cannot be easily disentangled, I begin with the question of choice in part because choices are made with respect to different packages of goods and in part because some aspects of the question of choice have received some attention in liberal political theory.[11]

Sometimes partial membership occurs because people have ascriptive characteristics unrelated to their individual choices, but sometimes it occurs because individuals have made their own choices. Residents of Puerto Rico and the District of Columbia exemplify the first group,[12] while long-term resident aliens and American Indians who remain affiliated with some Native American tribal organizations are examples of people in the second.[13] Liberal political theory ordinarily is hostile to the distribution of benefits or burdens on the basis of ascriptive characteristics, and that hostility makes a great deal of sense in the present context when—but perhaps only when—the nation, or more generally someone other than the partial member's own community, imposes partial membership on a person. Michael Walzer's position appears sound and largely uncontroversial. According to Walzer, partial membership based on ascriptive characteristics is inconsistent with liberal commitments for two reasons.[14] The less important is that maintaining categories of ascriptive partial membership dulls the polity's commitment to liberal universalism.[15] The more important is that it creates real opportunities for the nation as a whole to exploit those it forces to be second-class citizens.[16]

Before examining the more difficult case of partial membership resulting from choices by a person's own community, we must consider partial membership that occurs because an individual chooses that status. Two central cases frame the inquiry: that of the long-term resident alien eligible for citizenship who chooses to refrain from becoming a citizen,[17] and that of a person living in the District of Columbia who could obtain all the benefits of being a full member by moving to Maryland or Virginia. Liberal political theory's emphasis on the importance of individual choice suggests that there might be nothing problematic about a liberal state's maintaining categories of partial membership occupied only by those who choose to accept limited membership. The central cases illustrate a key point here. A person who wishes to be a full member ordinarily can become one: A long-term resident alien can become a citizen, a resident of the District of Columbia can move to Maryland or Virginia.[18]

Neither becoming a citizen nor moving to obtain citizenship are cost-free, however. To become a full citizen is to make a conscious decision to relinquish, at least in form, a set of ties to another nation that may be important to a person's identity. For the person who chooses to become a naturalized citizen the benefits of full citizenship outweigh these psychological costs, as the choice itself demonstrates, but the costs do exist. Similarly, migration may be financially and psychologically costly.

Naturalization and migration can indeed be responses to the issue of partial membership,[19] but offering them as solutions raises important questions of fairness. Although a person who chooses to migrate finds the benefits of full citizenship to outweigh the costs of relinquishing or weakening other ties, the question of fairness is independent of the question of choice. Liberal political theory has to determine whether it is fair to put a person to the choice between the package of goods associated with partial membership and the package associated with full membership if the cost is, in some sense, large: it might be unfair, independent of a person's willingness to bear the costs, to impose large costs resulting from migration on partial members who must move to become full members.

What will be large and what small will, of course, be controversial.[20] As a U.S. citizen with no competing membership claims on me, I find it relatively easy to say that asking a long-term resident alien to become a naturalized citizen in order to obtain the full roster of benefits available to citizens does not impose large costs on the resident alien. But I confess to uneasiness about saying that, for I really cannot appreciate the psychic costs of relinquishing the attachment to one's nation of origin that naturalization entails.[21] I do, however, feel the force of the argument that I should not complain about the partial membership that flows from being a citizen of the District of Columbia when all I need do to become a full member is move a few blocks away.[22]

Suppose, then, that unfairly large costs ought not be imposed on a person who must migrate to become a full citizen. I believe that unfairness is relative to the packages of goods at issue. To see this, consider two cases in which the costs of migration are identical. In the first case the difference in the goods available to the partial and the full member is quite large, making the transition from partial to full membership quite valuable, while in the other the difference is significantly smaller. A person in the first case might be tempted to migrate given the specified cost of migration, while a person in the second case, facing the same cost, would not. But the fact that the transition is quite attractive might make it unfair to impose the fixed cost: it offers the person a choice that she ought not in fairness be induced to make.

If fairness is relative to the packages of goods, we can reduce the problem of unfairly large costs associated with the transition from partial to full membership by reducing the distinction between the packages of goods that partial and full members get. Of course, doing so also reduces the distinction between partial and full membership. The choice between the two statuses becomes almost inconsequential if one can get all, or almost all, of the benefits of being a full member (and suffer all or nearly all of the burdens) while remaining a partial member. It would not be a matter of real concern to liberal political theory. And, as noted at the outset, this might be a desirable result in light of the problematic place that issues of membership have in that theory.

What, then, are the different packages of goods offered to partial and full members? Clearly a liberal state must assure everyone subject to its jurisdiction minimal human rights: it may not say to resident aliens (whether long- or short-term), "We simply will not provide you with minimum police services."[23] The reason is that minimum human rights flow from the fact that a person is a human being, and from nothing else. Suppose, however, that a liberal state provides its full members with more than the minimum goods of various sorts required by universal human rights. Under what circumstances may it deny that excess to voluntary partial members?

We can divide the excess goods into two groups. One consists of goods closely associated with the very idea of full membership: voting, eligibility for high public office, and perhaps some other goods. I will call these *membership goods*. The other consists of other publicly supplied goods: public education, public assistance to the needy, the protection of general laws (including antidiscrimination laws).[24] These I call *optional publicly supplied goods*.

It might seem at first that membership goods define membership. Consider voting, something that most people would find at the heart of citizenship. We might think it inconsistent with the distinction between U.S. citizens and aliens, for example, to allow aliens to vote in U.S. elections. Similarly, what makes citizens of the District of Columbia and of the U.S. territories partial members of the U.S. polity is that they do not have the right to vote for full members in the House of Representatives and the Senate, nor, in the case of the territories, for the president and vice president.

The thought that membership goods define full membership might be mistaken, however. Some states allowed long-term resident aliens to vote in the nineteenth century, without obliterating the distinction between U.S. citizens and aliens.[25] As Abraham Lincoln put it in the Gettysburg Address, the United States is a nation dedicated to a proposition of political theory, and perhaps a person can be a full member of that nation as long as she or he is also dedicated to the propositions that define it as a nation.

Perhaps, however, we need to maintain *some* membership good or goods solely for full members, simply to ensure that the category of full membership is distinct from the categories of partial or nonmembership.

It could be, however, that the problematic role of citizenship in liberal political theory ought to induce us to reduce the significance of *anything* that serves to define the categories of full and partial members. We would then seek to reduce the costs associated with the distinction by keeping the class of membership goods rather small. U.S. Supreme Court decisions treat public employment as a teacher, police officer, or probation officer as membership goods, but treat public employment as a notary public, civil servant, or member of the bar as outside that class.[26] The lines the Court has drawn are not entirely clear, but one possibility suggests an underlying concern to keep the costs of the choice between membership and nonmembership low. Most of the jobs that the Court has found closely associated with membership are ones for which there are available substitutes in private employment markets—in private schools and private security agencies, for example. Denying access to the public forms of these jobs will have some impact on the economic opportunities of nonmembers, but the impact may not be large enough to be worrisome. In contrast, the Court has denied states the ability to preclude nonmembers from jobs for which there are no readily available private substitutes, the most obvious being membership in the bar.[27]

Gerald Rosberg has offered another argument that has the effect of minimizing the package of membership goods.[28] To understand his argument we must first consider the extent to which partial members can be denied optional publicly supplied goods such as public education and public assistance to the needy. Annette Baier asserts that voluntary partial members are properly second-class citizens with respect to optional publicly provided goods.[29] As Baier sees it, this is a natural entailment of the very fact that they are partial members: Full members can rightly demand that optional goods be provided to them first, and to partial members second.

In contrast, current U.S. law treats the denial to partial members of these goods as questionable,[30] apparently because they are denied membership goods and are therefore vulnerable to exploitation in the political process: They pay taxes and yet have no say in affecting the decision to deny them the benefits their taxes help provide.[31] Why this should be regarded as exploitation is unclear, however, at least where the partial member occupies that status because of individual choice. The partial member obtains the minimum requirements of universal human rights from the government, and is able to obtain any other goods from nongovernment sources (that is, through purchases on the market). If the market is itself not an institution of exploitation, it is not clear why relegating partial members to market sources is an instance of exploitation.[32]

Taking existing U.S. law as his starting point, Rosberg points out that the case for denying membership goods weakens as it becomes more difficult to distinguish those to whom the goods are denied from those who are concededly full members. The territorial linkage between long-term resident aliens and the nation is as strong as it is for full citizens, for example. Sometimes through legislative choice and sometimes in response to compulsion by courts interpreting the Constitution, the United States has gone a long way—though not all the way—toward ensuring that partial members have nearly all the optional publicly supplied goods that full members do. When the *only* distinction between full and partial members is that the partial members are denied membership goods, the justification for the distinction disappears and is replaced by a definition.[33]

We began this inquiry into the different types of goods in an effort to see whether the unfairness associated with forcing a very costly choice between full and partial membership could be eliminated by reducing the costs associated with that choice. The general strategy is to minimize the distinctive benefits associated with full membership, by reducing the number of membership goods and by extending the provision of optional publicly supplied goods. It should be clear that pursuing this strategy makes the distinction between full and partial membership less important. And, as already noted, that may be a desirable result in light of the general problems that questions of membership raise for liberal political theory.

Denying membership goods to those who wish to become full members thus seems incompatible with liberal premises. Perhaps a liberal nation-state may demand that such people incur some costs, through either psychological or physical mobility, although it is unclear how large those costs may be before they become troublingly unfair. The very existence of nation-states suggests another possible limitation. Consider again a person in England who asserts a desire to vote in U.S. elections, perhaps because she believes them more consequential for her than British elections, perhaps because she finds them more interesting. She is willing to give up her British citizenship but has no interest in living in the United States, even for the period necessary to establish her statutory eligibility to become a naturalized citizen. I am sure that few if any will find her claim to full membership by choice appealing. The existence of nation-states seems to mean that full members must have some sort of territorial affiliation with the nation of which they are members.

Locating the threshold of territorial affiliation is not easy, precisely because territory is such a problematic criterion for liberal theory anyway. Perhaps the best we can do is rely on criteria derived from the historical development of particular nations to determine how much territorial affiliation is enough.[34] Long-term resident aliens in the United States are distributed throughout the country; whatever the required territorial affiliation is, they must have it. Prior to the admission of Hawaii and Alaska to statehood, perhaps the threshold would have required some territorial contiguity, which would have meant that citizens of the District of Columbia had exceeded the threshold but citizens of Puerto Rico had not. After 1959, however, the remaining territorial threshold probably must be that the territory already have some political association with the United States.[35]

The preceding discussion of individual choice and the types of goods associated with membership has cleared the ground for a treatment of what is probably the most important variant of partial membership, and the one most relevant to the question of Puerto Rico's status. An organized political group of partial members might choose to maintain that status, even over the objection of those who prefer either full membership or independence. We can call this status *collective partial membership*. The discussion of voluntary partial membership provides the structure for the appropriate analysis. Just as the long-term resident alien makes a voluntary choice that the costs associated with nonmembership are justified by its benefits as she sees them, so the collective must believe that it receives benefits in exchange for forgoing full membership. And if this is true, it provides some reason for thinking that collective partial membership might be acceptable within a liberal state. In moving from individual to collective membership, we must acknowledge that any real-world form of collective partial membership will force partial membership on some individuals who would prefer to be full members.[36] We might find this acceptable, however, if the only consequence is that these dissenting members must bear the costs of moving to a place where they can become full members. And precluding the possibility of collective partial membership makes it impossible for those who prefer that status to achieve it, which seems inconsistent with a liberal commitment to individual choice.

We must identify something that collective partial membership provides to the group that is unavailable from full membership or independence, and for which the second-class citizenship aspects of partial membership are a fair price, if we are to justify that status.[37] In light of the fact that the group is likely to have some internal dissidents, assessing the price poses a familiar set of difficulties. Like the voluntary resident alien, those who desire partial membership necessarily have concluded that the benefits of that status exceed the costs of second-class citizenship: They see the cost as a fair price for whatever they secure from partial citizenship. The dissidents, of course, see things differently. They may believe that the benefits they receive from partial membership are smaller than the costs of second-class citizenship: to them, the price of partial membership is not fair. I doubt that there is any comfortable resolution to the problem of determining which perspective to use in assessing the fairness of the price for partial membership.[38]

Assume, however, that these difficulties can be overcome, perhaps because the internal dissidents come to agree that the costs of second-class citizenship are not as great as they fear. What then can the group achieve from partial membership that it cannot get from full membership or independence? The most obvious candidate is that the group may sustain a kind of autonomy as a partial member that would be vulnerable in the event the group became a full member.[39] Still, independence provides this, and every citizen of the independent nation is a full member (of it). Independence might be undesirable, however, if its price were too high. In particular, an independent nation would not be in a position to seek redistributive "foreign aid" in amounts equivalent to what it could receive if its citizens were full members of the larger nation with which it would be affiliated. As full members they would provide a political resource available for bargaining and trading within the national political system, and using that resource, its members can take part in the national political system of wealth distribution. As citizens of an independent nation, in contrast, all they can do is appeal to the "donor" nation's self-interest and to moral concern; such appeals are likely to be less effective than political bargaining within the nation.

It would be difficult to support the conclusion that partial membership is acceptable in the service of group autonomy if a degree of autonomy equivalent to that available with independence can be maintained with another nation by groups composed of people who are full members of the nation. Traditional liberal political theory acknowledges this by creating institutions that respect and attempt to preserve group autonomy to a certain degree. These are the institutions of decentralization, regulated by the political principle of subsidiarity, and of federalism, in which some degree of autonomy is given constitutional protection. Some forms of federalism have the important characteristic that, while insisting that all federal subunits ("states") respect fundamental human rights, they acknowledge the reasonableness of alternative specifications of the precise content of those rights. In such a federal system, a group controlling a subunit might be able to adopt regulations to preserve the group's autonomy that other subunits, and national majorities, might conclude were inconsistent with *their* understanding of fundamental human rights. So, for example, a national majority might conclude that free speech principles bar the nation from adopting regulations of sexually explicit speech while a local majority might conclude to the contrary, in the service of group autonomy.[40] Similarly, the province of Quebec might be able to regulate commercial signs by requiring that all external signs use French only, even though majorities outside Quebec would find such a restriction to be incompatible with their understanding of free speech principles. This sort of variation ought to be tolerable in a liberal society as long as each subunit's specification of general fundamental rights is not obviously inconsistent with those rights.

We must then ask: Why might decentralization and federalism be thought inadequate as compared with collective partial membership? Consider first the particular version of federalism in the United States. That version of federalism might not provide protection for cultural or group autonomy equivalent to that available in an independent nation. The U.S. Supreme Court's recent revival of interest in constitutional federalism might seem inadequate. Some decisions narrow the regulatory scope of national power, but the restrictions are not substantial and are unlikely to provide much constitutional protection not otherwise available from the subsidiarity principle that sometimes guides national policymaking.[41] Other decisions, seemingly more promising from the point of view of those interested in decentralization, protect the institutional interests of state governments as such.[42] Clearly, however, there is no necessary correspondence between those interests and the interests of state citizens in sustaining something distinctive about their overall culture, or even their political culture. Protecting the institutional interests of state government, then, offers only indirect, and probably modest, protection for the underlying interests of state citizens.

In addition, a territorially based federalism might be too rigid to provide what the group wants.[43] Some groups might be concentrated in locations that make territorial federalism a sensible solution, as with Puerto Rico and the District of Columbia. Other groups, however, may be more dispersed, as are many Indian nations. Territorial federalism is unresponsive to the changes that naturally occur in a dynamic society.[44] A system of constitutional federalism can adapt to these changes, primarily through a willingness to amend the constitution regularly.[45] A political system guided by the principle of subsidiarity is, however, more likely to address concerns about change more effectively.

The treatment of fundamental human rights in U.S. federalism illustrates another sort of rigidity. Described in the most general terms, federal systems make it possible that different subunits will specify fundamental rights in ways that vary from place to place without raising concerns that the underlying fundamental rights are being denied somewhere. U.S. federalism, however, does not allow that to occur. The Supreme Court has held that each right protected by the Bill of Rights is protected in exactly the same way everywhere in the country.[46]

These difficulties might lead some to conclude that their interest in group autonomy cannot be served by becoming a subunit within the United States. Whatever might be true of federalism and decentralization considered abstractly, the forms available in the United States might seem unacceptable. These people might seek to obtain concessions, departures from existing federalist principles, in exchange for giving up some of the benefits of full membership. Full membership, that is, would be traded off to secure a greater degree of protection for group autonomy than would be available in the existing U.S. federal system.[47]

But there is a more troubling concern. Perhaps *no* political institutions—the institutions of federalism, those of national independence, or those of partial membership—are strong enough to stand against the centralizing and universalist tendencies of liberal political theory set in a market-oriented economy. The homogenizing pressures of a national and transnational economy and culture make questionable the claim that institutions of government, no matter how robust, will actually preserve what the group seeks to preserve. These pressures undermine the argument for collective partial membership. If the group cannot get what it seeks from constitutional federalism or independence, it seems quite unlikely that it will get it from the weaker protections it receives as a collective partial member. Indeed, collective partial membership seems likely to make the group more vulnerable than nonconstitutional federalism, or subsidiarity as a political principle that guides national policymaking. The reason is that subsidiarity is likely to be vigorously pursued when subnational groups have some representation in national policymaking circles.[48] And yet representation is precisely what collective partial membership denies to the partial member.

Finally we must consider what is undoubtedly the most important real-world question about collective partial membership. Practical considerations always exist when a group is faced with choosing full membership, partial membership, or independence. These practical considerations may dominate whatever principled grounds the group has for choice.[49] I have argued that liberal political theory argues rather strongly in favor of either full membership, perhaps in a federal system, or independence. But what if the costs of either course are unacceptably high?[50]

I believe that the vision of constitutionalism associated with Abraham

Lincoln provides important guidance. Lincoln believed that the U.S. Constitution protected slavery where it existed. He also believed that slavery was inconsistent with the Constitution's deepest commitments. He argued that the tension between the actual Constitution and the nation's underlying commitments placed political actors under a duty to do what they could to set slavery on a course to as speedy an extinction as was practically possible. Translated to the context of the present discussion, the thought would be that political actors have a duty to reduce the costs associated with achieving either full membership or independence.[51]

Partial membership is in tension with liberal political theory. It seems impossible to defend when it is forced on individuals who would prefer to be full members, except insofar as the existing division of the world into separate nation-states justifies a nation in imposing some degree of territorial affiliation on those who would be full members. It is difficult to justify even when a group chooses collective partial membership, except to the extent that the costs of alternative courses have not yet been reduced to the point where full membership or independence are realistic possibilities. There may be a modest practical pay-off to this analysis: people should be nervous about maintaining the current status of Puerto Rico and the District of Columbia.[52]

Even that conclusion may have to be qualified, however. My arguments have been about what we might require a liberal state to do in connection with partial membership. The fact, if it is one, that some forms of partial membership in the United States might be inconsistent with those requirements may show that the United States is not a completely liberal state. Perhaps the U.S. commitment to liberal political theory is deep enough that such a diagnosis leads to the prescription that forms of partial membership should be eliminated as quickly as possible. But perhaps the diagnosis simply shows that liberal political theory is only one of the traditions to which the United States is committed.[53]

Notes

I would like to thank T. Alexander Aleinikoff and participants in the *Foreign in a Domestic Sense* conference (Yale University, March 27–29, 1998) for helpful comments on earlier versions of this essay.

1   As I discuss below, this formulation is slightly misleading, because issues of partial membership arise with respect to long-term resident aliens as well.

2   I have been unable to develop an alternative phrase here that would eliminate the ambiguity between *state organization*, describing the general principles of organizing a polity, and *state*, describing one of the units in the United States.

3   As argued below, collective choice itself comes in two versions, one in which the collective making the decision is external to the group that becomes full or partial citizens, and the other in which that group itself makes a (majoritarian) decision for full or partial citizenship.

4   The citation of the Declaration of Independence shows, of course, that the realization of liberal principles is often imperfect, even in liberal states. The Declaration referred to men rather than to people, and women and African Americans were less-than-full citizens for generations after the Declaration. The Declaration's statement should be taken as an expression of liberal ideals or aspirations rather than of liberal practices.

5   Martha Nussbaum, *For Love of Country: Debating the Limits of Patriotism* (1996), at 7.

6   Nation-states are defined by the distinction between people who are members and those who are not.

7   The most prominent statement of the difficulties is Joseph H. Carens, "Aliens and Citizens: The Case for Open Borders," *Review of Politics* 49 (1987): 251. A later discussion is Yael Tamir, *Liberal Nationalism* (1993), which provides a liberal defense for a quite watered-down nationalism. An eloquent brief statement is Eric Hobsbawm's conclusion to his historical inquiry into the rise of nationalism: "The owl of Minerva which brings wisdom, said Hegel, flies out at dusk. It is a good sign that it is now circling round nations and nationalism." Eric Hobsbawm, *Nations and Nationalism since 1780: Programme, Myth, Reality,* 2d ed. (1992), at 192.

8   I note a tension between the universalist aspirations of liberalism and the equally universal judgment that every liberal state will have some classes of partial members, such as children and the mentally impaired. The existence of such classes can be used to justify broader exclusions from full membership, on the ground that the broader classes share the characteristics that justify treating children and the mentally impaired as partial members. Such analyses, indeed, have been typical in defenses of treating women and ethnic minorities as partial members. I know of no good grounds on which to resist such arguments except by insisting that liberalism requires exceedingly strong justifications for the creation of classes of partial members, and that the justifications are strong enough with respect to children and the mentally impaired but not strong enough for any other group.

9   As we will see, the roughness of the territorial association that seems required to make sense of membership issues further complicates the question of Puerto Rico's status.

10 *See* Jules Coleman and Sarah Harding, "Citizenship, Justice, and Political Borders," in *Justice in Immigration,* ed. Warren Schwartz (1995), at 51 ("Political borders are arbitrary from the moral point of view."). Another concern has historically been associated with denial of membership, either full or partial: that the non- or partial members are too different culturally from full members to be part of the same polity. I do not address this concern here, believing that it is flatly incompatible with liberal political theory's pluralist commitments. For a brief discussion, see Mark Tushnet, "Immigration Policy in Liberal Political Theory," ibid. at 153–54.

11 See, e.g., Annette Baier, "Some Virtues of Resident Alienage," in *Nomos XXIV: Virtue 291,* ed. John W. Chapman and William A. Galston (1992); Michael Walzer, *Spheres of Justice* (1983).

12 At least if we put aside for the moment the question of whether a person's choice to reside in Puerto Rico or the District of Columbia counts as a choice of accepting partial membership.

13 Justice William Rehnquist's dissent in *Nyquist v. Mauclet,* 432 U.S. 1, 17 (1977), argued that it was inappropriate to apply a stringent standard of review to a statute barring long- (and short-) term resident aliens from a state program of financial assistance for college expenses,

because long-term resident aliens could remove themselves "from the disfavored classification" whenever they chose. See ibid. at 20.

14   See Walzer, supra note 11.

15   I believe that this is the best way to understand why, to Gunnar Myrdal writing in the 1940s, race relations in the United States were the American dilemma.

16   Walzer's version of the argument depends on his account of justice in the liberal state, according to which principles of allocation in one sphere—such as the political, where membership distinctions necessarily arise—ought not slop over into other spheres. Exploitation occurs because full members use the political power they have, and that partial members lack, to allocate goods in other domains. I do not believe, however, that Walzer's conclusion depends on his particular theory of justice in the liberal state.

17   For a discussion suggesting why some long-term resident aliens make such a choice, see Baier, supra note 11.

18   Liberal political theory would be hostile to policies that barred long-term resident aliens from becoming full citizens, and to policies that restricted mobility. The former situation is exemplified in the literature on citizenship by the case of residents of Turkish origin in Germany, whose difficulties in obtaining German citizenship are quite troublesome from a liberal point of view.

19   For present purposes, I mean *migration* to encompass the abandonment of prior attachments that naturalization entails.

20   I can report that in discussions of the District of Columbia question, District residents tend to think that asking them to move to Maryland or Virginia is unreasonable, while residents of states outside the region tend to think that it is not. I suspect that a parallel phenomenon occurs with respect to discussions of the status of Puerto Rico.

21   In this connection I note that Fre LePoole Griffiths, the resident alien who sought admission to the Connecticut bar in *In re Griffiths*, 413 U.S. 717 (1973), subsequently returned to the Netherlands, where she has become a judge.

22   There are of course psychic costs here as well, particularly the cost of relinquishing a commitment to living in a troubled city.

23   I assume in this example that there is a fundamental human right to minimum police services, a point that the purest libertarian might deny. But even such a libertarian would object to a regime that precluded resident aliens from purchasing private police services.

24   I must note, however, that identifying the elements in each category is itself a difficult enterprise. The scheme I have offered relies on traditional distinctions between civil rights (in the present scheme, universal human rights), political rights (here membership goods), and social rights (other publicly supplied goods). Those distinctions are grounded at least as much in historical development as they are in political theory, and it is not hard to see how rights to public assistance might come to be understood as falling in the same category as voting, for example.

25   For an argument that conferring voting rights on resident aliens is constitutionally permissible and consistent with deep U.S. traditions, see Jamin B. Raskin, "Legal Aliens, Local Citizens: The Historical, Constitutional, and Theoretical Meanings of Alien Suffrage," *University of Pennsylvania Law Review* 141 (1993): 1391.

26   *Ambach v. Norwick*, 441 U.S. 68 (1979) (holding that state may bar resident aliens from teaching positions); *Foley v. Connelie*, 435 U.S. 291 (1978) (same as to state police officer); *Cabell v. Chavez-Salido*, 454 U.S. 432 (1982) (same as to probation officer); *Bernal v. Fainter*,

467 U.S. 216 (1984) (holding that state may not bar resident alien from being notary public); *Sugarman v. Dougall*, 413 U.S. 634 (1973) (same as to general civil service positions); *In re Griffiths*, 413 U.S. 717 (1973) (same as to bar).

27   I believe that the distinction between jobs for which there are private substitutes and those for which there are not makes more sense of the cases than, for example, a concern for the extent to which the job is associated with the expression of civic concerns. The argument that a police officer plays a special role in *civic* life for which full citizenship is a prerequisite seems to me strained, for example. I note, however, that the "state-as-monopolist" theory does not make sense of the Court's decision to treat general civil service positions as outside the class of membership goods, for these are positions for which there are readily available private substitute jobs.

28   Gerald M. Rosberg, "Aliens and Equal Protection: Why Not the Right to Vote?" *Michigan Law Review* 75 (1977): 1092. Much of Rosberg's article applies then-current U.S. constitutional standards to the question of the resident alien's right to vote, but it concludes with some reflections on the issues of political theory with which I am primarily concerned.

29   Baier, supra note 11, at 298.

30   At least when the denials are authorized by state rather than national law.

31   See, e.g., *Graham v. Richardson*, 403 U.S. 365 (1971).

32   I suspect that the underlying intuition is that the market is indeed exploitative. If it is, however, the exploitation of partial members is only a particular instance of a more general phenomenon.

33   Long-term resident aliens *are* denied some publicly provided goods available to full members, which at least makes it possible to claim that they can be denied membership goods as well. Citizens of Puerto Rico and the District of Columbia, in contrast, are denied almost nothing other than membership goods. (Some publicly provided goods—federal subsidies of various sorts, for example—are differentially distributed to them, but the same is true with respect to the distribution of the same goods to citizens of individual states.)

34   Until recently people of German origin were entitled to German citizenship no matter how long in the past their ancestors' residence in Germany was. See Coleman and Harding, supra note 10, at 33. My sense is that liberal political theory finds this rule curious, and does so because it has difficulty understanding why any territorial connection is relevant to membership.

35   Otherwise, the very notion of membership would be called into question, as the earlier example of the citizen of the United Kingdom suggested.

36   Consider a referendum in which a 55 percent majority votes for some version of partial membership. A substantial minority would nonetheless prefer full membership, whether in the form of independence or statehood.

37   Consider in this connection the choice between full membership and independence. The latter can be justified when it provides benefits to its members that are unavailable when they become full members in some other nation. The structure of the case for collective partial membership must be the same.

38   One might think that it would be better to assess the price from the minority's point of view, as a way of offsetting the natural self-interest the majority has. Yet, it might be that the *local* minority is associated with a *national* majority. The local majority then would be a minority when the larger unit is considered. It then is again unclear which perspective to adopt.

39   I have changed my terminology here for convenience, referring to the group as a partial or full

member. I do not mean to reify the group, however, and retain the analytic commitment to treating groups as composed of individuals who are themselves the only proper subjects of liberal political theory.

40 Justice John Marshall Harlan, writing separately in the companion cases of *Roth v. United States* and *Alberts v. California*, 354 U.S. 476, 496 (1957), argued for this sort of divided interpretation of the First Amendment, although he did not specify that the reason for the state's greater authority lay in the desire of its citizens to sustain a distinctive culture.

41 *United States v. Lopez*, 514 U.S. 549 (1995) (invalidating by 5 to 4, with concurrences expressing concern that the decision not be taken too broadly, the federal Gun-Free School Zones Act of 1990).

42 *New York v. United States*, 505 U.S. 144 (1992); *Printz v. United States*, 521 U.S. 898 (1997).

43 My concern in this essay is primarily with liberal political theory, not with U.S. constitutional law. The U.S. version of federalism might allow a group to achieve or sustain a great deal of autonomy, but there might be limits. In particular, the Uniformity Clause, *United States Constitution*, art I, sec. 8, cl. 1 ("all Duties, Imposts and Excises shall be uniform throughout the United States"), might limit state-specific tax breaks. But see *United States v. Ptasynski*, 462 U.S. 74 (1983) (finding that a statute exempting certain "Alaskan oil" from coverage of tax does not violate the Uniformity Clause).

44 The most cogent defenses of something like territorial federalism in the United States rely far more on regional differences—"the West," "the Northeast," and the like—than on differences between states. Similarly, Europeans have discerned a trend toward regionalization that is in some tension with the nation-state–based centralization associated with the European Union. For a relatively early discussion, see Giandomenico Majone, "Preservation of Cultural Diversity in a Federal System," in *Comparative Constitutional Federalism: Europe and America*, ed. Mark Tushnet (1990), at 67.

45 Belgium provides the best, and perhaps the only good, example of such constitutional adaptation. See André Alen, ed., *Treatise on Belgian Constitutional Law* (1992), at 5 (describing constitutional reforms in 1970, 1980, and 1988, which transformed Belgium "from a unitary decentralised State . . . into a federal State *sui generis*").

46 See Geoffrey Stone et al., *Constitutional Law*, 3d ed. (1996), at 812 (citing cases). The Court has allowed regulation of obscenity that violates "local community standards," *Miller v. California*, 413 U.S. 15 (1973). Conceptually, this states a rule applicable uniformly throughout the country, but it does allow for local variation in application.

47 It is unclear to me, however, that as a matter of U.S. domestic law, Congress could bind itself and its successors to continue to provide the bargained-for extra protection. If that is so, there really is no trade-off, only an illusory bargain, and the case for partial membership would be almost completely undermined.

48 For the argument as to the United States, see Herbert Wechsler, "The Political Safeguards of Federalism," *Columbia Law Review* 54 (1954): 543; for the argument as to the European Union, see George Bermann, "Taking Subsidiarity Seriously: Federalism in the European Community and the United States," *Columbia Law Review* 94 (1994): 332.

49 But not always. Slovakia separated from the Czech Republic when it seems to me that all the practical arguments favored full membership in a strongly federated system. For a description of the separation process that unfortunately does not pay enough attention to detailing the practical issues, see Eric Stein, *Czecho/Slovakia: Ethnic Conflict, Constitutional Fissure, Negotiated Breakup* (1997).

50 How high the costs are, and whether they are unacceptably high, will of course depend on particular circumstances, about which nothing general can be said. Nor am I competent to say anything about them in the particular case of Puerto Rico.

51 These actors are located in both the nation with which the group is associated—here, the United States—and in the group itself—Puerto Rico and the District of Columbia. Obviously the costs associated with the two courses are different, and political actors would take different steps to reduce them. Must the costs of each course be reduced proportionally, or may political actors choose to reduce the costs, say, of achieving independence more rapidly than they reduce the costs of achieving full membership? I do not have a reasoned position on this question, but my intuition is that it would be wrong for political actors in the United States to skew the choice for Puerto Rico by reducing the costs of one course while keeping the costs of the other the same.

52 The pay-off is modest because the nervousness can be allayed by demonstrating the practical impossibility of achieving either statehood or independence.

53 For an extensive discussion of such a claim, see Rogers M. Smith, *Civic Ideals: Conflicting Visions of Citizenship in U.S. History* (1997).

Injustice According to Law:
The *Insular Cases* and Other Oddities

José Trías Monge

It is not unusual for law to lag behind reality. At times law is so outdistanced by events that it ceases to be a reliable guide to conduct and a means to social betterment. It becomes instead a formidable hurdle on the path to do what changed circumstances require. At that point law ceases to be law or at least to command respect.

Such is the case of the colonial policy that led to the *Insular Cases*[1] and was in turn affected by them. Such policy was largely shaped by the expansionist feelings that swept the United States in the late nineteenth century, and has stubbornly been kept alive after the world for which it was built has long been gone. The holdings of the *Insular Cases,* which validated the policy, read today as about as up-to-date and on target as those of *Scott v. Sanford*[2] and *Plessy v. Ferguson,*[3] although a lot can be learned from *Dred Scott* insofar as it wisely held that the Territorial Clause only applied to the territories existing at the time of the Constitution.

Late in the nineteenth century the United States contracted a dreadful disease, rampant in Europe for many years. It too decided to avail itself of an empire. The territories to be acquired were to be held for an indefinite period, presumably forever, and governed as Congress should in its wisdom determine, basically unencumbered by the Constitution.

The United States had had a decided interest in the Caribbean since early in the nineteenth century. Interest in Cuba was one of the reasons for the proclamation of the Monroe Doctrine on December 2, 1823.[4] President James K. Polk tried several times to purchase Cuba.[5] The phrase "Manifest Destiny" was coined during his presidency. In 1860, an effort was made to acquire five small Caribbean islands, including two belonging to Puerto Rico.[6] By the end of the century, naval theoreticians were underlining the strategic importance of Puerto Rico as guardian of the Mona Passage, one of two ways of reaching the Caribbean Sea from the Atlantic Ocean, control of which was thought to be indispensable for the security of the proposed canal through the Isthmus of Panama.[7] The Spanish-American War provided the opportunity to seize Puerto Rico, along with the Philippines and Guam.

Elihu Root, then Secretary of War, was chiefly responsible for devising the administration's theory concerning the status of the new territories. The Constitution was not to apply to them *ex proprio vigore*. They were to be indefinitely subject "to the complete sovereignty of [Congress], controlled by no legal limitations except those which may be found in the treaty of cession" (there were none).[8] There were things, Root believed, that Congress could not do, such as legislating without due process of law, but these were to him moral rather than legal constraints. Professor Abbot Lawrence Lowell of Harvard, later its president, wrote an influential article arguing that the Constitution allowed for two kinds of territories, those that are part of the United States, to which the Constitution would apply, and those that are not part of the United States, but possessions thereof.[9] To these unincorporated territories only the fundamental provisions of the Constitution would apply, as legal and not simply moral limitations. The Root-Lowell view would triumph in the courts.

Justice White, an ardent protectionist from Louisiana whose opinion would finally prevail, concluded in *Downes v. Bidwell,* the leading *Insular* case, that the United States could acquire territory and exercise unrestricted power in determining what rights to concede to its people. He stated, in a fateful phrase: "While in an international sense Porto Rico was not a foreign country, since it was subject to the sovereignty of and was owned by the United States, it was foreign to the United States in a domestic sense, because the island has not been incorporated into the United States, but was merely appurtenant thereto as a possession."[10]

The *Insular Cases* left the United States free to develop the policies which started taking shape during the military occupation of Puerto Rico: the acquisition of an empire was possible; the colonies were mere possessions of the United States and not a part thereof in a domestic sense; they were subject to the plenary powers of Congress and consequently to be governed as the Congress should determine, except that certain undefined fundamental provisions that operated as limitations to the powers accorded Congress by the Constitution had to be respected. Other elements of the policy, not at issue in the cases, were left undisturbed: self-governing powers should be extended with great caution and in small doses, the colonials not being ready for self-government; the colonies should be held indefinitely as something owned by the United States, no promise of independence or statehood being made; and cultural assimilation should be aimed at as a way of educating the people in the art of self-government and bringing them up as close as possible in the image of their owners.[11]

In an earlier case concerning Cuba, then under military government, but as to which the United States had disclaimed any purpose of exercising sovereignty, the Court had held that as between the United States and other countries, Cuba "was to be treated as if it were conquered territory. But as between the United States and Cuba that Island is territory held in trust for the inhabitants of Cuba to whom it rightfully belongs and to whose exclusive control it will be surrendered when a stable government shall have been established by their voluntary action."[12] This opinion was written by Justice Harlan, who a year later would file in *Downes* an eloquent dissent. The ownership of Puerto Rico by the United States was not to be impressed with such a fiduciary duty, as also suggested by the Puerto Rican patriot Eugenio María de Hostos. The power of the United States to acquire and govern colonies was rather breezily affirmed as part of "the law of nations," a notion that today would raise many an eyebrow. The difference between the majority and the minority in *Downes* was mainly as to whether conquered territory became a part of the United States, although Harlan would hold to the view that "[t]he idea that this country may acquire territories anywhere upon the earth, by conquest or treaty, and hold them as mere colonies or provinces—people inhabiting them to enjoy only such rights as Congress chooses to accord to them—is wholly inconsistent with the spirit and genius as well as with the words of the Constitution."[13]

The *Insular Cases* were based on premises that in today's world seem bizarre. They, and the policies on which they rest, answer to the following notions: democracy and colonialism are fully compatible; there is nothing wrong when a democracy such as the United States engages in the business of governing others; people are not created equal, some races being superior to others; it is the burden of the superior peoples, the white man's burden, to bring up others in their image; and colonies have no right to freedom or any other rights, except to the extent that the nation which possesses them should in due time determine.

The Fuller Court, which gave us *Downes* and other key cases, was not, to say the least, a distinguished one. This was the Court that upheld racial discrimination in the United States;[14] justified the use of injunctions against unions and the imprisonment of its leaders for conduct later considered to be protected by the Constitution;[15] employed the Due Process Clause to annul progressive social legislation, such as that limiting daily working hours;[16] and found income tax legislation unconstitutional.[17] Brown, the author of the first majority opinion in *Downes,* was the author of the majority opinion in *Plessy v. Ferguson,* where he wrote: "We consider the underlying fallacy of the plaintiff's argument to consist in the assumption that the enforced separation of the two races stamps the colored race with a badge of inferiority. If this be so, it is not by reason of anything found in the act, but solely because the colored race chooses to put that construction upon it. . . . If one race be inferior to the other socially, the Constitution of the United States cannot put them upon the same plane."[18]

Concerning Justice White, the author of the second majority opinion, which was destined eventually to prevail, Justice Holmes once commented that his fellow Justice was "built rather for a politician than a judge."[19] Another distinguished critic wrote much later, in words quite relevant to White's efforts in *Downes:* "What impresses later generations in White's opinions is less their substance than their extraordinary form. He moves portentously across the thinnest of ice, confident that a lifeline of adverbs—'inevitably,' 'irresistibly,' 'clearly,' and 'necessarily'—was supporting him in his progress."[20]

Justice Gray, the author of the third majority opinion in *Downes,* had a dismal record in civil rights issues. He voted with the majority in the *Civil Rights Cases,* in which the Court annulled the Civil Rights Act of 1875, which required equal treatment for every American citizen, regardless of color, in any place under the jurisdiction of the federal government.[21] The fourth member of the majority, Justice Shiras, was a railroad lawyer from Pittsburgh, ultraconservative in matters of social legislation, but with a liberal bent in civil rights cases. The last member, Justice McKenna, the sole McKinley appointee, was a congressman from California and part of the political machine of Leland Stanford, the railroad magnate. His lack of professional preparation has prompted comments like the following from students of the Court: "His mind uncluttered by the complex dicta of legal scholarship, McKenna tended to decide each case individually as it came before the Court, mostly on the basis of the application of 'common sense.' The net result of his erratic empiricism is a series of frequently conflicting opinions and votes. . . . The quilted patterns of McKenna's legal decisions largely defies logical analysis."[22]

The *Insular Cases,* in short, parallel the holding in *Plessy v. Ferguson.* As *Plessy* sanctioned racial discrimination in the United States, the *Insular Cases* approved discrimination between states and territories that are part of the United States but mere possessions, "foreign in a domestic sense." Properly deconstructed, the *Insular Cases* stand for just another version of the separate but equal doctrine, but with a twist: there is not even the mirage of equality. The cases blessed instead what Judge Torruella, Chief Judge of the First Circuit, has aptly termed the doctrine of separate and unequal.[23] Bluntly put, the *Insular Cases* simply sanctioned a naked exercise of power, understandable at a time when notions of Manifest Destiny were in the air, but unintelligible after the dream of empire faded.

The decision in *Downes* was not required by preceding cases. There were authorities on both sides of the question as to whether the United States could acquire and maintain colonies, as well as on whether territory so acquired could be governed at the pleasure of Congress.[24] Since the Court was mainly composed of nationalists, as well as economic and racial protectionists, it is not surprising that a majority in *Downes* felt more comfortable adopting the administrative policy favored by the government as most consonant with their position. The Court could easily have applied the *Neely* principle, adopted with reference to Cuba, and have subjected the holding of the colonies to a trust for their benefit, for an indefinite but limited period, as long, let us say, as necessary for them to achieve proper levels of education and living conditions and full self-government in any of its many faces. The times were not ripe, however, for such niceties, and the issue was never properly placed before the Court.

Yet, in the present world, where the need for decolonization of all non-self-governing peoples is generally recognized, the Fuller Court should not carry the full burden of the blame for the colonial policies that blossomed early in the century and are still in place. The *Insular Cases* simply reflected those policies, which have shown to be hardy and resilient. The *Insular Cases* could be left twisting slowly in the wind, as they well should be, and still such policies would continue to play havoc with the cry for justice rising from the colonies. It is not enough to show the *Insular Cases* for what they are. The policies themselves, which range over a wider area, need to be criticized also. Such policies do no honor to a great nation like the United States and unfairly single out the United States as one of the fast diminishing breed of empires, however well-intentioned.

The United States's record on colonial policy matters is, it is sad to state, dismal. Let us take a look at the case of Puerto Rico. In 1898, prior to the United States's invading Puerto Rico, the island enjoyed greater freedom and rights in certain areas than it does now. Puerto Rico had a parliament of its own, composed of a fully elected House of Delegates and an upper house the majority of which was also elected. The ministers or department heads were responsible to the parliament. The insular parliament had broader powers than those now held by the Legislative Assembly, it being able to legislate on matters concerning monetary policy, banking, import and export duties, the public credit, and certain other fields forbidden to it now. Puerto Rico could negotiate its own commercial treaties, and any economic treaties affecting the island, if adopted without its participation, were subject to its approval. Puerto Ricans were Spanish citizens, equal in all respects to mainland Spanish citizens. The Spanish Constitution applied in Puerto Rico in the same manner as in Spain proper. Puerto Rico had as full a right to representation in the Spanish parliament as any other province of Spain. Finally, the Autonomic Charter of 1897, which governed Puerto Rico's relations with Spain, clearly stated that it could not be changed except with Puerto Rico's consent.

In a relatively short time after the invasion, the United States did away with all these privileges and provided instead, in the first organic acts, for very limited powers of self-government.[25] It has taken Puerto Rico a hundred years to get back some of these powers, but some are still lacking or disputed, although, in so many ways, politically and economically, Puerto Rico is, of course, much better off now than it was then.

The United States, one notes with a heavy heart, has been unaccountably slow in decolonizing its wards, slower than most modern administering nations. None of them, except the Micronesian people to a certain extent, have attained a fully noncolonial status. As to the former Trust Territory of Micronesia, the Northern Marianas have become a commonwealth, with greater powers than those enjoyed by Puerto Rico, but this commonwealth still is unquestionably a colony in light of the decolonization criteria adopted by the United Nations, and is openly treated as a territory by the government of the United States.[26] The rest of the Micronesian territories are now Freely Associated States. They are members of the United Nations, but there are still questionable aspects to the relationship, such as the length of the independent agreements, which considerably affect the right to unilateral termination. The United States was the last nation to terminate a trust mandated by the United Nations. It took the United States over fifteen years to negotiate the corresponding agreements with what are now the Freely Associated States of Micronesia.

As respects the Caribbean, Puerto Rico was, immediately after the establishment of the Commonwealth, at the forefront of the rest of the islands. It no longer enjoys that status; it is now one of the most backward. On the road to independence, it is far behind twelve of the English former colonies which have attained it. As respects integration with the metropolis, Guadeloupe, Martinique, and French Guiana are now part of France on an equal footing with the rest of the departments, while there is no indication on the part of Congress of any desire to grant or even promise statehood to Puerto Rico. Finally, on the road to association, the Netherlands Antilles are far ahead of Puerto Rico in attaining fuller powers of self-government in association with the metropolis, not to mention Surinam, which has achieved independence. In all, Puerto Rico is now, politically, one of the least developed regions of the Caribbean peoples. Even economically, although the United States spends in Puerto Rico close to what it spends for foreign aid in the rest of the world, Puerto Rico's per capita income is lower than that of several Caribbean areas.

How has this come to pass? Why does the United States remain as one of the last colonial powers in the world? Is this compatible with its well-deserved reputation as the foremost defender of the values of freedom in the world? I would say that part of the blame falls on the fact that American territorial policy has been shaped out of the glare of national politics.

Before we proceed further, it is important to understand why it is that Puerto Rico is a colony of the United States, indeed the oldest colony in the modern world. Many Americans cringe at the use of such term, deeming it to be highly inaccurate and unfair, yet the first step toward realizing the anachronistic nature of the *Insular Cases* and the need for a new policy aimed at prompt decolonization is to take a hard look at the state of unabashed subjection in which Puerto Rico has been kept after more than one hundred years of American rule. What is being said here about the Commonwealth of Puerto Rico applies with greater reason to areas that still bear the label of "unincorporated territories."

Let us note a few examples. United States laws apply to Puerto Rico without its consent, as Congress may determine, in spite of decades of asking that the generic consent given in 1952 to such a questionable arrangement be turned into specific consent to particular laws, as in true associations between self-governing peoples. The Congress of the United States, moreover, assumes that its laws override even the provisions of the Puerto Rico Constitution. The president and other executive officers of the United States take action, such as negotiating treaties and issuing directives that affect Puerto Rico, without consultation with the Puerto Rican government. There is no equality or comparability of rights between American citizens residing in Puerto Rico and American citizens residing in the

United States. In spite of repeated statements by the Supreme Court of the United States and the Court of Appeals for the First Circuit to the effect that Puerto Rico is now sovereign over matters not ruled by the United States Constitution,[27] the United States government currently claims that sovereignty over Puerto Rico resides solely in the United States. In spite of contrary statements solemnly made before the United Nations by the United States government,[28] both the Congress and the executive branch of the United States act as if there were no compact between the United States and the people of Puerto Rico, and some key members of Congress and the administration even contend that none is possible. Even if it be held, as I believe, that the relationship between Puerto Rico and the United States is based on a compact that may not be amended except by mutual consent, the consent thus given by the people of Puerto Rico in 1950 to the present state of affairs is overbroad. You cannot consent, for example, to the unrestricted applicability of United States laws to Puerto Rico and then claim that you thereby have erased the colonial nature of such an arrangement. Puerto Rico clearly does not meet the decolonization standards set by the United Nations in 1960. The United States does not argue otherwise, but simply contends that the United Nations has no jurisdiction on the issue, the question supposedly being a domestic matter of sole concern to the United States and Puerto Rico. To sum up, there is no self-governing jurisdiction in the world over which another holds such broad powers.

In fairness to the United States, let us be clear as to the sense that the emotionally charged term *colony* is used in this essay. It is not employed in the usual pejorative sense of a people ruthlessly exploited by an evil empire. This has never been the case in the United States–Puerto Rico relationship. The United States has been most generous toward Puerto Rico and has clearly harbored nothing but good will toward its people. In 1942, the government of Puerto Rico and its citizens received a total of $9.7 million in aid. The total now exceeds $10 billion. The term *colony* is not employed either to deride or promote any particular status formula. The word is simply used to denote that the United States unnecessarily holds excessive powers over Puerto Rico, thoughtlessly preventing it from attaining a respected place on earth as a self-governing people freely associated to the United States, integrated to the United States as a state thereof, or separate from the United States as an independent nation. Again, the colonial nature of the present relationship is a question of maintaining old policies and old case law alive long after the reasons for their initial formulation have disappeared.

Under the aegis of the *Insular Cases* and the territorial policy represented by them, there have been other odd happenings. The meaning of some basic concepts dear to Western thought has been lost or altered. Let us examine part of the ancient lineage of the concept of "participation," especially in its relationship to law and government.

Participation in the making of the laws is, of course, a defining part of democracy. In representative democracies this is usually accomplished through participation of representatives of the people in the legislative organ. In areas in some way related or associated to a mother or core country, participation can also be attained through agreement that the laws of the latter do not apply to the former or that they may apply, but only at its request or with its consent as to each specific field or piece of legislation. Since Locke, it has been stressed that man "cannot by compact or his own consent . . . enslave himself to any man."[29] Other theorists, such as Rousseau,[30] have also recognized that laws extended to a people without their participation in the legislative process have no obligatory force. Kant provided the classical formulation of this principle when he listed, as inalienable rights of man, the liberty to obey only such laws in the formulation of which one participates, directly or indirectly; the right to civil equality, which does not allow one to recognize that anybody is his superior before the law; and the right to civil independence, which does not permit one to subject himself to the arbitrary will of another.[31] These principles were dear to the Founding Fathers.

On such rock was the great American democracy built. The simple truth is that democracy and colonialism are incompatible concepts. The *Insular Cases* and the policy that gave birth to them violate the most basic tenets of this Republic.

Another curiosity, often used to argue that the United States cannot enter into a valid compact with a dependency, unalterable except by common consent, is the notion that "one Congress cannot tie the hands of another." This idea has a long history. It came to the United States by way of Great Britain, where it was developed in the course of the battles between Parliament and the Crown. Parliament was finally able to proclaim its omnipotence, which, however, did not initially include the faculty to limit its own powers and approve laws that it later could not repeal. This made a lot of political sense then, as it allowed Parliament to undo any legislation forced upon a weak Parliament by a strong Crown.

The idea was later extended to British colonial law. When the concept of "dominion" was developed and the Statute of Westminster was approved in 1933, whereby Parliament stated that it would not legislate for the dominions except with their consent, it was long argued that Parliament could not so bind itself. The situation has changed since then. Now, respectable authorities hold that the alternative view, that Parliament can indeed renounce its omnipotence and enter into irrevocable compacts with its colonies, is at least as tenable, and indeed more sensible, than the older conception.[32]

The omnipotence notion goes farther back to disputations about the omnipotence of God. Can God undo the past? Can She take away the laws given to Moses, go back on Her word and violate the Covenant? Can God create a stone so heavy that She herself cannot lift it? In other words, does God have the power to act against Her own nature? Thomas Aquinas stated that God's "omnipotence" has limits.[33] He cannot undo the past, order that the Ten Commandments be disobeyed, act against the eternal law.

Congress's omnipotence is also limited. It cannot take back its word whenever it wants to. In the Northwest Ordinance of 1787 the Continental Congress extended certain rights to the people of those territories and covenanted that they would "forever remain unalterable unless by common consent."[34] Were those empty words? Later, cases have held that Congress may not reclaim lands that it has ceded away or modify the conditions under which bonds have been issued.[35] It is difficult to understand that Congress can be held to be so bound in land disposition or bond representations cases and yet be termed free to denounce at will commitments to territories designated as compacts. How could it be argued that Congress's solemn word to a territorial entity is worthless? How could it be held that Congress may grant independence to a territory or admit it to the Union as a state thereof, but that it is powerless to enter into a different kind of binding relationship with it? Long ago, a clerk in the Bureau of Insular Affairs of the War Department, later known as Justice Frankfurter, had this to say about constitutional obstacles to the relationships that Congress could enter with an unincorporated territory:

> The form of the relationship between the United States and unincorporated territory is solely a problem of statesmanship.
>
> History suggests a great diversity of relationships between a central government and dependent territory. The present day shows a great variety in actual operation. One of the great demands upon inventive statesmanship is to help evolve new kinds of relationship so as to combine the advantages of local self-government with those of a confederated union. Luckily, our Constitution has left this field of invention open.[36]

These are not idle musings. Many still consider that statehood and independence are constitutionally the only ways to attain freedom out of the status of unincorporated territory. In spite of the fact that the Supreme Court of the United States and the United States Court of Appeals for the First Circuit have held that Puerto Rico now holds a unique relationship with the United States, that it no longer is a territory thereof, many continue to hold the view that Puerto Rico is still what *Downes* said it was, an unincorporated territory or possession of the United States, "foreign in a domestic sense," something merely "appurtenant to the United States as a possession."

The United States Constitution certainly cries for a reading more consonant with the principles on which this great republic was founded. The mere ideas that Congress may have plenary powers to govern another people and that the decolonization alternatives open to other nations are not open to it do not make much sense in today's world.

May I say at this point that I am not arguing in this essay in favor of any given status option. My aim is simply to dispel legalisms which have clouded the decolonization issue. Status alternatives can and should be discussed on the merits, not on the basis of questionable allegations to the effect that this or that choice is legally unavailable or, without adequate factual research, that this or that option would have such and such dire consequences.

Another fanciful issue is the question of sovereignty. This old concept, which harks back to the sixteenth and seventeenth centuries, when it had a role in the development of the modern state,[37] has for a long time now been put to use in the field of colonial governance, besides at times having temporarily become a hurdle to the growth of associations of peoples like the European Community. Sovereignty has been primarily and wrongly used as a synonym of indivisible power and as an indispensable attribute of a nation. Present thinking about sovereignty deals with the concept in a very different manner. Sovereignty, like power, can be shared and does not necessarily rest in a single place.

In dealing with its territories, the Congress of the United States has been most anxious to assert at all possible junctions that sovereignty rests solely with the United States. Yet the United States is itself, like other federations, a prime example of sovereignty apportioned between various units and a central government. In the Covenant to Establish a Commonwealth of the Northern Marianas in Political Union with the United States, Congress could not refrain from declaring that such political union was "under the sovereignty of the United States of America."[38] As respects the freely associated states in Micronesia, however, which were not under the sovereignty of the United States but transferred in trust to the United States, it is clearly stated that they are fully sovereign. In Puerto Rico's case, the Supreme Court of the United States and the Court of Appeals for the First Circuit have repeatedly held that Puerto Rico is "sovereign over matters not ruled by the United States Constitution," but some important members of Congress act as if it were not so. "Sovereignty," again, is another of the concepts in territorial parlance which should be rethought, together with those of "participation," "plenary powers," "possession," "foreign in a domestic sense," and the like. Talk about "sovereignty" adds nothing meaningful to the realities of power and succeeds only in being offensive to the dignity of relationships based on the principle of equality or comparability of rights. Old talk about undivided sovereignty is part of the language of subjection and should have no place in the decolonization context.

The *Insular Cases* themselves, while waiting for their *Brown v. Board of Education*,[39] have suffered considerable erosion. Only the fundamental provisions of the United States Constitution are supposed to be a barrier to the plenary powers of Congress, but few constitutional provisions have been held not to be "fundamental" for such purpose, outside of, basically, the Uniformity Clause. The treatment of Puerto Rico's political status points to further signs of serious erosion. As stated, Puerto Rico's commonwealth status has been termed unique by the courts. This has been held to mean that Puerto Rico has ceased being a territory of the United States.[40] The *Insular Cases* conceived only of states and territories, incorporated and unincorporated. Now there is a different kind of entity. What exactly is it? In what does Puerto Rico's uniqueness consist?

The elements of consent, no matter the shortcomings of its implementation, represents the key factor. The fact that the relationship between the United States and a former possession or territory is or should be based on the principle of consent takes care of most of the difficulties created by the lack of participation and full sovereignty, provided that such consent is specific and not generic. Thus it can reasonably be stated that the United States is now composed of (1) states; (2) unincorporated territories like the Virgin Islands, Guam, and American Samoa (there being no incorporated territories at present); (3) peoples associated by compact to the United States, however imperfect and riddled with colonial features, like Puerto Rico and the Commonwealth of the Northern Marianas; and (4) freely associated states, like the Republic of the Marshall Islands, the Freely Associated State of the Republic of Palau, and the Federated States of Micronesia. The *Insular Cases*, as should be, are slowly becoming a relic.

Should the courts play a role in further developments? Not in a sweeping, abstract way. In highly particularized, well-defined, and limited situations, such as those wherein the issue involved was the interpretation of what was accomplished in 1952 when the Commonwealth of Puerto Rico was established, the courts have not hesitated to intervene and prevent efforts to slide back and act toward Puerto Rico as if it still were an unincorporated territory or possession of the United States. Such was the case when it was argued that the Constitution of the Commonwealth of Puerto Rico was just another act of Congress that Congress could amend at will and that Congress had to assent to amendments thereto. In rejecting such argument the Court of Appeals for the First Circuit stated: "The answer to appellant's contention is that the constitution of the Commonwealth is not just another Organic Act of the Congress. We have no reason to impute to the Congress the perpetration of such a monumental hoax."[41]

The courts have also turned back arguments that federal laws apply municipally in Puerto Rico, as if it were still an unincorporated territory;[42] or that Congress may exercise over Puerto Rico greater power than it does toward the states;[43] or that Puerto Rico totally lacks any measure of sovereignty;[44] or that the establishment of the Commonwealth did not change at all the relations between Puerto Rico and the United States.[45] Other well-focused issues may well arise, such as whether a federal law, permitting wiretapping or imposing the death penalty, all prohibited by the Commonwealth constitution, may trump the constitutional provision.

So much for Puerto Rico and, possibly, the Commonwealth of the Northern Marianas. But what about those areas that still bear the onus of being classified as "unincorporated territories"? The problem there is that movement toward self-government has been so excruciatingly slow—in the case of Guam even slower than Puerto Rico—that it could well be argued in the proper setting that the normal channels for change are clogged, as happened with the desegregation of the races, placing a democratic solution too far into the future. The plight of the remaining unincorporated territories is at least as poignant as that of those who suffered the indignities of the separate but equal doctrine in the case of desegregation. The discrimination is as visible and contrary to democratic values in the former as in the latter case, except that the discrimination going on against the peoples of these islands is out of the national public eye. In such a situation, it is respectfully submitted, the time may soon come in which the *Insular Cases* may well have to be revisited. It is becoming far too long to live under their premise of injustice according to law.

Notes

1   See basically *De Lima v. Bidwell*, 182 U.S. 1 (1901); *Goetze v. United States*, 182 U.S. 221 (1901); *Crossman v. United States*, 283 U.S. 221 (1901); *Dooley v. United States*, 182 U.S. 222 (1901); *Armstrong v. United States*, 182 U.S. 243 (1901); *Downes v. Bidwell*, 182 U.S. 244 (1901); *Huus v. New York and Porto Rico Steamship Company*, 182 U.S. 392 (1901); *Dooley v. United States*, 183 U.S. 151 (1901); *Fourteen Diamond Rings v. United States*, 183 U.S. 176 (1901).

2   *Scott v. Sandford*, 60 U.S. (19 How.) 393 (1857).

3   *Plessy v. Ferguson*, 163 U.S. 537 (1896).

4   W. H. Callcott, *The Caribbean Policy of the United States, 1890–1920* (1942), at 1–12.

5   Baxter Perkins, *The United States and the Caribbean*, rev. ed. (1966), at 92–93.

6   Callcott, supra note 4, at 29.

7   J. W. Pratt, *America's Colonial Experiment* (1950), at 16.

8   *Report of the Secretary of War*, 56th Cong., 1st sess., H. Doc. 21 (1899): 24.

9   Abbott Lawrence Lowell, "The Status of Our New Possessions—A Third View," *Harvard Law Review* 13 (1899): 155.

10 *Downes*, 182 U.S. at 341–42 (White, J., concurring).

11 See José Trías Monge, *Puerto Rico: The Trials of the Oldest Colony in the World* (1997), chap. 4.

12 *Neely v. Henkel*, 180 U.S. 109, 120 (1901).

13 *Downes*, 182 U.S. at 380.

14 *Plessy*, 163 U.S. 537.

15 *In re Debs*, 158 U.S. 564 (1895).

16 *Lochner v. New York*, 198 U.S. 45 (1905); *Allgeyer v. Louisiana*, 165 U.S. 578 (1897).

17 *Pollock v. Farmers' Loan and Trust Co.*, 158 U.S. 601 (1895).

18 *Plessy*, 163 U.S. at 551–52.

19 Freund, Sutherland, Howe, Mark, and Brown, *Constitutional Law*, vol. 1, 4th ed. (1967), at xiv.

20 Ibid. at xv–xvi.

21 109 U.S. 3 (1883).

22 J. F. Watts Jr., "The Justices of the United States Supreme Court, 1789–1960," in *The Justices of the Supreme Court: Their Lives and Major Opinions*, ed. L. Friedman and F. L. Israel, vol. 3 (1980), at 1479.

23 Juan R. Torruella, *The Supreme Court and Puerto Rico: The Doctrine of Separate and Unequal* (1985).

24 See, e.g., *Dred Scott*, 60 U.S. (19 How.) at 393; *Late Corporation of the Church of Jesus Christ of Latter Day Saints v. United States*, 136 U.S. 1 (1890).

25 For a history of these organic acts see José Trías Monge, *Historia Constitucional de Puerto Rico* (1980–1983, 1994), vol. 1, chap. 11 and vol. 2, chap. 16.

26 The list of factors for determining when a colony has achieved a full measure of self-government appears in Resolution 1541(XV) of the General Assembly, 15 UN GAOR Supp. (No. 16) at 29, UN Doc. A/4684 (1960).

27 *Posadas de Puerto Rico Assoc. v. Tourism Co.*, 478 U.S. 328 (1986); *Alfred L. Snapp & Son, Inc. v. Puerto Rico*, 458 U.S. 592 (1982); *Rodriguez v. Popular Democratic Party*, 457 U.S. 1 (1982); *Calero Toledo v. Pearson Yacht Leasing Co.*, 416 U.S. 663 (1974).

28 Report by Hon. Frances P. Bolton and Hon. James P. Richards on the Eighth Session of the General Assembly of the United Nations, April 26, 1954, printed for the use of the Committee on Foreign Affairs, 83d Cong., 2d sess. (Washington: GPO, 1954), at 241.

29   John Locke, *Two Treatises on Civil Government* (1960 [1690]), at 6.

30   Jean Jacques Rousseau, *The Social Contract* (1974 [1762]), at 12.

31   Immanuel Kant, *Metafísica de las costumbres* (1993 [1797]), at 46.

32   See H. L. A. Hart, *The Concept of Law* (1961), at 148.

33   *Summa Theologica* (1942 [1267–73]) first part, q. 25, art. 3 and ff.

34   *U.S. Statutes at Large* 1 (1789): 50.

35   See *Perry v. United States*, 294 U.S. 330 (1935); *Lynch v. United States*, 292 U.S. 571 (1934); *Murray v. City of Charleston*, 96 U.S. (6 Otto) 432 (1877).

36   Quoted in *Mora v. Torres*, 113 F. Supp. 309 (D.P.R. 1953).

37   See, e.g., *Oeuvres Philosophiques de Jean Bodin,* ed. P. Mesnard (1952); Carl F. Friedrich, *Politica methodice of Johannes Althusius* (1931).

38   *U.S. Statutes at Large* 90 (1975): 263.

39   *Brown v. Board of Education*, 347 U.S. 483 (1954).

40   *Córdova & Simonpietri Ins. v. Chase Manhattan Bank*, 649 F.2d 36, 41 (1st Cir. 1981).

41   *Figueroa v. People*, 232 F.2d 615 (1956).

42   *United States v. Figueroa Ríos*, 140 F. Supp. 376 (D.P.R. 1956).

43   Ibid.

44   *Rodriguez*, 457 U.S. 1.

45   *Examining Board v. Flores de Otero*, 426 U.S. 572 (1976); *Córdova & Simonpietri*, 649 F.2d at 41.

One Hundred Years of Solitude:
Puerto Rico's American Century

Juan R. Torruella

The relationship between Puerto Rico and the continental metropolis, and the rights—or more accurately, the disparity of the rights—that result from this relationship have for too long been relegated to the back burners of American constitutional thought and dialogue. It is particularly appropriate that the debate on this subject was revived on the one hundredth year[1] of the bittersweet relationship that binds Puerto Rico to the United States—a relationship that at times is reminiscent of Gabriel García Márquez's Macondo in his aptly named *One Hundred Years of Solitude*.[2]

That we came upon this centennial without a definitive resolution to this conundrum, and are still, at this juncture in history, engaged in this apparently interminable and mostly circular debate about Puerto Rico's destiny, is reason enough for this collection of essays. The time for us to reflect about the nature of things past, and of realistic prospects for the future, has long been overdue. One hopes that a second centennial will not find Puerto Rico and the United States in the same relationship, and that the divisive issues that sometimes keep us apart will soon be only of historical interest.

The central thrust of this essay is that the current commonwealth status is necessarily and unavoidably modifiable at the will of Congress, and that commonwealth status therefore is not and cannot become a permanent solution to the status dilemma. This basic fact narrows the field of possible alternative solutions to the problem of Puerto Rico's status, which should help both Puerto Rico and the United States to make an informed choice on the matter.

Introduction to the Status Debate

The starting point for the examination of the legal and constitutional relationship between the United States and the Commonwealth of Puerto

Rico is the search for a constitutional definition of the "Commonwealth of Puerto Rico." This may be easier said than done.

One is reminded of the fable of the four blind men who came upon an elephant and upon proceeding to touch him immediately started a heated debate as to what it was they had found.[3] The first, upon feeling his trunk, proclaimed that it was a kind of snake. The next man felt one of the elephant's legs and stated it was a tree. The third ran into its sides and argued that it was undoubtedly a wall. Finally, the fourth, upon touching the elephant's ears, concluded that he was dealing with a big fan. Similarly, in trying to determine what the "Commonwealth of Puerto Rico" is, commentators have appeared to be moving around, feeling their way blindly. There are several visions as to what this commonwealth is, and perhaps even more views as to what it should be. Some are based on the U.S. Constitution, while the basis for others is more difficult to pinpoint. The time has arrived, however, for us to take off our blindfolds, and look reality in the face.

Any inquiry into Puerto Rico's status must begin with the Constitution of the United States, as well as various Supreme Court and lower court decisions, most of which have helped immeasurably to confuse the issue. The fundamental problem is that, look as one may, one will not find any definition in the Constitution as to what the "Commonwealth of Puerto Rico" is. In fact, nowhere in this document will one find the term *commonwealth* even mentioned. The reason for this is really quite simple. The term *commonwealth,* regardless of what attributes one may choose to endow it with through hope or legislation, is not one which has direct constitutional reference. It is rather a body politic created by legislation. Although this legislation finds as its source of authority the Territorial Clause of the U.S. Constitution,[4] a provision that grants Congress almost unlimited powers over territories and possessions,[5] the Commonwealth of Puerto Rico, as such, lacks the constitutional recognition granted other entities of government that are specifically mentioned in that document, namely, the states,[6] the District of Columbia,[7] the territories and possessions,[8] and the Indian tribes.[9] These are the only subnational political entities specifically mentioned in the Constitution.

This, of course, is not to say that Congress cannot create an entity and call it by whatever name it chooses, be it "commonwealth," "free associated state" (the literal translation from the Spanish term "estado libre asociado," the name by which the "Commonwealth of Puerto Rico" is known in Spanish), or by whatever other title it deems convenient to meet the political needs of the moment. However, even the almost unlimited plenary powers granted to Congress under the Territorial Clause do have limits.

One such limitation is the Constitution itself, and it might be prudent to ask ourselves whether Congress can create something that is constitutionally different from a territory, a possession, or a state, particularly in the sense of a body politic with powers greater than those entities have. That question is addressed in greater detail later in this essay.

By a process of elimination, we know what the "Commonwealth of Puerto Rico" is not, at least constitutionally speaking. It is obviously not a state, for the enabling process in the Constitution that is required before a territory may become a state has not taken place.[10] Parenthetically, and to illustrate how labels can deceive and obscure the true nature of things, there are states of the Union, such as Virginia and Massachusetts, that have named themselves "commonwealths," but obviously they are not what Puerto Rico is. There are also groups of independent nations, voluntarily joined by common bonds of various kinds, whose bonds are subject to unilateral revocation by any of the parties thereto, which are jointly known as a "commonwealth of nations," such as the British Commonwealth. Obviously, neither Puerto Rico's status nor its relationship with the United States supports any legitimate claim that a British type of "commonwealth" exists between Puerto Rico and the United States. And there was, as those who collect stamps may be aware of, a "Commonwealth of the Philippines,"[11] which, before it became a republic in 1947, was considered by the U.S. Supreme Court to be an unincorporated territory of the United States.[12] This gets us closer to a definition of commonwealth.

What is an "unincorporated" territory of the United States? According to the Supreme Court—because again, this is terminology that is nowhere to be found in the Constitution—an unincorporated territory is a territory as to which, when acquired by the United States, no clear intention was expressed that it would eventually be incorporated into the Union as a state.[13] The distinction between being classified an incorporated versus an unincorporated territory is not an insignificant one, for in the infamous *Insular Cases* the Supreme Court held that only those rights in the Bill of Rights that are determined to be "fundamental" are applicable in unincorporated territories.[14] The Supreme Court has dealt with these issues on a case-by-case basis, but as an example of its rulings in this respect, it has held that the right to trial by jury is *not* a fundamental one and thus need not be given to criminal defendants in unincorporated territories.[15] In *Dorr*, the U.S. Supreme Court stated:

> We conclude that the power to govern territory, implied in the right to acquire it, and given to Congress in the Constitution in article 4, § 3, to

whatever other limitations it may be subject, the extent of which must be decided as questions arise, does not require that body to enact for ceded territory not made a part of the United States by Congressional action, a system of laws which shall include the right of trial by jury, and that the Constitution does not, without legislation, and of its own force, carry such right to territory so situated.

The Court has also ruled, based on that principle, that Congress can discriminate in the payment of Social Security benefits to the aged and benefits to children and the poor who reside in those areas.[16]

As was the case with the Philippines, Puerto Rico was categorized by the Supreme Court as falling into the unincorporated category,[17] even after Congress granted its residents United States citizenship in 1917.[18] Thus, up to 1952, when Public Law 600 was enacted granting local self-government to the residents of Puerto Rico,[19] there was no doubt in anyone's mind that Puerto Rico was, constitutionally speaking, an unincorporated territory. This unanimity of opinion is evidenced by the fact that the only question debated after the creation of the Commonwealth of Puerto Rico was whether Puerto Rico had ceased to be a territory.[20]

This unanimity was lost in the wake of Law 600, which "created" the Commonwealth of Puerto Rico, and contained in its preamble the enigmatic "in the nature of a compact" language,[21] thus fueling a seemingly never-ending debate about whether Law 600 transformed Puerto Rico's status, and, if so, in what way. Although the legislative history of this statute should make it perfectly clear that Congress intended no change in Puerto Rico's fundamental political relationship with the United States,[22] this unambiguous record has been largely ignored by most commentators and courts.[23] This does not exclude the U.S. Court of Appeals for the First Circuit, which is not beyond struthious conduct now and then.[24]

Of course, the fact that the "Commonwealth of Puerto Rico" is the product of legislation, rather than a status that has independent constitutional rank, has obvious consequences which are directly relevant to the topic of this essay, and which fundamentally affect any proposals that may be put forward regarding Puerto Rico's status.

The Unavoidable Impermanence of Commonwealth

It is often claimed that an integral component of commonwealth status is that the United States and Puerto Rico can enter into a binding pact which cannot be unilaterally altered by either party, including by Congress through subsequent legislation.[25] This hypothesis raises two related questions of constitutional dimension: (1) Can Congress permanently divest itself of its plenary powers over Puerto Rico? and (2) Can one Congress bind a subsequent Congress, in the sense that legislation passed regarding the status of Puerto Rico by one Congress would impede a later Congress from unilaterally modifying or revoking such prior legislation? The answer to both questions is no, for reasons explained below.

If past wisdom regarding constitutional law is any indication of how the Supreme Court might answer these questions—a proposition that admittedly calls for somewhat risky forecasting—one might very well conclude as to the first question that short of granting independence to Puerto Rico or allowing its entry into the Union as a state, Congress can no more permanently divest itself of its powers over Puerto Rico than it can permanently renounce any of its other constitutional powers and duties.[26] This is not necessarily to say that Congress must exercise all or any of its powers, or that it may not delegate some of them in a limited fashion. It would seem, however, that a permanent abdication or transfer of any of its powers would require an amendment to the Constitution.

The answer to the second question posed, whether one Congress can bind a subsequent one, is perhaps more categorical. It would appear to be a well-settled general proposition that each Congress is sovereign, in the sense that its legislative powers cannot be compromised by prior legislation.[27] This is a principle that even applies to treaties.[28] As an exception, Congress is limited in its ability to deprive individuals of their vested rights,[29] but this would seem to be inapplicable to status legislation.

Yet there are some who insist otherwise. For example, Professor Aleinikoff states that the "old constitutional chestnut [that] a sitting Congress may not bind a future Congress" is "hardly an absolute rule" because neither the granting of statehood nor the granting of independence "may be revoked; nor may land grants or other 'vested interests' be called back by a subsequent Congress."[30] Similarly, the Hon. José Trías Monge, former Chief Justice of the Puerto Rico Supreme Court, has recently argued:

> Another element of the colonial debris, one connected to the sovereignty conundrum, is the quaint notion that autonomist options based on the mutual consent idea are not open to the United States because supposedly one Congress cannot tie the hands of another. This is, of course, sheer nonsense, as the United States Department of Justice has pointed out on several occasions. Congress can obviously bind other Congresses by granting statehood, independence, *or any-*

thing in between. The Insular Cases interpreted the United States Constitution to mean that the United States could acquire and govern colonies. It would be simply astounding to hold that it cannot permanently divest itself of the power to govern them to the extent that the national interest should dictate.[31]

I have been unable to find any jurisprudential support in American constitutional law for this proposition.

Aside from the lack of any citation to pertinent authority, which could be excused at least in Trías Monge's case since his book was expressly intended for the general public rather than for lawyers, these statements are aimed at defeating a straw man. The contention that commonwealth cannot be a permanent status is not based on the claim that Congress can always revisit any decision made by a previous Congress. As noted by both commentators cited above, there are certain categories of congressional action that are effectively final and irrevocable. They err, however, in assuming—probably on the basis of the intuition that the greater power must always include the lesser—that the creation of a commonwealth falls within one of these categories. To the contrary, the one thing that these categories have in common is that their irrevocability flows directly from the Constitution. The Constitution, for example, provides for the creation of states, but not for their dissolution.[32] Similarly, an individual may not be deprived of his or her vested property interests without due process of law, including adequate compensation in appropriate cases.

The granting of independence to a territory is somewhat more difficult to categorize. Although it would be recognized by the Constitution insofar as it took the form of a treaty between sovereign nations,[33] independence is not truly irrevocable, since the United States could annex the now-sovereign territory. Of course, this would likely be a violation of various international treaties to which the United States is a signatory,[34] but under U.S. constitutional law, treaties may be unilaterally repealed. And if a treaty recognizing a nation's independence is revocable, it stands to reason that a mere statute creating a commonwealth is all the more subject to modification or repeal.

Conclusion

This essay has sought to establish certain baseline principles that should be kept in mind, not only in analyzing what has been, and what is, but also in charting the future, so that unwarranted expectations are not raised about things that cannot constitutionally be. Only when both the United States and Puerto Rico have agreed on which status choices are constitutionally permissible will a final decision be achievable.

As a practical matter, however, a final decision will remain out of reach until the U.S. Supreme Court provides an authoritative answer to the status question. Unfortunately, it is not unforeseeable that the Supreme Court may continue to avoid the issue, using what amounts to the well-known political question doctrine or other similar evasive tactics. But is this issue any more a political question than were the rights at issue in *Brown v. Board of Education,* in which the Court reversed *Plessy v. Ferguson*'s nefarious "separate but equal" doctrine that had been on the books for fifty-eight years?[35] Had the Court not reversed itself in *Brown,* it is doubtful that the political branches of government would have changed this judicially sanctioned apartheid. The same is true of the judicial doctrine established by the Court in the *Insular Cases,* which allows Congress to treat four million U.S. citizens not only in a separate manner but also unequally.[36] The political branches have shown themselves unwilling or unable to correct the errors and injustices of the *Insular Cases.* It is thus high time for the Supreme Court, a century after these cases were decided, to correct this constitutional aberration.

Notes

Although it may be unnecessary to state the obvious, there should be no doubt in anyone's mind that the opinions that I express here are but my own, and naturally, that I reserve the right to change them at any time that I am convinced, by the use of reason and better logic, of the error of my ways.

1   At the conclusion of the Spanish-American War, Spain ceded to the United States "the island of Puerto Rico and the other islands now under Spanish sovereignty in the West Indies, and the island of Guam in the Marianas or Ladrones." *Treaty of Peace between the United States and the Kingdom of Spain, U.S. Statutes at Large* 30 (1899): 1754, at 1755.

2   Gabriel García Márquez, *Cien Años de Soledad* (1967).

3   This traditional Indian fable is ultimately derived from a canonical Buddhist text, the Udana 6.4: Parable of the Blind Men and the Elephant.

4   "The Congress shall have Power to dispose of and make all needful Rules and Regulations respecting the Territory or other Property belonging to the United States." *United States Constitution,* art. IV, sec. 3, cl. 2.

5   "Congress possess[es] and exercis[es] the absolute and undisputed power of governing and legislating [for the territories]." *Dorr v. United States,* 195 U.S. 138, 140 (1904) (quoting *Seré v. Pitot,* 10 U.S. [6 Cranch] 332, 337 [1810]).

6   The states are an integral aspect of the federal constitutional structure, and are mentioned throughout the text of the Constitution.

7   Congress shall have the power "[t]o exercise exclusive Legislation in all Cases whatsoever, over such District (not exceeding ten Miles square) as may, by Cession of particular States, and the acceptance of Congress, become the Seat of the Government of the United States." *United States Constitution*, art. I, sec. 8, cl. 17; see also *United States Constitution*, Amendment 23.

8   See supra note 4.

9   Congress shall have the power "[t]o regulate Commerce with foreign Nations, and among the several States, and with the Indian Tribes." *United States Constitution*, art. I, sec. 8, cl. 3.

10   "New States may be admitted by the Congress into this Union; but no new State shall be formed or erected within the Jurisdiction of any other State; nor any State be formed by the Junction of two or more States, or Parts of States, without the consent of the Legislatures of the States concerned as well as of the Congress." *United States Constitution*, art. IV, sec. 3, cl. 1.

11   A civil government was established for the Commonwealth of the Philippines by the Philippine Organic Act. See Act of July 1, 1902, *U.S. Statutes at Large* 32 (1902): 691.

12   See *Balzac v. Porto Rico*, 258 U.S. 298, 305 (1922).

13   See generally ibid. at 304–12 (explaining distinction between incorporated and unincorporated territories).

14   The *Insular Cases*, strictly speaking, are the original six opinions issued in 1901 involving the status of the territories acquired as a result of the Treaty of Paris: *De Lima v. Bidwell*, 182 U.S. 1 (1901); *Goetze v. United States (Crossman v. United States)*, 182 U.S. 221 (1901); *Dooley v. United States*, 182 U.S. 222 (1901); *Armstrong v. United States*, 182 U.S. 243 (1901); *Downes v. Bidwell*, 182 U.S. 244 (1901); and *Huus v. New York and Porto Rico Steamship Co.*, 182 U.S. 392 (1901). However, a series of cases which involved the status of the territories of the United States, culminating in *Balzac*, supra note 12, are often included under this rubric.

15   *Dorr*, 195 U.S. at 149; *see also Balzac*, 258 U.S. at 312 (reaffirming *Dorr*).

16   See *Califano v. Torres*, 435 U.S. 1 (1978) (per curiam) (right to travel was not violated by provision of the Social Security Act, according to which persons residing in a state lost their supplemental security income benefits upon changing their residence to Puerto Rico).

17   "[N]either the Philippines nor Porto Rico [is] a territory which had been incorporated in the Union or become a part of the United States, as distinguished from merely belonging to it; and . . . the acts giving temporary governments to the Philippines, 32 Stat. 691 . . . , and to Porto Rico, 31 Stat. 77 . . . , had no such effect." *Balzac*, 258 U.S. at 305 (citing *Dorr* and *Downes*).

18   Residents of Puerto Rico, theretofore citizens of "Porto Rico," were granted U.S. citizenship by means of the Organic Act of Porto Rico of March 2, 1917, popularly known as the Jones Act. See *Jones Act, U.S. Statutes at Large* 39 (1917): 951.

19   Act of July 3, 1950, *U.S. Statutes at Large* 64 (1950): 319.

20   Cf. *United States v. Figueroa Rios*, 140 F. Supp. 376 (D.P.R. 1956) (U.S. Attorney argued that, even after the creation of the commonwealth, Puerto Rico remained a territory subject to Congress's plenary power under the Territorial Clause); *Mora v. Torres*, 113 F. Supp. 309 (D.P.R. 1953), *aff'd sub nom Mora v. Mejías*, 206 F.2d 377 (1st Cir. 1953) (question presented was whether the commonwealth remained a territory).

21   "Be it enacted by the Senate and House of Representatives of the United States of America in Congress assembled, That, fully recognizing the principle of government by consent, this act

is now adopted *in the nature of a compact,* so that the people of Puerto Rico may organize a government pursuant to a constitution of their own adoption." Preamble, Pub. L. 600, supra note 19 (emphasis added).

22   See S. Rep. No. 1779, 81st Cong., 2d sess. (1950); see also H.R. Rep. No. 2350, 82d Cong., 2d sess. (1952); S. Rep. No. 1720, 82d Cong., 2d sess. (1952); *Hearings before the Senate Committee on Interior and Insular Affairs on S. J. Res. No. 151,* 82d Cong., 2d sess. (1952); *Hearings before the House Committee on Interior and Insular Affairs on S. J. Res. No. 430,* 82d Cong., 2d sess. (1952).

23   See, e.g., Rafael Hernández Colón, "The Commonwealth of Puerto Rico: Territory or State?" *Revista del Colegio de Abogados de Puerto Rico* 19 (1959): 207; see also Juan R. Torruella, "¿Hacia dónde vas, Puerto Rico?" *Yale Law Journal,* 107 (1998): 1503, at 1506 n. 24 (listing authors who contend that Law 600 established a compact between Puerto Rico and the United States that can be modified only by mutual consent).

24   *Struthious* means "ostrichlike," which aptly describes the federal judiciary's collective tendency to avoid the difficult question of Puerto Rico's status. The First Circuit, which has appellate jurisdiction over federal cases originating in the U.S. District Court for the District of Puerto Rico (and which until 1961 also had jurisdiction to review the decisions of the Supreme Court of Puerto Rico), has faced, unsurprisingly, more appeals involving Puerto Rico's status than any other circuit. This has not prevented the court from failing to give a final and definitive answer to the question. Compare *United States v. Quiñones,* 758 F.2d 40, 42 (1st Cir. 1985) ("[I]n 1952, Puerto Rico ceased being a territory of the United States subject to the plenary powers of Congress as provided in the Federal Constitution. The authority exercised by the federal government emanated thereafter from the compact itself.") with *United States v. Rivera-Torres,* 826 F.2d 151, 154 (1st Cir. 1987) (stating that the Commonwealth of Puerto Rico remains subject to the authority of Congress under the Territorial Clause). See also *United States v. López-Andino,* 831 F.2d 1164, 1172 (Torruella, J., concurring) (noting that *Quiñones* was simply dicta) (cited with approval in *United States v. Sánchez,* 992 F.2d 1143, 1151 [11th Cir. 1993]).

25   See, e.g., José Trías Monge, *Puerto Rico: The Trials of the Oldest Colony in the World* (1997), at 170–71 (claiming that there is no constitutional bar to a future pact).

26   See, e.g., *Reichelderfer v. Quinn,* 287 U.S. 315, 318 (1932) ("The dedication [of land as a public park] expressed no more than the will of a particular Congress which does not impose itself upon those to follow in succeeding years."); *Connecticut Mutual Life Insurance Co. v. Spratley,* 172 U.S. 602, 621 (1899) ("[E]ach subsequent legislature has equal power to legislate upon the same subject."); *Stone v. Mississippi,* 101 U.S. 814, 817–18 (1879) ("All agree that the legislature cannot bargain away the police power of a State. 'Irrevocable grants of property and franchises may be made if they do not impair the supreme authority to make laws for the right government of the State; but no legislature can curtail the power of its successors to make such laws as they may deem proper in matters of police.' ") (citations omitted); *Newton v. Mahoning City Commissioners,* 100 U.S. 548, 559 (1879) ("Every succeeding legislature possesses the same jurisdiction and power with respect to [laws enacted in the public interest] as its predecessors. The latter have the same power of repeal and modification which the former had of enactment, neither more nor less. All occupy, in this respect, a footing of perfect equality. This must necessarily be so in the nature of things. It is vital to the public welfare that each one should be able at all times to do whatever the varying circumstances and present exigencies touching the subject involved may require. A different result would be fraught with evil.").

27   See ibid.

28   The *Restatement (Third) of Foreign Relations Law* (1986), sec. 115 provides:

> (1) (a) An act of Congress supersedes an earlier rule of international law or a provision of an international agreement as law of the United States if the purpose of the act to supersede the earlier rule or provision is clear or if the act and the earlier rule or provision cannot be fairly reconciled.
>
> (b) That a rule of international law or a provision of an international agreement is superseded as domestic law does not relieve the United States of its international obligation or of the consequences of a violation of that obligation.

Simply put, "[a]n act of Congress and a self-executing treaty of the United States . . . are of equal status in United States law, and in case of inconsistency the later in time prevails." Ibid. at sec. 115, cmt. a.

29   " '[E]very statute, which takes away or impairs vested rights acquired under existing laws, or creates a new obligation, imposes a new duty, or attaches a new disability, in respect to transactions or considerations already past, must be deemed retrospective.' " *Landgraf v. USI Film Products,* 511 U.S. 244, 269 (1994) (quoting *Society for Propagation of the Gospel v. Wheeler,* 22 F.Cas. 756, 767 [No. 13,156] [C.C.N.H. 1814] [Story, J.]). Although Congress can, in most instances, enact legislation with a retroactive effect, courts will give it such an effect only when the statute clearly indicates that such was Congress's intent. Furthermore, "[n]o person . . . shall be deprived of life, liberty, or property, without due process of law; nor shall private property be taken for public use, without just compensation." *United States Constitution,* Amendment V.

30   T. Alexander Aleinikoff, "Puerto Rico and the Constitution: Conundrums and Prospects," *Constitutional Commentary,* 11 (1994): 15, at 38.

31   Trías Monge, supra note 25, at 171 (emphasis added).

32   See supra note 10.

33   References to treaties are scattered throughout the Constitution. See, e.g., *United States Constitution,* art. I, sec. 10, cl. 1 ("No State shall enter into any Treaty, Alliance, or Confederation."); art. II, sec. 2, cl. 2 ("The President . . . shall have Power, by and with the Advice and Consent of the Senate to make Treaties, provided two thirds of the Senators present concur."); art. VI, cl. 2 ("This Constitution, and the Laws of the United States which shall be made in Pursuance thereof; and all Treaties made, or which shall be made, under the Authority of the United States, shall be the supreme Law of the Land; and the Judges in every State shall be bound thereby, any Thing in the Constitution or Laws of any State to the Contrary notwithstanding.").

34   See *Restatement (Third) of Foreign Relations Law,* supra note 28, at sec. 331. For example, the Kellogg-Briand Peace Pact, *U.S. Statutes at Large* 46 (1928): 2343, and the Charter of the United Nations, *U.S. Statutes at Large* 59 (1945): 1031, T.S. No. 993, both outlaw aggressive war and the acquisition of territory through conquest.

35   See *Brown v. Board of Education,* 347 U.S. 483 (1954) (overruling *Plessy v. Ferguson,* 163 U.S. 537 [1896]).

36   See Juan R. Torruella, *The Supreme Court and Puerto Rico: The Doctrine of Separate and Unequal* (1985).

A Tale of Distorting Mirrors: One Hundred Years of Puerto Rico's Sovereignty Imbroglio

Roberto P. Aponte Toro

In 1901 the United States Supreme Court, through a divided court with no majority opinion, decided *Downes v. Bidwell*.[1] In one of the opinions in that case, Justice White coined the phrase "foreign in a domestic sense" to describe the legal relationship between Puerto Rico and the United States.[2] This essay is an attempt to look both at the consequences of his description and at the attempt by political forces in Puerto Rico to escape the "hall of mirrors" that this characterization has created.

In the following pages I will introduce three different topics for discussion. First, I describe the "foreign in a domestic sense" imagery as an evasive light beam, a significant component of what in effect has become our Puerto Rican "hall of mirrors." By way of this interlocking images of distinct and confusing dimensions of the domestic, the Supreme Court of the United States adopted a now outdated conception of sovereignty[3] which has unfortunately paralyzed part of Puerto Rico's political process during this past century. Second, I discuss the reasons why I believe that this political impasse may finally find a breakthrough if we present it within the general context of U.S. policies toward Latin America and the Caribbean. Finally, I insist on the need on the part of the United States, for its own self-interest, to produce new dimensions of cooperative and participatory sovereignty,[4] consistent with modern principles of self-determination under both international law and domestic constitutional law. It is my argument that a search for a solution to the status problem offers the United States an opportunity to innovate. It may also be an opportunity for the United States to provide real twenty-first-century content to historical values which many thought outdated, the values of federalism. As Barry Friedman has argued, both defenders and detractors of federalism have in their struggle paid little attention to any serious assessment of its value. I propose among other alternatives that in its approach to Puerto Rico, the United States may seek to produce a new form of federalism—one in which a sovereignty formula different from that of the federated states may be put into practice as a frontier for innovation and responsible experimentation.[5]

The Foreign in a Domestic Sense Imbroglio

The phrase "foreign in a domestic sense," as it originated in 1901 in *Downes v. Bidwell,* was a pragmatic resolution of an American ideological dilemma: the dilemma of a society torn between an inborn idealism, often based on natural law postulates, and the growing pull toward expansionism and imperium.[6] This second pull came as a response to a perceived risk of potential internal moral decay, a thought which became a constant source of strain in that nation's collective psyche.[7] Faced with this dilemma, the Supreme Court offered a "juggle of words" as a "magic key" to unlock the conflicts that the new situation brought about.[8] One of the problems with the phrase, from the Puerto Rican perspective, is that it was only a short-term solution to what eventually would constitute a long-term American dilemma. Even more important for Puerto Rico, that solution never took into serious consideration the "other"[9] in the equation used to resolve the perceived problem. It has not done so yet, more than one hundred years later.

Puerto Rico came under United States jurisdiction at the end of the nineteenth century, at a time when there were few limits, either in international or in domestic law, as to what a country could do regarding the acquisition of territories.[10] A few months before the U.S. invasion, Puerto Rico had obtained from Spain the "Autonomic Charter," which at least in formal terms provided guarantees that no change would be effected in that charter without the island's prior approval.[11] It took four hundred years of civic struggle to obtain such a concession. But to no avail: the governing elite in America already had its own agenda for Puerto Rico.[12]

Whatever general moral principles, based on natural law notions, were then in vogue as to what should be done with territories such as Puerto Rico, the reality was that no controlling principle of international or humanitarian law was then in existence to protect them.[13] Even today, there is no neutral or truly effective international machinery in place to protect a small country from the will of an overpowering opponent.[14]

This lack of international standards is evident from most of the debates of the period.[15] There was almost no concern in the literature of the time regarding possible violations of international norms stemming from the actions of the United States.[16] The debate that in effect took place regarding the new territories did involve moral arguments, but those were used mainly to provoke internal reflection. Basically, they focused on the way Americans would look at themselves in their new role as imperialists.[17] It was a self-referential exercise. As a people, Puerto Ricans appeared in the "expansionist" discourses as invisible creatures, if not as a disdained population.[18]

This was a period of limited international standard setting and norm creation as regards acquisition of territories. The imperialist "virus" had again attacked Europe,[19] which with the United States constituted almost the totality of the so-called family of nations.[20] The United States offered, particularly to Europe, a new frontier of ideas regarding technology, as well as political change and creativity.[21] It was at the time an icon of democratic standard setting. As a result, this country found no external norm against which to measure its actions; rather, it found only its own internal limits, and a reservoir of moral strength in some American intellectuals of the period, who tried in vain to neutralize the worst aspects of American imperialist dreams and the rhetoric of the period.[22] Although that group represented a very small minority of the American intelligentsia, we must pay homage to them. Puerto Ricans miss them the more as they observe the current lack of involvement by most American academics in our common Puerto Rican problem.[23]

Throughout this century, the legal issues underlying Puerto Rico–United States relations, even when looked at as a domestic American problem, have not attracted the attention of major American casebooks and textbooks. With very few exceptions, not even U.S. international relations specialists have shown curiosity about the nature of those relations. As a result, Puerto Rico is present on nobody's map. It is almost invisible. For decades, not even the United Nations has been ready to acknowledge its plight. Indeed, blinded by the glare which all the turmoil of images reflected, at one point even the United Nations opted for eliminating Puerto Rico from the list of dependent sovereignties, and the General Assembly has not yet been willing to reopen the discussion of the case again.[24]

It is in such a context that one has to weigh the impact of the "foreign in a domestic sense" imagery. Embedded in the phrase is the implication that Puerto Rico, as far as its international personality goes, was a part of the domestic sphere of the United States, thus subjected to one of the orbits (unfortunately not a web)[25] of United States sovereignty. Puerto Rico was already inside, secure, and out of the reach of the sphere of influence of the

international community. As compared to the modern conceptions of su-
pranationality, as well as to the current evolution of the practice of sovereignty in contemporary states, the imagery seems to encompass a vague
description of what I refer to here (merely for heuristic purposes) as *sub,
infra, arrested,* or *frustrated* sovereignty.[26]

The phrase "foreign in a domestic sense" was in addition a very convenient construct for some short-sighted interests in the United States, as it
also depicted a noninclusive side. Puerto Rico was domestic, but only to an
extent.[27] Looked at from the center, we were extraneous. As a territory
Puerto Rico did not participate in the internal processes; the internal orbits
of participatory sovereignty did not count Puerto Rico in.[28] Thus reads the
text to which Puerto Ricans have been permanently subjected as a people.
That has been their predicament. And, very often, in that "hall of mirrors,"
the light was turned off. Then, there was nothing to look at, outside of
darkness itself. Only their own internal reflections in the long and lonely
night; no mirrors, no light. Left to themselves, some Puerto Ricans wanted
out; others had dreams of being let in; still others wanted in for certain
purposes, but not for others.

Living in fear, as all colonial people do, Puerto Ricans from one ideological leaning found themselves constantly sabotaging the alternatives of those
of other ideological leanings.[29] That seems to be one of the favorite colonial
pastimes. It also seems to be one of the favorite American spectator shows.
Laid back in their seats, the United States executive and Congress will
constantly reply that they only want to help, but do not know how; that it is
the Puerto Ricans' own fault; that they just do not get their act together.
That is the last of the false images in the hall of mirrors. In fact, a majority
of Puerto Ricans have come together many times, but to no avail. Waiting
for clear signs from the political branches, the third branch, the Supreme
Court, which originally through the *Insular Cases* offered legitimating consent to the empire, now carefully avoids the issue.[30] The face of dame justice
will be remembered in our case more for the blindfold than for the balanc-
ing act of the scales in her hands.

A brief summary of the areas of the federal Constitution which have been
found applicable to Puerto Rico in no way reflects the agony of this process
for the island. The colonial jurisprudence of the United States has not been
characterized by transparency, homogeneity, and certainty. Let us look at
some examples. As a legacy of the *Insular Cases,*[31] Puerto Rico is no longer a
foreign country within the meaning of the tariff laws.[32] Yet, for almost a
year, goods exported from Puerto Rico to the United States were found not

subject to the Uniformity Clause; thus some differences in the way tariffs are imposed were still possible.[33] As to criminal procedure guarantees, still today we do not enjoy the Sixth Amendment to a jury trial.[34] Yet, like other United States residents, Puerto Ricans are under the protection of "fundamental" constitutional rights.[35] Thus we are "in" as to tariffs and "out" as to the right to a jury trial, although we are also "in" regarding fundamental rights.

Today, over one hundred years after the United States entered Puerto Rico, no one can affirm or deny categorically whether the Commerce Clause applies *ex proprio vigore* to Puerto Rico.[36] Are Puerto Ricans "in" regarding the Commerce Clause, or are they "out"? Recently, the United States First Circuit Court of Appeals held that the Commerce Clause in its dormant state does apply, and Dean David Helfeld correctly asserts that regardless of whether legislation is traced to the Commerce Clause or the Territorial Clause, or to section 9 of the Federal Relations Act, its constitutionality will be sustained.[37] Thus, in this area, the answer to Puerto Rico's concern is "do not ask how, just assume you are in."

One hundred years after *Downes,* Congress still retains the same authority to discriminate regarding Puerto Rico. In the past it has used that authority both to help build and to destroy.[38] Through it Puerto Rico has benefited from exemptions to federal taxes.[39] But also through it Congress approved in 1948 the Sugar Act, restricting the amount of refined sugar exported from Puerto Rico which could enter the U.S. market and further crippling what was then Puerto Rico's dominant industry.[40] The most recent examples of such negative congressional discrimination are two federally funded programs: ssi and afdc.[41]

The imagery of sovereignty that emerged from the *Downes* decision, reflecting a now outdated view of how sovereign powers could be potentially distributed between different centers, is one which may find its origins in developments related to the emergence of international law in the seventeenth century, as a result of the Peace of Westphalia and further evolutions of that concept in Europe as a result of the contributions of Jean Bodin. The basic view then was that sovereignty was indivisible. This "indivisibility" guaranteed that no one could claim universal authority over national states.

In some historical periods such a view of sovereignty ended up being a way of justifying absolutism. In others, as in our case, it was used to establish an impervious, apparently conceptual, but in effect very real wall around our territory, within which the sovereign central authorities in Washington, be it Congress, the executive, or the Supreme Court, could distribute jurisdictional areas of authority as absolute, or shared, depending on what they considered expedient. The way in which this scheme was worked out provided the central government with even more leeway in the case of Puerto Rico than what was then considered acceptable in the case of a federated state.

It is my contention that both technological change as well as a corresponding social and political evolution have changed the context of any serious conversation regarding sovereignty in the twenty-first century. Nowadays, a jurisdiction is more than a territorial construct. Many new productive and valuable economic spaces that have emerged in this century are less susceptible to control by any country today than in the recent past. Countries now share new work spaces as well as creative resources, and a good part of the most ingenious energies of man are dedicated nowadays to evading cultural and economic control by any central sovereign, often with great success.

Puerto Rico, Globalization, and the U.S. Backyard

At this stage, let me turn the focus of my attention to what the United States may do in the future regarding Puerto Rico. Imagine that the United States is ready and willing to work out a solution with Puerto Rico. It is 1998, not 1898. In the last two hundred years America has for the most part been setting the agenda on human rights norms.[42] One U.S. president could be credited with the articulation of the rhetoric of self-determination, although he never made any attempt to apply it to Puerto Rico. In effect, it is particularly daunting to hear President Wilson say that "no right anywhere exists to hand peoples about from sovereignty to sovereignty as if they were property,"[43] when those words were uttered less than nineteen years after Puerto Rico and its inhabitants were in effect handed over as property from Spain to the United States at the latter country's initiative. Fortunately, and partly as a result of Wilson's words, today we enjoy a more or less general awareness that countries and peoples have a recognized right to self-determination.

The United States knows very well that often there is more than one way to get to the same place. A century ago it dealt with Puerto Rico in the context of new internal realignments regarding the annexation of foreign territories. That period had some of the characteristics of one of those "constitutional moments" Bruce Ackerman[44] has identified in his later writings: first, there was a war, the Spanish-American war; second, there were heated constitutional debates regarding acquisition of territories; third, in 1896 the United States had gone through what was apparently a critical election; and last of all, eventually, the Supreme Court in *Downes* set up a framework to quiet down the debates.

Although Europeans already were veterans on imperialism, the United States was new at it.[45] It was a period of high political tensions and lively academic exchanges.[46] Puerto Rico's political fortunes were in the short term defined by U.S. illusions of conquest. Looking at itself in the Puerto Rican mirror, the United States could fancy that it had crowned its glories by becoming a member of the exclusive imperialist club. If expansion was the future that Republicans were forced to delineate for their nation, nothing better to initiate that future than the acquisition of a few new territories, a few strategic pieces of real estate.[47]

I propose that this time around the United States would be well advised to deal with Puerto Rico in the context of United States decisions regarding its new relations with the rest of Latin America and the Caribbean region.[48] A decade ago the United States also won a war against communism, a war which was never fought as a total war. During the last several elections the United States has been trying to define, regarding its internal politics, how Hispanics will be accommodated within its power structure. Externally, it is also trying to define the direction and form of its further expansion both to the north and to the south. This brings me to my second point.

The name of the game this time is not late-nineteenth-century imperialism,[49] but early-twenty-first century capitalism under the modality of economic globalization.[50] In its struggle to expand its regional markets, the United States, sooner rather than later, must decide on the nature of the legal and institutional formula that it will use to integrate other economies with its own. As anyone can realize by looking at the example of the European Union, or at the history of the creation of the American market itself, free trade agreements will not be enough.[51] Free trade agreements may facilitate commerce, but they do not generally provide for the needed "common" institutions for optimal use of the factors of production present in a market.

A need for supranational or integrative institutions will soon be felt in the region. In order to stimulate effective demand in the area a social charter or general social welfare scheme will need to be put in place. Soon there may even be a need to liberalize U.S. immigration policies once again to establish the free movement of labor, in order to relieve what may become a strained job market in the United States.[52] How is the United States going to deal with such developments? How is it going to interact with those "associate" countries? Will it embrace them under the "foreign in a domestic sense" scheme used for Puerto Ricans in 1901? Or is it planning to incorporate those new partners for eventual statehood? In what other ways may we envision that the United States will work out with others the questions of cooperation and sovereignty?

To include Puerto Rico as an important element in the United States strategy of integration with Latin America does not by itself make the controversy as to the status of Puerto Rico self-correcting. Having reached a decision as to the form that United States policy within the region will take, arguments may still be raised as to why, in that context, either independence, statehood, or a special type of association may be the answer to the Puerto Rican problem. Yet the broader context of United States–Latin America–Caribbean integration may well provide the framework in which the Puerto Rican situation will at least gain scale and visibility. Left to itself, as a small, overpopulated, insulated piece of real estate in the Caribbean, a region which seems nowadays to be going nowhere, Puerto Rico does not have a chance to enter the United States's short-term agenda, and if it does, it may be for the wrong reasons.[53]

Puerto Ricans, at the same time, need to be realistic. On the one hand, through NAFTA and other recent developments, the center of gravity of the United States has moved toward the Pacific,[54] and farther away from Puerto Rico. Meanwhile, notwithstanding the dreams of becoming a bridge between the United States and Latin America that island politicians have articulated in the past, the island has never played such a role in reality. If there is any U.S. territory that is playing that role between Latin America and the United States, that is the city of Miami. In such a scenario there is no center-stage role to be played by Puerto Rico in the near future.[55] Yet the context of U.S. relations with Latin America and the Caribbean will provide the island its main chance of securing a seat at any negotiating table. With the hundredth anniversary of the invasion and the turn-of-the-century ceremonies related to the Foraker Act over,[56] Puerto Rico will again disappear from the U.S. agenda at least until 2017, the centennial of Puerto Ricans' advent into U.S. citizenship.[57] Its status situation should be dealt with before that happens, either within the context of trade liberalization and integration with Latin America and the Caribbean or as part of a package in the process of normalized relations between Cuba and the United States.[58] Once that opportunity passes, our fate, I repeat, will fade out of focus. The politics of *frustrated* sovereignty will reign again.

Puerto Rico should have a place of its own in any framework of a United States regional policy that may finally help raise the Caribbean countries from the depths in which they find themselves now.[59] Overall, this may serve the United States in facing the twenty-first century with a clearer understanding of the sovereign maze it has thrown itself into. It may offer the United States a chance to consider seriously new opportunities of shared sovereignty that this new world seems ready to adopt.

My proposal raises daunting questions both for the U.S. government and for Puerto Rican ideological sectors. Statehooders are already alluding to the important role that Puerto Rico may play as an internal laboratory for issues and programs regarding Latin America.[60] A similar culture and history, they argue, may offer Puerto Rico the chance to serve first as an experimental laboratory and later as a bridge toward Latin America and the Caribbean region.

Most of the emphasis in the statehooders' campaign, however, has been centered on a civil rights rhetoric and on an appeal to United States moral sensibility.[61] In the last few years, statehooders have put in place a credible effort to convince the executive branch and Congress to take a position regarding our status, upon the centennial of U.S. intervention in Puerto Rico. Significant financial resources and lobbying have been devoted to and against this effort with apparently limited success on both sides.[62] But statehooders must realize by now that something more than political fundraisers and politically correct declarations about democracy are needed. They need to convince the United States that what they have to offer to the Union represents a valuable contribution to the future viability of U.S. predominance in the world. It must be something economically, psychologically, or politically useful to the United States that none of the other states may provide[63]—something which may compensate for any real or perceived potential costs that statehood may represent for the United States. The question again may be simple: what new contribution may Puerto Rico offer that the rest of the states are unable to offer?[64]

Defenders of free association or other kinds of enhanced sovereignty may have in their favor an argument which they have seldom used. The United States already has fifty states within the federation. All of them enjoy the same constitutional privileges and limitations. They may be useful laboratories in regard to the same areas over which the Constitution provides them with authority, be it total or concurrent with the federal government. None of it directly involves the field of foreign commerce and foreign relations.[65] That does not have to be the situation regarding Puerto Rico, which under the Territorial Clause may be subject to discrimination both in its favor as well as to its detriment.[66] "Why," defenders of free association may ask, "should the opportunities that Puerto Rico may afford as a 'laboratory,' in areas for which states could not be used, be gratuitously thrown away?" Such a question, in the context of the many questions that Latin American integration schemes raise, may force many in the United States to rethink the role Puerto Rico may play. Even Florida, with its large Spanish-speaking population, may not play the role. Of course, that argument leaves open all concerns which defenders of autonomy may have regarding the Territorial Clause, and the almost absolute powers it leaves in the hands of Congress. Further refinements may have to be made in order to make this a workable and attractive alternative.[67]

Supporters of independence will certainly find themselves comfortable with the proposed United States approach toward decolonization. Independence may be seen as a foreign policy gesture on the part of the United States toward Latin America.[68] Furthermore, it may offer evidence to Latin America and other Caribbean countries that the United States is not really planning to assimilate or engulf Latin American economic partners. It had the chance to incorporate Puerto Rico and it did not. Any concerns that Latin American countries may have as to economic integration schemes leading eventually toward political assimilation may be assuaged by this action. In addition, the scheme provides separatists with a new redefinition of cooperation with the United States in which political ties are not really broken but redefined in a sovereign formula which now may be felt as more modern and less unbalanced. The experiences and contacts of a hundred years' relationship will still provide Puerto Ricans with a comparative advantage regarding the United States that a number of other countries in the region will not enjoy.[69]

Of course Congress may not have the will to look at more complex solutions, and will prefer simple ones. There is a cost, however, to the United States on passing up those potentially more complex arrangements. This may represent not only a short-term economic cost but also a long-term political cost, namely, losing the chance to experiment with integrative schemes between foreign countries and nonstate associated entities. Those short-term economic costs may eventually be translated into even greater long-term economic opportunity costs. In short, is there anything in the U.S. Constitution that prevents the United States from representing Puerto Rico in some negotiations, leaving others to be negotiated by Puerto Rico alone? Not that I know. Is that a more complex policy? Perhaps. Impossible to administer? No.

Evolving Constitutional Structures in a Global Economy

This brings me to my last point: We are witnessing a period of fluid and intermingling sovereignties. In March of 1998, I made a brief, ten-day trip to Europe, during which I offered Catalonian students a series of four lectures. Just before leaving for Barcelona, I came across an article written by Charles Tiefer, former Solicitor and Deputy General Counsel of the House of Representatives.[70] In it, Mr. Tiefer argues that the presidency of the United States is becoming in practice a broker of state interests. In his opinion, this is a result of the following developments: (1) the negotiation of recent global agreements has produced strong negative reactions at the state and regional levels and ended up splitting both parties in Congress;[71] (2) recent U.S. Supreme Court decisions regarding federal preemption have limited its usefulness in regard to implementation of international agreements;[72] and (3) lately, Congress has been uncooperative with the president regarding "fast track" authorization.[73] Mr. Tiefer argues that as a consequence of all these developments, the president heads today a confederation, not a federal structure. It is one similar to that originally experimented with in the United States in the eighteenth century.[74] American states and municipalities are requesting more participation, and, we may add, a space of their own, in negotiating and implementing international agreements.

A few days later, while on my way to Spain, I read on the plane a draft of a paper presented at a symposium at the University of Arizona Law School in late February 1996. In this paper, Professor Rudolf Geiger of the University of Leipzig writes about developments in the European Union.[75] He points out how, since the European Court of Justice 1994 decision regarding the division of competences between the EU and the member states as regards accession into the WTO, European policy has been changing course from one which for two decades almost exclusively centered on increasing supranational authority and recognizing implied external powers, to one which now is more aware of the need for greater member state participation in the approval of some trade agreements and which is less inclined to find implied external powers in a field not covered by the EU Common Commercial Policy. This article reaffirmed my suspicion that "federal" institutions, both in Europe and the United States, are going through an evolution in their attempt to accommodate still viable and useful underlying units of sovereignty.

Consequently, it was not a surprise to find a constant bombardment in the Spanish press of news regarding the petition of various Spanish autonomous regions demanding that the Spanish government allow them to par-

ticipate directly in the European Union Council of Ministers, its top structural organ.[76] The day of the petition Mr. Abel Matute, Spain's Foreign
Minister, immediately opposed it, arguing that the mechanism would be
too complex. However, by the next morning he had already been overruled
by the rest of the leadership of his government. The proposal was publicly
accepted by the leadership both of the Popular Party and the Socialist
Party.[77]

Thus it is evident that we are witnessing a period of accommodation at
both state and federal levels. At least in the case of the United States it will
not be the first occasion on which an accommodation within the constitutional structure for foreign economic relations has taken place.[78] The history of the United States has plenty of examples of such occurrences. One of
them, probably the one which has received the most attention lately, involves the mechanism for providing advice and consent to treaties previously negotiated by the executive branch. Throughout this century that
mechanism evolved from one formally based in the Treaty Clause, Article II,
section 2, in which it was required that the Senate, through a two-thirds
majority, approve the negotiated agreement, to one where congressional-
executive agreements, approved by a majority in both chambers, may serve
exactly the same purposes.[79] In the long run, examples such as this one show
the pragmatism, creativity, and capacity for accommodation of U.S. constitutional and political structures.

However, at least one example, the one which covers the events of the
Civil War, provides evidence of an opposite trait.[80] One may correctly question my optimism regarding the final outcome of the constitutional debates
we face today. Why should we expect tensions being exposed in the American constitutional framework today to be resolved this time in favor of
accommodation to the requests for participation of the subnational entities
instead of a repetition of the stalemate that ended up in the outbreak of the
Civil War? There are several explanations for my optimism. In the first
place, at least as regards Puerto Rico, some of the areas of authority generally requested by Puerto Rican political parties, such as sport sovereignty,
do not require changes to the United States Constitution. But there are
other more important explanations. The experience of the Civil War itself
is available for anyone to study and thereby avoid its result. Regarding
that event, one realizes that in the nineteenth century the resources com-
manded by the federal government were not even a shadow of the hege-
monic strength that the U.S. federal government possesses today.[81] The
United States today is a self-assured hegemon. In addition, it enjoys a very

integrated national market, which it was in effect trying to establish during the mid–nineteenth century. Eventually the process gained momentum as a result of the Civil War, and finally crystallized during the New Deal.[82] If anything, what we are recently seeing, both within the United States as well as Europe, is a tendency toward devolution, subsidiarity, and decentralization, even though at the same time the argument is made that external economic forces are devaluing the centralizing capabilities of the nation-state.

Recently there has been a rebirth of academic and governmental debate on federalism issues in the United States.[83] At times it looks ideological, but at other moments becomes very pragmatic, with parties switching allegiances or positions based on the nature of the issue.[84] Yet, probably because of the history of the issue of race, which historically has represented a litmus test distinguishing between supporters of states' rights or expanding federal authority and may be in the background of some of the rationalizations as to federalism within the United States, no one seems today to be dealing with nonnegotiable positions. The fact is that the United States is formally a federal structure, and no matter how far apart formal constitutional structure and sociopolitical reality may be today, federalism remains part of the United States political creed. More importantly, even present opponents of federalism, people with very strong arguments against its relevancy today, already concede that Puerto Rico, Native American tribes, and other offshore territories offer what they believe are the only examples of jurisdictions within the United States where federalism still makes sense.[85]

Of course, that said, we must concede that current discussions of federalism do not generally contemplate foreign commercial or economic relations as areas encompassed by those discussions on states' rights.[86] Current debates about the relevance of federalism today have been mostly based on the Tenth Amendment, which reserves to the states or to the people all powers not delegated to the federal government, and the Commerce Clause, which sets limits for further growth on the authority conferred to the Congress. That such, and no other, are the limits of the discussion on federalism today is definitely a true assessment of current debates. But it is a truth which does not tell the whole story.

There is a growing literature on the effect that the so-called globalized or integrated world economy is having both on states and on the federal structure.[87] The United States may have to ask itself, "Should we face the new demands of the twenty-first century for a globalized market with the same structures we have used for more than two hundred years to create an internal national market?" At the least, it may ask itself, "Shouldn't we be experimenting with United States territorial areas or other related sovereignties which are not subject to the same constitutional constraints as the states?" In effect, states as well as cities in the United States are already experimenting in areas of overlapping sovereignty, where the federal government has not acted. They are also establishing throughout the world twin-city projects as well as foreign trade offices. Puerto Rico already operates a number of them.[88] The federal government has not gone to war because of this.

Peter J. Spiro, from Houston University, has recently called our attention to the new players on the international stage at the end of the century.[89] Subnational governments (states and cities) are included in his list. At some point, not letting them negotiate with others, or at least be consulted, will represent an opportunity cost for the United States. What is even more dangerous, in order to attempt to represent centrally the multidimensionality of the interests of fifty or more states the United States will run the risk of creating a bigger national bureaucracy, one which will only offer more of the same as a solution to problems, and which eventually it may not have the capacity to activate, control, or handle.[90] One must remember that foreign commerce represented just a few years ago a fraction of the United States's gross national product, whereas today it represents a third. An increase in the numbers probably does represent a relative increase in the complexity of the apparatus being used to manage those foreign economic accords.[91]

At the nation's founding the framers of the U.S. Constitution left the regulation of commerce, both foreign and domestic, in the hands of Congress.[92] At the same time the president of the United States, through his power over foreign relations and his authority both to negotiate treaties and receive ambassadors, also had a very important role to play in this area. States, however, were never considered main actors in the area of foreign relations. That formal division of responsibilities does not, however, answer all potential questions which may be raised. What are the implications for the federal government when there is an area within the state's traditional jurisdiction, for example, criminal conduct, whose regulation may have international implications? What in effect happens when both federal and state governments may have concurrent jurisdiction over an area, and the federal government has not taken action? The answers to those questions, as case law reflects, have never been simple and clear-cut.[93] If anything, such cases suggest that the formal constitutional structure is quite a separate matter from the political accommodations that both courts and the different levels of government have to make when they face a real-life issue.

Coming back to my original argument, the other two instances in which there is evidence of contemporary change are the cases involving changes in constitutional doctrine regarding the European Union and the claims of Spain's autonomous regions. The European Union has shown over a period of more than four decades a capacity to work through similar dilemmas and come out of them strengthened.[94] How Spain will ultimately deal with the claims of the autonomous regions is a difficult situation to predict. Traditional historical cleavages and tensions in its social fabric, as well as the possibility that in the near future the European Union will not be able to dispense similar volumes of social funds to its less developed regions, particularly as new and underdeveloped East European countries become incorporated into the Union, make such predictions difficult.[95] Both factors may add to the amount as well as the intensity of the requests for additional participation by these regions. Similar claims may be made by other members of the Union, rendering the decision-making process substantially more complex and giving rise to the need for additional efforts to generate creative participatory solutions.[96]

In different ways, all the societies and federal structures mentioned here are responding to the new international challenges they face. In the case of Puerto Rico, it is precisely in the area of foreign trade and foreign relations that we have seen increasing efforts by both pro-statehood and pro-commonwealth administrations to create a special niche for Puerto Rico.[97] Be it within the context of existent U.S. domestic federal mechanisms (which according to some experts are finally waking up in response to international changes and corresponding domestic and local concerns),[98] or as part of a request for larger measures of autonomy from the federal government (regarding the capacity of nonstate, territorial, or commonwealth entities to negotiate agreements on their own, or as active parties to federal negotiating teams),[99] both statehood and commonwealth administrations have tried to join the trend toward participation in international commercial developments. It goes without saying that in the case of independence the claim to such authority seems to be intrinsic to the nature of the status itself. As we all realize, independence today seems synonymous with all sorts of cooperative arrangements between sovereign countries, a trend which seems to be emerging everywhere.[100]

The previously described developments bring me to two final ideas. Contrary to what some may believe, the fact that there is such fluidity in sovereign arrangements does not mean that nation-states are no longer important.[101] It has been in effect a sovereign state, the most powerful one that has ever existed, which has been at least standing idly, if not in the way, keeping

Puerto Ricans from reaching a solution to their current political problem. A second point is equally important: complexity is not a good enough excuse to prevent both the United States and Puerto Rico from being creative or accommodating.[102]

With all certainty, the web of sovereign relations in the world of the future is going to be more complex than the web of the one we are living in now. That is precisely the challenge for present and future generations. The reality is, however, that in societies premised on individual and collective human rights, both individual citizens and groups will not accept the alternative of reduced empowerment and participation regarding areas that affect them both directly and unequally.[103] Modern constitutions, which were conceived as charters of liberty, should not be used as excuses, nor as impediments to human progress.

A constitution provides boundaries, limits within which social and political actors will operate. Its text may represent the wisdom of a generation as it projects a vision for the future.[104] As a document, as a text, however, it has to be contextually interpreted at least at two different periods. In the first place, the context must take into consideration the founders' expressed intent, its contextual meaning at that time. But the interpreter must also look at the institutional and sociological context present at the current moment of interpretation, how the original purpose may be defeated in the present context, and what other internal or external developments have taken place which must be considered in the current application of its provisions.[105] I am not arguing here that there are never valid constitutional arguments or constitutional limits. But I do agree with Ackerman and others that most of those are time-bound and all of them are socially and politically constructed.[106] The past, of course, always has a very important say over the present generation. But a constitution, at least the United States Constitution, is a living, evolving document.[107]

United States federalism, notwithstanding the country's social and political evolution and the extent to which those changes may have altered its substantive content, remains internally a fundamental and, in effect, a normative principle. That is so at least until the United States formally declares itself a unitary government. For the purpose of this discussion, the main point is that on many occasions what looks at first impression to be a serious constitutional argument is in effect an excuse on the part of those with authority in order not to rethink the concept. Let me choose an example to illustrate my point. Congress, no doubt, has plenary powers over Puerto Rico. In some areas it can discriminate in our jurisdiction almost at will. Why, then, could not the island be granted direct and delegated foreign negotiating authority in areas where it wishes to have that authority? This is not an issue of U.S. constitutional limits. It is one of policy and political will. One may decide that to tolerate deviance may produce indirect negative effects over the federal system. Yet in the future it will be difficult to reconcile the need for the United States expansion with the argument in favor of strict domestic homogeneity. Supreme Court opinions such as *Harris v. Rosario,*[108] in which federal program benefits are denied to Puerto Ricans and discrimination in those programs is sustained, reflect that difficulty. Are we really talking in *Harris* about "constitutional principles"? Aren't we in fact pointing to instances of policy or issue-bound nonprincipled adjudication?[109]

Of course, I readily concede that there are real constitutional constraints. When a few years ago the Puerto Rican government attempted to negotiate a tax-sparing agreement with Japan, the U.S. Department of State objected.[110] Many Puerto Ricans argued that the objections raised by the Department of State had more to do with Puerto Rican internal politics than with any constitutional limitations.[111] That may have been the situation, yet there is no doubt that there were also solid constitutional arguments tied to policy determinations that imposed limits which had been transgressed in this case. The United States exercises sovereignty over Puerto Rico. The federal government is responsible for foreign relations. Since the United States had never before acceded to any international agreement conferring a tax-sparing arrangement, it was argued that once the United States authorized this agreement, in the future any foreign country could have requested from the United States that the same benefits be provided to its nationals, relying on GATT's "most favored nation" provision. Fair enough.[112]

Although I understand the argument and agree that it may have been a valid constitutional limit in this instance, it was not absolutely necessary for the Department of State to interpret the limitation so broadly. The founding fathers did not have an expansionist empire in mind as a model for the new republic. Although they never considered foreign economic relations as a reserved area for the states, they also never contemplated what the future situation with colonies would be. Colonialism was totally abominable to them.[113] Taxing was to the framers principally a state concern, not a federal one.[114] The agreement I refer to involved tax incentives for local domestic investments. Thus it is difficult to find support for the State Department's position in the original intent of the framers. Yet the U.S. State Department's position prevailed. Of course, the issue was never litigated.

In many instances in U.S. history, political and social structures have not allowed the U.S. Constitution to become an obstacle to human progress.[115] In those "constitutional moments," the changes and accommodation that took place did not even follow formal constitutional procedures. People were not made to serve constitutions; it is the other way around. Working under that premise both the United States and Puerto Rico could well be ready to face their future with confidence.

Conclusions

The time has come for the United States to decide what type of relationship, if any, it finally envisions with Puerto Rico, and to delineate its context. It may have to decide the role that Puerto Rico will play in the United States's strategic goals, as it enters into cooperation and integrative schemes with Latin America and the rest of the Caribbean region, and may have to identify the areas of sovereignty which it may be ready to share with Puerto Rico, and perhaps with other countries. That will be the way in which the United States will finally "self determine" as to Puerto Rico.[116] Then, it will be the moment for Puerto Ricans to decide if American plans and goals for Puerto Rico come within the ambit of what we envision to be our future. After all, this will be Puerto Rico's own collective process of self-determination.

The U.S. policy decisions and constitutional understandings regarding Puerto Rico that I propose here will not, for the most part, require United States constitutional amendments. To an extent, they may address common concerns of many states of the Union. Looked at from Puerto Rico's reference point, they may probably be felt differently. In the case of independence, for example, the federal government may negotiate concessions almost at will, under the Commerce Clause, the Treaty Clause, the Territorial Clause, and general foreign relations authority, somewhat limited only by GATT or other preexistent bilateral obligations, and then to the extent the United States may not want to extend similar concessions to the other countries or push for "waivers." No constitutional amendment is required for that.

In the case of free association, similar arrangements may be worked out under the Territorial Clause, which we have said provides the United States with great flexibility for positive or negative discrimination. A new agreement, arrived at in the context of a separate sovereignty, will codify and define more clearly the articles of the Constitution which have been found applicable *ex proprio vigore* and which now may be part of a negotiation under the Treaty Clause.[117] Depending on the way in which sovereign rights end up being distributed, the need for a constitutional amendment or accommodation, or lack thereof, may have to be faced.

Puerto Rico may, under the theory of the compact, benefit or be constrained by similar limitations in this area as states are. According to some interpretations of the relation between the United States and Puerto Rico as one based on an agreement "in the nature of a compact," the commonwealth has at least the same degree of autonomy as a state of the Union. To the extent that the federal government looks away while states and territories actively participate in the international sphere, there will be no need for any formal amendment to the U.S. Constitution. To the extent to which the commonwealth is perceived as less subject to the constraints of that "compact," it may distance itself from the limitations on states, but on the other hand, under the Territorial Clause it runs the risk of being subject to greater negative discrimination.

Lastly, if Puerto Rico became a state of the Union, that state would be able to influence foreign economic relations through the constitutional mechanisms already in place. Today, and particularly as a result of the negotiations leading to the approval of NAFTA and the WTO, a state, according to NAFTA and WTO implementation acts,[118] must be notified in advance of any commercial negotiation to be entered into by the United States, and be consulted as to that which may affect it; and it must also be notified of any foreign attack in the WTO on its domestic legislation, or on actions taken by its courts. Puerto Rico as a state should have the right to participate in the teams that will represent the United States in the dispute-resolution mechanism of the new organism.[119] To be consulted, of course, does not mean that the Puerto Rican position on the issues will be adopted, but it represents much more participation than the type states used to enjoy even five years ago.

The degree of direct state participation in international economic negotiations is still very limited and under a large cloud of constitutional reservations. Yet, I do not foresee in the immediate future any new rights-based claim by states as to that type of participation: States' participation will take place at the different levels of consultation and through their representatives in Congress. That kind of participation does not require any constitutional amendment.[120]

To an extent, Puerto Rico's position is both somewhat better and somewhat worse today than during the first fifty years of United States–Puerto Rican relations. Up to the middle of this century there was an understanding that the only mechanism available to the United States for international agreements was a treaty under the Treaty Clause. That meant that the president negotiated the agreement and the Senate ratified it. Puerto Rico did not have then, nor does it even have today, a say in the selection of the president or any representation in the Senate, but most U.S. international agreements are still applied to us.[121] The evolution, outside of the formal constitutional framework, toward the use of congressional-executive agreements, has at least provided the island with a chance in the House of Representatives to say something about an agreement, although its representation there has no vote on the floor. Even today, Puerto Rico is still a disenfranchised minority. It may be worse off today, since the bilateral and multilateral agreements that may now affect the island are both more and broader in scope than they were then.[122]

Be the choice independence, free association, or statehood, all Puerto Ricans claim and need a greater share of participation in the articulation and execution of sovereign powers. That is what Tiefer, Geiger, and Spain's autonomous regions tell us. That will be the world of the twenty-first century. If the United States finally takes a stand in the direction we propose, at the turn of the twentieth century, Puerto Ricans may finally look at ourselves in our mirrors, without any fear of facing a distorted image. It has taken a very long while, but no one should argue that it is too late. That will be the beginning of genuine real freedom for us, a defining moment when we begin to discover the truth that has eluded Puerto Rico for a century.

Notes

1 *Downes v. Bidwell*, 182 U.S. 244 (1901).

2 See Justice White's argument in his concurring opinion in *Downes*, ibid. at 182 U.S. 341–42.

3 Saskia Sassen observes that although sovereignty and territory remain key features of the international system, they have been reconstituted and partly displaced into areas outside the state and nationalized territory. That is, "sovereignty has been decentered and territory partly denationalized." Sassen proposes a reexamination of the way the concept of the nation-state is often used. See Saskia Sassen, *Losing Control? Sovereignty in an Age of Globalization* (1995), at 28.

4 For recent instances of domestic cooperative federalism in other areas and of a different nature, see Raymond W. Lawton and Bob Burns, "Models of Cooperative Federalism for Telecommunication," *Albany Law Journal of Science and Technology* 6 (1996): 71. See also A. Dan Tarlock, "Federalism without Preemption: A Case Study in Bioregionalism," *Pacific Law Journal* 27 (1996): 1629.

5 See Barry Friedman, "Valuing Federalism," in "Symposium: The Law and Economics of Federalism," *Minnesota Law Review* 82 (1997): 319: "We have not determined whether states really are laboratories for experimentation, and under what circumstances experimentation will flourish."

6   To see the interplay among contestants in those debates and how they were expressed in the
     Insular Cases, see Efrén Rivera Ramos, *The Legal Construction of Identity: The Judicial and
     Social Legacy of American Colonialism in Puerto Rico* (2001). See also Efrén Rivera Ramos, "The
     Legal Construction of American Colonialism: The Insular Cases (1901–1922)," *Revista Jurídica
     Universidad de Puerto Rico* 65 (1996): 225, at 272–98.

7   On American early-nineteenth-century concerns regarding potential corruption in any so-
     ciety, see G. Edward White, *The Marshall Court and Cultural Change: 1815–1835* (1991), at 54–
     61. White describes how Americans dealt with the cyclical theory of change, "which assumed
     degeneration of society over time." He explains the role of space and time in early American
     republican thought, noting that one important nineteenth-century argument in support of
     territorial expansion was that "the spread of republican institutions into inhabited land would
     help regenerate them and thereby might preserve the Republic against decay." Ibid. at 69.
     Similar arguments reappeared at the end of the century, when expansion was already reaching
     continental exhaustion. Ibid.

8   In his analysis of the *Insular Cases,* Rivera Ramos dissects *Downes*'s language and strategy of
     interpretation. The recent history of the United States at that time, he explains, "prevented the
     simple declaration that the new peoples were 'chattels' of the federal government." Instead,
     "people" and "locality" in the new territories were conflated. This conflation, in which "lo-
     cality," defined in terms of its "deficient" population, was ultimately privileged as the concep-
     tually determining category, made it possible to address the question as one relating to the
     power to "dispose" of the "territory." Rivera Ramos (1996), supra note 6, at 291–92; see also
     Rivera Ramos (2001), supra note 6.

9   For a discussion regarding the use of the "other" as a category, see Rivera Ramos (1996), ibid.
     at 290–91. See also Octavio Paz, *Laberinto de la Soledad* (1961), introduction.

10   On the status of international law at the outset of the twentieth century, see Lassa Oppenheim,
     "The Science of International Law: Its Task and Method," *American Journal of International
     Law* 2 (1908): 313.

11   See José Trías Monge, *Puerto Rico: The Trials of the Oldest Colony in the World* (1997), at 12–15.

12   See ibid. at 21–29. For a historical analysis of those plans from a European perspective, see
     Raymond Carr, *Puerto Rico: A Colonial Experiment* (1984), chap. 1. See also *Selections from the
     Correspondence of Theodore Roosevelt and Henry Cabot Lodge, 1848–1918,* vol. 1 (1925), at 267.

13   See supra note 10.

14   Recent incidents in Central America and the Caribbean would be enough to illustrate the
     point. The cases of Grenada, Panamá, and Nicaragua should be enough. In the case of Cuba,
     even if we are not referring to outright military intervention, at least since the 1960s, the eco-
     nomic blockade may represent an instance of economic warfare which some argue may be con-
     sidered illegal both at the wto as well as under modern precepts of international law. Even in
     the case of Nicaragua, where this nation finally obtained a favorable judgment in the Inter-
     national Court of Justice against the United States, it was never able to execute the sentence, and
     finally the post-Sandinista government abandoned the claim. A similar judgment could be
     made of early to mid-century Soviet presence in Latvia, Estonia, and Lithuania, which was
     apparently finally resolved by the events leading to the eventual dissolution of the Soviet Union.

15   Trías Monge offers an excellent short summary of these debates. See Trías Monge, supra note
     11, chaps. 2 and 4. None of the concerns had to do with any international law limitations. Most
     of them referred to the pragmatic problems which the administration of the new territories

created for the country. If there was any debate regarding colonialism in Puerto Rico, it was, on the part of the United States, self-referential. See ibid. at 28. See also Juan R. Torruella, *The Supreme Court and Puerto Rico: The Doctrine of Separate and Unequal* (1985), chap. 2. Such assessments are consistent with Lassa Oppenheim's and views of the state of international law at the time, see supra note 10.

16   See in particular William Graham Sumner's article, "The Conquest of the United States by Spain," *Yale Law Journal* 8 (1899): 168.

17   Sumner charges the "imperialists" precisely with disdaining the newly obtained populations: "We are told by all the imperialists that these people are not fit for liberty and self-government; that it is rebellion for them to resist our beneficence; that we must send fleets and armies to kill them if they do it; that we must devise a government for them and administer it ourselves; that we may buy or sell them as we please, and dispose of their 'trade' for our own advantage." Ibid. at 176–77.

Rivera Ramos extends his analysis further into the ideology manifested in the discourse of the *Insular Cases;* see supra note 6, at 284–300. See also Frank Guerra, *The Pamphlet Wars: The Original Debate over American Citizenship in the Insular Territories* (unpublished paper, on file with author).

18   See Guerra, ibid.; Rivera Ramos (1996), supra note 6; Torruella, supra note 15, at 28.

19   See Trías Monge, supra note 11, at 29; José A. Cabranes, "Puerto Rico and the Constitution," in "Judicial Conference," *Federal Rules Decisions* 110 (1986): 449, at 478; Raymond Carr, supra note 12, at 24.

20   In his description of the period Michael Akehurst explains: "By about 1880, however, Europeans had conquered most of the non-European states, which was interpreted in Europe as conclusive proof of the inherent superiority of the white man, and the international system became a white man's club, to which non-European states would be elected only if they produced evidence that they were civilized." Michael Akehurst, *A Modern Introduction to International Law,* 3d ed. (1979), at 19.

21   John Whiteclay Chambers II, *The Tyranny of Change: America in the Progressive Era, 1900–1917* (1980).

22   I refer here to people like William Graham Sumner, who was in effect an academic, but we may also include in our list Senator William E. Mason, who introduced a bill in the Senate regarding the Philippines which ordered the "People of the United States of America" not to attempt "to govern the people of any other country in the world without the consent of the people themselves." See Guerra, supra note 17, at 18.

23   Although I disagree with some of his premises, Arnold Leibowitz, one of the participants in the panel at Yale University where I discussed the first draft of this essay, has been one of the few exceptions. Mr. Leibowitz, although an intellectual, casts himself as a Washington insider on territorial issues, more than as an academic.

On the extent and causes of Puerto Rican isolation from U.S. mainstream academic concerns, see José A. Cabranes's commentary, supra note 19. Judge Cabranes quotes Chief Justice Rehnquist's remarks on the *Insular Cases* at Louisiana State University in 1983: "[E]ven the most astute law student of today would probably be completely unfamiliar with these cases; indeed when I went to law school more than 30 years ago, they rated only a footnote in Constitutional law casebooks." Cabranes, ibid. at 477. See also Antonio García Padilla, "Reseña," *Revista Jurídica Universidad de Puerto Rico* 57 (1988): 183, at 185–86.

24   While I was working on this essay the case of Puerto Rico was debated in closed chambers at

the United Nations. For the first time in seven years a resolution in support of free determination and independence came out of committee. To the extent to which the White House in a recent Senate hearing conceded that no substantial change in relations came about as a result of the establishment of the commonwealth in 1952, no other result could have been expected. The new White House's position contradicts the official one expressed at the General Assembly in 1953: "It was not, however, a political status choice and it did not change the Island's fundamental relationship to the United States, as your predecessor committee noted in approving it." See Committee on Energy and Natural Resources, *Hearing to Receive Testimony on H.R. 856, to Provide a Process Leading to Full Self-Government for Puerto Rico, and S. 472, To Provide for Referenda in Which the Residents of Puerto Rico May Express Democratically Their Preferences Regarding the Political Status of the Territory, and for Other Purposes,* 105th Cong., 2d sess. (July 15, 1998) (statement of Jeffrey L. Farrow).

    On the early discussion regarding Puerto Rico at the UN, see Trías Monge, supra note 11, chap. 12. For an excellent summary of the efforts of Puerto Ricans at that forum up until the late 1970s, see Carmen Gautier Mayoral, *Puerto Rico y la O.N.U.* (1978).

25   The use of the word *Web* as a descriptive category is a recent one. Social scientists and others had previously adopted the "orbit" imagery from the physical sciences and particularly the space race vocabulary. "Orbits" talk was prevalent in the late 1950s and 1960s. By the late 1980s, and particularly in the 1990s, computers and Internet terminology adopted the "web" imagery. One tends to enter or abandon a "web" at one's own discretion. The "orbit," on the other hand, envisions an extent of physical compulsion between energy fields to which the object in the orbit is subject. Orbits, of course, can also be entered or left, but the success of an object at doing it depends on the strength of the force which propels it. Webs on the other hand are "navigated."

26   Wolfgang Friedmann adverted in 1964 to the following characteristics of supranational institutions: First, the activities of states or groups are "merged in permanent international institutions." But those institutions "express purposes and functions of their own, and as they become more firmly established, they become increasingly emancipated from the states or groups establishing them. They develop a moral as well as a legal personality of their own." Wolfgang Friedmann, *The Changing Structure of International Law* (1964), at 38.

    As to the use of the term *arrested* in other contexts, see James Anderson, "Arrested Federalization? Europe, Britain, Ireland," in *Federalism: The Multiethnic Challenge,* ed. Graham Smith (1995), at 279.

27   According to *Downes v. Bidwell,* supra note 1, the extent to which Puerto Rico was considered within the "domestic" did not include the application of benefits or disadvantages generated by the Uniformity Clause. Thus, once the Foraker Act was approved, the United States could collect duties on imports from Puerto Rico, contrary to the previous decision in *De Lima v. Bidwell,* 182 U.S. 1 (1901), where it was not permitted, since Puerto Rico was not a "foreign country." See Rivera Ramos, supra note 6, at 246.

28   See David Helfeld, "How Much of the United States Constitution and Statutes are applicable to the Commonwealth of Puerto Rico?" in "Judicial Conference," *Federal Rules Decisions* 110 (1986): 449, at 468.

29   Frantz Fanon, *Los Condenados de la Tierra* (1965); Albert Memmi, *Retrato del Colonizado* (1969).

30   Judge Cabranes describes the original role played by the U.S. Supreme Court as follows: "[T]he following year, the Supreme Court in the *Insular Cases* blessed the colonial experiment

by holding that the new territories were not 'foreign territory,' but nevertheless not 'a part of the United States' for all Constitutional purposes." Cabranes, supra note 19, at 478.

Dean David Helfeld describes the current attitude of the U.S. Supreme Court regarding Puerto Rico in these terms: "While the court may be ready to interpret legislation and rectify statutory violations, in all probability it will continue to be most reluctant to declare unconstitutional Congressional legislation discriminatorily affecting Puerto Rico." David Helfeld, supra note 28, at 474.

31 For an analysis of the twenty-three cases which have come to be known as the *Insular Cases,* see Rivera Ramos (1996), supra note 6. For a discussion of some of these decisions, see Raúl Serrano Geyls, *Derecho Constitutional de Estados Unidos y Puerto Rico-Jurisprudencia, Anotaciones, Preguntas* (1986), at 496–561.

32 *Downes,* 182 U.S. 244. *De Lima,* 182 U.S. 1, decided before the approval of the Foraker Act that a similar duty had been illegally exacted because Puerto Rico was no longer "foreign." But now, through *Downes,* it was found that although Puerto Rico was not foreign, still it had not been incorporated. Thus it was not subject to the Uniformity Clause (see *United States Constitution,* art. I, sec. 8, cl. 1).

33 Helfeld, supra note 28, at 454.

34 Helfeld has expressed "doubts" as to the extent that *Balzac v. Puerto Rico,* 258 U.S. 298 (1922) is still a "good precedent." Ibid at 458. See also José Julián Álvarez González, "The Protection of Civil Rights in Puerto Rico," *Arizona Journal of International and Comparative Law* 6 (1989): 68.

35 Helfeld, ibid. at 457; Rivera Ramos, supra note 6, at 261–71; GAO, Report to the Chairman, Committee on Resources, House of Representatives, *U.S. Insular Areas: Application of the U.S. Constitution* (November 1997), at 23–24. The specification of what rights will be found fundamental has been left to a case by case determination.

36 Helfeld, ibid. at 469; see also GAO, ibid. at 29; *Trailer Marine Transp. Corp. v. Rivera Vázquez,* 977 F.2d. 1, 7 (1st Cir. 1992).

37 Helfeld, ibid.; GAO, ibid. See also *Trailer Marine,* ibid. at 6: "Whatever the ultimate source of its authority or its exact constitutional status, Puerto Rico today certainly has sufficient actual autonomy to justify treating it as a public entity distinct from Congress and subject to the Dormant Commerce Clause doctrine."

38 Helfeld, ibid. at 459.

39 Ibid.

40 Ibid.

41 Ibid. at 461–62. Helfeld explains that "Congress excluded Puerto Rico from the Supplemental Security Income program for elderly, blind and handicapped persons, 42 U.S.C.A. sec. 1381 et seq.; and in the program of Aid to Families with Dependent Children, 42 U.S.C.A. sec. 601 et seq., provided appreciably less benefits for needy children in Puerto Rico, 42 U.S.C.A. sec. 1308(a)(1), 1396(d)(b) (1976 ed. and Supp II)." Ibid. at n. 42. The Supreme Court validated these actions in two different cases: *Califano v. Torres,* 435 U.S. 1 (1978) (per curiam) (holding that the provisions of the Social Security Act making benefits for aged, blind, and disabled persons under the SSI program payable only to residents of the United States, which is defined as the fifty states and the District of Columbia, are not unconstitutional as applied to persons who upon moving to Puerto Rico lost the benefits to which they were entitled while residing in the United States); *Harris v. Rosario,* 446 U.S. 651 (1980) (per curiam) (holding that the lower level of reimbursement provided to Puerto Rico under the AFDC program does not violate the Fifth Amendment, and that Congress, under the Territorial

Clause, may treat Puerto Rico differently from a state so long as there is a rational basis for its actions).

42   The contributions made by the United States to the development of human rights doctrine is unquestionable. One may go back to the eighteenth century and find the American Declaration of Independence, the U.S. Bill of Rights, and the French Declaration of the Rights of Man and Citizen, as the pillars on which the twentieth-century architecture of human rights was designed. In the mid–twentieth century, the Nuremberg Trials, the Preamble of the UN Charter, and the 1948 Universal Declaration of Human Rights were to a great extent influenced by the international weight which the United States enjoyed. See Mark W. Janis and Richard S. Kay, *European Human Rights Law* (1990), at 1–9. On how the protection of those individual human rights has been played out in Puerto Rico, see Álvarez González, supra note 34, at 88.

43   Trías Monge, supra note 11, at 67. For President Wilson's statement before the Senate, see *Cong. Rec.*, 64th Cong., 2d sess. (January 22, 1917): 1742.

44   Bruce Ackerman, *We the People: Foundations* (1991); see also Bruce Ackerman and David Golove, "Is NAFTA Constitutional?" *Harvard Law Review* 108 (1995): 801.

45   See Trías Monge, supra note 11, at 29. Raymond Carr puts it in perspective: "Puerto Rico was a victim of 'imperialism' as that term was understood at the turn of the century. The United States was acting as other great powers had acted." Carr, supra note 12, at 24.

46   See Trías Monge, ibid. at chaps. 2–4; Guerra, supra note 17; Rivera Ramos, supra note 6.

47   Trías Monge describes how, in 1896, "the Republican platform called for the acquisition of Hawaii and the Danish Islands (now the U.S. Virgin Islands) as well as the independence of Cuba and the complete withdrawal of European powers from the Western Hemisphere." Trías Monge, ibid at 24.

The 1896 election has been identified as one of the classic examples of a "critical election." See Walter Dean Burnham, *Critical Elections and the Mainsprings of American Politics* (1970). Although President McKinley had second thoughts about direct U.S. intervention in the Cuban conflict, the developments brought about by the maneuvers of the Democrats eventually took the United States to war against Spain, and finally catapulted it into Puerto Rico.

48   For a description of the various potential scenarios which the United States faced in the 1970s as it defined its policy of economic integration in this hemisphere, see Roberto P. Aponte Toro, *Amor a la Americana* (1994), at 37–40.

49   John A. Hobson, *Imperialism: A Study* (1965 [1902]); Vladimir Illich Lenin, *El Imperialismo, fase superior del capitalismo* (1966).

50   There is a constant cascade of books on economic globalization coming out. For my analysis I have relied on Saskia Sassen, supra note 3. On globalization's impact on U.S. federalism, see Barry Friedman's "Federalism's Future in a Global Village," *Vanderbilt Law Review* 47 (1994): 1441; see also Richard J. Barnet and John Cavanagh, *Global Dreams: Imperial Corporations and the New World Order* (1995); John Naisbitt, *Global Paradox: The Bigger the World Economy, the More Powerful Its Smallest Players* (1995); Kenichi Ohmae, *The Borderless World: Power and Strategy in the Interlinked Economy* (1990).

The role of the state and of sovereignty in that new order is both more as well as less active or intrusive. In the new regime, the state, particularly when one refers to the United States, is able to see its language become the international lingua franca, most of its commercial institutions and practices being adopted by others, its codes assimilated by other countries, and so on. Yet, now more than ever, no state is able to control the use by its citizens of networks of communication, through porous frontiers and other means. See Sassen, ibid. at chap. 1.

51   In the case of the European Union, member countries went through different stages of integration at various levels of political cooperation. The United States went through similar stages. In its case, eventually two regions of the country settled their conflict through a civil war, whereby one side of the country imposed its economic model over the other in order to establish an integrated national market. See Jim Chen, "Of Agriculture's First Disobedience and Its Fruit," *Vanderbilt Law Review* 48 (1995): 1261, at 1299; William N. Eskridge Jr. and John Ferejohn, "The Elastic Commerce Clause: A Political Theory of American Federalism," *Vanderbilt Law Review* 47 (1994): 1355. Republicans were very active in consolidating that market: "The Lincoln platform was strikingly different from the Jacksonian one of the previous period, emphasizing the role of the national government in economic development (through railroad land grants, for example) and in redistributing social power (ultimately favoring the abolition of slavery and the badges of servitude it imposed)." Ibid. at 1376.

52   During the process leading to NAFTA's approval, two of its leading supporters, Gary Hufbauer and Jeffrey J. Schott, wrote on the effect it might or might not have on illegal immigration. They were very candid as to the limits of using NAFTA with those goals in mind. They even quoted articles arguing that shutting the door to immigration would be counterproductive to some sectors of the U.S. economy. See Gary Clyde Hufbauer and Jeffrey J. Schott, *North American Free Trade: Issues and Recommendations* (1992), at 126–27.

      With the strength shown in the last few years by the U.S. economy, unemployment has been reduced dramatically. Under the present conditions, it would have been expected that the United States would have fewer people looking for jobs. Although concerns about inflation have been articulated by economists, they have not materialized. One possible explanation for that situation is the effect that the trend toward outsourcing, and the transfer of certain labor-intensive operation to low-salary jurisdictions, may have had on disarming inflation.

53   The Puerto Rican press has denounced New Progressive Party (NPP) efforts to win support for statehood both in Congress and the White House through the creation of political action committees (PACs) and the provision of other types of financial contributions to U.S. politicians. There is a now prevalent belief in Puerto Rico that this is the way American politics is conducted. That belief gains credibility from constant reports in the U.S. media about illegal political contributions. But it is a belief that may run counter to one of the statehooders' stronger arguments, that is, that statehood is a "moral" crusade.

      When the U.S. national press made public the video tapes of one of the White House breakfasts made famous by the congressional investigations on political fundraising, one of the participants who was identified was a well-known contributor from Puerto Rico to the Democratic Party. In effect, he is not a statehooder but a commonwealth supporter. Whatever his ideological preferences are is not important for our argument. What matters is that this is the way many Puerto Ricans are looking at the political process in Washington.

54   Roberto P. Aponte Toro, "El Notariado Puertorriqueño en el Contexto del TLC de América del Norte," paper given at a joint meeting of Public Notaries from Mexico, Quebec, and Puerto Rico, San Juan, Puerto Rico, December 9, 1994, at 16 (on file with author).

55   Through the presidency of the Council of State Governors, Governor Rosselló hosted a number of regional meetings with Latin American and Caribbean leaders in Puerto Rico. He visited various Latin American countries while representing the council. I doubt that this is enough. In order to move ahead further in his agenda, a sustained effort must take place. One would need to enlist the assistance of the private sector, but Puerto Rico does not have one with the dynamism and risk-taking entrepreneurship found in Miami. Furthermore, Puerto

Rico is a less attractive place to do business today than it was two decades ago. The island faces serious problems in its infrastructure. In general, the situation regarding external transportation is worse in both Puerto Rico and the rest of the Caribbean than it was ten years ago.

Meanwhile, Miami, having overcome the public safety hysteria regarding tourists of a few years ago, is definitely taking charge of the South American and Caribbean markets. In effect, Miami has been chosen as the seat of the Free Trade Area of the Americas expansion negotiation for the first three years. See M2 Presswire (1998 WL 11306878). Texas is also playing an important role in those markets.

56   *U.S. Statutes at Large* 31 (1900): 77. For a good historical memory of events during the years immediately succeeding the approval of the law, see Trías Monge, supra note 11, at chap. 5.

57   On the issue of U.S. citizenship, see José Julián Álvarez González, "The Empire Strikes Out: Congressional Ruminations on the Citizenship Status of Puerto Ricans," *Harvard Journal on Legislation* 27 (1990): 309; Johnny H. Killian, Congressional Research Service, *Discretion of Congress Respecting Citizenship Status of Puerto Rico* (1989); Killian, Congressional Research Service, *Questions in re Citizenship Status of Puerto Ricans* (1990); José A. Cabranes, *Citizenship and the American Empire: Notes on the Legislative History of the United States Citizenship of Puerto Ricans* (1979); Raúl Serrano Geyls, "El Misterio de la Ciudadanía," *Revista del Colegio de Abogados de Puerto Rico* 40 (1979): 437. Lately the Supreme Court of the Commonwealth of Puerto Rico has recognized the existence of a Puerto Rican citizenship in *Ramírez de Ferrer v. Mari Brás,* 97 J.T.S. 134 (1997).

The concession or imposition of United States citizenship on Puerto Ricans in 1917 has been seen by some observers as a decisive moment in Puerto Rico–U.S. federal relations. Some argue that it turned the tide of the status discussion toward statehood. On the other hand, the proindependence movement actually began to grow after 1917, reaching the peak of its electoral support thirty-five years later. It was the social benefits to which Puerto Ricans became entitled under the expansive welfare state of the 1960s and 1970s which once again increased support for statehood and eroded the independence movement's base. Yet those benefits, at least at the time, had little to do with citizenship, and more with legal residence. Legal aliens enjoy some of the same benefits, including benefits that U.S. citizens living outside the United States may not enjoy. Even illegal immigrants enjoy certain protections and guarantees. In addition, arrangements under NAFTA and the Caribbean Basin Initiative (CBI) allow access to exports to U.S. markets; this right is also not associated with citizenship. Although the United States expresses reservations about dual citizenship, it effectively condones that framework. See Pablo Lizarraga Chavez, "Creating a United States–Mexico Political Double Helix: The Mexican Government's Proposed Dual Nationality Amendment," *Stanford Journal of International Law* 33 (1997): 119; Jorge Vargas, "Dual Nationality for Mexicans? A Comparative Legal Analysis of the Dual Nationality Proposal and Its Eventual Political and Socio-economic Implications," *Chicano Latino Law Review* 18 (1996): 1.

In sum, the extension of U.S. citizenship to Puerto Rico in 1917 should not constrain its decisions concerning Puerto Rican status in 1998. This does not mean that it is not in the United States's interest to offer statehood to Puerto Rico, but this must be a decision that stands on its own merits.

58   There are many good reasons to contemplate the proximate normalization of political and economic relations with Cuba as an excellent opportunity to finally close the Puerto Rican chapter. First of all, Cuba and Puerto Rico enjoyed up until the end of the nineteenth century a common history of Spanish colonialism and common efforts to overcome political malaise.

Both have also been proxies to superpowers during the last half of the twentieth century. That seems to be at an end now.

The Cuban exile community in Puerto Rico is very influential and has contributed significantly to the development of entrepreneurial skills in many of Puerto Rico's most dynamic economic sectors. Both Cubans in Cuba and in exile have shown a capacity to excel in areas where Puerto Ricans have not. That has been particularly so in commerce. Joel Kotkin mentions Cubans as the only group in this hemisphere which could fit the description of an economic "tribe." See Joel Kotkin, *Tribes: How Race, Religion, and Identity Determine Success in the New Global Economy* (1992), at 5.

Puerto Ricans, on the other hand, seem to be closer to the model of a democratic civic culture than Cubans. Even in Miami, Cubans seem to have problems in adapting to the requirements of a democratic civic culture, and in particular to compromise. A bonding between the two communities may produce a mix which could be favorable to both. Finally, both communities will end up at the end of the century with a good number of its members holding American citizenship, something about which the United States, due to its outdated conception of the role of citizenship, may be concerned.

59   Roberto P. Aponte Toro, "La Integración en América Latina y el Caribe," *Revista Jurídica Universidad de Puerto Rico* 68 (1999): 119, at 137–39.

60   Documento Justificativo, Negociado para Asuntos Hemisféricos, Departamento de Estado, Año Fiscal 1997 (on file with the author). See also Remarks by the Honorable Pedro Rosselló, Governor of Puerto Rico and Vice President of the Council of State Governments, delivered at a roundtable discussion on States, Provinces, and Global Affairs at the Annual Meeting and State Leadership Forum of the Council of State Governments, Cleveland, Ohio, December 10, 1996 (on file with the author). For a discussion relating to such a role see Efrén Rivera Ramos, "Colonialism and Integration in the Contemporary Caribbean," *Beyond Law* 6 (1998): 189.

61   In testimony at the Committee of Energy and Natural Resources of the Senate, former Resident Commissioner Carlos Romero Barceló was explicit in his use of such references ("It marks 100 years of Congressional indifference to the Puerto Rican dream of political equality"; "the democratic rights of the people of Puerto Rico have been ignored"; "the U.S. government became a part of this misrepresentation"; "We proudly march off to war under the stars and stripes, but we may not vote for the president who calls us to arms"; "There is a definite geographical discrimination.") Committee on Energy and Natural Resources, supra note 24, at 2–5.

62   A bill calling for a plebiscite which was supported by statehooders and the Puerto Rican Independence Party passed the U.S. House of Representatives by one vote, but died in the Senate. Statehooders, however, may claim that they raised the awareness of Congress on this issue to unprecedented levels. This argument, of course, may cut both ways. Congress may be more aware now of both the arguments favoring statehood as well as the arguments against statehood.

63   One may still argue that, even if another state may be able to supply the same benefit, Puerto Rico could do it better and more efficiently, or that former suppliers are unable to satisfy the whole of U.S. demand.

In addition, the Rosselló administration tried to convince the federal government of Puerto Rico's value to the United States for military defense and as regards its antinarcotics strategy. As a result, the United States has decided to move its Southern Military Command to Puerto Rico. With the constant improvements in technological defense capabilities, and the failures of military action against drugs, this value seems condemned to obsolescence. Furthermore, no one in Puerto Rico seriously believes that in the short term Puerto Rico will be freed from any strategic military role it may have for the United States.

64   The "states as laboratories" imagery originally appeared in Justice Brandeis's dissent in *New State Ice Co. v. Liebmann,* 285 U.S. 262, 311 (1932). According to it, states were free to experiment and "try novel social and economic experiments without risk to the rest of the country." More recently Justice O'Connor, in an opinion concurring in part and dissenting in part in *FERC v. Mississippi,* 456 U.S. 742, 788–89 (1982), brought back the same imagery, which has since regained its vitality.

65   Although recently there have been increasing debates regarding the "revolutionarism" of recent U.S. Supreme Court decisions on federalism, decisions which seem to reempower states, no one seems to be implying that states have now been given authority over those two areas, though Daniel Farber has implied that in those decisions states are in some measure "independent nations." See Daniel A. Farber, "The Constitution's Forgotten Cover Letter: An Essay on the New Federalism and the Original Understanding," *Michigan Law Review* 94 (1995): 615. See also Robert F. Nagel, "Real Revolution," *Georgia State University Law Review* 13 (1997): 985. For a recent article which supports the conventional view regarding the authority over foreign affairs and which addresses problems that it creates, see Ronan Doherty, "Foreign Affairs v. Federalism: How State Control of Criminal Law Implicates Federal Responsibility under International Law," *Virginia Law Review* 82 (1996): 1281.

66   Helfeld, supra note 28, at 463, 474.

67   In particular, the use of the Supremacy Clause to preempt state legislation when treaties are involved comes to mind. Since most treaties and agreements are either given advice and consent in the Senate, or in both chambers, and there is no Puerto Rican representation in the Senate, Puerto Rico finds itself dispossessed of any opportunity to affect the political process regarding those agreements. Someone, of course, will raise the argument, under the "theory of the compact," that under Public Law 600 Puerto Ricans abdicated any claim over the area of foreign relations. In effect, the same situation applies to the rest of the states as regards executive agreements, which do not follow the two-house process. However, at least they have the right to vote for the president.

In the past, Carl Friedrich dismissed the argument that through the approval of laws 600 and 447, Puerto Ricans renounced any preexistent claim to have a say in some matters. This has been referred to as "generic consent." In his opinion, that would constitute a negation of the principle of government by consent. I agree that it was so in 1954 when Professor Friedrich wrote "La Nueva Constitución de Puerto Rico." See Serrano Geyls, supra note 31, vol. 1, at 560. It is even more so today, forty-four years later.

68   The argument also may cut both ways. Although going back to Simón Bolívar there has been a historically documented interest regarding independence on the part of many Latin American leaders, statehooders still may raise the argument that shutting the doors closed for Puerto Rican statehood will be interpreted by Latin Americans as evidence of the unwillingness of the United States to really look at Latin Americans as equals. No one really knows how new Latin American leaders, many of them technocrats educated in the United States, and less ideologically oriented than in the past, will respond to any U.S. decision.

69   There is no doubt that the benefits that the new capacity to enter into international economic agreements would provide for Puerto Rico would have to be weighed against new potential losses. At least in theory, Puerto Rico may risk losing the weight of the bargaining power that

the U.S. presence represents at any bargaining table: the more the United States obtained at the table, the more it could distribute to its constituent units.

To analyze the issue in those terms is, however, to lose track of our argument. An authority that Puerto Rico may exert does not necessarily need to have as a counterpoint the loss of total authority over that area on the part of Washington. This is not a zero-sum proposition. In some occasions it may just represent a capacity to negotiate when Congress has not acted; in others it may mean absolute capacity to act over an area; and in still others it may imply joint and even trilateral or multilateral collaboration, both with Washington and foreign centers. We could not continue looking at Puerto Rico–U.S. relations in terms of exclusive sovereignties.

70   Charles Tiefer, "Free Trade Agreements and the New Federalism," *Minnesota Journal of Global Trade* 7 (1998): 45.

71   Ibid. at 48–54.

72   Ibid. at 52–72. See also *Barclays Bank v. Franchise Tax Bd.*, 512 U.S. 298 (1994); *Reeves, Inc. v. Stake*, 447 U.S. 429 (1980); *White v. Massachusetts Council of Construction Employers, Inc.*, 460 U.S. 204 (1983); *Big Country Foods, Inc. v. Board of Education*, 952 F.2d 1173 (9th Cir. 1992); *Wardair Canada, Inc. v. Florida Dept. of Revenue*, 477 U.S. 1 (1986); *Container Corp. of America v. Franchise Tax Bd.*, 463 U.S. 159 (1983); *Trojan Technologies, Inc. v. Pennsylvania*, 916 F.2d 903 (3d Cir. 1990) cert. denied 501 U.S. 1212 (1991).

73   Tiefer, ibid. at 46.

74   Tiefer describes the paradigm as follows: "[T]he new paradigm regarding federalism consists of a new form of 'weak' preemption in implementation following state 'partnering' in negotiation. In negotiating internationally on state issues, the President seeks volunteered concessions by the states and tailors his international proposals, negotiations, and actions to these state concessions. In this regard, the President functions partly as the national director of international relations and partly as a spokesperson and mediator for a league of sovereign states." Ibid. at 47.

75   Rudolf Geiger, "External Competences of the European Union and the Treaty-making Power of Its Member States," in "Symposium: NAFTA and the Expansion of Free Trade: Current Issues and Future Prospects," *Arizona Journal of International and Comparative Law* 14 (1997): 319.

76   L.R.A., "Las autonomías podrían participar en el Consejo de la Unión Europea," *El País Internacional*, Year XVI, #772, Madrid, Spain, March 9–18, 1998, at 9.

77   Ibid. The Popular Party had to abandon Mr. Matute's position as a result of the Socialist Party's support of the petition of the autonomous regions.

78   See Bruce Ackerman and David Golove, supra note 44. In reality, Ackerman and Golove's analysis refers to any kind of treaty. This particular article, however, appeared in the context of NAFTA and GATT's approval. It indirectly describes how this approval has impacted the foreign economic relations area.

79   Ibid. Some scholars often use the word *interchangeability* to refer to this characteristic of the paradigm. See, e.g., Ackerman and Golove, ibid.

80   The Civil War exception is particularly interesting for Puerto Rico. In the first place, prevalent social imagery during that period strongly influenced the vocabulary that the U.S. Supreme Court later used to manage the Puerto Rican imbroglio. See Rivera Ramos (1996), supra note 6, at 291. In addition, the Civil War defined in the United States a "constitutional moment," but more than that, opened the door for the "complete" integration of a U.S. national market.

The latter came about through the annihilation of one side's culture and economy by the other.

Contrary to what happened then, what I propose is a kind of cooperative enterprise, whereby Puerto Ricans may find their place in a global environment through both cooperation and competition with the United States, as this last country finds its way to a sustained global economy. The annihilation of Puerto Rico on the part of the United States, in any way, be it culturally or economically, consciously or by error, would constitute a very costly mistake.

81 In 1856, several years before the Civil War started, the federal government's budget expenditures equaled $69,751,000. See U.S. Department of Commerce, Bureau of Census, Bicentennial Edition—*Historical Statistics of the U.S.—Colonial Times to 1970*, part 2, series y-335-338, at 1104. In 1994, the most recent year from which we have statistics, it amounted to $1,630 billion; the U.S. Gross National Product in current dollars in 1995 was $7,297 billion dollars. See U.S. Department of Commerce, Economics and Statistics Administration, Bureau of the Census, Statistical Abstract of the United States (1997), at 298,838. The oldest statistics on GNP I could find were from the period 1869–1873, more than a decade and a half after the Civil War started. According to those figures the GNP amounted to $6.71 billion. See U.S. Department of Commerce, *Bureau of the Census with Cooperation of the Social Science Research Council* (Washington, D.C., 1960).

One has to realize that in the 1850s the United States was not one of the major world economies. Today the U.S. is the undisputed leader in terms of GNP.

82 See Chen, supra note 51; Eskridge and Ferejohn, supra note 51; Thomas Heller, "Legal Theory and the Political Economy of American Federalism," in *Integration through Law: Europe and the American Federal Experience*, ed. Mauro Cappelletti, Mónica Secombe, and Joseph Weiler (1986) vol. 1, bk. 1, at 254–79.

83 Robert F. Nagel of the University of Colorado explains that a number of scholars see radical potential in the Court's recent federalism decisions, and that some even consider them "revolutionary." See Robert F. Nagel, "Real Revolution," in "Symposium: New Frontiers of Federalism," *Georgia State University Law Review* 13 (1997): 985.

84 See Norman Redlich and David R. Lurie, "Federalism: A Surrogate for What Really Matters," in "Twentieth Annual Law Review Symposium—Fear and Federalism," *Ohio Northern University Law Review* 23 (1997): 1273.

85 See Edward L. Rubin, "The Fundamentality and Irrelevance of Federalism," in "Symposium," supra note 83 at 1009; Edward L. Rubin and Malcolm Feeley, "Federalism: Some Notes on a National Neurosis," *University of California Law Review* 41 (1994): 903.

86 See Friedman, supra note 50, at 1467. Of course Friedman's assessment does not incorporate cases subsequent to *García v. San Antonio Metropolitan Transit Authority*, 468 U.S. 528 (1985), which are in effect the actual symbols of the federalism revival. See *United States Term Limits, Inc. v. Thornton* 514 U.S. 779 (1995); *United States v. Lopez*, 514 U.S. 549 (1995); *Seminole Tribe v. Florida*, 517 U.S. 44 (1996); *City of Boerne v. Flores*, 521 U.S. 507 (1997).

87 See Friedman, ibid.; Tiefer, supra note 70; James T. O'Reilly, "Stop the World, We Want Our Own Labels: Treaties, State Voter Initiative Laws, and Federal Preemption," *University of Pennsylvania Journal of International Economic Law* 18 (1997): 617; Ronan Doherty, "Foreign Affairs v. Federalism: How State Control of Criminal Law Implicates Federal Responsibility under International Law," *Virginia Law Review* 82 (1996): 1281; Ackerman and Golove, supra note 44; Christine T. Milliken, "Incorporating Principles of Domestic Federalism within the

Framework of the World Trade Organization," *ASIL Proceedings*, April 7, 1995, at 327–34; Aponte Toro, supra note 48.

88   In the last few decades the Commonwealth established commercial offices in Germany, Argentina, Brazil, Chile, Costa Rica, Spain, and Mexico, as well as in some U.S. cities.

89   Peter J. Spiro, "New Players on the International Stage," *Hofstra Law and Policy Symposium* 2 (1997): 19.

90   Peter M. Senge, *The Fifth Discipline: The Art and Practice of the Learning Organization* (1990), at 61 ("Pushing harder and harder on familiar solutions, while fundamental problems persist or worsen, is a reliable indicator of nonsystemic thinking—what we often call the 'what we need here is a bigger hammer' syndrome.").

91   For interesting approaches to the issue of complexity, see Roger Lewin, *Complexity: Life at the Edge of Chaos* (1992); M. Mitchell Waldrop, *Complexity: The Emerging Science at the Edge of Order and Chaos* (1992); Stuart Kauffman, *At Home in the Universe: The Search for Laws of Self-Organization and Complexity* (1995). James N. Rosenau himself espouses the idea that there are limits even to the possibilities of the complexity framework. See James N. Rosenau, "Demasiados casos a la vez: La teoría de la complejidad y los asuntos mundiales," *Nueva Sociedad* 148 (1997): 70.

92   *United States Consitution*, art. I, sec. 8, cl. 3, gives Congress the authority to "regulate Commerce with foreign nations." Art. I, sec. 8, cl. 18 provides it with potential additional authority through the "Necessary and Proper Clause"; art. I, sec. 10 states:

>   No State shall enter into any Treaty, Alliance, or Confederation; grant Letters of Marque and Reprisal . . . No State shall, without the Consent of the Congress, lay any Imposts or Duties on Imports or Exports, except what may be absolutely necessary for executing its inspection Laws. . . . No State shall, without the Consent of Congress, lay any duty of Tonnage, keep Troops, or Ships of War in time of Peace, enter into any Agreement or Compact with another State, or with a foreign Power, or engage in War, unless actually invaded, or in such imminent Danger as will not admit of delay.

93   See Doherty, supra note 65.

94   Michael J. Baun, *An Imperfect Union—The Maastricht Treaty and the New Politics of European Integration* (1996), at 14. For a commentary referring both to the obstacles as well as the accomplishments of the European Union in the economic area, see Willem Molle, *The Economics of European Intergration: Theory, Practice, Policy* (1990), at 57–79.

95   Recently both the European Union and the North Atlantic Treaty Organization have had to address the issues regarding the incorporation of new entrants. See "E.U. Enlargement: 'First Wave' Screening Will Run to July, 1999," *European Report*, May 30, 1998.

96   Such are the kind of moments when a learning organization must show that it has the capacity to leave aside any "learning disability" it may have. It may be time for "metanoia," or a shift of mind. See Senge, supra note 90, at chap. 2.

97   See supra note 88. See also Rivera Ramos, supra note 60.

98   Milliken, supra note 87.

99   The first scenario will involve the type of participation that Spiro envisions in his article. See Spiro, supra note 89. See also Ruth Lapidoth, *Autonomy: Flexible Solutions to Ethnic Conflict* (1997), at 54. The second scenario, which will probably cover requests both of statehooders and some commonwealth supporters, will be played out in the framework Milliken describes. See Milliken, ibid.

100   It was in effect sovereign independent states that participated in the process of integration which took place in Europe. Sovereign states have been entering into different integration

schemes in North America (NAFTA), South America (MERCOSUR), Central America (Central America Integration System), and the Caribbean (Association of Caribbean States) in addition to the Andean Pact and others. Something similar has been taking place in Asia, and is probably going to begin soon in Africa. On Latin America, see Aponte Toro, supra note 59.

101 For an argument describing the way in which major states have in effect been further strengthened, see Sassen, supra note 3, at 25. Sassen explains that "global capital has made claims on national states, which have responded through the production of new forms of legality." In this context, corporate actors and states cooperate with each other and strengthen each other. "Views that characterize national states as simply losing significance fail to capture this very important fact, and reduce what is happening to a function of the global-national duality: what one wins, the other loses." She insists that national legal systems remain as the major, or crucial, institution through which guarantees of contract and property rights are enforced. Ibid.

102 See supra note 91.

103 On how this situation was played out in NAFTA's debates, see Aponte Toro, supra note 48. On the impact future economic agreements will have over states, see Friedman, supra note 50, at 1447–66.

104 I am not a "specialist" in constitutional law, and in no way do I want to enter the current debate on constitutional interpretation. Reading some of the court opinions on the *Insular Cases,* however, both concurring and dissenting, one may find similar views to mine as to the nature of constitutional interpretation in the Justices' opinions. Yet, our views on the particular cases are probably different. For an excellent analysis of the legal theory of the *Insular Cases,* as regards theories of interpretation and adjudication, contextuality, the judicial function, and the nature of rights, see Rivera Ramos (1996), supra note 6.

105 In particular, see Justice McKenna's dissent in *De Lima,* 182 U.S. 1, at 200.

106 Ackerman and Golove are explicit regarding the constitutional change toward interchangeability: "The intentions of the Framers have been redeemed—so long as we recognize that the relevant framers were the Americans who fought the Second World War and not those who fought the Revolution." Ackerman and Golove, supra note 44, at 803.

107 See *McCulloch v. Maryland,* 17 U.S. (4 Wheat.) 316 (1819); Benjamin Cardozo, *The Nature of the Judicial Process* (1921).

108 *Harris,* 446 U.S. 651.

109 For a critique of *Harris,* as well as of *Califano,* 435 U.S. 1, addressing invidious discrimination arguments, see Helfeld, supra note 28, at 461–62.

110 Ann Davidson, "Tax Sparing: a Question of Treasury Policy or Puerto Rican Politics?" *Tax Notes* 35 (May 25, 1987): 731, at 731–36.

111 Ibid.

112 Ibid. On "Most Favored Nation," see John H. Jackson, William J. Davey, and Alan O. Sykes Jr., *Legal Problems of International Economic Relations—Cases, Materials, and Text,* 3d ed. (1995), chap. 9.

113 Raoul Berger, *Federalism: The Founders' Design* (1987), chap. 3.

114 See *Gibbons v. Ogden,* 22 U.S. (9 Wheat.) 1, 199 (1824): "Congress is not empowered to tax for those purposes which are within the exclusive province of the states." As Raoul Berger finds, the recognition of a power to tax in the federal government caused a lot of controversy in the ratifying conventions. The founding fathers were well aware of the need to raise revenues in order to provide for armies and defense. Yet they took steps so that the right to tax could only

be exercised regarding the enumerated powers which the Constitution puts under the authority of Congress. See Berger, ibid.

For an article arguing for more federal control, see Daniel Shaviro, "An Economic and Political Look at Federalism in Taxation," *Michigan Law Review* 90 (1992): 895. Shaviro criticizes the conventional view exposed by Walter Hellerstein, quoting him: "Absent some pressing need for federal intervention . . . the states should be free to go their own way. Our constitutional system contemplates concurrent state and federal taxation, with considerable latitude accorded to the states in this domain." Ibid. at 896 and n. 5.

115 Ackerman, supra note 44; Ackerman and Golove, supra note 44.

116 Michla Pomerance asks the difficult question of what constitutes the "self" in "self-determination": "Is it Biafra or Nigeria? Northern Ireland, Ireland, or the United Kingdom together with Northern Ireland?" A. D'Amato, *International Law Anthology* (1994), at 254. A similar question may be asked of the United States–Puerto Rico relation. The argument that Puerto Ricans on the mainland should vote in a plebiscite, based on the idea that Puerto Ricans everywhere form one nation, raises additional questions, particularly if those Puerto Ricans expect to remain U.S. citizens. This would involve U.S. citizens potentially voting against U.S. sovereignty in Puerto Rico, but retaining their own citizenship and domestic political weight within the United States. A second question concerns how, procedurally, the United States would exercise a right to self-determination. A third concerns the role which the idea of a "compact" will play in this discussion. Consistent with the argument I am raising, Governor Kirk Fordice from Mississippi once called publicly for U.S. self-determination regarding the future of Puerto Rico through plebiscite votes. See Leonor Mulero, "Genera recelos la idea de la anexión," *El Nuevo Día,* August 5, 1998, at 6.

117 By the time of the approval of the Puerto Rican Federal Relations Act, through article 9 of that law, federal legislation not locally inapplicable was understood as applicable. Through that interpretation, many provisions from previous organic acts were found still in force. See 1 P.R. Laws Ann. § 59; 1 P.R. Laws Ann. § 158.

Former governor Rafael Hernández Colón has argued that free association could only be negotiated by Puerto Rico from the standpoint of independence. In the past, Governor Hernández Colón had argued that the status of free association guaranteed in the UN context the legality of commonwealth status, and that there was no need for a substantive transfer of powers before a noncolonial plebiscite took place. At that time, the opponents of commonwealth described his as a proposal for the transfer of authority "on paper."

If Hernández Colón's more recent argument is that the United States is not willing to accept any other form of free association than one negotiated from a separate sovereignty, he may be right in his assessment. In effect, that position finally found its way, through Resident Commissioner Romero's efforts, into the final bill on the plebiscite approved by the commonwealth legislature. If that is not Hernández Colón's argument, then he in effect has changed his previous position on the issue. Furthermore, he may be misreading what applicable international law today is, since the truth of the matter is that there are no clear UN guidelines in this area. Rafael Hernández Colón, *La nación de siglo a siglo y otros ensayos* (1998), at 48.

118 See Milliken, supra note 87.

119 Ibid.

120 Although that is my prediction in the short term, we must not underestimate the extent and degree of concern by states regarding new agreements.

121 That is so, irrespective of what *Carolene Products* may say. See *United States v. Carolene*

Products, Co., 304 U.S. 144 (1938). In this case the Supreme Court rejected a substantive due process challenge to a federal statute prohibiting the interstate shipment of "filled milk" on the grounds that the legislation rested upon a rational basis. But Justice Stone added a footnote suggesting that the Court would not be so deferential in the review of legislation "which restricts political processes" or "where prejudice against discrete and insular minorities may be a special condition, which tends seriously to curtail the operation of those political processes ordinarily to be relied upon to protect minorities, and which may call for a correspondingly more searching judicial inquiry." Ibid. at 152–53 n. 4.

122   International trade has increased dramatically as a result of recent agreements. See Raj Bhala, *International Trade Law: Cases and Materials* (1996), chap. 3 and xiv.

IV. Membership and Recognition

Law, Language, and Statehood: The Role of English in the Great State of Puerto Rico

José Julián Álvarez González

In 1998, the United States House of Representatives approved the "Young bill" by a one-vote majority.[1] That bill would have sponsored a plebiscite on Puerto Rico's political future. One of the alternatives was statehood. Thus, the United States began a process that could lead to a new state. Although the Senate failed to act on the Young bill and the Puerto Rico electorate thereafter refused to endorse statehood,[2] the issue will not become moot unless and until a final decision is taken concerning the political status of Puerto Rico. Any serious discussion of the prospect of statehood for Puerto Rico must address the single most important difference between that potential state and the first fifty: language.

Law and Reality: The "Official" Status of English in Puerto Rico

In a 1998 speech, the then-governor of Puerto Rico, Dr. Pedro J. Rosselló, stated that since 1902 both Spanish and English have been official languages of Puerto Rico.[3] This, however, does not reflect a sociological reality, but rather the peculiarities of Puerto Rican colonial politics.

ENGLISH IN PUERTO RICO: THE LAW
When the United States invaded it in 1898, as the Spanish-American War drew to a close,[4] Puerto Rico was a linguistically homogeneous society where few people spoke English.[5] There was no need for an official-language law. That need emerged—for the United States—after the invasion. Two years of military government saw English become a de facto official language. It was the language in which the military governors issued their general orders, as well as the native tongue of cabinet members. Congress's first organic act for Puerto Rico, the Foraker Act of 1900,[6] did not include an official-language provision. That dubious honor would come as a corollary to the colonial government of Puerto Rico created by that statute.[7]

The Foraker Act polarized the island's political parties. The pro-statehood Republican Party applauded it, while the autonomist Federal Party denounced it. The Federal boycott of the 1900 elections for the House of Delegates resulted in Republican control of all seats. This was the setting when on February 21, 1902, Spanish and English became official languages of Puerto Rico.[8] Since the governor and his cabinet were anglophones, the 1902 law was deemed necessary to allow them to function, as well as vital for the Americanization of Puerto Rico, a prime goal of colonial administrators.[9] The House of Delegates, dominated by pro-statehood delegates from 1900 until 1904, backed these efforts.[10]

The 1902 statute lasted until 1991. Then, when the United States Senate was considering Puerto Rico's political status, the governing pro-commonwealth Popular Democratic Party made Spanish the only official language, a measure which the pro-statehood forces opposed.[11] This may have been a strategic mistake. Puerto Rico, a homogeneous society,[12] does not need an official-language statute. The simple repeal of the 1902 statute would have sufficed. Making Spanish the sole official language only fueled partisan fires, without altering the sociological reality of the overwhelming predominance of Spanish. Upon returning to power in 1993, the pro-statehood New Progressive Party repealed the 1991 statute and again made both Spanish and English official languages.[13]

ENGLISH IN PUERTO RICO: THE REALITY

Spanish is the language of Puerto Rico.[14] Of the island's 3.8 million residents, 98.2 percent speak Spanish, 52.6 percent do not speak English at all, and 23.8 percent speak English "with difficulty."[15] At best, only 23.6 percent of the population is truly fluent in English.[16] Fluency in English, moreover, does not run along the lines of political status preferences, but rather reflects socioeconomic class and urban or rural dwelling.[17]

The 1902 statute exemplifies an abyss between law and reality. Spanish is the language of Commonwealth government proceedings: judicial,[18] legislative,[19] and executive.[20] At all public school levels, instruction is in Spanish pursuant to law, except for English-language courses.[21] While all formal proceedings in federal agencies are in English, Spanish translations are a fact of life.[22] Informal dealings with federal employees are usually conducted in Spanish, as most of them are native Puerto Ricans. Even in the federal District Court, whose formal business must be conducted in English pursuant to federal law,[23] judges and attorneys will often go into chambers to confer in Spanish.[24] In sum, the role of English as a language of government in Puerto Rico is negligible. It is essentially limited to some executive affairs and government forms, and to recording deeds in that language.[25] No one has a right to force the Commonwealth government to conduct a proceeding in English.

In the private realm, Spanish reigns, to the almost complete exclusion of English.[26] Politicians address crowds only in Spanish. Local cultural manifestations, such as literature, theater, and film, are almost exclusively in Spanish. Literature in English by island Puerto Ricans is uncommon, usually reserved for exportation. Hollywood movies are subtitled in Spanish. Although English is most often used in business affairs and in certain liberal professions, the influence of English in these contexts is similar to that felt throughout the Western world.[27] In spite of that influence, the language of the workplace is overwhelmingly Spanish.

That more than three-fourths of island Puerto Ricans are not fluent in English after a century of United States presence is not due to a collective genetic flaw. Undoubtedly, educational policies have had problems, but, besides the lack of need to master English in order to participate in Puerto Rican society, there may be a deeper factor at work. Many Puerto Ricans perceive English as a proxy for attempts at political and cultural domination, which have been resisted since 1898.[28] Even supporters of statehood evince their own version of this trait. They argue that the Spanish language and Puerto Rican culture are not negotiable[29] and refer to "*Jíbaro* Statehood," evoking the erstwhile Puerto Rican peasant. Some time ago, the most ardent exponents of this thesis were Resident Commissioner Carlos Romero Barceló and Governor Rosselló.[30] In recent years they have downplayed it.[31]

Self-Determination and the Official Status of English under Statehood

A long-standing debate in Puerto Rico centers on the role that English would play under statehood, if Puerto Rico became a state of the Union. As just shown, the prevailing view among statehood supporters is that statehood will not have a significant impact on Puerto Rico's culture or on the use of Spanish as *the* language of government, instruction, and common understanding. That view deserves critical attention, lest any voter be deceived by it, were it to prove unjustified. It also deserves the attention of the United States electorate and of its representatives in Congress, lest they be deemed to have embraced it tacitly, through their silence.

STATEHOOD AND THE REQUIREMENTS OF INTERNATIONAL LAW

In the past decade, Congress has reviewed the question of Puerto Rico's political status twice: in 1989–1991 and again in 1996–1998. These two congressional efforts to foster a solution to the status question have recognized Puerto Rico's right to self-determination under international law.[32] That is a welcome development. For too long the United States claimed that Puerto Rico was a domestic affair, off-limits to the world community.[33]

The relevant international legal standards are found in United Nations' Resolutions 1514(xv)[34] and 1541(xv).[35] Resolution 1514(xv) denounces colonialism, recognizes that all peoples have the right to self-determination and independence, calls for an end to all repressive measures against dependent peoples and for respect for their territorial integrity, and urges the transfer of all powers to the peoples of dependent territories. Resolution 1541(xv) sets principles to gauge whether member states must report on non-self-governing territories under their administration, an obligation that ceases whenever a territory attains one of three political conditions: full independence, integration to another nation-state, or free association to another nation-state.

Under any reasonable definition, Puerto Rico is a nation, with a separate culture, a distinct personality, and a characteristic language.[36] That is why Resolutions 1514(xv) and 1541(xv) apply to the Puerto Rican people. Even the avowed denier of the truism of Puerto Rican nationality Resident Commissioner Romero recently conceded that Puerto Rico may be a nation from a sociological but not a legal standpoint.[37] That was a telling admission. The concept of nationality *is* cultural and sociological.[38] Its legal relevance ensues when law ascribes some consequence to that concept, as the international law of self-determination does.

Congressional recognition of Puerto Rico's right to self-determination has important consequences for language under statehood. While Resolution 1541(xv) accepts integration as a legitimate solution to a colonial problem, it also requires that integration take place without any discrimination concerning fundamental rights,[39] and only after the subject territory has "attained an advanced stage of self-government"[40] and its people act in an "informed and democratic process,"[41] "with full knowledge of the change in their status."[42] Thus it is crucial that a plebiscite ballot on the status of Puerto Rico clearly explain the consequences of statehood for Spanish as a language of government.

STATEHOOD, INTERNATIONAL LAW, AND CONGRESS:
AN EXERCISE IN AVOIDANCE

The statehood option, as framed in the two recent congressional processes on Puerto Rico, does not comply with these principles of international law.

The 1989–1991 process did not comply by studied silence; the 1998 process, by insufficient specification.

In the 1989–1991 process, statehood advocates requested that the plebiscite bill expressly recognize that Spanish would be an official language of a state of Puerto Rico.[43] The then-Chairman of the Senate Committee on Energy and Natural Resources, Senator J. Bennett Johnston, rejected that proposal, claiming that it was better to "just be silent on the question, just leave it out altogether."[44] On such an important issue for the overwhelming majority of Puerto Ricans, however, silence is inadmissible. Johnston argued that addressing the language issue could lead federal legislators to conclude that Puerto Rico is too distinct and separate to join the Union.[45] That is precisely why silence on that issue, rather than being golden, would be fraudulent. In the end, opposition to statehood, particularly because of linguistic and cultural issues, derailed the 1989–1991 process.[46]

In 1998, Rep. Gerald Solomon (R-N.Y.), then-Chairman of the Rules Committee and an official-English supporter, forced the House to address this issue. He required an open debate on the Young bill, where he and others could present amendments.[47] While his amendment to make English the official language of government in the United States was defeated, a substitute amendment was approved instead.[48]

That amendment, incorporated into the bill approved by the House, devotes three provisions to language. First, section 3(b), states that under statehood "the official English language requirements of the Federal Government shall apply to Puerto Rico in the same manner and to the same extent as throughout the United States."[49] Second, section 3(c), states that "[i]t is in the best interest of the [United States] for Puerto Rico to promote the teaching of English as *the* language of opportunity and empowerment in the United States in order to enable students in public schools to achieve English language proficiency by the age of 10."[50] Lastly, section 4 requires that in the event of a vote for statehood, the president shall submit to Congress a transition plan, which "*shall* . . . include proposals and incentives . . . including teaching *in* English in public schools [and] promote the use of English by the United States citizens in Puerto Rico in order to ensure . . . efficiency in the conduct and coordination of the official business activities of the Federal and State Governments."[51]

It appears that the House is suggesting that Spanish cannot be *the* language of instruction in a state of Puerto Rico,[52] and that efficient coordination requires that Spanish *not* be *the* language of government in Puerto

Rico. If that is the intent of Congress, it should appear clearly on the ballot, in order to comply with international law and to avoid voter confusion.

Language Requirements and the Federal Constitution

The Constitution is silent concerning a language of government. English, however, is the de facto national language of the United States.[53] In the last two decades a movement has been afloat to make English the official language of government. At the federal level, various constitutional amendments have been proposed.[54] Such efforts, as yet unsuccessful, began in 1981 and have not abated.

It has been suggested that this movement will never succeed at the federal level.[55] Yet there is no evidence that it is dying; quite the contrary is the case, as even its opponents admit.[56] The success of this drive at the state level has been swift and dramatic. In 1981, only two states had official-language laws.[57] By 1998, English was an official language of twenty-two states.[58] Other states are weighing similar measures.[59] Moreover, the issue of the constitutionality of official-English statutes has attracted considerable attention in academic journals.[60]

Some argue that a federal law which attempted to force the Puerto Rican government to function in English would be unconstitutional.[61] They claim that making an English-language requirement a condition for statehood would violate the equal footing doctrine; that no independent federal powers exist to justify a federal official-language statute applicable to states; and that such a statute would violate state sovereignty as well as individual rights to equal protection of the laws and freedom of expression.[62] I find no solace in these arguments, which do not seem so obviously right as to provide an adequate assurance of the protection of Spanish under statehood.[63] Many such arguments rely on unstable 5–4 Supreme Court majorities.[64] No people should rest their future on constitutional quicksand.

THE EQUAL FOOTING DOCTRINE

A judicial creation originating in a 1911 decision concerning the site of the capital of Oklahoma,[65] the equal footing doctrine holds that, in admitting a state, Congress may not impose conditions that would place it "upon a plane of inequality with its sister States in the Union."[66] There is, however, a significant difference between the site of a state capital and the language its government uses to communicate with the public.[67] Where to locate a state capital is an eminently local decision, which should not concern the federal government or other states. The choice of which language a state government communicates in with its citizens, citizens of other states, and legally admitted aliens involves important issues of federalism that interest the whole nation, since it may affect interstate commerce, the effective right of interstate travel, and the privileges and immunities of United States citizenship.[68]

Congress has imposed English-language requirements on new states four times: Louisiana in 1811,[69] Oklahoma in 1906,[70] and New Mexico and Arizona in 1910,[71] all states with a substantial number of non-English speakers.[72] Evidently, Congress believes that the plane of equality among the states presupposes a common language. It seems unlikely that the Supreme Court would intervene to invalidate whatever decision Congress made on government language in a state of Puerto Rico.[73]

The equal footing argument may ultimately backfire. Faced with a threat that an English-language condition would be assailed *after* statehood,[74] Congress could decide to follow historical practice and refuse to consider statehood for Puerto Rico until there is an English-speaking majority on the island.[75] Senator Daniel Patrick Moynihan has written concerning Puerto Rico:

> Congressional resistance [to a plebiscite which includes statehood as an alternative] arises largely from the question of whether the island should have the option to choose statehood whilst retaining Spanish as an official language. In two centuries, the United States Congress has admitted thirty-seven new states to the original union of thirteen. But always a stated or unstated condition was that English be the official language. Louisiana, for example, might and did retain the *Code Napoléon,* but trials were to be in English. This position may seem arbitrary, but it is defensible. *E pluribus unum.*[76]

OTHER FEDERAL POWERS AND STATE SOVEREIGNTY

Those who rely on the equal footing doctrine admit that a condition to statehood would be valid if Congress has independent powers over the subject.[77] But they argue that Congress lacks such powers, especially under the Commerce Clause, and that the principle of state sovereignty would preclude a language requirement. Such arguments, however, would read into the Constitution the sovereign right of every state to impose upon its sisters a multilingual confederation. Citizens of the United States need not be motivated by nativist or racist impulses[78] in order to oppose such a result.[79]

The Commerce Clause and state sovereignty arguments are two sides of the same coin.[80] If the Commerce Clause does not authorize Congress to enact a language of government applicable to all states, its enactment would infringe upon state sovereignty. However, the state of the law in this area is highly unstable.[81] If jurists cannot make up their minds, it is not appropriate to ask Puerto Rican voters to make such a momentous decision against this background of absolute uncertainty.

Other federal powers should not be ignored. The Congressional Research Service has failed to address Congress's power under section 5 of the Fourteenth Amendment[82] or its spending power to create conditional grant programs.[83] The CRS recognizes that "[t]he setting of language policies *per se* is not beyond Congress' reach,"[84] and cites several congressional actions, anchored on these two federal powers, which have resisted constitutional attack.[85] However, it does not deal adequately with these two potential moorings for a federal language law.

Katzenbach v. Morgan[86] held in 1966 that section 5 of the Fourteenth Amendment enabled Congress to set certain language policies. Congress had prohibited state English literacy requirements as applied to persons who completed the sixth grade in Puerto Rico. But *Morgan* does not prohibit Congress from setting uniform English literacy requirements.[87] It has been argued that Congress may act under this power to establish a national language of government, in order to enforce the privileges and immunities of national citizenship and the right of interstate travel.[88] Thus an analysis of section 5 powers may prove crucial in the enactment of a federal language law.

Concerning conditional grants, the Court has interpreted the spending power[89] broadly, upholding statutory conditions on the receipt of federal funds.[90] It has held that such conditions do not violate state sovereignty, since the states may reject the funds.[91] This question is crucial for Puerto Rico. For example, the Elementary and Secondary Education Act,[92] which funds public education, is a conditional grant program.[93] If Congress were to add a requirement on language of instruction, it would radically alter a central factor in the preservation of Puerto Rican culture and identity.[94] It seems extremely unlikely that a state of Puerto Rico would decide to forgo all federal aid and finance its costly public school system entirely out of its own treasury.

INDIVIDUAL RIGHTS

While federalism-based arguments exclusively concern a federal statute that attempted to impose English as the language of government of a state or of all states, individual-rights arguments are equally applicable to federal and state attempts to legislate an official language.

Equal protection of the law. The typical equal-protection arguments against a federal official-English statute hinge decisively on application of some kind of heightened scrutiny. That would require the Supreme Court to do something that it has consistently avoided for decades: find a new suspect class, in this case composed of people who speak languages other than English.[95] Members of that class have lost all claims to a right to government communications in their native tongues or to participation in governmental affairs in those tongues.[96]

Thus equal protection is not a propitious argument against language laws.[97] It would be an ironic twist if after refusing to find that Puerto Rican residents are a suspect class for purposes of their exclusion from certain welfare programs,[98] the Supreme Court were to find otherwise concerning their inclusion in a federal statute of general applicability.

Freedom of expression. Another argument against official-English laws relies on freedom of expression. The Ninth Circuit relied primarily on this ground to invalidate Arizona's constitutional provision on official language[99] in the *en banc* 6–5 *Yñiguez* decision that the Supreme Court vacated on a mootness rationale.[100] Freedom of expression was also the principal ground in the Arizona Supreme Court's subsequent invalidation of that provision.[101] Both courts termed the provision, which orders all state employees to "act in English and no other language,"[102] "by far the most restrictively worded official-English law to date."[103] Both courts struck it down because it inhibited too much speech.[104]

The First Amendment analysis in both decisions is problematic. First, both courts held that choice of language is speech, not conduct or symbolic speech, thus clearing the way for application of the strongest First Amendment standards.[105] However, neither decision identified a particular message against which the Arizona provision was directed. There is a crucial difference between regulating specific words that carry a communicative impact and regulating the language used irrespective of its message. The Arizona provision could be characterized as a manner restriction, not directed at any particular message, and therefore subject to less stringent First Amendment review.[106]

Most importantly, both decisions emphasize the narrowness of their holding, which should not satisfy any Puerto Rican who claims that language and culture are not negotiable. In *Yñiguez* the Ninth Circuit refused to find an affirmative right to government communications in native tongues.[107] *Ruiz* agrees, and goes further, stressing that Arizona need not "provide any service in a language other than English,"[108] and that no "governmental entity in Arizona has a constitutional obligation to provide services in languages other than English, except, of course, to the extent required by federal law."[109] *Ruiz* also (1) assumes the validity of the enabling act requirements that Arizona public schools operate in English and that all state officers and legislators be functional in that language;[110] (2) argues that if the Arizona provision were similar to less restrictive provisions in other states, "it might well have passed constitutional muster;"[111] and (3) assumes "that the government may, under certain circumstances and for appropriate reasons, restrict public employees from using non-English languages to communicate while performing their duties,"[112] but asserts that the vice of the Arizona provision is that its "reach is too broad."[113]

In sum, the vindication in *Yñiguez* and *Ruiz* of the rights of non-English speakers does not transform them into full-fledged members of the Arizona political community. They can be excluded from public office or employment and from jury duty. They have no right to receive written governmental communications in their native tongue. Their sole "right" is to have that meaningless document explained to them in their native tongue, but only if they are able to find some state employee who is able and willing to speak that language.

Only the recognition of a constitutional right to governmental services in native tongues would lend coherence to the *Yñiguez* and *Ruiz* holdings, but such a development seems highly unlikely in the foreseeable future. If *Yñiguez* and *Ruiz* are the best that courts can do to invalidate a state official-English provision, I would not be confident that such provisions, or a comparable federal statute, would find a similar fate at the Supreme Court. Moreover, the emphasis in both decisions on the extreme restrictions of Arizona's provision suggests that even if the First Amendment rationale is sound, it could be unavailable for other types of language statutes.[114]

Even if the Supreme Court endorsed the *Yñiguez* and *Ruiz* rationales, they could produce unexpected results in the Puerto Rican context. If Congress admits Puerto Rico into the Union with no language restrictions and if Puerto Rico courts continue holding that local law does not require that a proceeding be conducted in any language but Spanish, what would be the federal constitutional rights of non-Spanish-speaking United States citizens in Puerto Rico? According to both *Yñiguez* and *Ruiz*, they only would have the constitutional right to receive governmental information in English *if* they could find a Puerto Rican public employee who was able and willing to provide it. *E pluribus unum*?

OFFICIAL ENGLISH AND PUERTO RICO: RECAPITULATION

The chances of enactment of a declaration of English as the official language of government in the United States seem good in the long run, in view of its broad electoral support.[115] If that declaration occurs through a federal statute, there is great uncertainty as to whether the Supreme Court would uphold it. The people of Puerto Rico should not be forced to place their vernacular on this table of constitutional roulette. Moreover, if a federal statute were held invalid, the Constitution may be amended, as many have urged.[116] Against that dealer's blackjack, no insurance is available.[117]

In the long run, the chances for success of the amendment route increase each time another state approves an official-English statute. That is the strategy of its supporters, whose initial attempts at a constitutional amendment failed.[118] If approved, that amendment would pose a formidable obstacle to the survival of Spanish as the principal language of Puerto Rico.

To force Puerto Ricans to gamble, without adequate knowledge and understanding, on a matter so essential to their integrity as a people is neither "informed consent" nor "full knowledge of the change in their status," as Resolution 1541(xv) requires. The United States must resolve this issue of language rights before Puerto Rico is asked to vote on whether to join the Union. Puerto Rico already was a guinea pig in a United States constitutional experiment, as the *Insular Cases* clearly show.[119] It is simply unconscionable to subject it to another such experiment.

Quebec, Puerto Rico, and Bilingualism in the United States

Supporters of official English, arguing against Puerto Rican statehood, have pointed to Quebec to buttress their claim that the United States should not take on a problem that has vexed Canada since its birth.[120] Supporters of Puerto Rican independence also have evoked Quebec to underscore the uniqueness of Puerto Rican statehood.[121] Others have replied that millions of Spanish speakers in the United States prove that the Quebec analogy is fallacious.[122] In this debate, those who stress the similarities between Puerto Rico and Quebec are on firmer ground.

Quebec's geographic and economic position make it a much more important issue in Canadian politics than Puerto Rico could ever aspire to be for the United States.[123] But from a sociological standpoint, the predominance of Spanish in Puerto Rico is even stronger than that of French in Quebec, while bilingualism is more pervasive in Quebec than in Puerto

Rico.[124] And the sense of separate identity of Puerto Ricans considerably exceeds that of the Québecois.[125]

The importance of English in Quebec is also due to the presence of 800,000 anglophones, immigrants from the rest of Canada and from other countries, who hold a major share of the means of production.[126] Canada has "colonized" Quebec similarly, although not as extensively, as the United States colonized territories where many non-English speakers lived, such as Louisiana, Hawaii, and New Mexico.[127] A small island with a world-record population density, Puerto Rico has never been open to such colonization, and most probably never will be.[128] Its small segment of anglophones cannot assume the role that United States citizens played in controlling the economic and political life of the territories, or even the role that anglophone Canadians have played in Quebec.

Some have claimed that the persistence of minority languages in the United States proves that Puerto Rican statehood would not present a different problem.[129] That is a serious misconception. Bilingual education programs in the United States are transitional; their aim is to permit students to master English as soon as possible.[130] No federal program exists to permit students to maintain their native tongue, and no court decision has ever held that there is a constitutional right to such a program.[131] That is worlds apart from the situation of French in Quebec and of Spanish in Puerto Rico.

More importantly, what statehood leaders claim is not that Puerto Ricans will be able to continue speaking Spanish at home and have regular Spanish classes at school, but that the principal language of government, instruction, and common understanding in a state of Puerto Rico will be Spanish. No linguistic community in the United States is making such a claim; of those who did make it in the past, none succeeded.[132] Hispanic communities in the United States lack political and cultural cohesion, and the rate of anglicization of their newer generations parallels that of other minorities.[133] If realized, the Puerto Rico statehood leaders' claims would challenge the *e pluribus unum* notion of the United States. However, if poststatehood political realities turn out to be less rosy, Puerto Rico as we know it might be doomed.

I do not assume that law will overpower culture, but neither can I assume the opposite. Their relationship is one of reciprocal influence.[134] I am concerned that the influence of a federal language law over Spanish in Puerto Rico would be sufficiently substantial in the long run as to present an independent reason against statehood. Even if such a law did not displace

Spanish as the main vehicle of private communications, it would sufficiently affect Puerto Rican culture and identity to change it in ways that are unacceptable to the overwhelming majority of Puerto Ricans. Such a law would certainly make English truly an official language of government and would allow anglophones to demand that state functions be conducted in that language.[135]

Additionally, one cannot view the impact of law over culture in isolation. There are other events, besides a statute, that may affect the preservation of Spanish in Puerto Rico. Some of these are already occurring, and statehood would only accelerate them—to wit, extensive cable TV penetration, education of children of the elite in anglophone private schools, and return migration of mainland Puerto Ricans, whose offspring mostly speak only English.[136] As long as Puerto Rico has some control over the language of government and public instruction, these factors by themselves may not prove decisive. Without such control, however, the prospect may be quite different.

The pervasive worldwide influence of English is undeniable. But that influence has not induced other societies to adopt English as their main vehicle of government communication, to the detriment of their vernacular. While no one contests that Puerto Ricans should have the opportunity to learn English, it is an entirely different proposition to level the road for a future displacement of one language over another.

The failure of the United States in its attempt to impose English on Puerto Rico during the first fifty years of this century does not prove that it is impossible.[137] Although statehooders supported such plans,[138] they were not a majority. For the majority the issue was one of *them*—the Americans— against *us* Puerto Ricans.[139] If statehooders become a majority, this will present a scenario more conducive to the imposition of English.

Self-Determination for Puerto Rico and for the United States

The decision to admit a state whose culture, language, and way of life are very different is as momentous for the United States as for Puerto Rico. It calls for an ample debate, larger than that of 1898.[140] It is perplexing that the prospect of Puerto Rican statehood is almost completely ignored in the current debate over language policy in the United States, though such an event could radically alter the terms of that debate.

The people of the United States must address a myriad of questions. Do culture and language matter in structuring a political organization? Are modern federations whose components have diverse cultural and linguistic traits truly similar to American federalism? If not, is the difference related to those divergent cultural and linguistic traits? If it is, does that mean that a federation whose components exhibit such contrasting traits *must* be looser and less centralized than that of the United States? Is the United States ready and committed to redefine its notion of federalism? Would a state of Puerto Rico only be a step in a larger political reorganization in the Americas? Is the United States contemplating this?[141]

Or does the United States believe that modern multilingual and multi-cultural federations will eventually assume an integration more closely re-sembling its own? Does it believe that the relationship between Scotland, Lombardy, Flanders, and Catalonia will in time resemble that of California, Mississippi, Iowa, and Vermont? Does it predict that cultural and linguistic differences between the fifty states and Puerto Rico will wane after state-hood or will prove to be politically insignificant? Do Puerto Ricans share that belief? Is it important whether they share it? What would be the conse-quence of an erroneous prediction by the United States or by Puerto Rico?

However it answers these and other questions,[142] the United States *must* spell out, much more clearly than it has, its expectation concerning lan-guage in Puerto Rico.[143] If it is expected and welcomed that a state of Puerto Rico may continue communicating with its residents in Spanish and that no one will have a right to *force* that government to function in English, aside from translations in the penal and like contexts, the plebiscite ballot should so state. However, if the expectation is otherwise, which seems to be the convoluted message of the Young bill, that also should be spelled out clearly in the ballot. Only then will there be a true process of self-determination, for both parties.

Conclusion: Language, Statehood, and the Specter of Secession

A defective process of self-determination which led to statehood would be a recipe for certain trouble in the future. But even an adequate process does not guarantee everlasting tranquility. Although it has been disputed, I sub-scribe to the view that the right to self-determination is not extinguished once exercised.[144] Many writers—perhaps already a majority—argue that secession may be a valid exercise of self-determination in appropriate circumstances.[145]

The leader of the Puerto Rican independence movement has argued for a right to secession after statehood.[146] If statehood does not prove to be the panacea that its supporters preach, or if their linguistic and cultural claims prove unrealizable, other sectors of the Puerto Rican society may demand another exercise of self-determination. Even under some more restrictive views on the international right to secession, the people of Puerto Rico have a much better normative claim to the territory that comprises their small island archipelago than the descendants of those who, by invading it in 1898, "tainted [the situation] with the 'original sin' of colonialism."[147] Would the United States refuse to recognize that claim? Would it bombard San Juan in the twenty-first century?

The issue of language in Puerto Rico—under statehood or under any form of relationship with the United States—is very serious, as serious as the issue of Puerto Rican statehood itself. It will not go away through inattention or neglect. After one hundred years of United States neglect of Puerto Rico—benign or not—that should be abundantly clear.

Notes

This is a substantially abridged version of an article published in *Law and Inequality Journal* 17 (1999): 359, which in turn was an expanded and footnoted version of the address the author delivered at the Foreign in a Domestic Sense Conference (Yale Law School, March 27–29, 1998).

1   *United States–Puerto Rico Political Status Act,* H.R. 856, 105th Cong., 2d sess. (1998).

2   On December 13, 1998, the pro-statehood government of Puerto Rico held a referendum among five alternatives: (1) commonwealth, defined as a colonial status; (2) free association; (3) statehood; (4) independence; and (5) none of the above. "None of the above," defended by the pro-commonwealth Popular Democratic Party, garnered a majority of the vote (50.2 percent), followed by statehood (46.5 percent), independence (2.5 percent), free association (0.3 percent), and colonial commonwealth (0.1 percent). John Marino, " 'None of the Above' Wins," *San Juan Star,* December 14, 1998, at 5.

3   Address at the Foreign in a Domestic Sense Conference, supra note 1, item three (on file with author).

4   Concerning that war, see generally Ángel Rivero, *Crónica de la Guerra Hispanoamericana en Puerto Rico* (1922); Julius W. Pratt, *Expansionists of 1898* (1936), at 1; José Trías Monge, *Historia Constitucional de Puerto Rico,* vol. 1 (1980), at 144; José Trías Monge, *Puerto Rico: The Trials of the Oldest Colony in the World* (1997), at 21–29.

5   See María M. López Laguerre, *El Bilingüismo en Puerto Rico* (1989), at 8.

6   Act of April 12, 1900, *U.S. Statutes at Large* 31 (1900): 77.

7   Under the Foraker Act, the president, with the advice and consent of the Senate, appointed the governor, the judges of the Supreme Court, and the members of the upper house of the legislative assembly (the Executive Council). Only the lower house, the House of Delegates, was an elective body. José Julián Álvarez González, "The Protection of Civil Rights in Puerto Rico," *Arizona Journal of International and Comparative Law* 6 (1989): 68, at 91 and n. 12.

8   Law of February 21, 1902, 1 P.R. Laws Ann. § 51 (1982), repealed; Law No. 4 of April 5, 1991, 1 P.R.

Laws Ann. § 56 (Supp. 1993), repealed; Law No. 1 of January 28, 1993, 1 P.R. Laws Ann. § 59 (Supp. 1997). The English text of this last statute may be found in PR-Legis 1 (1993) (Westlaw).

The 1902 Act provided: "In all the departments of the insular government and in all the courts of this island, and in all public offices the English language and the Spanish language shall be used indiscriminately; and, when necessary, translations and oral interpretations shall be made from one language to the other so that all parties interested may understand any proceedings or communications made therein."

9   See Trías Monge (1997), supra note 4, at 55.

10   Ibid. at 52–60.

11   Law No. 4 of April 5, 1991, 1 P.R. Laws Ann. § 56 (Supp. 1993), repealed. See Edgardo Meléndez, *Movimiento Anexionista en Puerto Rico* (1993), at 275–77. See also Carmelo Delgado Cintrón, ed., *El Debate Legislativo sobre las Leyes del Idioma en Puerto Rico* (1994), especially Luis Muñiz Argüelles, "The Status of Languages in Puerto Rico," at 69–82.

12   Law No. 4 of April 5, 1991 (Statement of Motives), PR-Legis 4 (1991) (Westlaw).

13   Act No. 1 of January 28, 1993, PR-Legis 1 (1993) (Westlaw).

14   This section relies on my personal knowledge and on Muñiz Argüelles, supra note 11; Raúl Serrano Geyls and Carlos Gorrín Peralta, "Puerto Rico y la Estadidad: Problemas Constitucionales," *Revista del Colegio de Abogados de Puerto Rico* 42 (1981): 1.

15   U.S. Dept. of Commerce, Bureau of the Census, *1990 Census of Population—Social and Economic Characteristics—Puerto Rico* (1993), at 46 [hereinafter Census].

16   Ibid.

17   Ibid. at 32, 71. The Census statistics are confirmed in a 1993 private study. See "Resumen del Estudio del Ateneo Puertorriqueño Respecto al Uso, Dominio y Preferencia de los Idiomas Español e Inglés en Puerto Rico" [hereinafter *Ateneo Study*], in Delgado Cintrón, supra note 11, at 83–84.

18   As held by the Puerto Rico Supreme Court in spite of the 1902 statute. See *People v. Superior Court*, 92 P.R.R. 580, 588–89 (1965) (rejecting right to trial in English, holding that "the language of the Puerto Rican people . . . has been and continues to be Spanish . . . and that is a reality that cannot be changed by any law"). See also P.R. R. Crim. P. 96(d) (criminal jurors must speak Spanish); P.R. R. Civ. P. 8.5 (all documents must be in Spanish). The pro-statehood legislature of Puerto Rico endorsed *People v. Superior Court* when it restored the official status of English in 1993. Act No. 1 of January 28, 1993, PR-Legis 1 (1993) (Westlaw) (Statement of Motives).

Under Puerto Rican law, anyone who does not speak Spanish will need an interpreter to testify. The state will provide interpreters only to criminal defendants. *People v. Superior Court*, 92 P.R.R. at 590. See also *Jackson v. Cintrón García*, 665 F.2d 395 (1st Cir. 1981) (criminal trial in Spanish with right to a translation satisfies due process).

19   Although the Puerto Rico Constitution requires legislators to be literate in Spanish *or* in English (P.R. Constitution, art. II, sec. 5), modern legislators never use English, save for isolated instances in which some have sought to show their support for statehood. See, e.g., Pepo García, "Llega el 'English only' al Senado," *El Nuevo Día*, April 23, 1997, at 14 (Senator Kenneth McClintock-Hernández took the floor in English to defend a resolution in that language).

20   In the executive branch there are some exceptions to this norm, but they are both rare and of minor importance. For a collection of such exceptions, see Serrano Geyls and Gorrín Peralta, supra note 14, at 43–46.

21   See Law No. 68 of August 28, 1990, art. 1.02, ¶ 3, 1990 Leyes de Puerto Rico 364, PR-Legis 3RS 68

(1990) (Westlaw) ("It is hereby provided that education shall be imparted in Spanish, the vernacular language. English shall be taught as a second language."). This provision codified a 1949 administrative policy, which had reversed a 1905 policy that attempted to impose English as the language of instruction, pursuant to the Americanization goal. The legislature expressly reaffirmed the Spanish instruction policy when it restored the official language status of English in 1993. *See* Law No. 1 of January 28, 1993, PR-Legis 1 (1993) (Westlaw) (Statement of Motives).

For a broader discussion of this subject, see, e.g., Aida Negrón de Montilla, *Americanization in Puerto Rico and the Public-School System: 1900–1930* (1971); Dennis Baron, *The English-Only Question: An Official Language for Americans?* (1990), at 166–70.

There is bilingual education in some public classrooms, a practice which originally sought to develop the Spanish-language proficiency of anglophones. This was a mandate of Congress. The 1978 amendments to the Bilingual Education Act provided that Puerto Rico could serve the needs of students with limited proficiency in Spanish. See Pub. L. 95-561 of November 1, 1978, § 721(d), *U.S. Statutes at Large* 92 (1978): 2275. Recently, there have been a few, localized experiments with English immersion laboratories. See P.R. Dept. of Education, *Project for the Development of a Bilingual Citizen* (1997). It is too early to evaluate their chances for success.

22 See Serrano Geyls and Gorrín Peralta, supra note 14, at 48–50. In most agencies there are Spanish versions of the standard English language forms.

23 *Puerto Rico Federal Relations Act,* § 42, *U.S. Code* 48 (1995) § 864.

24 Muñiz Argüelles, supra note 11, at 79.

25 Concerning the latter activity, see 30 P.R. Laws Ann. § 2210 (1993).

26 The pro-statehood legislature also admitted this in 1993: "Through this measure, the Legislatures does not pretend to establish by legislative fiat, a condition of bilingualism alien to the everyday reality of the Puerto Rican People." Law No. 1 of January 28, 1993, PR-Legis 1 (1993) (Westlaw) (Statement of Motives).

27 D. Baron, supra note 21, at 177–79.

28 See, e.g., Trías Monge (1997), supra note 4 at 86; D. Baron, supra note 21, at 170, 197.

29 In 1976, the statehood party stated this on page 1 of its platform. Reece B. Bothwell, *Puerto Rico: Cien Años de Lucha Política* (1979), at 1293. In 1984, that party approved a resolution demanding that Spanish be the official language of any state of Puerto Rico, declaring that "Spanish language and culture will not be a matter of negotiation upon [Puerto Rico's] request for admission as the 51st State of the Union," and announcing that under statehood "education will still be offered in Spanish, and English will be taught, as well as other languages." Laurence H. Tribe, "Memorandum of Law Re: NPP Statehood Resolutions," at 20 (October 12, 1984) (co-authored, on behalf of the Popular Democratic Party, with the law firm of Covington & Burling) (on file with author).

30 For Romero's views, see Carlos Romero Barceló, *La Estadidad Es para los Pobres* (1976), at 13; Carlos Romero Barceló, "Puerto Rico, U.S.A.: The Case for Statehood," *Foreign Affairs* 59 (1980): 60, at 60, 64, 65, 69, 72, 78. For Rosselló's, see *Ponencia del Dr. Pedro J. Rosselló,* in Delgado Cintrón, supra note 11, at 395–96 ("Spanish is not negotiable under any circumstance or political change.") (my translation).

31 See Meléndez, supra note 11, at 270–71, 276 n. 26.

32 S. 712, 101st Cong., 2d sess., as preliminarily approved by the Senate Committee on Energy and Natural Resources on September 6, 1990, Report 101–20, § 1(1); H.R. 856, supra note 1, §§ 2(6)–(9), 3.

33   See Trías Monge (1997), supra note 4, at 136–40.

34   15 UN GAOR Supp. (No. 16), at 66, UN Doc. A/4684 (1960).

35   15 UN GAOR Supp. (No. 16), at 29, UN Doc. A/4684 (1960).

36   José Julián Álvarez González, "The Empire Strikes Out: Congressional Ruminations on the Citizenship Status of Puerto Ricans," *Harvard Journal on Legislation* 27 (1990): 309, at 313 n. 14. See also Rubén Berríos Martínez, "Puerto Rico's Decolonization," *Foreign Affairs* 76 (1997): 100, at 102–3. For similar arguments by two sitting Justices of the Supreme Court of Puerto Rico, see *De Paz Lisk v. Aponte Roque*, 124 D.P.R. 472, 507 (1989) (Negrón García, J.), and *Ramírez de Ferrer v. Mari Brás*, 97 J.T.S. 134, 208 (1997) (Hernández Denton, J.).

37   According to Romero, "Puerto Rico in geopolitical terms is not a nation. One might consider Puerto Rico a nation in *sociological* terms, but not in geopolitical position. We are a *community*." *Cong. Rec.*, 105th Cong., 2d sess. (March 4, 1998): H829 (emphasis added). Romero's concept of "community" is curious. No other "community" in the United States has an international legal right to self-determination, except, perhaps, the original inhabitants of the several states and territories. See, e.g., Raidza Torres, "The Rights of Indigenous Populations: The Emerging International Norm," *Yale Journal of International Law* 16 (1991): 127, at 156.

      For other similarities between Puerto Ricans and Native Americans, see Álvarez González, supra note 36, at 313 n. 14. One of these concerns language. The move to educate Native Americans exclusively in English, see Michael DiChiara, Note, "A Modern Day Myth: The Necessity of English as the Official Language," *Boston College Third World Law Journal* 17 (1997): 101, at 103, roughly coincided with instruction in English in Puerto Rican public schools, see supra note 21.

38   Rafael Garzaro, *Diccionario de Política*, 2d ed. (1987), at 245 ("Nationality is a psycho-sociological category.") (my translation). See also Elie Kedourie, *Nationalism* (1966), at 62–68.

39   UN Gen. Ass. Res. 1541(XV), Principle VIII. The United Nations Charter denounces linguistic discrimination. UN Charter arts. 1(3), 13(b), 55(c), and 76(c). Other international legal sources of linguistic rights are Article 2 of the Universal Declaration of Human Rights of 1948, Gen. Ass. Res. 217, UN GAOR, 3d sess. (1948), Article 2(2) of the International Covenant on Economic, Social, and Cultural Rights of 1966, 993 U.N.T.S. 3 (1966), and Articles 2(1), 14, 24(1), 26, and 27 of the International Covenant on Civil and Political Rights of 1966, 999 U.N.T.S. 171 (1966).

40   UN Gen. Ass. Res. 1541(XV), Principle IX(a).

41   Ibid.

42   Ibid. Principle IX(b).

43   S. 712, 101st Cong., 1st sess. (1989): tit. II, § 17.

44   *Political Status of Puerto Rico: Hearings before the Senate Comm. on Energy and Natural Resources on S. 170, S. 711, and S. 712*, vol. 1, 101st Cong., 1st sess. (1989): 370 [hereinafter *1989 Hearings*]. Johnston (D-La.) retired in 1992 and became a lobbyist for statehood in 1996. Leonor Mulero, "De cabildero Johnston," *El Nuevo Día*, March 7, 1997, at 18.

45   *1989 Hearings*, ibid. vol. 1, at 371. For Johnston's further views on this subject, see ibid. at 364–72; vol. 2, at 779–80; vol. 3 at 388–92.

46   E. Meléndez, supra note 10, at 274 (quoting Senators Wallop [R-Wyo.], Nickles [R-Okla.], and Conrad [D-N.D.]). See also Rafael Hernández Colón, "Reflexiones sobre la Autodeterminación Puertorriqueña (1989–1991)," *Revista Jurídica Universidad de Puerto Rico* 65 (1996): 431.

47   Robert Friedman, "Young Finally Shepherds Status Bill to House Floor," *San Juan Star*, March 4, 1998, at 4; Gerardo Reyes, "Possibility of Statehood Stirs Language Debate in Puerto Rico," *Miami Herald*, March 4, 1998, at 1A.

48   Robert Friedman, "Young Bill Passes 209 to 208," *San Juan Star,* March 5, 1998, at 5; Leonor Mulero, "Por virazón la victoria," *El Nuevo Día,* March 5, 1998, at 4. The substitute amendment was sponsored by Rep. Young and by key backers of his bill: Reps. Dan Burton (R-Ind.), Bill McCollum (R-Fla.), and George Miller (D-Cal.). See Mulero, ibid.

49   H.R. 856, supra note 1, § 3(b). That statement is misleading, since currently there are no federal language requirements applicable to state governments. The situation concerning the federal government is not much different. See D. Baron, supra note 21, at 1. Recent attempts to enact such legislation, however, have garnered significant support. In 1996 the House approved a bill to make English the official language of the federal government. See *The English Language Empowerment Act of 1996,* H.R. 123, *Cong. Rec.,* 104th Cong., 2d sess. (August 1, 1996): H9771–72 (approved by the House by a vote of 259 to 156). It was again filed in 1997, after the Senate did not act in 1996. See H.R. 123, 104th Cong., 1st sess.

Key sponsors of the Young bill voted in favor of the 1996 measure. These include Reps. Young, Burton, and McCollum. All three again co-sponsored the 1997 bill. This is the second time that main players in a process for Puerto Rico's self-determination happen to be supporters of official English, as was the case with Senators Johnston and McClure (R-Idaho), the main figures in the 1989–1991 process. See Álvarez González, supra note 36, at 347–48 n. 157.

50   H.R. 856, supra note 1, § 3(c) (emphasis added).

51   Ibid. at § 4(b)(1)(C)(i) and (ii)(I) (emphasis added).

52   See also Juan M. García Passalacqua, " 'English-now' Is Key Effect of House Vote," *San Juan Star,* March 15, 1998, at V2.

53   See *Meyer v. Nebraska,* 262 U.S. 390, 401 (1923); *Frontera v. Sindell,* 522 F.2d 1215, 1220 (6th Cir. 1975).

54   Two of the latest proposals are H.R. J. Res. 109, 104th Cong., 1st sess. (1995), and H.R. J. Res. 171, 103d Cong., 1st sess. (1993).

55   See, e.g., Bill Piatt, *¿Only English? Law and Language Policy in the United States* (1990), at 28–29.

56   See, e.g., Deborah E. Richardson, Note, "The Quebec Independence Vote and Its Implications for English Language Legislation," *Georgia Journal of International and Comparative Law* 26 (1997): 521, at 524; Michael A. T. Pagni, Note, "The Constitutionality of English-Only Provisions in the Public Employee Speech Arena: An Examination of *Yñiguez v. Arizonans for Official English,*" *Hastings Constitutional Law Quarterly* 24 (1996): 247, at 248–49; Michele Arington, Note, "English-Only Laws and Direct Legislation: The Battle in the States over Language Minority Rights," *Journal of Law and Politics* 7 (1991): 325, at 325–29.

The rapid increase in popular support for a *federal* official language law is shown by two polls. In 1990, 54.4 percent of respondents favored making English the official language of government in the United States. By 1992, the figure had risen to 64.5 percent. Raymond Tatalovich, *Nativism Reborn? The Official English Language Movement and the American States* (1995), at 178.

57   Those two states are Nebraska and Illinois, whose laws date back to the nativist era following World War I. See Tatalovich, ibid. at 33–62, 65–69.

58   Alabama, Arizona, Arkansas, California, Colorado, Florida, Georgia, Hawaii, Illinois, Indiana, Kentucky, Mississippi, Montana, Nebraska, New Hampshire, North Carolina, North Dakota, South Carolina, South Dakota, Tennessee, Virginia, and Wyoming. See Chris Boehler, Note, "*Yñiguez v. Arizonans for Official English:* The Struggle to Make English the Official Language," *Houston Law Review* 34 (1998): 1637, at 1640.

59   In 1996, ten states had similar bills then pending in the legislature. See Pagni, supra note 56, at 248 and n. 4.

60   Besides the works already cited, see the following, which question the constitutionality of such measures: Yxta Maya Murray, "The Latino-American Crisis of Citizenship," *University of California Davis Law Review* 31 (1998): 503, at 546–59, 582–89; Susan Kiyomi Serrano, Comment, "Rethinking Race for Strict Scrutiny Purposes: *Yñiguez* and the Racialization of English Only," *University of Hawaii Law Review* 19 (1997): 221; Lori A. McMullen and Charlene R. Lynde, Comment, "The 'Official English' Movement and the Demise of Diversity: The Elimination of Federal Judicial and Statutory Minority Language Rights," *Land & Water Law Review* 32 (1997): 789; Karla C. Robertson, Note, "Out of Many, One: Fundamental Rights, Diversity, and Arizona's English-Only Law," *Denver University Law Review* 74 (1996): 311; Leila Sadat Wexler, "Official English, Nationalism and Linguistic Terror: A French Lesson," *Washington Law Review* 71 (1996): 285; Martina Stewart, "English-Only Laws, Informational Interests, and the Meaning of the First Amendment in a Pluralistic Society," *Harvard Civil Rights–Civil Liberties Law Review* 31 (1995): 539; Juan F. Perea, "Demography and Distrust: An Essay on American Languages, Cultural Pluralism, and Official English," *Minnesota Law Review* 77 (1992): 269; Frank M. Lowrey IV, Comment "Through the Looking Glass: Linguistic Separatism and National Unity," *Emory Law Journal* 41 (1992): 223.

Some articles have recently appeared supporting the constitutionality of official English laws. See Boehler, supra note 58; Michael W. Valente, Comment, "One Nation Divisible by Language: An Analysis of Official English Laws in the Wake of *Yñiguez v. Arizonans for Official English,*" *Seton Hall Constitutional Law Journal* 8 (1997): 205.

61   These include: Paul Gewirtz, Statement before the Senate Committee on Energy and Natural Resources, *1989 Hearings,* vol. 1, supra note 45, at 339–40; Johnny H. Killian, Congressional Research Service, *Power of Congress to Impose Use of English as Condition on Admission of Puerto Rico as a State* (1997) [hereinafter *CRS Language Memorandum*]; Grupo de Investigadores Puertorriqueños, *Breakthrough from Colonialism: An Interdisciplinary Study of Statehood* (1984), 1379–1478 [hereinafter *Breakthrough*].

62   Gewirtz, ibid. at 339–46; *CRS Language Memorandum,* ibid. at 8–23 (expressly refusing, ibid. at 12 n. 18, to address individual rights claims); *Breakthrough,* ibid. at 1147, 1456–78.

63   For a rejection of all such claims, see Tribe, supra note 29, at 28–46.

64   See infra note 80 and accompanying text.

65   *Coyle v. Smith,* 221 U.S. 559 (1911) (invalidating congressional requirement that the capital of Oklahoma remain at Guthrie until 1913).

66   Ibid. at 565.

67   See also Tribe, supra note 29, at 26.

68   Ibid. at 26–30.

69   Louisiana Enabling Act, § 3, *U.S. Statutes at Large* 2 (1811): 641, at 642 (all government proceedings must be in English).

70   Oklahoma Enabling Act, § 3, *U.S. Statutes at Large* 34 (1906): 267, at 271 (public schools "shall always be conducted in English").

71   Joint Enabling Act for New Mexico and Arizona, §§ 2, 20, ¶¶ 4, 5, *U.S. Statutes at Large* 36 (1910): 557, at 559, 570 (public schools "shall always be conducted in English"; state officers and legislators must be able to function in English without the aid of an interpreter).

72   For a discussion of these four precedents from different perspectives, see Gewirtz, supra note 61, at 346–48; *CRS Language Memorandum,* supra note 61, at 8–11; *Breakthrough,* supra note 61, at 1147; Tribe, supra note 29, at 24–26; Trías Monge (1997), supra note 4, at 185. In none of these four territories was the role of English as insignificant as it is in Puerto Rico. In New

Mexico, for example, on the eve of statehood the court system operated in English, albeit with frequent need for translators. D. Baron, supra note 21, at 99.

73   See also Serrano Geyls and Gorrín Peralta, supra note 14, at 75–79.

74   See Georgie Anne Geyer, "Puerto Rico Status Act Leaves U.S. Open to Bilingualism," *Chicago Tribune*, February 27, 1998, at 25 (quoting a legislative aide to Rep. Solomon, who claimed the statehood leaders made that threat).

75   Serrano Geyls and Gorrín Peralta, supra note 14, at 75. See also D. Baron, supra note 21, at xv–xvi (explaining that, with the exception of Louisiana, statehood was always withheld until territories contained English-speaking majorities).

76   Daniel Patrick Moynihan, *Pandaemonium: Ethnicity in International Politics* (1993), 73–74.

77   Gewirtz, supra note 61, at 326–27, 342–46; *CRS Language Memorandum*, supra note 61 at 8–11. For a similar argument by one who believes that Congress may impose language requirements, see Tribe, supra note 29, at 27.

78   That is the usual indictment of the official English campaign. See, e.g., Tatalovich, supra note 56, at 32, 243–57; B. Piatt, supra note 54, at 20–23; Perea, supra note 60, at 361–62.

79   D. Baron, supra note 21, at xiv, xviii, 5–7, 22–23, 28, 31, 41 (accepting that, for some, the monolingual tenet may be based upon a philosophical notion of the connection between language and nationality, instead of on racism). Promoters of English as the official language of the United States have included Benjamin Franklin, John Adams, Thomas Jefferson, John Quincy Adams, John Marshall, Theodore Roosevelt, Oliver Wendell Holmes, and Franklin D. Roosevelt. See ibid. at 2, 28–29, 64–67, 134, 148–49, 169.

As others have stressed (see Lowrey, supra note 60, at 292), the generally widespread voter approval for official-English measures makes it difficult to explain that success exclusively in racist terms. State referenda have produced lopsided margins everywhere, except in Arizona: 83.9 percent in Florida, 73.25 percent in California, 64 percent in Colorado, and 88.5 percent in Alabama. Tatalovich, supra note 56, at 101, 122, 158, 182. The Arizona amendment passed with only 50.5 percent of the vote (ibid. at 145), after an especially acrimonious campaign (ibid. at 131–46), but it was the most restrictive official-language law in the United States. Ibid. at 23.

80   See, e.g., Stephen E. Gottlieb, "Does Federalism Matter to Its Devotees on the Court," *Ohio Northern University Law Review* 23 (1997): 1179, at 1180.

81   As the CRS admits, *CRS Language Memorandum*, supra note 61, at 13–19, its argument assumes that the collective effect of *Gregory v. Ashcroft*, 501 U.S. 452 (1991) (5–4 decision), *New York v. United States*, 505 U.S. 144 (1992) (6–3), *United States v. López*, 514 U.S. 549 (1995) (5–4), and *Printz v. United States*, 521 U.S. 898 (1997) (5–4), is to implicitly overrule *García v. San Antonio Metropolitan Transit Auth.*, 469 U.S. 528 (1988), and *South Carolina v. Baker*, 485 U.S. 505 (1988). *García*, another 5–4 decision, had overruled *National League of Cities v. Usery*, 426 U.S. 833 (1976), yet another 5–4 decision, which in turn had overruled *Maryland v. Wirtz*, 392 U.S. 183 (1968). It seems that this area of constitutional law is currently characterized by *stare indecisis*. See generally John E. Nowak and Ronald D. Rotunda, *Constitutional Law*, 5th ed. (1995), sec. 4.8.

82   *CRS Language Memorandum*, supra note 61, at 12–13. The CRS asserts that section 5 "is particularly preemptive of state powers, in ways that the powers conferred by Article I of the Constitution are not." Ibid. at 13. It then states, in a puzzling non sequitur: "But for purposes of imposing upon the States an English-only, or an official-English, requirement, it is to the authority under the commerce clause that one must look." The CRS never explains why Congress's power over language must stand or fall on Commerce Clause analysis, and may not rely on the "particularly preemptive" section 5.

83   Ibid. at 12, 24. The CRS treatment of this issue is even more perfunctory. It states:

> Briefly, it should be noted that it is likely that Congress has power to condition receipt of federal moneys upon Puerto Rico as a State agreeing to adopt English to the degree Congress chooses. . . . The condition would be imposed after Puerto Rico's admission to the Union, because the spending power is ordinarily contractual, not coercive. That is, since a State may choose to receive or to reject the proffered funds, it may accede to or reject the condition in its discretion. *This approach to the issue raises analytically different questions, which are not dealt with here.* (Ibid. at 24; citations omitted, emphasis added)

The question is analytically different only because the CRS chose to limit its analysis to the validity after statehood of conditions imposed before statehood. But the critical question is whether Congress could force Puerto Rico, before or after statehood, to conduct all or part of its governmental operations and educational system in a language other than Spanish. Still, what little the CRS did say speaks volumes.

84   Ibid. at 12.

85   Ibid. at 12–13, 24.

86   *Katzenbach v. Morgan,* 384 U.S. 641 (1966) (holding valid the congressional enfranchisement of persons educated in Spanish in Puerto Rico).

87   That is, at least as long as the Supreme Court continues to refuse to hold that English literacy requirements violate equal protection. See *Lassiter v. Northampton County Bd. of Elections,* 360 U.S. 45 (1959). Some commentators go beyond this and argue that Congress, acting under section 5, may even dilute Fourteenth Amendment rights. See, e.g., Archibald Cox, "The Role of Congress in Constitutional Determinations," *University of Cincinnati Law Review* 40 (1971): 199, at 259–60. But see *City of Boerne v. Flores,* 521 U.S. 507 (1997).

88   Tribe, supra note 29, at 28–30, 32–39.

89   *United States Constitution,* art. I, sec. 8, cl. 1.

90   *Charles C. Steward Machine Co. v. Davis,* 301 U.S. 548 (1937); *Helvering v. Davis,* 301 U.S. 619 (1937); *Oklahoma v. United States Civil Service Comm'n,* 330 U.S. 127 (1947); *South Dakota v. Dole,* 483 U.S. 203 (1987).

91   See, e.g., *Pennhurst State School & Hospital v. Halderman,* 451 U.S. 1, 17 (1981); *Bell v. New Jersey,* 461 U.S. 773, 790 (1983); *South Dakota v. Dole,* 483 U.S. 203, 213 (1987).

92   Pub. L. 89–10, April 11, 1965, as amended, *U.S. Statutes at Large* 79 (1965): 27.

93   See, e.g., *U.S. Code* 20 (1990) §§ 2721–22.

94   Other amendments to that program have been proposed, such as the elimination of Title VII, which covers bilingual education. For a description of such an amendment, see Tatalovich, supra note 86, at 15–16.

95   Julian N. Eule, "Judicial Review of Direct Democracy," *Yale Law Journal* 99 (1990): 1503, at 1567–68; Kathryn J. Zoglin, "Recognizing a Human Right to Language in the United States," *Boston College Third World Law Journal* 8 (1989): 15, at 24. It is unnecessary to consider the fundamental-rights strand of equal protection in this context, since the fundamental right at issue would be freedom of expression. It is well settled that if the fundamental right itself is not violated, equal protection will not require a different result. See J. Nowak and R. Rotunda, supra note 80, at sec. 14.40.

96   State cases rejecting such claims include: *DaLomba v. Director of the Division of Employment Security,* 337 N.E.2d 687 (Mass. 1975); *Commonwealth v. Olivo,* 337 N.E.2d 904, 911 (Mass. 1975); *Castro v. California,* 466 P.2d 244 (Cal. 1970); *Guerrero v. Carleson,* 512 P.2d 833 (Cal. 1973), *cert. denied,* 414 U.S. 1137 (1974); *Jara v. Municipal Court,* 578 P.2d 94 (Cal. 1978); *Alfonso v. Bd. of*

Review, 444 A.2d 1075 (N.J.), *cert. denied,* 459 U.S. 806 (1982); *Hernández v. Dept. of Labor,* 416 N.E.2d 263 (Ill. 1981). Similar federal cases include: *Carmona v. Sheffield,* 475 F.2d 738 (9th Cir. 1973); *Frontera v. Sindell,* 522 F.2d 1215 (6th Cir. 1975); *Guadalupe Organization, Inc. v. Tempe Elementary School,* 587 F.2d 1022 (9th Cir. 1978); *García v. Gloor,* 618 F.2d 264 (5th Cir. 1980), *cert. denied,* 449 U.S. 1113 (1981); *Pabón v. MacIntosh,* 546 F. Supp. 1328 (E.D. Pa. 1982); *Soberal-Pérez v. Heckler,* 717 F.2d 36 (2d Cir. 1983), *cert. denied,* 466 U.S. 929 (1984); *Viález v. New York City Housing Authority,* 783 F. Supp. 109 (S.D.N.Y. 1991); *García v. Spun Steak Co.,* 988 F.2d 1480 (9th Cir. 1993), *cert. denied,* 510 U.S. 1190 (1994); *Toure v. United States,* 24 F.3d 444 (2d Cir. 1994).

97   For other pessimistic views, see Murray, supra note 60, at 583; Arington, supra note 56, at 335–37.

98   *Califano v. Torres,* 435 U.S. 1 (1978) (per curiam); *Harris v. Rosario,* 446 U.S. 651 (1980) (per curiam).

99   *Arizona Constitution,* art. XXVIII.

100   *Yñiguez v. Mofford,* 730 F. Supp. 309 (D. Ariz. 1990), *aff'd sub nom. Yñiguez v. Arizonans for Official English,* 69 F.3d 920 (9th Cir. 1995) (*en banc*), *vacated as moot sub nom. Arizonans for Official English v. Arizona,* 520 U.S. 43 (1997). The Supreme Court stated that it expressed "no view on the correct interpretation of Art. XXVIII or on the measure's constitutionality."

101   *Ruiz v. Hull,* 957 P.2d 984 (Ariz. 1998), *cert. denied,* 525 U.S. 1093 (1999). Denial of certiorari in *Ruiz,* of course, carries no precedential weight. See *Maryland v. Baltimore Radio Show,* 338 U.S. 912, 917–18 (1950). It may only mean that the Court is not ready yet to address this issue on the merits. See also the special concurrence of Justice Martone in *Ruiz,* 957 P.2d at 1003, ¶¶ 74–76, which suggested some justiciability problems in that case.

102   *Arizona Constitution,* art. XXVIII, secs. 1(3)(a)(iv), 3 (1)(a).

103   *Yñiguez,* 69 F.3d at 927; *Ruiz,* 957 P.2d at 994. Both decisions quote Arington, supra note 56, at 337.

104   *Yñiguez* expressly relied on the overbreadth doctrine, 69 F.3d at 931–48. While *Ruiz* formally disclaimed reliance on that doctrine, 957 P.2d at 999 n. 11, it stressed at several points that the vice of the Arizona provision was its too broad inhibition of speech. See ibid. at 993, 996, 997–98, 999–1000.

105   *Yñiguez,* 69 F.3d at 934–36; *Ruiz,* 957 P.2d at 996.

106   See also Boehler, supra note 57, at 1651–64; Valente, supra note 59, at 222–27.

107   69 F.3d at 936–37.

108   957 P.2d at 987.

109   Ibid. at 1002–3.

110   Ibid. at 990, quoting Act of June 20, 1910, ch. 310, §§ 20(4), (5).

111   957 P.2d at 994–96 (referring to Wyoming, Montana, and California).

112   Ibid. at 996.

113   Ibid.

114   See, e.g., Murray, supra note 60, at 584; Arington, supra note 56, at 337–39.

115   See Valente, supra note 60, at 208 n. 18 (polls show that between 65 percent to 86 percent of the population favors making English the official language of government in the United States).

116   See supra note 94.

117   It has been argued that an English-language amendment "would surely destroy any chance of Puerto Rican statehood." Joseph Leibowicz, Comment, "The Proposed English Language

Amendment: Shield or Sword?" *Yale Law and Policy Review* 3 (1985): 519, at 548. What would such an amendment destroy if enacted *after* Puerto Rico becomes a state?

118   DiChiara, supra note 37, at 523–24.

119   See *Downes v. Bidwell*, 182 U.S. 244 (1901). *Downes* was a test case framed in Congress in 1900 through enactment of the Foraker Act. See Jaime B. Fuster, "The Origins of the Doctrine of Territorial Incorporation," *Revista Jurídica Universidad de Puerto Rico* 43 (1974): 259, at 278–88, and Juan R. Torruella, *The Supreme Court and Puerto Rico: The Doctrine of Separate and Unequal* (1985), at 32–39. See also Efrén Rivera Ramos, "The Legal Construction of American Colonialism: The Insular Cases (1901–1922)," *Revista Jurídica Universidad de Puerto Rico* 65 (1996): 225, at 240.

120   U.S. English, Issue Briefing, "Avoiding an American Quebec: The Future of Puerto Rico and the United States," http://www.us-english.org/prissue.htm (as of March 25, 1998); Patrick Buchanan, "Let Puerto Rico Be a Nation," *New York Post,* May 16, 1990, at 1. Another official English supporter who opposes the Quebec model is former Speaker Newt Gingrich. "Citing Quebec Referendum, Calls Bilingualism Divisive," *International Herald Tribune,* October 31, 1995, at 8.

   Several senators echoed that point in 1991, while considering S. 244 (102d Cong., 1st sess.), the successor to S. 712. See Hernández Colón, supra note 46, at 458–59, 461–62, 464–65, quoting Senate Comm. on Energy and Natural Resources, 102d Cong. 1st sess., Business Meeting, February 20, 1991, at 19–20 (Sen. Ford), 28–29 (Sen. Conrad), 33–34 (Sen. Wallop) [hereinafter *S. 244 Hearings*].

121   See, e.g., Rubén Berríos Martínez, "Independence for Puerto Rico: The Only Solution," *Foreign Affairs* 55 (1976): 578, at 583; Rubén Berríos Martínez, supra note 36, at 110; Manuel Rodríguez Orellana, "Quebec y Puerto Rico: Un Hemisferio y Dos Soledades," *Revista Jurídica Universidad de Puerto Rico* 67 (1998): 1079. For another recognition of the Quebec–Puerto Rico analogy, see Wexler, supra note 59, at 377 n. 21.

122   See, e.g., Romero Barceló (1980), supra note 30, at 63, 68–69, 72. The rejection of the Quebec-Puerto Rico analogy, premised on cultural and linguistic diversity in the United States, was also central to the remarks of several senators during the debate on S. 244 in 1991. See *S. 244 Hearings,* supra note 120, at 23–25 (Sen. Bradley), 31–33 (Sen. Wirth), 46–48 (Sen. Akaka), quoted in Hernández Colón, supra note 46, at 459–60, 462–63, 466–67. The argument against the Quebec-Hispanic analogy is powerfully made, but without any reference to Puerto Rico, in Richardson, supra note 56.

123   On the Québecois question, see generally Jonathan Lemco, *Turmoil in the Peaceable Kingdom: The Quebec Sovereignty Movement and Its Implications for Canada and the United States* (1994); Jeremy Webber, *Reimagining Canada: Language, Culture, Community and the Canadian Constitution* (1994).

124   While only 23.6 percent of Puerto Rico's residents are truly fluent in English, just 1.8 percent do not speak any Spanish. See supra notes 14–17 and accompanying text. Puerto Rico is as monolingual in Spanish as the United States (97 percent) is in English. See D. Baron, supra note 21, at 177. In contrast, in Quebec there coexist a sizeable group (18 percent) whose native tongue is not French, of which little more than half are functional in that language, with a majoritarian segment (82 percent) whose native tongue is French, of which one-third are fluent in English. Lemco, supra note 123, at 10, 18.

125   A 1990 poll revealed that 55 percent of Quebec's residents consider themselves first as citizens of that province. Lowrey, supra note 60, at 260 n. 198. Meanwhile, a 1993 study revealed that the comparable figure in Puerto Rico is 91 percent. *Ateneo Study,* supra note 17, at 84–85.

126   See Sheila M. Arnopoulos and Dominique Clift, *The English Fact in Quebec*, 2d ed. (1984), at 230, 238.

127   Baron, supra note 21, at 2, 10, 83–87, 95–104.

128   *Breakthrough*, supra note 61, at 1475–76. According to Trías Monge, "only if all the people in the rest of the world moved to America, would the United States have a population density similar to that of Puerto Rico." Trías Monge (1997), supra note 4, at 2.

129   See sources cited supra note 54.

130   Baron, supra note 21, at 11–12, 173, 192; Richardson, supra note 56, at 532 n. 74. That was also the main thrust of the most important Supreme Court decision on the subject, *Lau v. Nichols*, 414 U.S. 563 (1974) (forcing non-English-speaking children into the regular curriculum violates section 601 of the Civil Rights Act of 1964, *U.S. Code* 42 (1994) § 2000d). *Lau* was reaffirmed in specific legislation. *U.S. Code* 20 (1994) § 1703(f). See also the Bilingual Education Act, *U.S. Code* 20 (1988) §§ 3281–3386. Federal courts have refused to approve bilingual education programs which do not comply with the transitional requirement. See, e.g., *Cintrón v. Brentwood Union Free Sch. Dist.*, 455 F. Supp. 57, 64 (E.D.N.Y. 1978).

131   Baron, supra note 21, at 10–11.

132   Baron, ibid. at 64–132 (discussing historical attempts to preserve German in Pennsylvania and other states, French in Louisiana, and Spanish in the Southwest).

133   Baron, ibid. at 188, citing Calvin Veltman, *Language Shift in the United States* (1983), at 214; Kenneth Karst, "Paths to Belonging: The Constitution and Cultural Identity," *North Carolina Law Review* 64 (1986): 303, at 352.

134   For a superb case study of the reciprocal influence of law and social reality, see Rivera Ramos, supra note 119.

135   Serrano Geyls and Gorrín Peralta, supra note 14, at 74.

136   See Muñiz Argüelles, supra note 11, at 74, 76.

137   That is a traditional argument of pro-statehood writers. See, e.g., Bothwell, vol. 4, supra note 29, at 474–75.

138   Trías Monge (1997), supra note 4, at 60; Serrano Geyls and Gorrín Peralta, supra note 14, at 34–36.

139   Cf. John Hart Ely, *Democracy and Distrust* (1980), at 158–59 (arguing that invalid stereotypes are those of the "we/they" type, where those who make the rule have no reason to feel empathy with those against whom that rule operates).

140   See, e.g., editorial, "Go Slow on 51st State," *Boston Herald*, March 7, 1998, at 12 ("Americans everywhere need to debate whether a culture so different from the mainland culture can fit into the union, and whether it should be admitted if a substantial minority doesn't want in— likely true for Puerto Rico.").

141   For some approaches to these questions, see Baron, supra note 21, at 6 (centrality of language to political organization); Lowrey, supra note 60, at 319 (questioning whether linguistic pluralism is feasible in the United States political system); Edward L. Rubin, "The Fundamentality and Irrelevance of Federalism," *Georgia State University Law Review* 13 (1997): 1009 (the United States is no longer a federal but a unitary state, with a modest degree of decentralization); Richardson, supra note 56, at 532 (stressing the loose nature of the Canadian federation).

142   The last time such questions were posed was during Senate consideration in 1991 of a plebiscite for Puerto Rico. See supra notes 43–46 and accompanying text; see also Hernández Colón, supra note 46. The outcome was that the process was aborted, which suggests that many senators found tentative answers.

143   Accord Trías Monge (1997), supra note 4, at 185, 192.

144   See, e.g., Lung-Chu Chen, "Self-Determination and World Public Order," *Notre Dame Law Review* 66 (1991): 1287, at 1310; Efrén Rivera Ramos, "Self-Determination and Decolonisation in the Society of the Modern Colonial Welfare State," in *Issues of Self-Determination,* ed. William Twining (1991), at 115, 124.

145   See, e.g., Surya P. Sharma, *Territorial Acquisition, Disputes, and International Law* (1997), at 248; Frederic L. Kirgis Jr., Editorial Comment, "The Degrees of Self-Determination in the United Nations Era," *American Journal of International Law* 88 (1994): 304, at 306; Lea Brilmayer, "Secession and Self-Determination: A Territorial Interpretation," *Yale Journal of International Law* 16 (1991): 177, at 192.

　　　　For views against the recognition of a right to secession, see, e.g., Lee C. Buchheit, *Secession: The Legitimacy of Self-determination* (1978); Cass R. Sunstein, "Constitutionalism and Secession," *University of Chicago Law Review* 58 (1991): 633.

146   Berríos Martínez, supra note 36, at 110.

147   Brilmayer, supra note 145, at 194, citing Michla Pomerance, *Self-Determination in Law and Practice* (1982), at 27. See Brilmayer, ibid. at 199–201, for a discussion of the factors that help determine whether a territorial claim is sound. The case of Puerto Rico, even after statehood, and particularly if statehood were granted without overwhelming support, would satisfy all of Professor Brilmayer's factors.

Puerto Rican National Identity and United States Pluralism

Ángel Ricardo Oquendo

When Gabriel García Márquez visited Puerto Rico not too long ago, someone asked why he had never written about the island. The Colombian Nobel Prize winning novelist responded: "If I told the truth about Puerto Rico, everyone would say I was making it up."[1] Indeed, the Puerto Rican experience is in many ways too outlandish even for magical realism. Despite being a territory of the world's largest exporter of democratic rhetoric, Puerto Rico is the only place in all of Latin America where not even a pretense of democracy exists: Puerto Ricans have absolutely no electoral say with respect to the institutions that enact and execute the supreme laws of the land.[2] Moreover, even though it has lost virtually all of its economic and strategic value to the United States, the island continues to receive increasing amounts of U.S. federal transfer payments—up to about eleven billion dollars a year—out of imperial, bureaucratic inertia.[3] Finally, most Puerto Ricans take an immense pride in their national culture and in their distinctness from the United States, yet the population overwhelmingly supports keeping Puerto Rico part of the United States.[4]

The first two antinomies show that U.S. foreign and economic policy at times works in mysterious (actually bizarre) ways. This phenomenon is in itself fascinating, but I am more interested in exploring the third paradox, which points to what appears to be a profound tension in the soul of the Puerto Rican people. How can Puerto Ricans, on the one hand, universally celebrate their national cultural difference and, on the other hand, want ever closer ties with the United States? I will start out by rejecting simplistic explanations. One such account would contend that Puerto Ricans are crassly irrational, insofar as they have inconsistent goals—independence from and absorption into the United States. Another, equally discardable explication would cynically assert that Puerto Ricans see their first and foremost aim as receiving U.S. dollars even if they have to give up deeply held patriotic convictions.

I would instead propose understanding the seeming contradictory Puerto Rican positions as an intelligible and sincere quest to cultivate very close relations with the United States while maintaining a separate national identity. Most Puerto Ricans prefer to continue or strengthen rather than to cut off their bond to the U.S. federation primarily in order to secure monetary support from and free access to the United States. At the same time, they have no overwhelming urge to embrace U.S. traditions, symbols, values, and principles. They genuinely want to remain Puerto Rican, to demarcate themselves from other U.S. citizens, to preserve their own ways, and to speak their own language.[5]

The two political parties that advocate a permanent relationship with the United States have, accordingly, adopted platforms that also call for the protection of the national culture. The Popular Democratic Party has been asserting for fifty years that under the current territorial status (or an improved version) Puerto Ricans can achieve the goal of safeguarding their national identity.[6] The New Progressive Party, in turn, has gone so far as to contend that this objective is realizable even if Puerto Rico becomes a full member of the Union. This party has come up with the formula of "Jíbaro statehood," a national or folkloric statehood, in order to achieve, simultaneously, national cultural separation from and political annexation by the United States.[7]

Even the third party, which calls for Puerto Rican independence, proposes yet another variation on the theme of combining strong U.S. political ties with national sovereignty. The Puerto Rican Independence Party espouses the creation of a separate nation that would nonetheless remain significantly within the U.S. political and economic orbit. It advocates a transition period of ten years or longer, within which the United States would maintain the current level of financial support.[8] The payments would arrive not as individual entitlements but rather as block disbursements to the sovereign government of Puerto Rico.[9] Even after this transition period ended, Puerto Rico would presumably expect U.S. foreign aid at a level comparable to that received by nations with special U.S. links, such as Israel. A key part of the separatist economic agenda would, at any rate, be the attraction of high levels of U.S. private investment through tax and other incentives.[10] Even under independence, moreover, continued free movement between the island and the mainland would be crucial in order to avoid building a wall right through the middle of the Puerto Rican community.[11] Puerto Ricans would have the opportunity, under the party's plan, of acquiring double citizenship.[12] Finally, through a series of additional bilateral agreements, the Republic of Puerto Rico would intricately bind its destiny to that of the United States. The two sovereign nations would thus have a common market and currency.[13] Notwithstanding the party's general goal of demilitarization, a deal to allow U.S. military bases to stay on and a significantly coordinated defense policy would be practically unavoidable.

Puerto Ricans are virtually unanimous in their conviction that the national culture is not negotiable. There is equally broad agreement that there should be some kind of interdependence with the United States on matters of economics, immigration, defense, and citizenship. Opinions diverge only on how exactly to set up these interconnections. In a way, the political disagreement in Puerto Rico is therefore about details. The discussion typically heats up probably due to the history of political repression and violence by the United States and because partisan politicking consistently distorts what is at stake. Perhaps a more constructive conversation would take place if the focus were not first on the three competing formulas but rather on the right mix of competence sharing with the United States. Deciding thereupon whether one should call the arrangement thus ultimately opted for the fifty-first state of the Union, a free associated state, a free associated republic, or an independent nation would, one would hope, be less controversial.

Before arriving at this deliberative juncture, however, it is necessary to answer the question of whether and how Puerto Rico can defend its national culture despite its (dangerous?) liaisons with the United States. The challenge becomes all the greater as the proximity between the two peoples increases. In this essay, I will therefore focus my attention on the problem of preserving Puerto Rican cultural sovereignty in the context of a permanent internal (or domestic) relationship with the United States—such as an association of the kind that exists now or, even more important, complete integration.

My argument will address three objections to the assertion that Puerto Rico could uphold its national culture within the United States. Each of the first two criticisms rests on a misconception of the U.S. polity. The third is a more serious challenge. Treating the Puerto Rican national culture as a public good and affording it intense official protection appears to clash not only with the concept of a federal unity of equals but also with the political culture—that is to say, the specific understanding of democracy and human rights—prevailing in the United States. In light of this problem, the only solution is an asymmetrical federalism, which would allow Puerto Rico to adhere to its own separate political culture. Though this kind of political settlement is severely problematic politically, it should be up to the peoples of Puerto Rico and the United States to decide whether to take this route.

National Cultural Consensus

When it comes to politics, there appears to be rampant disagreement in Puerto Rico. The divergence of opinion seems to reach a climax, of course, when the question is: What should be the political status of the island? The three main political parties, which break down according to status preference, have all made the furtherance of the national culture a central part of their platform. The pro-statehood New Progressive Party, despite striving for the complete annexation of the island by the United States, has managed to market itself as a defender of the national culture.[14] Party leaders assert that the national culture and language are not negotiable.[15] In fact, the statehood movement became a serious contender in the political arena only when it began to present itself as committed to Puerto Rican values and traditions.[16] Since its foundation in 1967, the New Progressive Party has been propounding the notion of a "jíbaro" statehood.[17] Within this vision, Puerto Rico would become not just another state of the Union but rather an "other" or a different kind of state. The idea is that even as a state, the island would be able to keep its own national character. The "jíbaro" is the Puerto Rican peasant, who in the nineteenth century became the Puerto Rican national symbol.[18] As a "jíbaro" state, Puerto Rico would be in a position to advance a national cultural agenda and even to have a degree of international recognition of its separate identity in sports and cultural events.

Relying on this vision, the New Progressive Party gave credibility to the statehood option and won the elections in 1968. Luis A. Ferré then became governor and ended the Popular Democratic Party's twenty-year political hegemony. Since 1968, the New Progressive Party has taken turns with the Popular Democratic Party at governing the island and has made statehood the second preferred formula, running closely behind the status quo option and leaving the independence choice far behind.[19]

The Popular Democratic Party, for its part, supports keeping a version of the current political status. It maintains that commonwealth status is the only way in which Puerto Rico can preserve its national identity while having a permanent domestic relationship with the United States. A group of former independence advocates, the most prominent of whom was Luis Muñoz Marín, founded the Popular Democratic Party in 1938. In light of the island's chronic underdevelopment, these individuals tempered their patriotic fervor and focused on improving the economy. They concluded that the political ties to the United States were essential in order to secure capital investment, maintain access to the U.S. consumer market, and continue receiving substantial financial aid from the U.S. federal government. The party's forefathers also saw in the United States mainland an open space that could help mitigate Puerto Rico's massive unemployment and over-population problem.

The Popular Democratic Party's promoters, however, did not want to give up altogether their nationalistic aspirations. They sought to preserve Puerto Rico's cultural identity and links to Latin America and Spain. They accordingly conceived a political status which would give Puerto Ricans "the best of two worlds": the cultural sovereignty benefits of independence and the economic security of statehood.[20] Today, party members contend that the Puerto Rican national legacy would be at risk with the full political incorporation of the island into the United States.[21]

The Puerto Rican Independence Party, predictably, has striven to present itself as the political organization with the deepest commitment to the national culture. It insists that only with complete political sovereignty will it be possible to guarantee the survival and flourishing of the Puerto Rican way of life.[22] The Independence Party has nevertheless been steadily losing support since the 1950s, partly due to the repression of its adherents by local and U.S. authorities,[23] but mostly because of the Puerto Rican economy's increased dependence on U.S. welfare. The success of the two other parties presenting themselves as guardians of the national culture has been a "coup de grace."[24] The Independence Party has thus faced the difficult task of convincing the population that, despite the apparently deep financial cost, independence is the only means of guaranteeing national and cultural prosperity.

All of the three main political parties have, accordingly, made a thriving national culture a crucial goal of their political programs. As political parties, their very existence hangs on their capacity to read the preference of the Puerto Rican people. They have all embraced this national cultural objective because they have correctly sensed a broad consensus on this issue. "There is a very strong cultural nationalism," Juan Manuel Carrión observes, "so strong indeed that even advertising companies exploit it to sell beer and cigarettes."[25]

Most Puerto Ricans advocate holding onto their national culture in the context of a permanent domestic relationship with the United States, as is shown in the fact that since 1968 they have consistently elected one of the two parties that favor this kind of arrangement. In fact, the New Progressive Party and the Popular Democratic Party typically obtain a combined total of over 90 percent of the votes. Even though it usually manages to send two or three representatives to the legislature, the Puerto Rican Independence Party has yet to win a single municipal election and the party's candidate for governor never receives the endorsement of more than 4 percent of the voters.

There have been three local referenda on the political status of the island. Puerto Ricans opted for the commonwealth formula in the two first plebiscites organized by the insular government, in 1967 and 1993. Support for this political recipe sank from 61 percent to 49 percent from the first to the second. The decline suggests disenchantment with the status quo, particularly if one considers that during the second vote an improved version of the free associated state was at stake. In contrast, the full integration option jumped from a 39 percent to a 46 percent approval rate. The independence movement boycotted the first referendum, and in the second less than 4 percent of participants favored separation.[26]

The New Progressive Party-led government put together a third plebiscite in 1998.[27] Puerto Rico faced the choice of being (1) a U.S. territory, (2) a free associated republic, (3) a state of the Union, (4) an independent nation, and (5) none of the above. The results were clearly disappointing for the New Progressive Party. The annexation option was not able to muster more than the 46 percent support obtained in 1993. Furthermore, slightly over 50 percent of the voters embraced the category labeled "none of the above," which the Popular Democratic Party favored to repudiate full integration as well as the territorial definition of the current status. While the independence ideal's performance—almost 3 percent—was a letdown, the first two options bombed, each registering less than 1 percent.[28]

The U.S. Congress has never offered Puerto Ricans a binding vote on their status. The legislative bills that would have taken the U.S. Congress in this direction in 1993 and 1998 died without final action. The first time, the responsible committees of each chamber never sent the projects for a plenary vote. The second time around, the House of Representatives endorsed a bill on the issue but the Senate shelved its own legislative proposal at the committee level. The explanation for this lack of interest in scheduling a referendum is the strong opposition in the United States to the full integration of Puerto Rico. This U.S. resistance to welcoming Puerto Rico to the Union is based only partially on racial or linguistic intolerance. There are more important political and economic reasons. As a state, Puerto Rico would send, on the basis of its population, more U.S. Representatives to Washington than about half of the fifty existing states. Moreover, equal treatment to that of the states would enable the island to receive much more U.S. funding than it does now, and, due to its low income level, Puerto Rico would receive much more federal aid per capita than any of the other states.

The U.S. Congress has at times attempted to justify its inaction by pointing to the lack of agreement among Puerto Ricans. This kind of rationalization misses the mark on three grounds. First, it neglects the fact that there is solid concurrence, expressed by all three Puerto Rican political parties, that Congress should organize a binding referendum. Second, it disregards that Congress could undoubtedly contribute to the development of a Puerto Rican consensus on what the island's status should be by spelling out what the options are, presenting them to the Puerto Rican electorate, and promising to honor the people's preference. Finally, an excuse of this sort fails to face up to the reality that Puerto Ricans have converged politically on what the essentials of the U.S.-Puerto Rican relationship should be. All three political parties posit maintaining strong economic ties with the United States and, more significantly, structuring Puerto Rican collective life around the defense of the national culture.

The Puerto Rican National Culture as a Public Good

What does it mean to assert that the Puerto Rican national culture is a collective good, which the state must look after and enhance? This kind of claim does imply that the national culture is valuable, but not just that. Something may have value to certain individuals only. The government may even decide to protect that something out of an interest in preserving individual preferences. It is therefore key first to explore the notion of a public good.

One may start with the example of someone who keeps his first milk tooth in an etui. The tooth is valuable to her and at most to a few other people. A collective good must touch many more people. A public park provides a case in point. Most members of the community cherish the park because each enjoys its benches, grass, paths, and fountains and perhaps associates important memories with the place. Despite thus being an asset to a large group of individuals, a public park is *not* a public good in the sense I am entertaining. As I have described it, the park is worthwhile to the community members as individuals or as parts of small groups, such as families or groups of friends. To be a collective good something must be valuable not just to each individual, but rather to all individuals. A historical monument captures what I have in mind. Its main value stems from the perspective of the members of a community not as individuals but as a group. They treasure the monument for what it means to them as a community. In part, it defines their collective existence. If the individuals did not constitute a community, the monument would have no value or meaning to them; they would not even have come to the idea of building the structure in the first place.

Needless to say, the worth of a public good is ultimately traceable to the individuals who constitute the collectivity. One does not have to anchor the good's value in a mystical metaphysical entity, such as a general or universal will. One simply has to understand that though it is individuals who embrace the good, they do so while thinking of themselves as part of a community. They would have a completely different attitude—perhaps one of indifference—toward the thing if they were not able thus to exercise their imaginations.

A national culture, to be sure, is not a self-standing or immutable object. It is a reality created and continually transformed by the people—at times consciously, at times not—relying on numerous internal and external influences.[29] To a degree, it is more an activity than a good. To declare it a matter of public concern, therefore, is to affirm that it is a collective endeavor whose pursuit is worthwhile to the community of individuals involved.

From this perspective, the national culture not only derives its value from the collectivity's perspective. It also gives content to the community's identity. In other words, not only do the individuals have to think of themselves as a community to appreciate the national culture, but they are also able to visualize themselves in such terms partly because of their shared national culture. There is, accordingly, a symbiotic relationship between national culture and identity.

Most Puerto Ricans not only regard their national culture as a public good, but also believe that that culture needs official protection. This conviction feeds off the feeling that the national culture is at risk. Though this latter perception seems generally justified, it is crucial to stay clear of hysterics. In the past, reports of the death of the Puerto Rican national culture have been greatly exaggerated.[30] If anything, that culture has shown an impressive vibrancy and resilience throughout this century.[31] Upon its invasion in 1898 and subsequent occupation of the island, the United States engaged in a concerted effort to destroy the national culture in Puerto Rico and impose U.S. cultural norms.[32] The attempt to "Americanize" Puerto Ricans reached a climax with the plan to make English the language of instruction in the public schools of Puerto Rico.[33] This entire campaign, which lasted officially until 1949,[34] failed miserably partly because Puerto Ricans refused to give up their national identity, but mostly because it is impossible even for willing participants successfully to undergo the kind of cultural metamorphosis contemplated by the U.S. authorities. Following this tragic episode in the history of U.S.-Puerto Rican relations, Puerto Rican individuals have continued making significant efforts, sometimes even sacrifices, in order to assure their national culture's survival and vitality. Since 1952, the Puerto Rican government has regularly purported to be part of this national crusade, irrespective of which party has been in power.

The United States has been far more effective in "Americanizing" Puerto Rico at the level of legal and political institutions. On the one hand, not only is there a hierarchically supreme layer of U.S. federal law in Puerto Rico, but also local legal institutions have often mindlessly transplanted U.S. law onto the Puerto Rican legal system. Throughout most of this century, the Puerto Rican legislature has copied legislation from the various states and the judiciary has adopted U.S. common law methods, precedents, and doctrines. The result, as José Trías Monge points out, was an amorphous and incoherent legal amalgam.[35] In the last three decades and at the behest of the Puerto Rico Supreme Court (most insistently during Trías Monge's tenure as Chief Justice), however, Puerto Rican law has consistently returned to its civil law origins.[36] On the other hand, the 1952 Constitution institutes an executive, a legislature, and a judiciary strikingly similar to those prevailing in the various states of the Union. At the same time, the U.S. Congress vetoed those provisions of the Puerto Rico Constitution recognizing social welfare rights, which seemed to be antithetical to the U.S. constitutional ideology.[37]

Not surprisingly, the United States's influence has been even greater on Puerto Rico's economy than on its politics or law. Puerto Rico's economy has gone through many different phases, but U.S. domination has been a constant throughout. To this day, most private economic activity takes place under the aegis of U.S. companies or their subsidiaries. Locally based private efforts, moreover, usually follow U.S. standards. Public economic undertakings, in turn, issue from insular governmental agencies, which typically copy the ways of their counterparts in the states.

In sum, the U.S. occupation of Puerto Rico has threatened the economic culture more than the legal and political culture, and far more than the social culture.[38] Curiously, the sense of Puerto Ricans that their national culture is at risk relates more to the social than to any other cultural sphere. Puerto Ricans are less concerned about U.S. economic or political hegemony than they are about losing their sociocultural bearings. Is their feeling that their social culture is at peril sheer paranoia?

Even though Puerto Ricans' social culture—their language, their customs, their music, their art, their dance, their cuisine—has demonstrated an impressive capacity to stay afloat and even flourish in the midst of an overwhelming U.S. presence, it would be a mistake to assume that that culture has suffered no decay at all. The influence of the U.S. way of life has been more significant in Puerto Rico than anywhere else in Latin America.[39] Among upper and middle classes, there is at times greater familiarity with and affinity for U.S. culture than Puerto Rican or Latin American culture. The members of these classes often speak a Spanish loaded with Anglicisms and English expressions.[40] Frequently, they prefer U.S. music, films, food, and clothes and they are quick to adopt U.S. customs.

This phenomenon of assimilation has been less pronounced within the lower classes. Puerto Rican author Luis Rafael Sánchez has argued that these classes and their "déclassé" culture have constituted the most effective barrier to U.S. cultural domination.[41] Because of their limited access to U.S. mass and sophisticated culture, the members of these classes have been able to hold on to and develop their own cultural experience. They have thus been the guardians of an authentic and self-sustaining national culture. They have directly produced a lively popular culture, which has often inspired more intellectualized cultural expressions.[42] Impressively, they have been in a position to perform this role despite their extensive migratory experience. Part of the explanation is that those individuals within classes that do migrate tend to live among their own, isolated from the rest of the U.S. citizenry, and to go back and forth between mainland and island. Of course, the lower classes have not been completely immune to cultural colonialism. They have felt the impact of U.S. cultural domination to a greater extent than their equivalents in other Latin American countries.

The prepotency of U.S. culture is bound to become greater now and in the future with the advent of the age of mass communication, the Internet, and globalization. Peoples everywhere will from now on experience a North American cultural bombardment. Puerto Ricans will inevitably feel the brunt of the attack, due to their political and economic proximity to the United States. The measures they took in the past to defend their national culture may prove insufficient under this new set of circumstances.

Again, it is crucial not to exaggerate the danger. As already noted, cultures are always in transition and exposed to external influences. A strong culture is able to absorb and transform the exogenous. Brazilians refer to this phenomenon as "cultural cannibalism": the capacity of their culture to devour and digest all kinds of cultural influences.[43] The Puerto Rican culture has proven to be in a position to domesticate and benefit from U.S. cultural imports in the past and it will probably continue to do so in the future. Nevertheless, Puerto Ricans will have to display creativity and act collectively through their political institutions.

Through their state, Puerto Ricans seek to create a situation in which they can appreciate and contribute to their own culture. Yet they need not isolate themselves from the United States culturally. A culture sustained through ignorance and fear would be very fragile indeed. The fact that a majority of Puerto Ricans are linguistically and educationally cut off from U.S. culture is, in the long run, not an insurance policy for, but rather a Damocles sword hanging over, Puerto Rico's cultural sovereignty. Puerto Rican cultural policy should aim at eliminating this state of deprivation. It should seek, on the one hand, to make Puerto Ricans fully bilingual in addition to well versed in the U.S. cultural code, and, on the other hand, to bring about a reflective national cultural pride.

Public schools must play a paramount role in this mission. They have to improve across the board to generate a robustly educated population which is completely in command of its language and cultural identity. Spanish philosopher Miguel de Unamuno's assertion that "the study and knowledge of other languages advances the study and improvement of our own"[44] is true not only of language but also of culture generally. If Puerto Rican students have a firm base in their own culture, they will be in a position to appropriate and "cannibalize" U.S. cultural exports.

Beyond the educational system, a nationally committed Puerto Rican government must bolster the national culture in other areas of life. It has to create space for the culture in the workplace, in commerce, in telecommunications, in the entertainment industry, in the arts. It must use incentives as well as sanctions to advance Puerto Rican cultural development. It has to become the vehicle through which Puerto Ricans can safeguard collectively a public good that they cannot protect at the individual level.

In a way, the Puerto Rican government has been making efforts in this direction since the existing Constitution's approval in 1952. The Puerto Rican Institute of Culture, created in 1955, has been in charge of defending and advancing Puerto Rican culture.[45] The Institute supports Puerto Rican folklore, art, literature, music, architecture, and cinema. The Puerto Rico government also funds the Puerto Rican Atheneum, which has been engaged on behalf on the national culture since 1876.[46] Even the New Progressive Party has emphatically endorsed this kind of cultural engagement.[47]

Puerto Rico's government already engages in this kind of action in specific areas of cultural activity such as cinema. It approaches the Puerto Rican film industry, for instance, as a national treasure, which individual Puerto Ricans may not be in a position to sponsor at the necessary level. The U.S. film industry has clear comparative advantages due to economies of scale in production, promotion, and distribution. Puerto Ricans therefore end up massively favoring the U.S. imports, perhaps because for the same price they would obtain an inferior local product or because advertising works on them like the sirens' voices on Ulysses. Puerto Rico's government, therefore, tries to encourage in a profound way the realization of Puerto Rican pictures through subsidies and tax incentives.[48] In order to launch the Puerto Rican cinematic industry, of course, the government would have to commit itself further to, and show an even more extreme partiality toward, Puerto Rican cinema.

The government can also promote the national culture by raising Puerto Rico's international profile. Culturally engaged groups benefit enormously from their contacts with their peers across the globe. They thus position themselves not only generally to learn from others but also specifically to interact culturally with non-U.S. associations. Of particular significance in this respect are ties with Latin American entities, through which Puerto Ricans can increase their understanding and appreciation of their own Latin American national culture. An international presence, moreover, enables Puerto Ricans broadly to attain their own recognition and that of others of their separate and national identity.

Just because it shows a solid commitment to a national culture, of course, a state does not unavoidably degenerate into an intolerant and repressive machine. It can, on the one hand, guarantee basic individual liberties so that persons not interested in or even adverse to the Puerto Rican culture can privately express and live out their own cultural preferences or animosities. It may, on the other hand, open up the national culture to all, welcoming everybody and all kinds of interpretations to the collective cultural project. The Institute of Puerto Rican Culture already purports to "encourage freedom and pluralism in the artistic, humanistic expression."[49] Only by embracing these two strategies will the Puerto Rican government be in a position to claim legitimacy for its national cultural endeavors.

The discussion has been far too general, and brief, but sufficient to give an idea of why Puerto Ricans take an immense pride in their culture and nonetheless feel that that culture needs the state's protection. The national culture is thriving but continually under threat. It will—in the eyes of Puerto Ricans—suffer irreparable harm if the state does not come to its rescue. From this perspective, the government of Puerto Rico—regardless of whether the island becomes independent, remains a territory, or turns into the fifty-first state of the Union—has a duty to stand up for the national culture.

The Liberal State's Equidistance from National Cultures

It is possible to argue against nationalistic ambitions along the following lines: To be part of the United States, one must embrace the U.S. national consciousness. One has to give up any other national affiliation one might have and blend in culturally. This is what being one nation (under God?) is all about. If Puerto Ricans want to remain within the United States and, especially, if they would like to become a state, they must sacrifice their national peculiarities and assimilate. Everybody else who has joined the U.S. family has had to do the same. No state has had any kind of cultural privileges when entering the federation. There is no reason why Puerto Rico should be an exception.

This argument, which often finds echo in Puerto Rico among those who favor independence and even the status quo,[50] clearly runs on a distorted picture of the United States; U.S. society comes across as a senseless beast that devours its own children. Yet the United States is a much more complex animal. Granted, there have been times of nativism in U.S. history and even today the country occasionally reverts to these jingoist instincts. All the same, this strand is neither predominant nor what the United States ultimately aspires to be, as expressed in its constitution and best traditions.

At one level, the United States is an association of states, which in principle are sovereign. The reach of state sovereignty, to be sure, has progressively decreased since the Declaration of Independence, as the federal government's areas of competence and influence have grown exponentially. At this federal level the United States does not, however, radiate a monolithic national ethos. Instead, it purports to follow the principles of a political liberalism of sorts, as defined by John Rawls.[51]

After providing a philosophical justification for the principles of political liberalism, Rawls develops the notion of an "overlapping consensus." Through this concept, he explains the stability of, and provides additional reasoned support for, a society organized around the previously defended norms. The principles of political liberalism rest on a thin conception of the good and are therefore compatible with various conceptions of the good life. Individuals and groups who do not share a full-fledged religious or philosophical conception can nonetheless pledge allegiance to the same set of politically liberal institutions. The complete rationalization that each person or community gives for upholding these institutions will vary. The stability of a state built along these lines stems from the fact that people adhering to comprehensive views will tend to be loyal. Only individuals who embrace unreasonable religious or philosophical perspectives—that is, who deny the fundamental principles of political liberalism—will not be in a position to be part of the principled convergence.

In elaborating his theory, Rawls is thinking of the problem of divergence in philosophical and religious doctrines. Yet one can bring the concept of an overlapping consensus to bear on the issue of national diversity within a single society. One would thus probably end up with something like Jürgen Habermas's notion of constitutional patriotism. Habermas contends that, though national pluralism is an ineluctable feature of modernity, this fact need not create insoluble crises for the state. For the modern state purports to unify its citizens not on the basis of common national language, ethnicity, or culture, but through a shared political culture. In other words, the state acts exclusively on the basis of a general set of norms—democratic principles, the notion of rule of law, and human rights—to which a very heterogeneous citizenry can assent. Beyond this political culture, the state agenda takes no particular content—religious or national. The citizens come together through and identify with a constitution embodying that political culture.

Rawls discusses political liberalism with the U.S. experience in mind. Habermas explicitly mentions the United States as an instance of the postnational state he describes. The U.S. federation thus does not impose a comprehensive national perspective but rather proposes a Rawlsian overlapping consensus or a Habermasian constitutional patriotism.[52] The U.S. Constitution and particularly the Bill of Rights bind federal authorities to a set of ideals generally corresponding to the political liberal principles and the political culture referred to by Rawls and Habermas, respectively. The federal government accordingly has no business coercing individuals in Puerto Rico into giving up their nationality or embracing an alternative one. On the contrary, it has a duty to guarantee their right to insist on their national distinctness.

All states of the Union share and express in their own constitutions a similar conception of the government's proper role. If any state wanted to deviate from this political and philosophical norm, the federal authorities would have to step in and force that state back into compliance. The Fourteenth Amendment of the U.S. Constitution—adopted in the aftermath of the Civil War—requires states to honor general principles of equality and due process. Federal precedents have, furthermore, relied on the Due Process Clause to make most of the Bill of Rights—which spans the first ten amendments and includes, among others, rights to freedom of expression and of conscience, against unwarranted searches and seizures, to a fair criminal trial by jury, against cruel and unusual punishments—applicable to the states. The Fifteenth Amendment, finally, demands state respect for certain democratic norms. The U.S. Constitution, therefore, calls on the federal government to assure that states abide by the common liberal political culture.

The government of Puerto Rico, as part of the U.S. constitutional scheme, may not get involved directly in matters of national culture. It has, however, the authority and obligation to make space for its residents to further their national culture. It must not only permit national cultural manifestations to bloom, but also must stop any person or entity from thwarting these displays. It obviously does not have to take in and enforce anything like a U.S. national perspective.

In sum, Puerto Ricans need not commit national cultural suicide to be part of the United States. They may remain faithful to their nationality, as individuals and even as a group. What they may not do is recruit their political institutions in this effort. When Pedro Albizu Campos, who headed the Puerto Rican Nationalist Party, declared Puerto Rico "the grave of U.S. liberalism," he demonstrated that he was not fully aware of the ambitions and possibilities of that political philosophy. When he dismisses the annexation option in the following terms, he exposes once again his narrowmindedness on the issue: "Given the impossibility of transforming this Hispanic-American nation into an Anglo-Saxon community, it is absurd to deal with statehood, which would require asking the United States to dismantle its national unity."[53] Puerto Rico does not have to become an "Anglo-Saxon community" nor capitulate to a rigid notion of "national unity," to become a state of the Union. It is precisely "U.S. liberalism" which bans any such prerequisites to membership in the United States.

The Pluralist State's Embrace of National Diversity

At this point, one can imagine still another reservation with respect to the Puerto Rican national culture's prospects within the confines of the United

States: most Puerto Ricans expect not just acquiescence but the actual aiding and abetting of their cultural ambitions. The culturally neutral liberal state—at the federal and local levels—will do them no good. They need a government that will support them and provide them with the means to carry out their national cultural mission. Their predicament is precisely that they cannot on their own protect and develop their national culture. If they are left to their own devices, that national culture will in all likelihood stagnate. A government that stands by and promises not to get involved is certainly of no help.[54]

An appropriate response might start with the concession that the neutrality-obsessed liberal state depicted in the previous section is inadequate. One might then turn to Michael Walzer's reflections on toleration and insist on the legitimacy of active official encouragement of national groups. Walzer asserts that government, particularly in the United States, may regard pluralism as a good and spend energies promoting diversity. The state may, accordingly, subsidize ethnic or national groups. It need not be indifferent to national cultural issues or limit its role to one of nonintervention.[55]

Walzer maintains that the threat to social unity in contemporary immigrant societies, such as the United States, is not that subgroups, including those based on nationality, are too prominent and are pulling the society apart. He contends that, on the contrary, it is the weakness of these associations that hinders broad societal cohesion. His reasoning unfolds as follows. In the United States the only unifying force is a common political culture. Citizens typically participate not as individuals but as members of particular subgroups in the institutions that embody the shared principles of democracy, legality, and human rights. These civic associations, which may rest on union, gender, or religious or national affiliations, serve as training grounds for political engagement inasmuch as within their ranks their members must already be intersubjectively active. Moreover, participation in the broader collective spectrum usually takes place through these subgroups. Social solidarity has been breaking down because these associations themselves and citizens' links to them have been breaking down. The individual today belongs to multiple communities and it is ever more difficult for her to identify solidly with any particular one of these.

Walzer therefore believes that the government must help reinvigorate these associative subgroups. In thus renouncing its indifference to the collectives formed around specific concepts of the good life, the state not only acts legitimately but also contributes to social stability. Of course it is ultimately up to the individuals themselves whether they want to bond with or distance themselves from a given subgroup. This political reality, to be sure, imposes limits on associations' capacity to keep members in line but, at the same time, guarantees basic individual freedom from coercion. With respect to national groups, Walzer would say that the state must empower them to reproduce their way of life and to bring their peculiar perspective to the society-wide political deliberation. The state may, for instance, subsidize their organizational efforts and their cultural activities.

Habermas embraces a similar approach when he asserts that the state may actively encourage multiculturalism as a collective good. He maintains that the state may provide the means through which groups and individuals can protect and develop their culture. Habermas nonetheless cautions that it is pointless for the state to try, on its own, to safeguard the survival of cultural communities as if they were endangered species.[56] If the peoples concerned are not themselves willing to strive for their own continued existence, any state effort will be hopeless.

Both Walzer and Habermas insist, however, that the state must be impartial or neutral when engaging in cultural politics. They do not mean, of course, to take back what they said about the state's cultural engagement. Nor do they thus intend to assert that the government must provide equal support to the various groups in absolute terms. Their idea is instead that the official assistance to national subgroups must be equal in relative terms. Thus a traditionally disadvantaged community may receive more aid than a historically privileged one.

The United States, conceived as a pluralist state along these lines, may engage in and allow official support for the Puerto Rican culture. Under this logic, the federal and Puerto Rico governments may even invest in and promote the Puerto Rican national culture to a greater extent than that of other national groups. It would be necessary to show that that national culture has suffered substantial discrimination throughout the years that calls for compensation or is generally in a position of disadvantage vis-à-vis other national cultures.

Of course every state of the Union spends some effort promoting the history and traditions of its residents. Yet what is at stake here is far more. The government of Puerto Rico, with the connivance and perhaps even assistance of its U.S. counterpart, would be upholding not any culture that emerges on Puerto Rican soil, but rather the Puerto Rican national culture. Though it has no precedent in the United States, this approach finds support in the pluralist vision described. One might justify carving out an exception for Puerto Rico on the grounds that it is the only major territorial unit in the United States inhabited overwhelmingly by citizens with a distinct national culture.

Asymmetrical Federalism's Concessions to National Sovereignty

Up to now, I have argued against the notion that to be part of the United States Puerto Ricans must give up their cultural nationality, individually or even as a group. As a liberal state, the United States must, on the contrary, make sure *not* to interfere with Puerto Ricans' national identity. I have noted, moreover, that the governments of Puerto Rico and the United States may foment the Puerto Rican national culture in the name of pluralism.

Carried to their full extent, however, the previously described Puerto Rican national cultural ambitions do not fit within the liberal or pluralist model. A liberal pluralist state would allow and even subsidize efforts by Puerto Ricans to live and reproduce their national culture. They would thus receive official acknowledgment and encouragement on a par with other national groups, such as Italian Americans or Irish Americans. Yet many Puerto Ricans seem to want not merely the status of "another minority group in a pluralist society" but rather that of a "nationality, a different people." They appear to have an interest not merely in public notice and general subventions but rather in an intense identification with their national culture on the part of the current commonwealth or a future federal state of Puerto Rico, with the acquiescence and perhaps encouragement of the U.S. federal government.

Construed along the lines I have proposed, Puerto Rican cultural ambitions amount to a version of what Charles Taylor has denominated a claim to recognition. Taylor explains what he means as follows:

> The recognition I am talking about here is the acceptance of ourselves by others in our identity. We may be 'recognized' in other senses—for example, as equal citizens, or right-bearers, or as being entitled to this or that service—and still be unrecognized in our identity. In other words, what is important to us in defining who we are may be quite unacknowledged, may even be condemned in the public life of our society, even though all our citizens' rights are firmly guaranteed.[57]

Many Puerto Ricans demand, however, not just the kind of acknowledgment a pluralist state might grant, meaning general words of encouragement and subventions on a par with those received by other cultural groups. They want their state government's preferential support for and identification with their national perspective. They seek thus to be in a position to act as a political community and collectively recognize themselves. From the federal government, they expect recognition as this kind of self-constituting and self-empowering collectivity.

This kind of protection for the Puerto Rican national culture is not only unprecedented in the U.S. federation but, additionally, goes beyond the limits of the pluralism depicted in the previous section.[58] Michael Walzer conceives of the nationalities within the U.S. "union of nationalities"[59] as rather informal groups, which live dispersed throughout the country and do not constitute a corporate political unit. In other words, they do not have any kind of official self-government. Walzer agrees with Habermas, moreover, that the state may not violate broad notions of ethical neutrality, at least in relative terms. Though the state need not be "perfectly indifferent to group culture," Walzer insists that it must be "equally supportive of all groups."[60] If culturally active along the lines just traced, the Puerto Rican government would have excessive control over the national culture's definition and membership and would show too much partiality toward one of the national groups within its borders. If the federal government supports or even consents to this kind of endorsement of national culture, it would make itself an accomplice in the violation of the principles of liberal pluralism.

Within the pluralist model, the U.S. and the Puerto Rico governments may subsidize Puerto Ricans and their national culture more than any other group only to the extent that they constitute a disadvantaged minority. These subventions would amount to a compensation and reparation for past discrimination. The Puerto Rico government may not, however, see itself as the representative of the Puerto Rican people in any special sense. It must embody, on rigidly equal terms, the goals shared by all persons residing in Puerto Rico. It has to be the collective voice and arm not only of Puerto Ricans but also, without distinctions, of U.S. natives and other U.S. citizens who happen to live on the island. Its prerogatives in national cultural affairs do not go beyond those of New York State, which may similarly provide extra support for its Puerto Rican community only insofar as necessary to make up for prior injustices but must otherwise remain generally impartial.

Puerto Rico's situation, of course, is different from that of any other state of the Union because Puerto Ricans are not a minority among others but actually a staggering majority of well over 90 percent of the population. This fact does not, however, entitle the Puerto Rico government to side with its Puerto Rican constituency. The pluralist standpoint would actually go out of its way to ban partiality toward the Puerto Rican national culture under these circumstances, for any such bias would constitute an injustice against overwhelmingly outnumbered minorities, such as U.S. natives and other non–Puerto Ricans residing on the island.

The freely associated state or a future fully integrated state of Puerto Rico, naturally, cannot disregard the wishes of 90 percent of the people it represents. It must, nonetheless, ignore all requests that that group makes as a national or ethnic unit and against the will of all other groups. Otherwise it would be in breach of the pluralist dogma. It may, therefore, attend to the needs of the Puerto Rican majority only on matters that do not involve making special ethnic concessions. With respect to these issues, incidentally, Puerto Ricans would probably not vote as a block. They would presumably break down in the same proportions as the rest of the citizenry.

Liberal pluralism, accordingly, would allow for no "Institute of Puerto Rican Culture," strictly speaking, but at most an "Institute of Culture," which would simply promote cultural expression on the island irrespective of its ethnic or national identification. The institute would not be able categorically to exclude "Anglo" cultural projects, just as the state of Montana may not refuse funding for Greek American or African American events. The contention that the excluded groups traditionally have no significant presence in the state and are therefore not really part of the collective ethnic identity is irrelevant. The governments of Puerto Rico and Montana, respectively, have no business delineating and watching over Puerto Rican and Montanan culture.

Liberal pluralism as practiced in the United States, moreover, would condemn Puerto Rico's language policies. The commonwealth is, and a future entirely integrated state of Puerto Rico would be, committed to keeping Spanish as an official and as the vernacular language. From this standpoint, the state government would conduct its business (including public school teaching) in Spanish and take measures to encourage the use of Spanish in everyday life. The state would thus show itself to be too biased in favor of, and too identified with, the Puerto Rican majority. Just as it bans these practices, U.S. liberal pluralism would prohibit similar action by any other state—even (or especially) if the Spanish-speaking community attained majority status.

In this regard, a counterargument is available which would challenge the premises of U.S. liberal pluralism. U.S. liberal pluralism shows with respect to this issue that it is not evenhanded but rather tilted toward the English-speaking majority and, more abstractly, to individuals of English origin. Though probably historically and practically ineluctable, this imbalance is a scar, for which the United States can partially make up through a tolerant language policy.[61] Declaring English the official language as well as categorically precluding states from operating in foreign languages would, accordingly, be out of the question.

To sum up, liberal pluralism would ban state support of the Puerto Rican national culture beyond the aid afforded other groups or beyond what making up for past discrimination would require. From the liberal pluralist vantage point, moreover, it is illegitimate for the government to present itself as principally representing Puerto Ricans. The state must actually take pains in order *not* to side consistently with the overwhelming majority. Inasmuch as it purports to subsidize preferentially and identify intensely with the Puerto Rican culture, the current commonwealth is, and a future fully integrated state of Puerto Rico would be, in violation of the U.S. political culture as expressed by liberal pluralism. As long as Puerto Rico is part of the United States, the state government is under an obligation to honor this prevailing political culture and, in case of breach, the federal authorities must step in. Only with respect to language would Puerto Rico be able legitimately to favor its national majority.

In many ways, the conflict in Puerto Rico between local efforts to uphold the national culture and federal liberal pluralism resembles that in Quebec. Charles Taylor describes the Québecois situation as follows: In Canada as a whole, the prevailing view is that the state should remain neutral vis-à-vis the particular conceptions of the good life of its citizens.[62] That is, political institutions must create a space in which individuals are able to choose their way of life freely, without any official interference. According to this liberal theory, any state encouragement of a particular existential perspective is unfair to people adhering to other viewpoints and violates the individuals' autonomy, meaning their right to decide on the best outlook on their own.

In contrast, Quebec separatists take a communitarian stance inasmuch as they believe that the state may and actually should side with particular cultural values. They regard French culture as a collective good that might disappear unless the state takes affirmative steps. In other words, if the state merely leaves it up to individuals, they will tend to assimilate to the English culture, which predominates in the nation as a whole and which the United States powerfully exports from the south. From this perspective, the state has a duty to stand up and save this besieged culture. It is no surprise that people brought up in this culture are the ones who tend to take this kind of position.

Analogously, in Puerto Rico a deep official commitment to the national culture at the local level clashes with the political culture at the federal level. This conflict takes place under not only a liberal but also under a pluralist interpretation of that political culture. It therefore seems that Puerto Rico has to give up its thoroughgoing state engagement in national cultural affairs in order to be part of the United States. As a freely associated state or as a future state of the Union, Puerto Rico may, of course, conduct business as usual despite running on a collision course with the prevailing U.S. political culture for a while. Yet Puerto Rico would face immense political (and perhaps even constitutional) pressure and would eventually have to yield.

One might question the need for the extraordinary commitment to national culture that many Puerto Ricans desire. Why should the governments of Puerto Rico and the United States do more than merely allow Puerto Ricans on their own to develop their national identity or at most offer them some state subventions? Does the proposed official national support for culture not amount to treating the Puerto Rican community as an endangered species? If the Puerto Ricans are not willing or able to preserve their national culture on their own or even with some governmental aid, why should anybody—let alone the state—feel an obligation to step in? Would such a governmental policy not be patronizing and ultimately doomed to fail, inasmuch as Puerto Rican individuals do not have the motivation or the means to uphold their national culture?

To begin answering these queries, one has to understand the specific predicament that a threatened national culture may face. Needless to say, if those who are part of that culture have no real interest in upholding it, it is illegitimate and hopeless for the state to try to take their place. Yet, it may be that, while these individuals do perceive their national culture as a public good whose survival is a matter of fundamental concern for them, they face a collective action problem. It may be, in other words, that even though they collectively will the flourishing of the national culture, they make choices at an individual level that prevent them from realizing their collective aim. They cannot coordinate their actions and, as a consequence, bring about an outcome that they recognize as suboptimal or even disastrous.

I have in mind, obviously, the classic prisoner's dilemma, in which it is individually rational but collectively irrational for two isolated codefendants to confess.[63] Puerto Rico provides a case in point. Most Puerto Ricans regard their national culture as a public good that they are able truly to protect only collectively. The kind of threat to the culture at issue would not be such if they were in a position simply to act on their preferences and go on with their cultural life without any worries. The difficulty lies precisely in that if the existing situation runs its course and they continue to make their individual choices as always, there will be a cultural dead weight loss. The problem simply cannot find a solution through the "invisible hand" celebrated by Adam Smith.[64] Puerto Ricans need to band together as a polity and undertake extreme measures to guarantee the thriving of their national culture.

Obviously, the fact that Puerto Ricans reasonably believe that they need their government's assistance in order to preserve their treasured national culture does not mean that it is legitimate for the government to take this role. In fact, liberalism and even pluralism as described above repudiate this kind of official state action, basically because it is unfair to, and discriminates against, those who are not part of the privileged cultural world of the nation. Taylor's response to this charge is that as long as it does not violate fundamental rights, the state may endorse a particular national perspective. The state may, according to Taylor, side with one of its national groups when it adopts policies with respect to commercial speech or public school instruction language. It may not do the same, however, when legislating in the area of voting rights or rights of criminal defendants.

Drawing a line between rights that are fundamental and those that are not is not only difficult but may, at times, appear arbitrary. Further, if this basic charter of rights includes anything like an equality or antidiscrimination principle, then the kind of discrimination that Taylor wants to endorse would not pass muster under a liberal interpretation. Instead of protecting cultural dissidents through a universal liberal set of fundamental rights, therefore, a nationally oriented state should propose its own reasonable collection of individual rights to guarantee a sphere of liberty to all persons who do not want to be part of the national-culture crusade. One also has to recognize that the state's identification with the majority culture may not be legitimate in all cases. Some states may not have the moral option of taking sides in cultural politics. Only those that are able to show that their national culture is genuinely at risk and that their cultural policies do not aim at oppressing disadvantaged minority groups will have this kind of national cultural prerogative. When the favored majority culture is already dominant and carries with it a heavy history of oppressiveness against others, one should be extremely wary with respect to its official protection.

A related point is that sometimes, due to extensive ethnic and cultural miscegenation, a national culture develops that belongs as much (or perhaps even more) to disadvantaged groups as to the elite. Under this scenario, which José Luis González maintains holds true in Puerto Rico,[65] it is not terribly problematic when the state embraces the national culture. For the national culture then is liberating and in no way intimidating to others.

From this contextual viewpoint, one would defer to the efforts of Puerto Rico's government in favor of its main ethnic constituency, but not to those of the U.S. government. This does not mean, of course, that there are no limits to what the Puerto Rico government may legitimately do in this regard. Some actions on behalf of the national culture will constitute too much of an affront to the dignity of minority groups, even relatively privileged ones, such as U.S. natives. The limits on the official cultural efforts will come from the particular principled charter of individual rights already alluded to.

If Puerto Rican cultural aspirations clash with U.S. liberal pluralism, it appears that they must yield if Puerto Rico is to remain within the United States. For liberal pluralism contains the "political principles" upon which rests the minimal "social unity" or "overlapping consensus," to use Rawlsian terminology. In Habermasian jargon, liberal pluralism exhausts the "political culture" through which the United States achieves "social integration" and defines its "constitutional patriotism." If it insists on its cultural policies, Puerto Rico will not meet the minimum requirements to stay within the United States and will call into question what the United States is all about.

What about adopting for Puerto Rico the solution that Taylor advocates for Quebec, in order to allow the two conflicting sets of political principles or political cultures, each of which one can reasonably defend within its own context, peacefully to coexist? Taylor's "binational" interpretation of the federal compact suggests a way in which the U.S. federation might evolve to recognize fully Puerto Rican cultural distinctness. This arrangement, which I referred to earlier as asymmetrical federalism, would transform the larger political entity into a multinational state.[66]

Taylor believes that Canada as a whole should adopt an extremely thin political culture, which includes only a very basic concept of democracy and human rights, and that each province—or, at the very least, Quebec—should have the right to choose between the Anglo-Canadian liberal and the Franco-Canadian communitarian conceptions of political culture. Taylor evokes his vision thus:

> Suppose that we lived in a country where the common understanding was that there was more than one formula for citizenship and where we could live with the fact that different people related to different formulae. Suppose that we wanted to preserve our common political values, our mode of liberal democracy, and our ways of providing for our common needs—which in fields such as medical care are so different from those of our immediate neighbours.[67]

Social integration would thus rest not only on the shared political culture but also on a particular idea of economic solidarity.

Taylor would concede that complete sovereignty would readily enable Quebec to embrace its own preferred, communitarian political culture and thus to attain the recognition it longs for. He admits specifically that the formal trappings of sovereignty—the exchange of ambassadors, a seat in the United Nations, and so on—is what it means to be internationally recognized. This, incidentally, is why it is very hard to conceive of the independentist movement in Quebec willingly making a deal for a renewed federation short of sovereignty; for the legal status of a sovereign country is essential to their goal.[68]

Such international recognition would allow the Québecois, most significantly, to bolster their sense of common cultural identity. Yet Taylor cautions that Quebec does not need full sovereignty, but only "some kind of political personality," in order to reach the same goals. He insists that within the kind of federation he supports, which is "founded on the duality that is basic to the country," Quebec can achieve this goal.[69] "A public acceptance that the country is the locus of two nations," he proposes, "could allow the international recognition that has hitherto always been muted."[70] More importantly, binational federalism would allow Quebec to adhere to its own set of political principles without having to secede. The provincial government would be in a position to act with partiality toward and to identify intensely with the national culture. The Québecois community would thus be able collectively to give itself the longed for recognition.

Walzer, in fact, suggests that this kind of federalist solution offers the only hope of democratic and egalitarian survival not only for Canada but for all "composite states" with "groups of people who share some but not all of the characteristics of a distinct historical community and who retain a strong territorial base."[71] This seems to be almost an invitation to consider the applicability of asymmetrical federalism to the case of Puerto Rico. Puerto Rico not only constitutes a community with a history and a territorial base distinct from those of the United States, but also with its own peculiar political culture. Construed broadly as a composite or binational state, the United States would be able to permit Puerto Rico the intense official devotion to its national culture described above. Puerto Rico could thus retain commonwealth status or become a state of the Union and nonetheless take a different path on matters of culture. Puerto Ricans would be in a position to achieve the recognition Taylor has in mind, not only internationally but also internally. Their government would have the authority to treat preferentially and embrace the Puerto Rican national culture.

One way of arriving at this solution would be to decide that the United States is throughout a union of nations, with each state representing a separate nation and having the opportunity to decide on its own matters of political culture. However, much as it once might have been a real option, this model has been rejected in the United States. In addition, it would not be possible philosophically to justify allowing all of the states of the Union to side with the cultural perspective of the ethnic majority along the lines that I have suggested above for the case of Puerto Rico.

A more reasonable way of permitting Puerto Rico to pursue its own particular political culture while staying within the United States would be to maintain the current relations among the fifty states of the Union and to create a special binational relationship between them all and Puerto Rico. The fifty states would share with each other a common political culture but with Puerto Rico only some principles of political and economic solidarity. An even clearer way of describing this kind of arrangement would be as an asymmetrical federation. The fifty states' links with each other and with the federal government would be equal and roundly symmetrical, whereas Puerto Rico's federal bonds would be unique and distinct from those of the rest of the states.

Puerto Rico thus would be able legitimately to continue its current cultural policies. It would have the right to preserve the Puerto Rican Culture Institute as well as state funding of the Puerto Rican Atheneum. It would be entitled to maintain its tax incentives for Puerto Rican films. It would be able rightfully to keep its current international profile in order to reinforce the sense of common cultural identity. It could, as a matter of fact, intensify its engagement in all these areas. It could, accordingly, strengthen its national cultural policy and increase its international presence, particularly in Latin America. Furthermore, there would be no doubt as to the legitimacy of Puerto Rico's language policy.

This kind of asymmetrical federalism could emerge tacitly as well as through explicit agreement. One might contend that the commonwealth is, and the future state of Puerto Rico would be, *sub silentio*, in a relationship of this sort with the rest of the United States. Insofar as they consider their cultural aspirations important, however, Puerto Ricans ought to insist on explicit guarantees. Otherwise, the United States might at any moment use its political and legal mechanisms to crush Puerto Rican national ambitions. If it decided to do so, it would have strong political and legal arguments to justify its actions.

Concluding Thoughts

As I suggested at the outset, asymmetrical federalism gives rise to substantial difficulties both in the abstract and as applied to the relationship between Puerto Rico and the United States. To begin with my general point, it is not clear why different nationalities ought to relate to each other through such a political formula and not as separate nation-states. One may start by examining Charles Taylor's response to this question in the case of Canada.

Why does Taylor not simply favor independence, which is the most direct way toward a separate political culture and toward the recognition of Quebec as a distinct society? For one, he thinks that there are "economic and technological" reasons to keep the nation together. He probably means that Quebec and the rest of Canada will be in a stronger position to achieve their economic and technological development goals if they have a single federal government make decisions. He suggests that the same logic has led the European Community to create supranational structures responsible for adopting unified policy on these matters.[72] Second, Taylor seems to believe that Quebec will be in a better position to preserve its status as a distinct society—with its own political culture and worthy of recognition— within a federation with the rest of Canada than as a sovereign state.[73] The underlying idea is that the threat to Quebec's integrity comes not just from anglophone Canada but also from the United States, and that Quebec can best resist the U.S. cultural invasion in an alliance with the rest of Canada. Finally, Taylor fears that in an independent Quebec ultranationalists will take over. He contends that few things are more spiritually destructive to a community than when ultranationalism wins out and a full-blooded affirmation of the idea of language and culture as a source of identity in its most extreme variant is made the basis of social life. Not only does this breed a willingness to sacrifice everything else on the altar of the nation, but nationalism itself becomes an obsession with power. He laments "the stultifying, repressive obsession with the nation, which is one of the standing dangers in modern civilization."[74] Taylor's preoccupation with ultranationalism, of course, resembles Habermas's concern about ethnonationalism.[75]

I do not want to take a specific position on Quebec. Regardless of how persuasive these three arguments are for keeping Quebec within the Canadian federation, my interest is in reflecting briefly upon whether they bear at all on the Puerto Rican question. The first (economic) reason is always mentioned to support keeping Puerto Rico part of the United States. Yet a sovereign Puerto Rico could conceivably obtain through international agreements many of the economic benefits of being linked to the United States: for example, a large common market or substantial financial aid. An independent Puerto Rico would additionally have regulatory tools that it could theoretically use to invigorate its economy.

Taylor's second contention does not apply to the case of Puerto Rico. There is no threat to the national culture outside the United States against which solid U.S. ties might serve as a protection. On the contrary, outside the territory that the United States and Puerto Rico occupy in the Western hemisphere lies Latin America. Shielding Puerto Rico from Latin America through its U.S. links serves not to fortify but rather to undermine the Puerto Rican national culture. The path toward a more solid Puerto Rican national culture inevitably passes through Latin America.

Thirdly, in Puerto Rico as well as in Quebec, the chances of the ultranationalists taking over after a victory for independence are no greater than those of rabid antinationalists calling the shots following a defeat. The way to avoid these two extremes is the same: to uphold and defend a local political culture that requires the government—whether independent or not—to provide a reasoned defense of its cultural policies and to honor a sacred sphere of individual liberty.

More generally, Taylor's thin federation proposal, if carried to its ultimate consequences, would create a situation in which there would barely be national unity at the federal level. The relationship between the national community and the rest of the country would be no different from that between two independent states that agree to a bilateral scheme to enforce a broad bill of international human rights. The two asymmetrically federated entities, like two sovereign states, would maintain a separate political identity and converge only on a discrete series of norms regarding democracy, legality, and human rights. The continued economic integration of the country as a whole would not undermine the analogy, inasmuch as the two sovereign states could sign a transnational economic consolidation pact.

Genuine political integration requires agreement not only on a thin but also on a thick political culture. What distinguishes a nation-state from the international community is precisely that the former recognizes a very specific assortment of political principles, whereas the latter endorses a relatively abstract set. Therefore, national political integration is rather complete, while its international counterpart is only partial. Of course, there are no absolutely clear-cut criteria for deciding when a political entity is integrated enough to constitute a nation-state. Yet, to the extent that a nation-state must enjoy a high degree of political integration, a national subgroup may seek independence in order to carry out political integration on different terms.

On this analysis, the European Union may ride on a thin political convergence only so long as it remains an association of sovereign states. Under such circumstances, it will suffice to have broad democratic guidelines and a general convention of human rights. In order to become a nation-state, the Union must achieve full political integration around a well-developed political consciousness.[76] Habermas, accordingly, refers to the need for "a Europe-wide *political* culture" and explains that "[a] European constitutional patriotism must . . . coalesce out of the various nationally and historically impregnated interpretations of the same universal principles of law." Europe would thus have to come together politically to the extent Switzerland has: "The case of Switzerland demonstrates that such a common political and cultural self-understanding can stem from the cultural orientation of different nationalities." Needless to say, if it ever reaches this stage, the European Union will have to be ready to face the specter of internal nationalist independence movements striving for secession in order to enact a different political culture.

In addition to these reservations I have with respect to asymmetrical federalism as a means to achieve cultural sovereignty, I have concrete doubts about an asymmetrically federalist solution to the case of Puerto Rico. If Quebec has not been able to persuade Canada to go along, Puerto Rico's chances are close to nil, inasmuch as its bargaining position within its existing federal system is immensely weaker than that of Quebec. It is unrealistic to believe that Puerto Rico will be able to negotiate an asymmetrically federalist deal with the United States.

It is, nonetheless, a mistake to start with a discussion of the merits and feasibility of asymmetrical federalism. It is similarly wrongheaded to begin arguing about whether Puerto Rico should be a state, a commonwealth, or an independent nation. To return to my recurrent theme, the debate in Puerto Rico should first focus on how to configure the U.S.-Puerto Rico relations. Puerto Ricans should discuss with their U.S. interlocutors which functions should fall upon the Puerto Rican government and which should be shared with the U.S. government. A constant of this conversation ought to be that the national culture is not negotiable. Once the people of Puerto Rico and of the United States settle all these issues, my hope is that it will be easier for them to decide whether they want to relate to each other federally or internationally. Maybe they will then be in a position to reflect objectively upon the merits and the plausibility of each of these two options.

Notes

I would like to thank Phillip Blumberg, Mark Janis, and Rick Kay for their critical comments on earlier drafts.

1   Elea Carey, "Spark's Novel Was Worth the Wait," *Commercial Appeal* (Memphis, January 22, 1995), at 3G.

2   U.S. federal law—which in this century has expanded immensely and now covers vast parts of public as well as private law in the United States—applies in Puerto Rico as in any state of the Union. Yet Puerto Ricans have no real representation in the legislative body that produces this law. They send no senators or representatives to the U.S. Congress. They only have a resident commissioner—with voice but no vote (except in committee)—in the U.S. House of Representatives. They do not participate in U.S. presidential elections, though (oddly enough) they do take part in U.S. presidential primaries. They therefore lack ultimate electoral influence over the president who nominates, or the Senate which consents to, the judges who sit in the federal court in Puerto Rico. See, e.g., José Trías Monge, *Sociedad, derecho y justicia* (1986), at 22. Even in Cuba, the most undemocratic regime in Latin America, the people go through the ritual—though it may not be much more than that—of voting for the individuals who enact the supreme law of the land.

3   Puerto Ricans receive these funds even though they do not pay a cent in federal income taxes.

4   Juan Manuel Carrión poses a similar question: "How can one also account for the dichotomy within a cultural nationalism, which expresses itself with great force but which in its political manifestations shows weakness?" Juan Manuel Carrión, *Voluntad de nación: Ensayos sobre el nacionalismo en Puerto Rico* (1996), at 105; see also 232.

5   See Ramón López, "Reveladora encuesta sobre el idioma," *Diálogo* (January 1993), at 14 ("The overwhelming majority of Puerto Ricans consider themselves culturally different from U.S.-Americans.") (referring to a poll conducted for the Puerto Rican Atheneum); Raymond Carr, *Puerto Rico: A Colonial Experiment* (1984), at 296–97 (Puerto Rican "traits and values . . . are distinct from those of North America. . . . Moreover the [Puerto Rican] tribe has preserved its own language."); ibid. at 268 ("In a survey made in the early 1970's, an overwhelming majority of middle-class schoolteachers saw" Puerto Rico as culturally distinct from the United States.) (citing Luis Nieves Falcón and P. Cintrón de Crespo, *Los maestros de instrucción pública de Puerto Rico* (1973), at 99–141; Carrión, supra note 5 ("Puerto Ricans want to continue being different from Americans while keeping the benefits of the U.S. welfare state; they want to see these benefits increased up to a level of parity with that of the states of the Union.").

6   See Carr, ibid. at 297.

7   Ibid. (The term *jíbaro* is explained below. See infra note 18 and accompanying text.) See also Carrión, supra note 4, at 30–31. Carrión unfairly accuses the New Progressive Party of abandoning the idea of a jíbaro state and of returning to pre-1967 "pitiyanki"—i.e., U.S. adulatory—conceptions, upon perceiving, following the collapse of a U.S. congressional attempt to implement a plebiscite process, "that Puerto Rican culture constitutes an obstacle for statehood." Ibid. at 155; see also 160, 168. See also Carr, supra note 5, at 277 ("Universalism, by which the intellectuals of the PNP meant Western values as mediated by America, could be used if not to deny the existence of a specific Puerto Rican culture, at least to denigrate it.").

8   *Programa del Partido Independentista Puertorriqueño 1996 (http://www.pip.org.pr/prog96.htm)* at 90 [hereinafter *Programa (PIP)*].

9   Ibid.

10   Ibid.

11   See Carrión, supra note 4, at 179 ("A 'reciprocal citizenship' treaty must be worked out, which takes into account that Puerto Ricans residing in the United States are part of our nation.").

12   *Programa (PIP)*, supra note 8, at 90.

13   Ibid.

14   In its rules and regulations, the New Progressive Party states: "The New Progressive Party promotes Puerto Rican culture together with the Spanish language as the vernacular and the English language as the second official language of Puerto Ricans." New Progressive Party, Rules and Regulations, Statement of Purpose, http://www.pnp.org/ReglasTodo.htm. In its platform, the party declares: "We shall support the activities of the Institute of Puerto Rican Culture in its effort to help hundreds of public and private entities promote cultural engagement." New Progressive Party, 1996 Platform, Cultural Matters, § 101, *http://www.pnp.org/ A_SOCIAL.htm#cultura;* see also § 114 [hereinafter *Platform (NPP)*].

15   Carlos Romero Barceló, one of the founders of the New Progressive Party as well as a former governor and Resident Commissioner, has explicitly proclaimed that Puerto Rico's language and culture are not negotiable. See José Luis González, *Nueva Visita al Cuarto Piso* (1986), at 84 (see also 104); Carr, supra note 5, at 297 ("[I]t is significant that modern statehooders have had to acknowledge that Spanish will remain an official language if Puerto Rico becomes the fifty-first state.").

16   See Carr, ibid. at 145 ("Although many early statehooders were ruthless Americanizers, the PNP rejects with indignation the charge that it is indifferent to Puerto Rican culture."). But cf. ibid. at 267–68 ("All [parties other than the New Progressive Party] make the defense of Puerto Rican culture a center of their programs; a culture distinct from that of mainland America.").

17   Ibid. at 297. See Carrión, supra note 4, at 30–31; but cf. 155, 160, 168.

18   See Manuel Antonio Alonso, *El Jíbaro: Cuadro de Costumbres de la Isla de Puerto Rico* (1974).

19   See Fernando Picó, *Historia General de Puerto Rico* (1986), at 278–80.

20   This was the Popular Democratic Party's slogan in the 1993 plebiscite, in which the party promoted an improved version of the current political status as offering " 'the best of two worlds,' the benefits of statehood and independence without the disadvantages of these two political formulas." Carrión, supra note 4, at 173; see also 232.

21   See Carr, supra note 5, at 297.

22   Ibid. See also González, supra note 15, at 40 (There is a "good cultural reason to struggle for independence.").

23   See Carrión, supra note 4, at 176.

24   The platform of the Puerto Rican Independence Party, not surprisingly, underscores the

tardiness and questions the authenticity of the other parties' commitment to the national culture. *Programa (PIP)*, supra note 8, at 86 ("Even those who in the past reduced culture to its folkloric expressions while promoting policies of assimilation and incarcerating those who defended our culture and nationality today proclaim themselves defenders of our culture and national identity.").

25 See Carrión, supra note 4, at 2; see also 30.

26 See *Información, Plebiscito 93, Comisión Estatal de Elecciones de Puerto Rico,* http://www. ceepur.org/ [hereinafter *Información*].

27 See generally, Juan Cavestany, "Los puertorriqueños rechazan por tercera vez la integración plena en Estados Unidos," *El País*, December 14, 1998; Julio Ghigliotty, "La quinta por mayoría absoluta," *El Nuevo Día*, December 14, 1998.

28 See *Información*, supra note 26.

29 See Mario Vargas Llosa, "Sirenas en el Amazonas," *El País*, December 8, 1998 ("A culture is not a concentration camp or an immutable condition of being. It is a human creation that is subject to transformation. It is a spiritual landscape that changes at the rhythm of human action, just like dunes change at the whim of the wind.").

30 See Mark Twain, cable from London to the Associated Press (1897) ("The reports of my death have been greatly exaggerated.").

31 Carrión, supra note 4, at 104.

32 See González, supra note 15, 105–6, 111–12.

33 See Carr, supra note 5, 279–81, 297.

34 See María M. López Laguerre, *El Bilingüismo en Puerto Rico* (1997), at 24–40; Luis Muñiz Argüelles, "The Status of Languages in Puerto Rico," in *El debate legislativo sobre las leyes del idioma en Puerto Rico,* ed. Carmelo Delgado Cintrón (1994), 69–82; González, supra note 15, at 105; Alfonso L. García Martínez, "Language Policy in Puerto Rico 1898–1930," *Revista del Colegio de Abogados de Puerto Rico* 42 (1981): 87; Alfonso L. García Martínez, *Idioma y política en Puerto Rico* (1976); Aida Negrón de Montilla, *Americanization in Puerto Rico and the Public-School System, 1900–1930* (1971); Juan J. Osuna, *A History of Education in Puerto Rico* (1949).

35 Trías Monge, supra note 2, at 27–28, 38–40.

36 See *Valle v. American International Insurance,* 108 D.P.R. 692 (1979).

37 See Carr, supra note 5, at 79. See generally José Trías Monge, *Historia Constitucional de Puerto Rico* 3 (1982), at 270–312.

38 Carr, supra note 5, at 117.

39 Ibid. at 290.

40 See González, supra note 15, at 112–13; Carr; supra note 5, 293–94.

41 See Luis Rafael Sánchez, *No llores por nosotros Puerto Rico* (1990).

42 See generally, José Luis González, *El país de cuatro pisos y otros ensayos* (1980).

43 See José Oswald de Andrade, "Manifiesto Antropófago," *Revista de antropofagia* 1 (1928): 1.

44 Miguel de Unamuno y Jugo, "Comunidad de la lengua hispánica," in *La raza vasca y el vascuence: En torno a la lengua española* (1974), at 172.

45 18 *P.R. Laws Ann.* § 1198 (1992). See also Picó, supra note 19, at 271; Carr, supra note 5, at 276.

46 See 18 *P.R. Laws Ann.* § 1202 (1992); 1995 PR ALS 381; 1995 PR ALS 125; see Picó, supra note 19, at 221.

47 See *Platform (NPP)*, supra note 14, Cultural Matters, § 101; see also § 114.

48 See 13 *P.R. Laws Ann.* § 9047 (1996); 13 *P.R. Laws Ann.* § 8630 (1996); 13 *P.R. Laws Ann.* § 10002 (1996); 7 *P.R. Laws Ann.* § 1243 (1994); 18 *P.R. Laws Ann.* §§ 1302–3 (1992).

49 18 *P.R. Laws Ann.* § 1198(a)(20) (1992).

50 See Carrión, supra note 4, at 181 (arguing that it is "utopian" to expect real respect for "national identities and ethnic differences"); see also 207.

51 John Rawls, *Political Liberalism* (1993). See also John Rawls, *A Theory of Justice* (1971).

52 Interestingly enough, an early annexationist, José Celso Barbosa, advocated an "intelligent patriotism," which in some ways appears to parallel the notion of constitutional patriotism. He wrote: "Fatherland is not just the land where one is born. Our liberties and rights are fatherland too." José Celso Barbosa, "Conversación familiar," in *Antología del pensamiento puertorriqueño, 1900–1970*, ed. Eugenio Fernández Méndez (1975). Barbosa, however, pleaded for the U.S.-Americanization of Puerto Rico and a yielding to the English language. See generally Carrión, supra note 4, at 212–13.

53 Rubén Berríos Martínez, "Definición y convergencia," *Partido Independista Puertorriqueño* (http://www.pip.org.pr/artdef.htm) (quoting Pedro Albizu Campos).

54 Of course, neither of the parties advocating keeping Puerto Rico within the United States proposes that the government of Puerto Rico be culturally indifferent in this sense.

55 Michael Walzer, *On Tolerance* (1997), at 37; see also 34.

56 See Jürgen Habermas, "Multiculturalism and the Liberal State," in "Symposium: Race and Remedy in a Multicultural Society. Address," *Stanford Law Review* 47 (1995): 849, at 850 ("There cannot be a 'preservation' of cultures in the same sense as most of us advocate the preservation of animals or other species. The reproduction of traditions and cultural forms is an achievement which can be legally enabled, but by no means granted. Reproduction here requires the conscious appropriation and application of traditions by those native members who have become convinced of these traditions' intrinsic value. The members must first come to see that the inherited traditions are worth the existential effort of continuation."). See also Jürgen Habermas, *Die Einbeziegung des Anderen: Studien Zur Politischen Theorie* (1996), at 259. Walzer would endorse this Habermasian contention. He declares: "Pluralism has in itself no powers of survival; it depends upon energy, enthusiasm, commitment within the component groups; it cannot outlast the particularity of cultures and creeds." Walzer, supra note 55 at 65. Walzer asserts further that "early pluralists . . . were surely right to insist that [ethnic vitality] should not artificially be kept alive, any more than it should be repressed by state power." Walzer, supra note 55, at 74; see also 76–77.

57 Charles Taylor, *Reconciling the Solitudes: Essays on Canadian Federalism and Nationalism* (1993), at 190. See generally 48, 52, 58, 142–43, 162, 169, 188 and 190–96; Charles Taylor, "Multiculturalism and the Politics of Recognition," in *Multiculturalism*, ed. Amy Gutmann (1992).

58 Juan Manuel Carrión avers that "the fundamental problem that the statehood movement has always faced is the repudiation by many U.S.-Americans of the idea of admitting as a federal state a culturally different entity such as Puerto Rico." Carrión, supra note 4, at 168.

59 Michael Walzer, *What It Means to Be an American* (1991), at 9.

60 Walzer, supra note 55, at 37; see also 34.

61 José Luis González expresses grounded skepticism about the United States's willingness to show this kind of flexibility on language matters. González, supra note 15, at 104.

62 See Taylor (1993), supra note 57.

63 According to Robert Axelrod, Merril Flood and Melvin Dresher invented the prisoners' dilemma game in 1950 and A. W. Tucker formalized it shortly thereafter. Robert Axelrod, *The Evolution of Cooperation* (1984), at 216 n. 3. But see R. Duncan Luce and H. Raiffa, *Games and*

Decisions: Introduction and Critical Survey (1957), at 94 (attributing the prisoners' dilemma game to A. W. Tucker). The game first appeared in Luce and Raiffa's book. It illustrates how the pursuit of a rational strategy by individuals can bring about a collectively irrational result. Social theorists have used the prisoners' dilemma game to illustrate how, in some contexts, individuals can best serve their particular interests through concerted action.

64   Adam Smith, *An Inquiry into the Nature and Causes of the Wealth of Nations* (1937 [1776]), at 423.

65   See generally González, supra note 42.

66   For a discussion of the multinational state, see Will Kymlicka, *Multicultural Citizenship: A Liberal Theory of Minority Rights* (1995).

67   Taylor (1993), supra note 57, at 199.

68   Ibid. at 53; see also 52: "Of course, political independence has a more direct relation to realization. Political sovereignty is itself a realization, one that puts a people on the map."

69   Taylor (1993), supra note 57, at 56, 57. Allen Buchanan believes, however, that Quebec can already afford its national culture sufficient protection under the existing arrangements. See Allen Buchanan, *Secession* (1991), at 61.

70   Taylor (1993), supra note 57, at 57; see also 102 ("Ideally for French Canadians, 'English' Canada should be a nation, in the sense of a constituent entity of a binational state.").

71   Walzer, supra note 59 at 56 ("Thus autonomy may be an alternative to independence, loosening the bonds of the composite state a way to avoid their fracture. Instead of sovereignty, national and ethnic groups may opt for decentralization, devolution, and federalism; these are not incompatible with self-determination, and they may be especially appropriate for groups of people who share some but not all of the characteristics of a distinct historical community and who retain a strong territorial base. Whether composite states can survive as federations is by no means certain, but it is unlikely that they can survive in any other way—not at least, if they remain committed (even if only formally) to democratic government or to some sort of social egalitarianism.").

72   Taylor (1993), supra note 57 at 58.

73   See, e.g., ibid. at 199 ("[W]e might even allow ourselves to see that what is specific to each component—yes, even the French language in Quebec—can more effectively be defended within a broader Canadian frame.").

74   Ibid. at 58; see also 57.

75   Compare Jürgen Habermas (1996), supra note 56, at 154–84.

76   See generally Jürgen Habermas, *Faktizität und Geltung* (1992), at 651. Habermas speaks of "a new political self-consciousness corresponding to the role of Europe in the 21st century world."

Puerto Rican Separatism and United States Federalism

Richard Thornburgh

The status of Puerto Rico has been debated for at least the past one hundred years. The debate has matured, but not waned over that time. As Attorney General of the United States and Chairman of the Domestic Policy Council, I was personally involved in the formulation of the Bush Administration's policy on Puerto Rico's status, as was President Bush himself. In 1991, I testified before the U.S. Senate Committee on Energy and Natural Resources on legislation to resolve the status of Puerto Rico,[1] and the Bush Administration was disappointed that neither the House nor Senate produced legislation at that time which could win the support of Congress as a whole.

In my view, too much emphasis was placed on whether the definitions of status options would be acceptable to the political parties in Puerto Rico, and not enough attention was paid to status definitions which would be fair and meaningful to the individual men and women of Puerto Rico as free people exercising the God-given right of self-determination. Congress has a duty to create an ongoing process to resolve the status question in a manner determined to be in the national interest, and which a majority of the residents of Puerto Rico determine to be in their own best interest in light of the status definitions and process prescribed by Congress.

This problem of presenting clear choices based on accurately defined options still impedes the debate in Congress over status resolution, although the legislation most recently under consideration was much more process-oriented and less result-oriented than previous proposals.[2] This is welcome, because the goal is a process that gives the tools of self-determination to the people concerned, not the achievement of a particular outcome. The people may not want to use those tools, but if the status quo continues it should not be because Congress failed to create a process for democratic determination of the status question.

The single issue which most encumbers the debate on terms for a status resolution process for Puerto Rico is whether Congress is willing to adopt some new paradigm of federalism that would enable Puerto Rico to become a "nation-within-a-nation," so that the difficult choice between statehood and true separate nationhood would not be necessary to achieve a permanent and fully self-governing status. While it avoids a stark choice, the position of "pseudo nationality" is complicated because Congress cannot by statute cede in any degree permanent separate sovereignty, nationality, and citizenship to Puerto Rico, while at the same time enabling Puerto Rico to retain the benefits of U.S. sovereignty, nationality, and citizenship. This will be true no matter how commonwealth status is reformulated in pursuit of greater autonomy and separatism, as well as under any form of associated republic or free association status. At the point the United States recognizes a separate Puerto Rican sovereignty, nationality, and citizenship, in the constitutional and legal sense, then it will be inevitable that U.S. sovereignty, nationality, and citizenship in Puerto Rico will end.

History and U.S. law show that U.S. citizenship will end in one of two ways. When the independent nation of the Philippines succeeded the Philippines commonwealth, U.S. nationality and territorial citizenship for persons who acquired it based on birth in the territory ended and all persons so situated became aliens under U.S. law. Those residing in the United States were repatriated to their homeland in the new republic of the Philippines, except for those who met residency requirements in the states of the Union and thereby were permitted by Congress to become candidates for naturalization. The other option, exemplified in the case of the succession from Spanish to U.S. sovereignty, provides for an election of allegiance to be allowed, requiring a choice of nationalities but not allowing dual nationality to be created by U.S. law or as part of the succession process.

There can be only one national citizenship in a federal system like that of the United States, and only one source of supreme law. The attempt to create a new category of state in union with the United States but with separate nationality under the American flag has failed and cannot succeed under the constitution and government structure of the United States. This essay presents a brief analysis of Puerto Rico's current political status followed by a case study of the attempt in the Puerto Rican renunciation cases to convert cultural nationalism into constitutional and legal separatism.

Some Fundamental Limits on the Power of Congress
to Cede Authority under the Current Status

For the people of Puerto Rico and of the United States, informed self-determination requires that certain fundamental constitutional issues be clarified. First and foremost, Congress must confirm for the people of Puerto Rico that Puerto Rico is still governed ultimately by the Congress pursuant to the Territorial Clause of the U.S. Constitution,[3] and that the Supremacy Clause[4] guarantees that federal law controls in Puerto Rico, as in the States and all territories of the United States. In 1991, I testified before Congress on legislative proposals to provide a framework for informed self-determination, and at that time I urged that the process also be based on clear direction from Congress as to what options should be presented for a vote by the Puerto Rican electorate.

The political status legislation which emerged in Congress in 1990 and 1991 did not receive the support needed for enactment into law during my tenure as Attorney General. In addition, the status referendum conducted in Puerto Rico under local law in 1993 without congressional support or recognition failed to clarify Puerto Rico's status for reasons that included a confused and misleading ballot. Because I believe it is time to resolve the issue of Puerto Rico's political status, I followed the subsequent development of legislation in the House and Senate with keen interest. In my view, this legislation represented significant progress in establishing the principles which must be respected in any legitimate self-determination process to resolve the status question.

I note with concern, however, that it continues to be the position of some that the present "commonwealth" arrangement should be "improved" (or "enhanced") and made permanent. Some advocates of permanent commonwealth in Puerto Rico also seek separate nationality and powers of consent over federal law, powers that even states of the Union do not have under the U.S. Constitution. These individuals would present Congress and the people of Puerto Rico with a definition of "commonwealth" that cannot be implemented. Specifically, Congress is not able to transform the current commonwealth status for Puerto Rico as created by statute into a permanent status guaranteed by the U.S. Constitution. Speaking plainly, that is the principal difference between a statute and a constitution. There is an irreconcilable constitutional conflict that prevents the establishment of a permanent, fixed commonwealth status for Puerto Rico. Only states have a permanent, constitutionally guaranteed status under the federal system, and, without a constitutional amendment, nothing done by the Congress can bind future Congresses in the treatment of Puerto Rico.

The need for a permanent status resolution approved by Congress is made even more clear to me because of my experience as a former Under-Secretary-General of the United Nations. As the highest ranking American official in the United Nations organization, I came to understand thoroughly that the national constitutional processes of the member states define the status of territories under their sovereignty. As discussed below, those in Puerto Rico who assert that the UN decolonization process determines Puerto Rico's status in a way that is binding on the United States are simply incorrect.

The Status of Puerto Rico: A Constitutional Framework for Self-Determination

In any future political-status vote in Puerto Rico it will be necessary to ensure that the voters understand each of the options presented to them: statehood, separate nationhood, and continued commonwealth status. There generally appears to be an understanding of the statehood and separate nationhood options. Unfortunately, there appears to be a great deal of misinformation about the commonwealth option. The people of Puerto Rico have been told that they may adopt a permanent and apparently self-executing "improved commonwealth" proposal. As with the options of statehood or separate nationhood, commonwealth status (however defined) could become effective only when Congress votes to adopt a specified status relationship. To resolve the status issue, Congress must vote to accept the terms of any option approved by the voters of Puerto Rico. Therefore, just as with the status options of statehood and separate nationhood, an initial referendum on status cannot include a definition of *commonwealth* that is merely a collection of proposals for benefits that might be possible. Rather, the definitions must inform the voter as to the constitutional structure of each status and the political process through which any option chosen by the people can be realized.

The foundation for all discussions of Puerto Rico's future status and relationship with the United States must rest on an unambiguous understanding of Puerto Rico's current status. Puerto Rico is presently an unincorporated territory of the United States. Puerto Rico is within the national sovereignty of the United States, but is not a state of the Union. Therefore, unlike in a state of the Union, Congress exercises sovereignty in Puerto Rico, including application of U.S. laws and treaties, under the Territorial Clause of the U.S. Constitution.

The Territorial Clause reads, "The Congress shall have Power to dispose of and make all needful Rules and Regulations respecting the Territory or other Property belonging to the United States."[5] That clause gives Congress the ultimate authority to govern Puerto Rico. The current "commonwealth" structure of federal territorial administration includes internal self-government under the Constitution of Puerto Rico, approved by Congress and the people of Puerto Rico in 1952. Like a state of the Union, the "commonwealth" is an autonomous political entity which exercises sovereignty over matters not governed under the U.S. Constitution. However, this is a statutory and permissive authorization of local sovereignty, subject to the Territorial Clause authority and full sovereignty retained by Congress.

The constitutional structure and political process through which Puerto Rico can pursue improvements to "commonwealth" have been in place for the four decades since the current "Commonwealth of Puerto Rico" structure of local self-government was established pursuant to U.S. Public Law 81-600 in 1952. This does not mean that changes to the present commonwealth structure which may be proposed as improvements are unattainable simply because Congress has failed to adopt those changes in the past. However, any definition of *commonwealth* cannot be adopted unless it is consistent with constitutional principles and informs voters of unavoidable realities. The voters of Puerto Rico must be aware of the following facts and analysis that define the options for Puerto Rico's political-status relationship with the United States.

Relevant History

The following events constitute the constitutional and legal context in which any status legislation must be considered by Congress.

1. The United States exercises sovereignty with respect to Puerto Rico pursuant to the Treaty of Paris proclaimed by President McKinley on April 11, 1899. Article IX of that treaty provided that, as of that date, persons residing in Puerto Rico who either were not eligible for or did not elect to continue allegiance to Spain or any other nation henceforth would be held under the laws of the United States and international law to owe allegiance to and have the nationality of the United States. Article IX provided further that the "civil rights and political status of the native inhabitants" of Puerto Rico "shall be determined by the Congress."

2. In 1952, Congress provided for Puerto Rico's self-government structure under a local constitution approved by Congress and adopted by the U.S. citizen residents of the territory in 1952, as authorized by U.S. Public Law 81-600. Puerto Rico remains an unincorporated territory of the United States and is self-governing in its internal affairs and administration.

3. On September 27, 1953, the General Assembly of the United Nations

approved Resolution 748(VIII), recognizing the establishment of commonwealth internal self-government in Puerto Rico. Section 9 of that resolution, however, expressly recognized that further self-determination would take place in Puerto Rico "in the eventuality that either of the parties to the mutually agreed association may desire any change in the terms of this association."

4. On November 14, 1993, in a political status plebiscite conducted under Puerto Rican law, without congressional recognition or sponsorship, less than a majority of the voters approved the "enhanced commonwealth" option on the ballot. In light of the fact that the current commonwealth relationship was established in 1952 on the basis of consent by the voters of Puerto Rico, this result underscores the need for a further process of self-determination to resolve the political status of Puerto Rico based on majority consent within Puerto Rico and the approval of Congress.

5. On January 23, 1997, the Puerto Rican Legislature approved Concurrent Resolution 2, which requested the 105th Congress "to respond to the democratic aspirations of the American citizens of Puerto Rico" by approving measures to bring about "a plebiscite sponsored by the Federal Government, to be held no later than 1998."

6. The UN resolution cited before, like the UN Charter itself, is not self-executing, and resolution of Puerto Rico's status can only be accomplished through the U.S. constitutional process. Pursuant to the U.S. Constitution, an area under the sovereignty of the United States that is not included in a state "must necessarily be governed by or under the authority of Congress,"[6] that is, pursuant to the Territorial Clause of the Constitution.

Defining Commonwealth

The following analysis is a brief attempt to sort out fundamental constitutional issues that have become obscured from Congress and the people of Puerto Rico as a result of decades of confusion and misrepresentation of the current status.

1. In 1952, Congress approved establishment of the present commonwealth structure of internal self-government and sovereignty over local affairs in Puerto Rico. Congress did this by exercising the authority reserved to it by the Territorial Clause of the U.S. Constitution. The Territorial Clause remains the source of constitutional authority for Congress to adopt legislation with respect to Puerto Rico, including the authority to approve any proposed change to the existing commonwealth structure.

2. In Puerto Rico, as in a state of the Union, the U.S. Constitution, treaties, and laws of the United States are the supreme law, as made applicable to Puerto Rico by Congress and under rulings of the Supreme Court of the United States.[7]

3. Unlike the condition of a state of the Union under the U.S. Constitution, the "Commonwealth of Puerto Rico" structure of government is not a constitutionally guaranteed or fully self-governing political status. Rather, "commonwealth" in the case of Puerto Rico is a form of local self-government established under a statutory authorization by Congress and instituted under a local constitution approved by Congress and adopted with the consent of the people of Puerto Rico in the manner prescribed by Congress. The political status of Puerto Rico remains that of an unincorporated territory, administered locally under this form of constitutional self-government, limited to internal matters and subject to the plenary authority of Congress under the Territorial Clause.

4. Unlike that of a state of the Union, the form of internal self-government established by Congress for Puerto Rico with the consent of the people in 1952 is not a permanent structure, provision, or feature of the U.S. Constitution or the constitutional process of the United States. In contrast, the sovereignty of a state of the Union and the people thereof who have full constitutional citizenship is a permanent feature of the U.S. Constitution. This is expressly recognized in the federal constitution, including the Tenth Amendment. The grant of internal sovereignty for Puerto Rico and a statutory form of citizenship for Puerto Ricans flow from Congress exercising the discretion retained under the Territorial Clause.

5. Puerto Rico is thus "like a state" in some respects but does not have a full measure of self-government. Under the current system, U.S. citizens of Puerto Rico are subject to U.S. sovereignty and law but remain disenfranchised in the federal political system. This disenfranchisement is the direct result of Puerto Rico's commonwealth status, for as long as Congress exercises ultimate sovereignty through the Territorial Clause, Puerto Ricans will not possess the full panoply of political rights exercised by U.S. citizens in the states of the Union. This is why clarification of the actual nature of commonwealth is so important. Informed self-determination, leading to full self-government, cannot take place as long as the myth of commonwealth as a form of permanent "associated" statehood stands without rebuttal. To empower the people of Puerto Rico, it must be confirmed that territorial commonwealth cannot be "enhanced" so as to "justify" permanent disenfranchisement and less than equal citizenship.

6. Acting under the Territorial Clause, Congress has authority to provide for application of provisions of the U.S. Constitution in Puerto Rico. By statute, Congress can extend the rights, privileges, and immunities of U.S. citizens under the Constitution, laws, and treaties of the United States to Puerto Rico. Conversely, Congress can limit application of certain rights, privileges, and immunities in Puerto Rico. It is also within congressional authority under the Territorial Clause to provide for Puerto Rico's autonomy and sovereignty over internal matters and local affairs. However, U.S. laws apply to Puerto Rico and are enforceable only as long as such statutes are in effect. Congress retains authority under the Territorial Clause to amend or repeal any or all such statutory provisions.

7. The Territorial Clause authorizes Congress to establish procedures for consent by the people of Puerto Rico to the terms and structure of internal self-government under applicable federal statutes. However, a future Congress would not be bound or prevented thereby from changing U.S. law or policy to provide for self-government and self-determination through other means, including statehood or separate sovereignty.

8. In the case of the Commonwealth of the Northern Mariana Islands,[8] Congress required that any proposal by the local government to change the islands' commonwealth structure be approved by Congress. Congress also chose to require the consent of the people of the territory before Congress could impose changes to the local commonwealth structure. Of course, Congress exercised its discretion in the specific context of the Commonwealth of the Northern Mariana Islands. The requirement of consent is a feature of the form of internal self-government agreed to by Congress and enacted by statute, not the political status of the territory or the form of statutory "union" which exists at this time.

9. Congress retains the power to incorporate more fully any such "commonwealth" territory into the U.S. constitutional system, or to reverse the political integration process by advancing self-government options other than continuation of the current commonwealth form. The U.S. Supreme Court has consistently and explicitly recognized the plenary authority of Congress over nonstate areas pursuant to the Territorial Clause.[9] Such congressional authority is recognized and limited by U.S. Supreme Court rulings, such as *Balzac v. Porto Rico,* that the federal government must respect "fundamental rights" in exercising its powers in nonstate areas under U.S. sovereign control.[10] *Balzac* and its progeny require that Congress consider due process and equal protection principles in structuring the measures required to resolve the Puerto Rican status question consistent with the national interest.

10. The present statutory U.S. citizenship of persons born in Puerto Rico does not arise from or exist by virtue of the Constitution of Puerto Rico, or the Puerto Rico Federal Relations Act pursuant to which that local constitution was instituted.[11] Eligibility of persons born in Puerto Rico for U.S. citizenship results entirely from an exercise of congressional discretion. Statutory citizenship initially was prescribed by the organic act of Puerto Rico.[12] In 1940 Congress amended the territorial organic act by removing the provisions governing the citizenship status of Puerto Ricans and including that statutory citizenship in Section 202 of the Nationality Act of 1940. When the Constitution of Puerto Rico was being approved in 1952, Congress again revised the statutory U.S. citizenship provision for Puerto Ricans in Section 302 of the Immigration and Nationality Act. The revision of U.S. citizenship for Puerto Ricans was codified at 8 U.S.C. § 1402, and Congress has chosen not to amend that provision further since 1952.

11. The definition and conferral of U.S. citizenship for persons born in Puerto Rico as described above was not part of the process for establishment of the "Commonwealth of Puerto Rico" structure of constitutional government. U.S. citizenship was conferred by separate statute and was not subject to consent or approval in the process described in section 1 of P.L. 81-600 (48 U.S.C. § 731b) as being "in the nature of a compact." The reference to U.S. citizenship in the Preamble to the Puerto Rican Constitution does not alter the legal nature of citizenship for Puerto Ricans. Nor did approval of the Puerto Rican Constitution convert statutory U.S. citizenship conferred under the Territorial Clause into the same constitutionally guaranteed citizenship arising from birth in a state of the Union.

12. The history of citizenship for Puerto Ricans confirms beyond debate that the nationality and U.S. citizenship of persons born in Puerto Rico is a matter governed by U.S. laws enacted by Congress unilaterally—albeit with broad popular support and acceptance among Puerto Ricans. This unilateral exercise of Territorial Clause authority to define the citizenship status of persons born in Puerto Rico is consistent with Article IX of the Treaty of Paris. Clearly, U.S. nationality and citizenship are not within the scope of delegated internal sovereignty exercised by the people of Puerto Rico under the commonwealth structure of local self-government.

13. Congress has the power to alter, regulate, or even terminate the current rights, privileges, immunities, and benefits of U.S. citizenship for persons born in Puerto Rico. No one can anticipate or predict the circumstances under which Congress would exercise those powers, but the historical precedents created in the case of the Philippines and other U.S. territories make it clear that this is a matter subject to the discretion of

Congress and that such discretion is based primarily on political criteria rather than constitutional or legal factors. Inherent in any definition of commonwealth status is the fact that the U.S. citizenship of persons born in Puerto Rico is secured by statute and not by the U.S. Constitution itself.

14. While the "fundamental rights" analysis of *Balzac* would apply to actions of the United States in Puerto Rico, the U.S. Constitution itself is not thereby made applicable to Puerto Rico as in a state of the Union. The people of Puerto Rico need to understand that Congress retains authority to alter the status of Puerto Rico or to end U.S. citizenship for persons born in Puerto Rico in favor of some other status. The U.S. Supreme Court, in *Balzac* and other cases, recognizes that the Constitution applies differently in territories than it applies in states, and the Court simply requires Congress to act consistently with due process and equal protection principles in unincorporated territories.

15. If the commonwealth status continues, Congress will continue to exercise plenary authority over Puerto Rico's governance. Congress could choose to extend federal taxation in Puerto Rico and/or choose to reduce spending levels. Without changing Puerto Rico's internal constitutional government, Congress also could decide to begin to reverse the decades of inclusion in domestic legislation and in federal programs. This potential unilateral alteration of Puerto Rico's form of internal autonomy and "disintegration" from the Union would have dramatic implications for the people of Puerto Rico. For example, Congress could choose to revert to a citizenship regime similar to that imposed in 1900 by the Foraker Act,[13] in which U.S. citizenship would end for persons born in the territory and be replaced by an exclusive territorial citizenship with such rights and benefits as Congress deems appropriate. If the local population rejects the option of integration leading to statehood, Congress could logically conclude that such dis-integration is necessary and appropriate in order to stop enlarging the class of disenfranchised U.S. citizens who by their own choice will not become full citizens.

16. Extending the Fourteenth Amendment to Puerto Rico by statute cannot limit the discretion of Congress to amend or repeal that statutory exemption. The Supreme Court in *Rogers v. Bellei* recognized Congress's unquestioned authority to place restrictions or conditions on forms of U.S. citizenship conferred by statute.[14] It is axiomatic that Congress, in passing 8 U.S.C. § 1402, did not and could not offer the permanent or constitutional protection of the Fourteenth Amendment to the people of Puerto Rico. Similarly, the protection of persons born in a state of the Union would not

under *Afroyim v. Rusk*[15] prevent Congress from changing laws defining the citizenship of people born in Puerto Rico.

As is clear from the preceding analysis, the national interest requires that Congress come to grips with the need to resolve the status of Puerto Rico before it becomes even more difficult for the Congress and the people of Puerto Rico to understand the real choices facing them. If the definition of *commonwealth* in a referendum informs voters that the people of Puerto Rico will be able to propose what they regard as improvements to the current commonwealth structure, that definition also must make it clear that approval of such a ballot by Congress does not constitute a commitment on the part of Congress to approve such changes to commonwealth as may be proposed by Puerto Rico. In addition, it also must be clear that no political-status relationship between Puerto Rico and the United States established by statute under the Territorial Clause can bind a future Congress.

The purpose of these observations is not to defend the status quo or the degree of federal authority over Puerto Rico. Rather, the goal is to illuminate and reveal the inherent difficulties under our Constitution of perpetuating indefinitely a less than fully self-governing territorial status for a large population of U.S. citizens. In America, we believe the rights and status of citizens should be guaranteed, rather than permissive. Basic civil rights should be secured by the Constitution and not subject to the discretion of the Congress. Full empowerment and equal citizenship will not exist in Puerto Rico as long as it is a territorial commonwealth.

Any ballot definition which does not make these truths apparent will lack constitutional legitimacy, as well as simple honesty.

Local Judicial Separatist Agenda and the Federal Response

On November 17, 1997, the Governor of Puerto Rico signed into law a statute approved by the Legislature of Puerto Rico defining a "citizen of Puerto Rico" as a person with United States nationality and citizenship who is a lawful resident of Puerto Rico. In this way, the elected branches of the territorial government affirmed the principles of U.S. constitutional federalism as embodied in the local Puerto Rican Constitution, and recognized a singular U.S. nationality-based citizenship under the American flag.

In reaffirming the centrality of U.S. citizenship and nationality, the elected branches of local government simply restated the overwhelming intent of Puerto Rico's voters. On November 14, 1993, over 95 percent of voters voted for "permanent" U.S. nationality—a feature of the proffered options of both statehood and commonwealth in that Puerto Rican plebiscite. The overwhelming mandate expresses the loyalty and patriotism of the 3.8 million American citizens of Puerto Rico.

Despite the expressed will of the Puerto Rican people and in contrast to the measures adopted by elected leaders, local territorial courts have issued rulings pushing separatism. On November 18, 1997, the local territorial Supreme Court issued a ruling suspending enforcement of a decades-old statute requiring U.S. citizenship in order to vote in local elections in Puerto Rico.[16] A majority on the territorial Supreme Court is composed of members appointed by a former governor who supports a perpetual "commonwealth" status for Puerto Rico in which the territory would have some of the attributes of both a state of the Union and a separate nation. The local court exempted Juan Mari Brás, a man who claimed to have renounced his U.S. nationality, from the local U.S. citizenship requirement for voting. It based this decision on a doctrine that a separate legal "nationality" for Puerto Ricans exists within the U.S. constitutional system. While there are many nationalities within the United States in the sense of cultural heritage and identity, there is and can be only one legal and constitutional form of national citizenship.

In addition to running afoul of the one legal nationality principle, the local Supreme Court's decision also constitutes an official action by a co-equal branch of the territorial government to nullify application of federal law. Ultimately, the local court's attempt to defy principles of federalism and the application of the federal Constitution caused the federal government to clarify and reiterate the supremacy of federal law in Puerto Rico. The result was to lead the federal government to reassert its rule over Puerto Rico, in effect treating the decision of the territorial Supreme Court as irrelevant and not worthy of response.

Specifically, the local court ruled in the Juan Mari Brás case that a person who has been certified by the U.S. State Department to be an alien, and who therefore can remain in the United States only with a visa, can instead remain in Puerto Rico and enjoy all the rights of a separate Puerto Rican nationality and citizenship—even though he has not complied with the immigration and nationality laws of the United States.

Aware of the local court's decision, the State Department adopted a policy of denying certification of loss of citizenship to persons who intend to remain in Puerto Rico based on a claim of local citizenship. The State Department did this on January 27, 1998, in the case of a copy-cat renunciation by one Alberto Lozada Colón. The State Department properly concluded that persons residing in Puerto Rico lack the intent to relinquish U.S. citizenship because they continue to accept the benefits of U.S. citizenship including the benefit of continued residency in a territory of the United States. The State Department's decision will prevent further copy-cat cases and provides the basis for bringing the previous cases into compliance with U.S. immigration law, thereby rendering moot the action by the Puerto Rico Supreme Court in contravention of federal supremacy, as it relates to nationality law, as long as Puerto Rico remains under U.S. sovereignty.

Applying federal law, the United States District Court for the District of Columbia resoundingly affirmed the State Department's decision. As discussed more thoroughly below, the court's decision should lay to rest the legal claim that a separate Puerto Rican nationality exists under the current political status relationship. Subsequently, the State Department corrected the anomaly created by Mari Brás by withdrawing its certification of the loss of U.S. nationality by Mari Brás. Federal policy as to the existence of a single nationality within the United States is now clear once again. However, this episode underscores the importance of resolving Puerto Rico's status. To help sort out the issues of nationality and citizenship related to status, the following principles and legal requirements must be recognized.

Just as states have sufficient sovereignty under the Tenth Amendment to determine the qualifications of voters, Congress acting pursuant to its Territorial Clause powers in 1952 (P.L. 81-600) delegated to Puerto Rico sufficient sovereignty over its internal affairs under the local constitution to prescribe the qualifications of voters. However, Puerto Rico's local sovereignty is a statutory delegation of the authority of Congress to govern territories, and is not a vested, guaranteed, or permanent form of sovereignty like the states have under the Tenth Amendment. Even if Puerto Rico's status was guaranteed under the federal constitution, no state of the Union, much less an unincorporated commonwealth territory, has the power to declare that the citizenship of the state or territory survives legally effective renunciation of U.S. nationality and citizenship.[17] Yet that is precisely what the territorial court in Puerto Rico attempted to do in the case of Juan Mari Brás, as discussed in detail below.

While Puerto Rico has powers of local government which in some respects are like the states to the extent consistent with federal law and the U.S. Constitution, Puerto Rico does not have the sovereignty or constitutional authority to ignore the Supremacy Clause of the federal Constitution by creating a separate nationality.[18] Congress alone determines and regulates nationality under Article I, Section 8 of the Constitution. In the local court's ruling in the Mari Brás case, however, a person certified by the U.S. Department of State to be an alien under U.S. immigration laws, and who has refused to obtain a visa in compliance with the Immigration and Nationality Act, was recognized by the local court as having certain rights and privileges of a fictitious separate Puerto Rican national citizenship.

In 1997, Congressman George Gekas warned about creeping separatism in Puerto Rico's local judiciary and abuse of U.S. citizenship renunciation processes.[19] This wake-up call was sounded when a local trial court judge ruled that it was unconstitutional under the Constitution of the Commonwealth of Puerto Rico for the legislative branch of the local government to make U.S. citizenship a voter eligibility requirement in elections in Puerto Rico—as it is in other states and territories in the United States.

A trial court in Puerto Rico held that Mari Brás should be allowed to vote in local elections even though he had gone to Venezuela and taken an oath renouncing his U.S. nationality and citizenship in the manner prescribed by Congress. Mari Brás then went to Cuba, and returned to Puerto Rico. He was admitted back into U.S. territory by INS officials based on his U.S. birth certificate, without disclosure that the State Department had issued him a Certificate of Loss of Nationality.

Claiming a separate Puerto Rican nationality, Mari Brás then sought certification of his eligibility to vote. His vote was challenged by U.S. citizen voters who do not want their own votes diluted by noncitizens ineligible to vote under Puerto Rican law. Although the elected representatives of the people of Puerto Rico in the territorial legislature had decided many years ago to make U.S. citizenship a voter qualification under the local election law, the trial judge threw out that statute so Mari Brás could cast a ballot. That ballot was sealed pending an appeal of the case to the territorial Supreme Court, which ultimately ordered that the ballot be counted based on the local court's recognition of a separate Puerto Rican nationality existing independently of the federal constitution or laws.

A federal court decision now makes clear the obvious: legally, there is no separate Puerto Rican nationality. In *Lozada Colon v. Department of State,* the court explicitly rejected the notion that an individual could renounce U.S. citizenship and continue to reside in Puerto Rico on the basis of a separate Puerto Rican citizenship.[20] In that case, the court stated:

> Plaintiff's arguments boil down to a disagreement with the Secretary of State as to whether or not he meets the relevant criterion of "intent" needed to expatriate. Plaintiff argues that he meets all of the elements:

He left the United States, went to the consular's office in the Dominican Republic, and took a formal oath of renunciation. In rejecting Plaintiff's renunciation, the Department notes that Plaintiff demonstrated no intention of renouncing all ties to the United States. While Plaintiff claims to reject his United States citizenship, he nevertheless wants to remain a resident of Puerto Rico. The Immigration and Nationality Act makes it unmistakably clear that Puerto Rico is a part of the United States for such purposes. See 8 U.S.C. § 1101(a)(38) (providing that the term "United States" for the purposes of the statute refers not only to the 50 states of the United States, but also Puerto Rico, Guam, and the Virgin Islands). Indeed, after attempting to renounce in the Dominican Republic, Plaintiff returned to Puerto Rico without making any effort to be documented as an alien under the Immigration and Nationality Act. *In other words, while claiming to renounce all rights and privileges of United States citizenship, Plaintiff wants to continue to exercise one of the fundamental rights of citizenship, namely the right to travel freely throughout the world and when he wants to, to return and reside in the United States.*[21]

With those words, Judge Stanley Sporkin rejected the argument that there exists a separate Puerto Rican nationality under the current political structure. The court's reasoning applies to all U.S. citizens who claim to renounce their citizenship to make a political point but who wish to continue living as U.S. citizens by enjoying the benefits attendant to that citizenship. Persons like Mari Brás, who purported to renounce his U.S. citizenship but continued to live, work, and receive benefits in Puerto Rico, cannot have it both ways. If such persons truly want to renounce their U.S. citizenship, they must become aliens in the United States, including Puerto Rico and other U.S. territories. As aliens, their right to travel to, reside in, or receive other benefits in Puerto Rico are limited under the Immigration and Nationality Act and other federal laws. All aliens must have a visa or other legal authorization to enter and reside in the United States.

The purported renunciants have no such intent. Instead, they proclaim that they have renounced their U.S. citizenship at a U.S. embassy in a foreign country (in Mari Brás's case it was in Venezuela), then they return to Puerto Rico. True renunciants generally establish a residence in a foreign country, travel to the U.S. embassy to renounce their U.S. citizenship, and continue to reside in that foreign country. Thereafter, any travel to the United States, including Puerto Rico, is conducted pursuant to whatever legal requirements attach to residents of that foreign country.

To demonstrate the intent required to renounce U.S. citizenship under law,[22] Lozada Colón, Mari Brás, and similar purported renunciants signed forms indicating they understood the following consequences of renunciation:

> 2. Upon renouncing my citizenship I will become an alien with respect to the United States, subject to all the laws and procedures of the United States regarding entry and control of aliens.
>
> . . .
>
> 5. If I do not possess the nationality of any country other than the United States, upon my renunciation I will become a stateless person and may face extreme difficulties in traveling internationally and entering most countries.[23]

It seems clear that the purported renunciants either did not understand the above statements or never intended to comply with any of the law's requirements as explained in the Statement of Understanding. The purported renunciants refuse to comply with "the laws and procedures of the United States regarding entry and control of aliens." Indeed, the purported renunciants seek to remain in Puerto Rico, an area specifically included within the definition of the United States by the law.[24] Lozada Colón, Mari Brás, and all similarly situated purported renunciants did not intend to obtain either the nationality of another country or to comply with the laws of the United States regarding entry and control of aliens. Accordingly, these purported renunciants have not established the intent to accept the consequences inherent in renouncing their U.S. citizenship.

8 U.S.C. § 1481(a) prescribes the procedure for renouncing citizenship in a legally effective manner and requires renunciants to execute an oath voluntarily and intentionally relinquishing "all rights and privileges" of U.S. nationality and citizenship. The right to reside in a territory under the sovereignty of the United States, including Puerto Rico, is generally a right and privilege of U.S. nationality and citizenship. In the case of noncitizen aliens, residence in a U.S. territory is a privilege flowing from compliance with the visa requirements of the federal Immigration and Nationality Act.

Mari Brás and similar purported renunciants have not truly expatriated themselves because they lack the actual intent to live as aliens in Puerto Rico. Their actions demonstrated an intent to exercise rights and privileges of U.S. citizenship in contravention of 8 U.S.C. § 1481(a)(5). This statute and its implementing regulations[25] require the Secretary of State to prevent abuse of and fraud in the renunciation procedure. The Secretary properly restored integrity to our system of citizenship by withdrawing recognition of the loss of citizenship of Juan Mari Brás. Puerto Rico is not a separate nation, able to confer citizenship independent of that of the United States. Indeed, that is an essential characteristic of the status option of independence; it does not exist under the other two options that may be presented to the voters of Puerto Rico.

The Puerto Rico Supreme Court attempted to delimit the constitutional nature of this separate Puerto Rican nationality by claiming that it exists within the framework of the United States–Puerto Rico relationship and is not equivalent to citizenship of an independent country. Instead, the local court seeks to establish a separate constitutional nationality and legal citizenship which has rights and privileges separate from U.S. nationality and citizenship in Puerto Rico. This alternative nationality and citizenship is claimed by the Puerto Rican separatists as a right binding on the United States in perpetuity which cannot be ended without the consent of Puerto Rico.

The opinion of the court in *Davis v. District Director, Immigration & Naturalization Service*[26] includes an excellent explanation of why the separate-state-citizenship-as-separate-nationality argument must fail in the case of the states of the Union. Certainly a territory with a local commonwealth constitution authorized by an act of Congress (P.L. 81-600) does not have greater sovereignty than a state of the Union. While the people of Puerto Rico consented to the establishment of the Commonwealth of Puerto Rico structure of local government with respect to internal affairs of the territory, this does not create a local sovereignty or basis for separate nationality and citizenship *superior* to that of the states of the Union. That is what the result would be if, as the Puerto Rico Supreme Court has ruled, "citizenship of Puerto Rico" constitutes a form of citizenship superior to that of citizenship of a state of the Union.

Those who argue that Puerto Rico could become a Quebec-like situation if it is ever admitted as a state must recognize that the real danger of a Quebec-like problem is if the current ambiguous status continues and this nation-within-a-nation ideology is imposed by local authorities without a fully informed act of self-determination by the people of Puerto Rico. The local judiciary's ruling in this case is an attempt to usurp the authority of Congress under the Territorial Clause in Article IV, section 3, clause 2 and section 8 of Article I (Congressional authority "to establish a uniform rule of naturalization") to determine the nationality and citizenship of persons born in Puerto Rico, an authority also recognized in Article IX of the Treaty of Paris, under which the United States became sovereign in Puerto Rico. The United States has not ceded or restricted that authority by agreeing to establish internal self-government under the commonwealth structure.

The failure of the judicial branch of the local constitutional government to respect the separation of powers under the local constitution does not bode well for the viability of continued territorial status under the commonwealth structure. Like the results of a locally conducted plebiscite in 1993 in which less than a majority of the voters approved a modified form of the current status, the court's ruling in this case suggests that the present status is not acceptable to the people. However, the territorial commonwealth status cannot be made acceptable by defining it as something other than what it really is—whether that redefinition occurs by unrealistic ballot wording or revisionist judicial rulings which attempt to transform unincorporated territory status into a form of permanent statehood, without going through the admissions process under Article IV of the federal Constitution, and at the same time seek separate nationality.

Puerto Rico is not a state, but an internally self-governing territory of the United States. Likewise, the "people of Puerto Rico" are not a separate nationality, but a body politic consisting of persons with U.S. nationality and citizenship who reside in Puerto Rico. This includes those born there and those who were born or naturalized in a state of the Union and reside there.[27]

The issue of nationality of persons born in Puerto Rico was resolved in 1904 when the Supreme Court of the United States interpreted Article IX of the Treaty of Paris to mean that the "nationality of the territory" was that of the United States, and that the inhabitants of the territory, in this case Puerto Rico, had the same U.S. nationality as the territory in which they live.[28] U.S. citizenship based on birth in Puerto Rico is a statutory right conferred by Congress in 1917 under the Territorial Clause of the U.S. Constitution based upon the U.S. nationality of persons born in Puerto Rico under Article IX of the Treaty of Paris. Any other interpretation of Article IX of the treaty is implausible, and is not the law of the United States as determined by the United States Supreme Court.

Similarly, the "citizen of Puerto Rico" status relied upon by the local judges seeking to establish a separatist legal doctrine in this case was created by Congress in 1900 in an exercise of Territorial Clause powers.[29] This "citizen of Puerto Rico" status created by Congress under the Foraker Act was codified by the local legislature (itself created by Congress under the Foraker Act) in section 10 of the territorial Political Code. However, this became a vestigial and now archaic provision which was codified at 48 U.S.C. § 733 and applied only to the 288 people who opted to remain in that territorial citizenship status as "citizens of Puerto Rico" instead of becoming U.S. citizens in 1917.

In 1927 Congress superseded the Foraker Act as to all persons other than those approximately 288 Foraker Act citizens of Puerto Rico by enacting the federal statute now codified at 48 U.S.C. § 733a, which provides that the "citizen of Puerto Rico" status which exists under the Constitution of Puerto Rico is no different from citizenship of a state of the Union—essentially a legal residency status with rights and privileges conferred under the local constitution to the extent consistent with federal law. A statutory citizenship status such as that of "citizen of Puerto Rico" under the Foraker Act is a subcategory of U.S. nationality which can exist side by side with (but because of the unincorporated territory status of Puerto Rico is less than equal to) full U.S. citizenship for a person born and residing in the states. The same is true of the statutory U.S. citizenship extended to persons born in Puerto Rico under the Jones Act of 1917. Compared to "citizen of Puerto Rico" status under the Foraker Act, U.S. citizenship under the Jones Act is more complete, but still not fully equal to that of persons born or naturalized in the states of the Union (and thereby enjoying citizenship protected by the Fourteenth Amendment).

Thus there was never a constitutional or legal "citizenship of Puerto Rico" created through the exercise of the inherent sovereignty of the people of Puerto Rico. This was confirmed by the Legislature of Puerto Rico on November 14, before the ruling in the Mari Brás case, when Article 10 of the Puerto Rico Political Code,[30] which defined "citizens of Puerto Rico," was amended to clarify that Puerto Rican citizenship was a form of legal residency rather than nationality. The local Supreme Court's thesis that the legislature enacted the statute restricting voting to U.S. citizens without knowledge of the Mari Brás case certainly does not apply to the amendment to the definition of Puerto Rican citizenship. That amending statute defining citizenship of Puerto Rico was signed into law by the governor before the local judiciary issued its ruling in the Mari Brás case. Remarkably, the court's ruling merely ignores the new citizenship statute, which is the law of Puerto Rico.

The irony is that "citizenship of Puerto Rico" under the Foraker Act is not a form of nationality, but a subordinate citizenship status created by Congress in an exercise of its Territorial Clause power to carry out the authority to determine the status of the inhabitants of Puerto Rico under Article IX of the Treaty of Paris. Thus the separatists who support Mari Brás are trying to project separate nationality by adopting an essentially colonial status imposed by the Congress in the early days of territorial administration. Section 10 of the original Political Code of Puerto Rico, relied upon heavily by Mari Brás, is a vestige of that colonial era.

It should be noted that section 10 of the original Political Code of Puerto Rico, the local statute relied upon by the trial judge to invent a new nationality/citizenship status for Mari Brás so he could vote, is currently codified under a territorial "citizenship" law found at 1 *P.R. Laws Ann.* § 7. For reasons set forth below, these local citizenship provisions do not govern or alter the nationality and citizenship status defined by Congress under 8 U.S.C. § 1402.

Under the Fourteenth Amendment of the U.S. Constitution and applicable federal law including 8 U.S.C. § 1402, the term *citizenship* is coextensive with and has the same meaning as *nationality* only for those born or naturalized in a state of the Union. The creation by Congress of a separate statutory citizenship status under the Foraker Act for persons born in Puerto Rico did not create a separate nationality. Rather, it defined a separate statutory status under federal law for persons who have U.S. nationality, but not a constitutionally defined equal citizenship status because neither their nationality nor citizenship is guaranteed by the Fourteenth Amendment. This is due to the fact that their nationality and citizenship arise from birth in a territory which is under U.S. sovereignty but not a state of the Union.

In addition to the lack of voting rights in national elections or voting representation in Congress for U.S. citizens born or residing in Puerto Rico, this less than equal form of statutory U.S. citizenship which is not constitutionally guaranteed is one of the reasons why unincorporated territory status has been described by the U.S. Supreme Court as necessarily and inherently a temporary form of territorial administration until full integration or independence is achieved through the constitutional process of self-determination.[31]

Neither the "citizen of Puerto Rico" status created by federal law under the Foraker Act nor the "citizen of Puerto Rico" status under local territorial law exists as a result of self-determination. In addition, both the previous federal form of that citizenship status and the form which exists under local jurisdiction are superseded by 8 U.S.C. § 1402. To the extent the residents of Puerto Rico have exercised sovereignty and self-determination in these matters, it has been through adoption and approval of the local constitution defining and conferring local jurisdiction on local authorities within limits of the federal Constitution. One such limitation is that Congress alone has the power to determine matters, including the law of nationality, within the federal sphere of authority.[32]

In addition, the current local constitution and laws instituted with the consent of the U.S. citizen residents of Puerto Rico supersede the previous local territorial administration and local citizenship status under the former organic act, as well as the previous local "citizen of Puerto Rico" status, to the extent of any inconsistency. In this regard, quite interestingly, Article IX, section 5 of the Constitution of the Commonwealth of Puerto Rico replaces the term for local "citizen of Puerto Rico" status under the territorial citizenship statutes cited above with the status of "citizen of the Commonwealth of Puerto Rico." The annotations to Article IX, section 5 of the local constitution as codified in Puerto Rico include references to "informal" historical materials which suggest that the nature of "citizenship of Puerto Rico" under section 10 of the Political Code is carried forward in 1 *P.R. Laws Ann.* § 7 without modification. Even if that is correct, however, Article IX, section 5 makes it clear that any local citizenship status exists in the context of the federal and territorial constitutional structure.

Within that federal-territorial constitutional structure approved by the voters in 1952, immigration and nationality law is a matter within the federal sphere of power and the territorial sphere of power is limited to local law consistent with the federal residency definition of "citizen of Puerto Rico" found at 48 U.S.C. § 733a, including the definition of local "citizen of Puerto Rico" status created for purposes of local jurisdiction under 1 *P.R. Laws Ann.* § 7. This reinforces the point that the local "citizenship" law exists and must be construed in a manner compatible with the commonwealth structure for internal self-government under a local constitution and compatible with the federal constitution as required by 48 U.S.C. § 731d.

The notion that the term "citizen of Puerto Rico" as used under section 10 of the former Political Code is an independent source of authority for the court's decision in this case ignores the fact that section 10 of the earlier territorial code was not consented to by the residents of Puerto Rico. In contrast, Article IX, section 5 of the Constitution of the Commonwealth of Puerto Rico was instituted with the consent of the governed. Thus in 1952 the people of Puerto Rico consented to a constitutional process under which nationality and nationality-based citizenship currently are determined under the federal constitution, and only local citizenship in the context of territorial law is within local jurisdiction.

In this context, the notion that the local legislature cannot rely upon the federal law of nationality as a requirement for voter eligibility due to the existence of a vestigial local form of "citizenship" ignores the fact that the local constitution itself recognizes applicable federal law—including that governing nationality-based U.S. citizenship. Even more fundamentally, in approving the local constitution, the people of Puerto Rico never consented to have the local government, especially the courts, determine their "citizenship" in the context of nationality, or to elevate local citizenship status to the level of an alternative to U.S. nationality and citizenship.

Even if they had, the application of the Supremacy Clause of the federal Constitution would preclude it because Congress has preempted the local government in this matter. There is nothing more fundamental under both 48 U.S.C. § 731b, the federal law authorizing a local constitution in 1950, and under the Constitution of the Commonwealth of Puerto Rico as approved by the people in 1952, than the requirement that the commonwealth act compatibly with applicable measures under the federal Constitution as the threshold test for the exercise of local jurisdiction by the local constitutional government.

Conclusion

The local election law in Puerto Rico requiring U.S. citizenship to vote in local elections was enacted by the democratically elected representatives of the people. The local statute approved by the Legislature of Puerto Rico properly recognizes that only the United States can define and confer nationality and citizenship for people born in Puerto Rico as long as it is within U.S. sovereignty.

The attempt of local courts to recognize, and thereby exercise the sovereign power to create, an alternative separate nationality and citizenship status in lieu of the federally defined status has been repudiated by the federal government through executive action in the Mari Brás matter and through court decision in *Lozada Colon*.

Only if the people of Puerto Rico, acting through their constitutional process and in an exercise of self-determination, requested that the U.S. Congress approve legislation to end the current U.S. nationality and citizenship of persons born in Puerto Rico, and Congress in fact did so, would a different result appear to be permitted by the U.S. Constitution.

In that event, presumably, a process leading to separate sovereignty, nationality, and citizenship for Puerto Rico would commence. Previously, neither the electorate in Puerto Rico nor the local legislature has expressed significant levels of support for that approach to resolving the ultimate status of Puerto Rico. If the local courts distort federal and local law to pretend to create a political status that does not exist, the voters of Puerto Rico will be denied the ability to make a fully informed determination of their political status. Without an act of fully informed self-determination, the people of Puerto Rico will abdicate their ability to control their own destiny.

Notes

1   *To Provide for a Referendum on the Political Status of Puerto Rico: Hearings on S.244 before the Senate Committee on Energy and Natural Resources,* 102d Cong., 1st sess., S311–31 (1991): 186.

2   See, e.g., *United States–Puerto Rico Political Status Act,* H.R. 856, 105th Cong., 2d sess. (1998), and S. 472, 105th Cong., 2d sess. (1998).

3   *United States Constitution,* art. IV, sec. 3, cl. 2.

4   Ibid., art. VI, cl. 2.

5   Ibid., art. IV, sec. 3, cl. 2.

6   *National Bank v. County of Yankton,* 101 U.S. (11 Otto.) 129, 133 (1879).

7   *United States Constitution,* art. VI, cl. 2.

8   *U.S. Statutes at Large* 90 (1976): 263.

9   *Harris v. Rosario,* 446 U.S. 651 (1980) (per curiam); *Downes v. Bidwell,* 182 U.S. 244 (1901); *Crespo v. U.S.,* 151 F.2d 44 (C.C.A. Puerto Rico), cert. denied, 327 U.S. 758 (1945).

10   *Balzac v. Porto Rico,* 258 U.S. 298 (1922).

11   Act of July 3, 1950, *U.S. Statutes at Large* 64 (1950): 319.

12   *Jones Act, U.S. Statutes at Large* 39 (1917): 461.

13   *U.S. Statutes at Large* 31 (1900): 79.

14   *Roger v. Bellei,* 401 U.S. 815 (1971).

15   *Afroyim v. Rusk,* 307 U.S. 253 (1967).

16   *Ramírez de Ferrer v. Mari Brás,* Supreme Court of Puerto Rico, No. CT-96-14 (November 18, 1997) (official translation).

17   See discussion below of *Davis v. District Director, Immigration & Naturalization Service,* 481 F. Supp. 1178 (D.D.C. 1979).

18   See *Rodriguez v. Partido Popular Democratico,* 457 U.S. 1 (1982).

19   See *Cong. Rec.* (April 29, 1997): E766.

20   2 F. Supp. 2d 43 (D.C. Cir. 1998).

21   Ibid. at 46 (emphasis added).

22   See *U.S. Code* 8 § 1481(a)(5).

23   7 FAM 1253, Exhibit 1253d.

24   See *U.S. Code* 8 § 1101(a)(38).

25   *Code of Federal Regulation* 22 §§50.40–50.50.

26   481 F. Supp. 1178 (D.D.C. 1979).

27   See *U.S. Code* 48 § 733; see also *Gonzales v. Williams,* 192 U.S. 1 (1903).

28   See *Gonzales*, 192 U.S. 1; *U.S. Code* 8 § 1402; Johnny H. Killian, Congressional Research Service *The Nature of U.S. Citizenship for Puerto Ricans,* (1996).

29   See Foraker Act, *U.S. Statutes at Large* 31 (1900): 79, sec. 7.

30   1 *P.R. Laws Ann.* § 7.

31   *Reid v. Covert,* 354 U.S. 1, 14 (1957) (stating that the Territorial Clause gives Congress the power "to provide rules and regulations to govern temporarily territories with wholly dissimilar traditions and institutions").

32   See *U.S. Code* 48 § 731d.

The Bitter Roots of Puerto Rican Citizenship

Rogers M. Smith

On November 18, 1997, the Supreme Court of Puerto Rico ruled that independence activist Juan Mari Brás remained a citizen of Puerto Rico even though he had formally and voluntarily renounced his United States citizenship at the U.S. Embassy in Caracas, Venezuela in 1994.[1] The U.S. consul in Venezuela had then provided Mari Brás with an official "Certificate of Loss of Nationality of the United States." If he became resident within the fifty states, he could no longer exercise the franchise to which he had previously been entitled. But because Mari Brás was nonetheless still a Puerto Rican citizen, Justice Fuster-Berlingeri wrote for the Court, he could still vote in Puerto Rican elections. The justice argued that section 2.023 of Puerto Rico's Electoral Law, which appeared to require that voters be U.S. citizens, should not be interpreted to do so in the case of people like Mari Brás. He was a native-born resident of Mayagüez, Puerto Rico, long engaged with the politics of Puerto Rico, whose parents were also both native-born Puerto Ricans. When enacting the Electoral Law in 1977, Fuster-Berlingeri wrote, the Legislative Assembly of Puerto Rico had almost certainly not contemplated the electoral rights of such persons, "whose *Puerto Rican nationality is unquestionable*" (italics in the original).[2]

Those words in particular and the holding in general appeared to give significant legal recognition to Puerto Rican nationality and citizenship as legal-political statuses that are distinct from United States nationality and citizenship. As such, the decision was applauded by champions of Puerto Rican independence like Mari Brás and by many other Puerto Ricans who did not favor independence but did feel themselves to be part of a distinctive Puerto Rican nation.[3] In many respects, the claim of many Puerto Ricans to some sort of nationality of their own seems to me a strong one, given that *nationality* can mean a people sharing common cultural, linguistic, and historical identities and experiences, as Puerto Ricans certainly do.

Nationality in any of those senses, as well as others, would be compatible with a variety of different sorts of relationships with the United States, including equal statehood.[4] Nothing in this essay is intended to disparage any of those possibilities.

I believe, however, that it is unwise to build claims for Puerto Rican nationality on the legal framework laid out by Justice Fuster-Berlingeri in the *Ramírez v. Mari Brás* decision. The opinion traces Puerto Rican nationality to the status of "Puerto Rican citizen" that originated legally in the Foraker Act of 1900. It was at that point, the Justice argues, that "the people of Puerto Rico became a political community, with its own citizenship."[5] But the type of political community and citizenship thus created, I will argue, were and are profoundly constituted and contaminated by U.S. policies and ideologies of imperial domination and racial subordination. It would be better for Puerto Ricans to repudiate that heritage definitively and to rest their claims on quite different legal and moral grounds.

It is notable in this regard that since the *Mari Brás* decision, the U.S. State Department has refused to permit other Puerto Ricans simply to renounce their U.S. citizenship while retaining Puerto Rican citizenship. It reportedly also revoked its recognition of Mari Brás's own expatriation.[6] In April 1998, Judge Stanley Sporkin of the U.S. District Court for the District of Columbia tersely sustained the State Department's discretionary power to deny Certificates of Loss of Nationality under such circumstances, though he refused to address "the much debated political question as to the status of Puerto Rico and its nationals in relation to the United States."[7] Ironically, despite that express disavowal his very wording revealed how natural it seems to speak of Puerto Rico as having its own "nationals." Nonetheless, this State Department policy and its judicial validation show that, contrary to some claims in Justice Fuster-Berlingeri's opinion, the legal status of Puerto Rican citizenship created by the Foraker Act remains in the eyes of the U.S. government what it has always been. U.S. officials still treat it as a status crafted in the interests of the United States by a United States government that wields ultimate sovereignty over Puerto Rico, even though Puerto Ricans are not and never have been represented in that government as equal citizens.

The Origins of Puerto Rican Citizenship in the Foraker Act

Although the legal status of "Puerto Rico citizenship" has not changed in those most basic regards since its creation in 1900, we live now in a world that is thankfully far removed from the one in which the Foraker Act was passed. This distance can, however, leave us ignorant of just how and why the Puerto Rican citizenship defined in that law came to be. In brief, this peculiar "citizenship" was spawned by American turn-of-the-century racism.

The late nineteenth century was a time when political reactions against the racially egalitarian transformations of Reconstruction, reinforced by prestigious postwar doctrines of separate and unequal racial evolution, created an increasingly hospitable climate for the rebuilding of systems of white supremacy in the United States. By the 1890s, most American political leaders and intellectuals openly and routinely endorsed the alleged racial superiority of peoples of northern European descent and their "manifest destiny" to, quite literally, rule the world. Historians generally agree that the Spanish-American War of 1898, which led to the U.S. acquisition of Puerto Rico, did not arise from any great economic or military necessity pressing on any party involved. It resulted essentially from the desires of some U.S. leaders to win a war, build a larger empire, and prove to the European powers that Americans, too, were one of "the great masterful races," as the feisty Teddy Roosevelt put it. When various circumstances made it inconvenient to hold Cuba in the wake of the war, many U.S. leaders came to regard Puerto Rico both as a symbol of American supremacy and as an important strategic asset for protection of the Panama Canal and America's expanding interests in Central and South America generally.[8]

The reason the United States could acquire Puerto Rico by warring with Spain was, of course, that Spain was itself an imperial power that had taken control of the island over four hundred years earlier. Since that conquest was completed, there had been only one armed revolt by Puerto Ricans against their Spanish governors, an 1868 uprising that championed independence but few other changes, so that it had little popular support and was quickly suppressed.[9] Though there were signs of a developing sense of a distinctive island cultural identity, most Puerto Ricans, it seems, had long been content to be Spanish subjects, without a legally recognized, independent Puerto Rican nationality.[10] But in November of 1897, tensions over Cuba led Spain to sign "Autonomic Charters for Cuba and Puerto Rico," establishing the first home rule governments in Havana and San Juan. Puerto Ricans won rights to full representation in the Spanish parliament, the *Cortes,* as well as in Spanish treaty negotiations affecting Puerto Rico. They also could veto Spanish commercial treaties they saw as harmful to their interests, and they could set the tariffs and duties on their imports and exports themselves via their own two-chamber parliament. Their executive officer, the governor-general, remained an appointee of the Spanish crown, and resident Spaniards as well as native Puerto Ricans were eligible to serve in this new Parliament of Puerto Rico.[11] Still, Puerto Ricans might then be said to have possessed a measure of independent, self-governing "citizenship" as well as Spanish subjectship; but that status was not legally explicit.

If it existed at all, it was extraordinarily short-lived. Eight days after the first meeting of the Puerto Rican Parliament in 1898, U.S. troops invaded the southern port of Guánica. They encountered little resistance; indeed many Puerto Ricans welcomed them enthusiastically. It was, after all, clear that resistance was futile, and many saw imperial governance by the fast-growing United States as not obviously worse than the often brutally repressive imperial governance they had recently experienced under declining Spain. In December of 1898, the Treaty of Paris ending the war provided that Congress would determine the "civil rights and political status of the native inhabitants of the territories hereby ceded to the United States," including Puerto Rico.[12] Puerto Ricans themselves had no meaningful say in the writing of this treaty, nor would they have an official voice in the congressional deliberations that would determine their fate.[13]

The question then arose: what limits, if any, did the Constitution of the United States set on the rights and statuses Congress could define for Puerto Ricans, as well as for the other new territorial inhabitants? Were they essentially identical to the colonial subjects of European empires, the status Americans had rejected for themselves over a century before, or were they necessarily republican citizens of the United States, just as Americans had become? In 1899, those issues were widely debated in American academic, political, and popular forums. Though voices championing human rights could be heard, among both proponents and opponents of America's new colonial empire, racial themes predominated.

The degree to which that was true has been somewhat obscured by the great scholarly attention paid to a set of articles in the *Harvard Law Review* during 1899, which argued the question of the Constitution and the colonies in rather dry, technical, legalistic terms. Many historians have recognized that the most seminal essay in the series was by A. Lawrence Lowell, a Harvard political scientist who would later become his university's president. Rejecting two "extreme" positions—that the Constitution did not apply to any territories at all, or that the Constitution "followed the flag" in full force wherever Americans took it—Lowell defined an influential middle ground. He developed what he acknowledged to be a neglected if not novel distinction between territories "incorporated" into the Union and "unincorporated" territories. In incorporated territories, the Constitution applied completely. In contrast, only its most basic principles were judicially enforceable in unincorporated territories. And it was, Lowell maintained, entirely Congress's choice whether a territory should be incorporated, and hence whether its inhabitants should have constitutional rights, or not.[14]

Although it took time, the Supreme Court would eventually endorse Lowell's "incorporated/unincorporated" distinction, and it remains accepted, though controversial, legal doctrine to this day.[15] But whatever its merits as a matter of territorial jurisprudence, and I think them dubious, the incorporation doctrine's original underlying motivations are far more transparently unconstitutional and immoral than scholars have emphasized. The broader rationale for the distinction was laid out by Lowell in a popular article in the *Atlantic Monthly* published earlier in 1899, an essay that has received insufficient attention. It demonstrates beyond any reasonable doubt that the incorporation doctrine was self-consciously part of the ignoble retreat from racial equal protection that dominated this era in America's constitutional history.

Lowell argued in the *Atlantic* that the westward-expanding United States had long been "one of the greatest and most successful colonizing powers the world has ever known," and he suggested that this history reflected at bottom the unalterable fact that "the Anglo-Saxon race is expansive." The United States had always also, however, had traditions endorsing the "theory that all men are equal politically." To be sure, the United States had never fully followed that theory. It had instead pretended that members of the native tribes and African Americans were "not men," a view that Lowell saw as proof of the "political good sense and bad logic of the English-speaking race." But the question remained whether in 1899 the theory should be followed in regard to the nation's new colonial acquisitions.[16]

Lowell said no. He prefaced his argument by noting that after the nation's commitment to the "theory of political equality" reached a high point with the enactment of the Fifteenth Amendment banning racial qualifications for voting, support for egalitarianism then "began to ebb." Lowell's own egalitarianism had ebbed along with the country's. He confessed that he had initially been "shocked" when Chinese were excluded from immigration on racial grounds, but he said he had come to recognize this policy as "sound." Only the "Anglo-Saxon race" had been made capable of self-governance by "centuries of discipline." Not only Asians but also persons of the "Spanish race" had not been so accustomed. It would be "sheer cruelty" to extend equal political rights to such races prematurely. The acquisition of powers of self-governance by Puerto Ricans must be "gradual and tentative" and guided by appropriate "experts, with a highly specialized training," such as Harvard social scientists. (For the Philippines, as it turned out, a Yale man would do).[17]

It was, then, because non-Anglo-Saxons were racially unfit for equal rights that Lowell thought legal grounds had to be found, or contrived, to deny that the Constitution extended equal political and civil rights to the new territorial inhabitants. The "incorporated/unincorporated" distinction was really a distinction between territories with populations racially qualified to be equal citizens and those racially fit only for lesser statuses. That fact peeked through in the last line of Lowell's *Harvard Law Review* article. There Lowell devoted most of his attention to justifying the distinct status of "unincorporated" territories in terms of legal precedents and did not discuss race; but he concluded that "many" of the constitutional rights guaranteed to U.S. citizens should be seen as "inapplicable except among a people whose social and political evolution has been consonant with our own."[18] Those words might seem reasonable enough in many contexts, but when read in light of late-nineteenth-century evolutionary theories of race and Lowell's near-contemporaneous endorsement of such theories, they appear far more ominous.

Although Lowell's article and others on the subject were rarely cited explicitly, subsequent congressional debates over the status of the colonies only made such racial concerns even more prominent.[19] For example, the most celebrated contribution to congressional discussions of the fate of the colonies was a 1900 Senate speech delivered by a young reform-minded Republican senator from Indiana, a Roosevelt ally named Albert Beveridge. In a symphonic orchestration of late-nineteenth-century racist themes, he argued that the colonial question was

> deeper than any question of party politics; deeper than any question of the isolated policy of our country even; deeper even than any question of constitutional power. It is elemental. It is racial. God has not been preparing the English-speaking and Teutonic peoples for a thousand years for nothing but vain and idle self-contemplation and self-admiration. No! He has made us the master organizers of the world to establish system where chaos reigns. He has given us the spirit of progress to overwhelm the forces of reaction throughout the earth. He has made us adepts in government that we may administer government among savage and senile peoples. Were it not for such a force as

this the world would relapse into barbarism and night. And of all our race He has marked the American people as His chosen nation to finally lead in the regeneration of the world. This is the divine mission of America, and it holds for us all the profit, all the glory, all the happiness possible to man. We are the trustees of the world's progress, guardians of its righteous peace. The judgment of the Master is upon us: "Ye have been faithful over a few things; I will make you ruler over many things."[20]

The galleries thundered applause. Newspapers ran enthusiastic headlines. Beveridge was placed on the committee to decide the fate of the colonial inhabitants, and his policies largely prevailed. The colonial inhabitants would be governed not as equal citizens but as wards of Anglo-Saxon "trustees."[21] Some administration leaders did propose absorbing Puerto Rico completely into the United States by establishing unrestricted trade and full U.S. citizenship for Puerto Ricans, but opposition to those egalitarian policies quickly triumphed. The only real battle was over whether it was too dangerous for the United States to have any extended connection with these lower races at all. Such "mongrels" might only introduce "ignorance and inferiority" and "pestilence" into America's great nation.[22] Though Puerto Ricans did not seem quite so low as Filipinos, it seemed a risky precedent to grant anything like equal membership to either community. To avoid such dangers, the organic act for Puerto Rico, or Foraker Act, passed later that session labeled Puerto Ricans "citizens of Porto Rico," not United States citizens. It also constructed a civil government for the island that was subordinate to Congress and funded by a special tariff on Puerto Rican international trade. The organic act's principal author, Senator Joseph Foraker, made it clear that his bill was not intended to give Puerto Ricans "any rights that the American people do not want them to have."[23]

The legal status of "citizen of Puerto Rico" invoked in the *Mari Brás* decision, then, is one that did not exist until it was created, not by Puerto Ricans but by the U.S. Congress in 1900, implementing an authority the United States had acquired through armed conquest. Legally the status was further justified by treaty and constitutional doctrines, also constructed entirely without Puerto Rican participation, that established virtually unlimited congressional power over Puerto Ricans. Though it labeled Puerto Ricans a separate race from "Americans," it did not involve any recognition of Puerto Ricans as having an independent nationality of their own. After all, African Americans had long been recognized as a separate race and denied genuinely equal citizenship, but the United States had never accepted any claims of independent African American nationality. Puerto Rican citizenship was similarly a category Congress created for a certain subset of its nationals. And Congress created that category expressly as another subordinate status, inferior to U.S. citizenship, and inferior explicitly because America's political and intellectual leaders regarded Puerto Ricans as not just a separate but as yet another unequal race, incapable of full self-governance.

The citizenship created by the Foraker Act thus seems to me a highly undesirable anchor for any legal claim of meaningfully equal and autonomous Puerto Rican nationality. It rests on express denials of both those claims. And so long as Puerto Rican citizenship remains a status created and defined by a Congress in which Puerto Rico is not represented, it is inextricably still a subordinate status, however much Congress or some Puerto Ricans may extol it as equitable and just.

Sweet Fruit from Bitter Roots?

Even so, the Foraker Act was admittedly passed long ago. Later in Justice Fuster-Berlingeri's *Mari Brás* opinion, he contends that the original tainted character of the Puerto Rican citizenship it created has been cleansed by subsequent developments. The opinion rightly places little reliance on the 1917 Jones Act conferring U.S. citizenship on Puerto Ricans, for that law did not alter Puerto Rico's status as an unincorporated territory, unrepresented in the Congress that governed it, and unprotected by many fundamental constitutional guarantees. Such U.S. citizenship represented neither equal membership in the American polity nor recognition of any autonomous national status for Puerto Ricans. It was, indeed, but another perfumed kind of colonial subjectship. Unsurprisingly, in 1917 it was opposed by the elected (but non-voting) representative of Puerto Rico to the U.S. Congress and by the Puerto Rican House of Delegates. The mass of Puerto Ricans did not have any formal opportunity even to express an opinion on the matter.[24]

But, the *Mari Brás* opinion contends, the "situation changed radically during the 1950–1952 constitutional process" when the Commonwealth of Puerto Rico was established. During that time "an overwhelming majority of the Puerto Rican voters" did approve U.S. Public Law 600, which led to the creation of the new Puerto Rican Commonwealth Constitution. This

process meant, Justice Fuster-Berlingeri contends, that "the public authority and governmental powers of the people of Puerto Rico were not, as
before, merely delegated by Congress, but, rather, *stemmed from itself and
were free from higher authority*" (emphasis in the original). When in 1952
Congress passed and the president signed Public Law 447 approving this
new Puerto Rican constitution, moreover, they acknowledged this new self-
constituted public authority of the Puerto Rican people; or so the Justice
avers. True, certain federal relations with the United States continued to
exist, but in his view those constraining relations had been rendered "obligations which the people imposed on itself," not products of conquest any
longer. "It is inconceivable," he writes, "that all this happened merely to
approve another piece of legislation of the United States Congress, or to
further the United States Congress' absolute powers over the Island of
Puerto Rico." Rather, at this point Puerto Rican citizenship and nationality
became legally cognizable entities independent of U.S. citizenship and nationality. As a result, although "Puerto Rican citizenship" was "initially
established by federal law," the justice maintains, "its legal foundation no
longer rests on such federal law" but rather on the "Constitution of the
Commonwealth of Puerto Rico."[25]

There is no doubt that Puerto Ricans gained richly warranted expanded
powers of self-governance over their internal affairs in the 1950–52 process.[26] Even so, in these portions of the opinion Justice Fuster-Berlingeri
claims too much. The changes he describes simply do not go far enough to
transform the Puerto Rican citizenship created by the Foraker Act into a
status stemming from the Puerto Rican people themselves and tantamount
to independent nationality.

Leave aside the very real questions about whether the choices given
Puerto Ricans during the 1950–52 process, which were essentially either to
approve the commonwealth or maintain the status quo, varied enough to
make the expressions of public opinion on which the Justice relies truly
meaningful. Let us instead take his argument on its own terms.

As even Justice Fuster-Berlingeri acknowledges, Puerto Ricans gained
only a limited measure of sovereignty through these changes. Even after
1952, the "exclusive authority of the Commonwealth solely addresses internal, self-government matters."[27] Ultimately, moreover, as the opinion's citations make all too clear, it remains the courts and Congress of the United
States that decide what matters are "internal" enough to be free of congressional regulation. Furthermore, as a matter of U.S. law, all these were
still changes initiated by congressional statute and approved by congressio-

nal statute. As such, they are legally alterable by congressional statute. U.S. officials have said that their government will not act unilaterally in these regards, viewing the commonwealth arrangements as a "compact" that can be altered only by mutual consent. And it is true that, if the Congress nonetheless did try to act unilaterally, Puerto Ricans would probably resist and international law authorities today would probably support their position. Such measures would make it all too clear that Puerto Rico remains fundamentally a colony, a status the United States claims to have transformed, with UN approval.[28] Yet even if that approval were withdrawn, it is not likely that Congress or the U.S. courts would view the United States as legally incapable of such unilateral changes in the status of Puerto Rico, and the United States would probably have the force to make its view stick.

In any case, the "compact" is a double-edged sword. Even if it does require that changes occur only with the agreement of both U.S. and Puerto Rican authorities, it thereby perpetuates a U.S. veto power over Puerto Rican decisions to alter their internal governing arrangements, even as it leaves the United States unencumbered in regulating all external matters. Those "external" regulations can have profound internal consequences, as the recent State Department decision not to allow Puerto Ricans to renounce their U.S. citizenship without also losing their Puerto Rican citizenship dramatically illustrates. Here a policy governing Puerto Ricans' relationship with the U.S. government, a policy in which Puerto Ricans have no formal say, has the consequence of potentially rendering Puerto Ricans disenfranchised aliens on their own home island. There could be no starker demonstration that, under current arrangements, Puerto Rican citizenship is still not regarded by the U.S. government as an independent nationality; and the veracity of the U.S. view is underlined by the fact that Puerto Ricans have so few institutionalized avenues to challenge it. Hence, as Justice Fuster-Berlingeri candidly notes, even many Puerto Rican "architects of the Commonwealth" now argue that all these limitations on Puerto Rican self-governance mean that "Puerto Rico is still a colony of the United States." The consent it gave to continuing U.S. power over the island, one has argued, "was excessively generic."[29]

If this characterization is correct, and it seems inescapable to me, then it also follows inescapably that, even after 1952, the Puerto Rican citizenship relied upon in the opinion retains the key characteristics it had when it was created by the Foraker Act. It remains in reality a variety of colonial subjectship, involving highly qualified powers of internal self-governance, exercised under conditions and within constraints written, approved, and interpreted by U.S. governmental authorities who have never been directly or indirectly electorally accountable to Puerto Rico, and with only limited Puerto Rican participation along the way to render these processes somewhat less despotic in form than they otherwise would be.

I do not wish to overstate the case. A subordinate status does not necessarily mean practical experiences of massive oppression. As colonial subjectships go, modern Puerto Rican "citizenship" is in fact a rather convenient and unburdensome variety, and it is not surprising that many Puerto Ricans do not seem discontent with it. Many U.S. citizens residing in the fifty states would probably gladly forgo their representation in Congress and their vote in presidential elections in exchange for relief from federal taxes. But whatever its financial advantages, contemporary Puerto Rican citizenship is still a status conceived in racism; expressive of the proposition that all men are not created equal; and supportive of a federal government that, in regard to Puerto Rico, does not derive its just powers from the consent of the governed in any regularly verifiable way. As such, it remains an ineradicably poor foundation for positions defending the autonomous nationality and citizenship of the Puerto Rican people.

Conclusion

None of the above is meant to imply that the specific holding in the *Mari Brás* decision, that Juan Mari Brás could be a Puerto Rican citizen and a voter in Puerto Rico despite renouncing his U.S. citizenship, was legally incorrect, much less morally or, dare we say it, politically incorrect. I have criticized the route by which those conclusions were reached, not the conclusions themselves. Here I can only sketch the outlines of a more appropriate alternate route.

First let me observe that when Justice Fuster-Berlingeri argues that the Puerto Rican nationality of Juan Mari Brás is "unquestionable," he does not really seem to be appealing to the Foraker Act's creation of Puerto Rican citizenship, even though that is the main legal argument his opinion develops. He seems implicitly to be relying on the recognition that Mari Brás is a native-born, lifelong resident of Puerto Rico, descended from Puerto Rican parents, who has throughout much of his long life championed the political cause of Puerto Rican independence. Hence, whether nationality is seen as a matter of *jus soli* or *jus sanguinis,* place of birth or parentage, as the international lawyers view it, or as a matter of personal consensual political commitment and involvement, as modern liberal, democratic, and republican political theorists tend to view it, Juan Mari Brás has very powerful claims to be a Puerto Rican national, if Puerto Rican nationality exists at all.

To be sure, the legal, theoretical, and polemical literatures on what constitutes a "nation" and "nationality" are vast and growing, especially since these issues have become increasingly contentious in a postcolonial, post–Cold War world of rapidly altering borders. I do not seek to settle those difficult issues here, either generally or in regard to Puerto Rico particularly. I only insist, again, that under many definitions of a "nation," including those stressing common historical experiences, shared territory, a unifying language, distinctive cultural traditions, longtime existence as some kind of distinctive political community, and existence as an "imagined community," thought of as such by a large yet broadly identifiable population of self-conceived members, Puerto Ricans qualify and have long qualified.

But if Puerto Ricans can therefore plausibly be termed a "nation," Puerto Rico has nonetheless never been an independent nation-state as a matter of international law. It moved from a longstanding if recently relaxed form of Spanish subjectship to imperial governance by the United States in 1898 without any intervening period of genuine freedom. And because, in terms of international law, independent nationhood and independent statehood tend to be virtually synonymous, that legal and political history is the strongest argument against Puerto Rican nationality.

But if the argument is put on such legal and historical grounds, then we also have to inquire by what legal right the United States has claimed ultimate sovereignty over Puerto Rico. Admittedly, its authority in this regard originally had the sanction of international law, which did not become at all hostile to colonialism until after World War II, and which remains permissive enough in this regard to be plausibly satisfied by the 1952 "commonwealth" arrangement. That arrangement satisfied the UN that Puerto Rico was sufficiently self-governing to be no longer a "colony" as UN agreements define that status.[30] U.S. law is, however, a different question. I do not think the U.S. Constitution or American political principles more broadly can sanction the status of Puerto Rico from 1898 up through today as legitimate.

That contention is of course a highly charged one and I cannot make a detailed case for it here. I will simply note, without mincing words, my belief, first, that the Spanish-American War was an unjust, unprovoked, and racist war of aggression by the United States which could not result in legitimate acquisitions. Its conduct may have been constitutional in form, as a duly declared war, but in substance it was an illicit exercise of federal powers outside and against any valid constitutional purposes. Second, the claim that the Constitution applied to territorial inhabitants only to the most limited extent, justified by the "incorporated/unincorporated" distinction, also seems to me legally unfounded as well as clearly racist in motivation. It was, as Lowell virtually acknowledged, an innovation with little precedential support contrived to avoid the results of clear and fundamental American constitutional principles. Third, the manner in which Puerto Ricans, as residents of a still "unincorporated" territory, are denied not only electoral representation in the U.S. government that claims ultimate sovereignty over them, but also full protection of the Bill of Rights and other constitutional guarantees, seems to me a violation of the equal protection clause of the Fourteenth Amendment, as well as a violation of various specific rights. It is a form of second-class citizenship, originally unilaterally imposed, significantly inferior even to that possessed by (often voluntary) inhabitants of "incorporated" territories. As such, it does not seem to me consistent with the Constitution even if it should be genuinely embraced by most Puerto Ricans in a referendum with a full panoply of possibilities made available to them, a circumstance that has never really occurred.

These points support the conclusion that the governing authority asserted by the United States over Puerto Rico is and always has been substantially illegitimate, in violation of the U.S. Constitution and the nation's broader political principles. Where that leaves the issue of Puerto Rican nationality is in important respects unclear, but it does clearly mean that the United States is not entitled to decide the status of Puerto Rico, at least not any further than Puerto Ricans wish them to do. Puerto Ricans should be seen as legally entitled to decide their status for themselves (a power that is arguably at the heart of national identity).

If one accepts these conclusions, then it seems perfectly appropriate for the Supreme Court of Puerto Rico to speak of Puerto Rican "nationality," to hold that a person can be a Puerto Rican national and citizen and not a U.S. citizen, and to rule that such a person can participate in processes of self-government in Puerto Rico.[31] Such actions represent at least some Puerto Ricans deciding on their status for themselves, without giving any unwanted weight to their imposed U.S. identity. On this line of argument, however, these conclusions are appropriate not because the Foraker Act provides legal authority for the status of Puerto Rican citizenship or nationality, but precisely for the opposite reason. The Foraker Act and the statuses it creates are here seen as irredeemably invalid measures that cannot stand as legitimate constraints on the authority of Puerto Ricans to define their own legal and political identities.

It is perhaps understandable that the Supreme Court of Puerto Rico preferred to try to read the legal history so that the Foraker Act and its legal descendants could be claimed as authority in support of its decision, not as barriers to it. Yet that reading requires asserting the occurrence of a "radical" transformation that, in truth, has yet to happen. Perhaps saying that it has occurred will help it to do so; yet it seems at least equally likely that saying this may allow the status quo to continue in important respects unchallenged. Etymologically, *radical* refers to roots, so that truly "radical" change requires tearing an unwanted plant up by its very roots. The legal roots of the current status of Puerto Ricans are bitter indeed. It is not enough, I believe, simply to spray the plant with legal herbicide. The roots must be torn up, if Puerto Ricans and the United States are to move beyond the twisted weeds of colonial subordination and racism that grew from those roots into open and flourishing fields of genuine freedom.

Notes

1   *Ramírez de Ferrer v. Mari Brás,* Supreme Court of Puerto Rico, No. CT-96-14 (November 18, 1997) (official translation).

2   Ibid. at 1–2, 30, 35–36.

3   Lance Oliver, "Court Rules Citizenship Does Exist," *Orlando Sentinel Tribune,* November 24, 1997, at A6; "Puerto Rican Citizenship Fillip," *Financial Times,* USA ed., November 21, 1997, at 6.

4   If, however, *nationality* is defined as membership in a political community recognized as fully independent and sovereign by municipal and international law, then Puerto Rico could not be both a nation and one of the United States. But it is now common to define nationhood in ways that do not require the existence of a nation-state—as a community sharing a common culture, history, territorial origin, ethnicity, or religion, among other senses—and Puerto Ricans can plausibly claim to be a nation according to at least some of these definitions even if they do not possess and do not seek full political independence from the United States. For a brief overview of conceptions of nationality and a defense of Puerto Ricans' claim to nationhood, see Nancy Morris, *Puerto Rico: Culture, Politics, and Identity* (1995), at 11–15, 17–18. Leading discussions of nationality and nationalism include Benedict R. O. Anderson, *Imagined Communities: Reflections on the Origin and Spread of Nationalism* (1983); Ernest Gellner, *Nations and Nationalism* (1983); Eric J. Hobsbawm, *Nations and Nationalism since 1780: Programme, Myth, Reality* (1990); Etienne Balibar and Immanuel Wallerstein, *Race, Nation, Class: Ambiguous Identities* (1991).

5   *Ramírez v. Mari Brás,* No. CT-96-14, at 22.

6   See, e.g., Lance Oliver, "Citizenship Questions Not Settled," *Orlando Sentinel,* February 2, 1998, at A6; Oliver, "Puerto Rico Citizens Face Alienation," *Orlando Sentinel Tribune,* May 4, 1998, at A12 (describing State Department refusals to allow Puerto Ricans to maintain Puerto Rican citizenship while renouncing U.S. citizenship).

7   *Alberto O. Lozada Colon v. U.S. Department of State,* 2 F. Supp. 2d 43 (D.C. Cir. 1998).

8   This discussion and the historical sections of this essay generally draw on Rogers M. Smith,

Civic Ideals: Conflicting Visions of Citizenship in U.S. History (1997), at 430–39. The Roosevelt quotation is found in Stanley Karnow, *In Our Image: America's Empire in the Philippines* (1989), at 85, and see also pp. 10, 79–80, 119.

9   Morris, supra note 4, at 21–22; Adalberto López, "Birth of a Nation: Puerto Rico in the Nineteenth Century," in *The Puerto Ricans: Their History, Culture, and Society,* ed. Adalberto López (1980), at 78–81.

10 See generally López, ibid. at 25–88.

11 Ibid. at 87–90; Morris, supra note 4, at 22–23; Juan R. Torruella, *The Supreme Court and Puerto Rico: The Doctrine of Separate and Unequal* (1985), at 14–15.

12 *Treaty of Peace between the United States and the Kingdom of Spain, U.S. Statutes at Large* 30 (1899): 1754, art. IX, par. 2, at 1759 ("Treaty of Paris"), cited in Torruella, ibid. at 24.

13 López, supra note 9, at 90–91; Torruella, supra note 11, at 16–24; Morris, supra note 4, at 23, 26–27; *Ramírez v. Mari Brás,* No. CT-96-14, at 21.

14 Abbott Lawrence Lowell, "The Status of Our New Possessions—A Third View," *Harvard Law Review* 13 (1899): 155. See also Smith, supra note 8, at 433–39.

15 See, e.g., *Downes v. Bidwell,* 182 U.S. 244, 302–3, 306, 311–15, 336, 342; *Hawaii v. Mankichi,* 190 U.S. 197, 224, 227 (1903); *Balzac v. Porto Rico,* 258 U.S. 298, 308–11 (1922) (with Chief Justice William Howard Taft definitively affirming the unincorporated/incorporated territories distinction). The U.S. Supreme Court continues to cite *Downes v. Bidwell, Balzac v. Porto Rico,* and the unincorporated/incorporated territories distinction to support restrictions of the scope of the Bill of Rights. See, e.g., *U.S. v. Verdugo-Urquidez,* 499 U.S. 259, 268 (1990).

16 Abbott Lawrence Lowell, "The Colonial Expansion of the United States," *Atlantic Monthly* 83 (1899): 145.

17 Ibid. at 149–54.

18 Lowell, supra note 14, at 176. In arguing for the yet more extreme position that the Constitution imposed few if any limits on congressional treatment of any inhabitants outside the existing states, Harvard law professor James Bradley Thayer had previously been even more blunt than Lowell, though only a bit more elaborate on race. At various points he referred to questions raised by "the presence of an alien and inferior race" and the task of "governing a barbarous or semi-barbarous people." Though he did not think the legal status of territorial inhabitants turned on such factors, that was chiefly because he thought the Constitution capaciously permitted every population to "be governed as is necessary to govern them, according to the actual circumstances of the case." He expected that a "civilized nation in modern times" would in fact "restrain itself within narrower lines than the Constitution requires" in regard to such populations, "from mere policy, and from its own sense of humanity and justice." But the U.S. government could do just about whatever it thought it needed to do. James Bradley Thayer, "Our New Possessions," *Harvard Law Review* 12 (1899): 464, at 474, 483. Similar racial references are sprinkled through other major legal essays on the new colonies written during this period (see, e.g., Carman F. Randolph, "Constitutional Aspects of Annexation," *Harvard Law Review* 12 (1899): 291, at 304–5 (suggesting that the "character of its people" renders the Philippines "unfit for statehood"); Simeon E. Baldwin, "The Constitutional Questions Incident to the Acquisition and Government by the United States of Island Territory," *Harvard Law Review* 12 (1899): 393, at 415 (arguing that the Constitution must be fully enforced in the territories even when dealing with "the half-civilized Moros of the Philippines, or the ignorant and lawless brigands that infest Puerto Rico"; see

also pp. 407, 411). But unlike Lowell's *Atlantic* article, most do not explicitly rely on such racial concerns to answer the legal questions involved any more than Thayer did.

19   See, e.g., Torruella, supra note 11, at 32–39; José A. Cabranes, *Citizenship and the American Empire: Notes on the Legislative History of the United States Citizenship of Puerto Ricans* (1979), at 39–41.

20   *Cong. Rec.*, 56th Cong., 1st sess. (1900): pt. 1:711.

21   As president, Harvard's Theodore Roosevelt would pick the Yale man as a suitable trustee for the Philippines—his White House successor and future Supreme Court Chief Justice William Howard Taft.

22   *Cong. Rec.*, 56th Cong., 1st sess. (1900): pt. 2:1996; pt. 3:2105, 2162; pt. 4:3610. Cf. Cabranes, supra note 19, at 39–41. This classic essay somewhat confuses this point by asserting that "racist overtones were most clearly discernible in the remarks of those who opposed American imperialism." Ibid. at 39. Racism was overt and pervasive throughout virtually all sides of these debates. See also Torruella, supra note 11, at 33–35; Karnow, supra note 8, at 109–10, 137.

23   *Cong. Rec.*, 56th Cong., 1st sess. (1900): pt. 3:2473–74. The Foraker Act employed the misspelling "Porto Rico," following an error in the English version of the Treaty of Paris. Though "Porto" is a Portuguese word, the U.S. government did not bother to correct it in official documents until 1932. Cabranes, supra note 19, at 1 n.1, 6, 22–44; Torruella, supra note 11, at 32–39; Smith, supra note 8, at 431–32.

24   *Ramírez v. Mari Brás*, No. CT-96-14, at 23–25, 34; *Balzac*, 258 U.S. 298.

25   *Ramírez v. Mari Brás*, ibid. at 3–6, 14, 32.

26   Ibid. at 25–26.

27   Ibid. at 7.

28   Ibid. at 9–13.

29   Ibid. at 7–11, 26–27.

30   For a discussion of pertinent UN policies, see ibid. at 9–12, citing particularly Resolution 748(VIII), United Nations General Assembly, November 27, 1953.

31   More broadly, it further seems appropriate for Congress to recognize the right of Puerto Ricans to determine unilaterally their ultimate political status. I would also add that, in light of the history of unjust treatment by the United States accompanied by some undeniably real benefits of affiliation with the United States, it seems to me proper for the United States today to offer Puerto Ricans the option of statehood as well as independence or some intermediate status, whatever Puerto Ricans wish to choose. But squaring some possible intermediate statuses, including the current commonwealth status, with the U.S. Constitution is a tricky business, for reasons I have noted. The answers to those difficult questions are fare for an essay far more extensive than this one.

A Note on the *Insular Cases*

Christina Duffy Burnett

Any student of the relationship between law and American expansionism will quickly find that the *Insular Cases* come up time and again, as they do in this book. These early-twentieth-century U.S. Supreme Court opinions (also known as the *Insular Tariff Cases*) introduced and developed the "doctrine of territorial incorporation," and with it the category of "unincorporated territories," which shaped and continue to govern the status of territories taken by the United States in 1898 and thereafter. Yet the careful reader will have noticed differences in the lists of opinions cited under this rubric even within this volume.[1] A review of the literature on the *Insular Cases* reveals similar variations. Although there seems to be nearly universal consensus that the series culminates with *Balzac v. Porto Rico* in 1922, and that *Downes v. Bidwell* is the single most important of these cases, authors rarely provide a complete list.[2]

Addressing these uncertainties, Efrén Rivera Ramos, one of the contributors to this volume, has sought to resolve them by compiling a list of twenty-three Supreme Court decisions handed down between 1901 and 1922.[3] He includes there nine decisions handed down in 1901, another thirteen cases decided between 1903 and 1914, and the generally acknowledged culmination of the series, *Balzac*, decided in 1922.

There is a good reason to stop at *Balzac*. That case produced the last significant development in the doctrine—the statement that "incorporation" could not occur without a clear statement of congressional intent—in a unanimous Supreme Court opinion explicitly endorsing the doctrine.[4] Since 1922, Supreme Court opinions dealing with territories have provided very little additional insight into the content of the doctrine of incorporation, and in particular, into its consequences for the status of unincorporated territories. Although the doctrine requires an analysis of the status of a territory prior to a court's determination of which constitutional rights (and federal laws) constrain governmental action in (or "apply" to) that territory, Supreme Court opinions since *Balzac* are noteworthy, if anything, for applying this case-by-case analysis while assiduously avoiding clarification of the status of unincorporated territories (that is, of the nature of their relationship to the United States). With regard to Puerto Rico, for instance, the Court has held that due process and equal protection guarantees are in force on the island, but has declined to determine whether they are so by virtue of the Fifth or the Fourteenth Amendment to the Constitution.[5] An answer either way would provide revealing information concerning Puerto Rico's precise relationship to the federal government, its place in the constitutional scheme, and its degree of sovereignty (if any), but the Court seems unwilling to say anything too conclusive about these matters.

Two earlier opinions, however, are almost never counted among the *Insular Cases*, and perhaps should be. These companion cases, both called *Neely v. Henkel* and also decided in 1901, slightly predate the usually cited set of opinions.[6] They were decided on January 14, 1901, just days after oral arguments in the first group of *Insular Cases*. In the *Neely* cases, the Court examined the status of Cuba in order to decide whether a U.S. citizen accused of embezzlement under Cuba's Penal and Postal Codes could be extradited from the United States and tried under the island's justice system. In deciding that the accused was indeed subject to extradition, the Supreme Court in *Neely* explained that Cuba was a foreign country despite the United States's occupation of, and exercise of temporary sovereignty over, the island, according to the terms of the resolution on Cuba's independence and the Treaty of Paris.[7]

The *Neely* cases—the Court wrote an opinion in *Neely I,* deciding *Neely II* by reference to the first one—belong on a complete list of the *Insular Cases* because their account of why Cuba was a "foreign country" while at the same time subject to U.S. sovereignty forms an integral part of the Court's broader analysis in the *Insular Cases,* which dealt with the related questions of when a place remains foreign regardless of a U.S. presence there, when it ceases to be foreign and becomes domestic territory, when it becomes a part of the "United States," and what relationship these different stages have to the exercise of U.S. sovereignty. The peculiar innovation of the *Insular Cases* was the determination that there is a difference between the latter two stages—that is, that territory can become "domestic" without becoming part of the "United States" in a constitutional sense. The *Neely* cases shed further light on this idea by describing a situation in which the United States could continue to exercise sovereignty over a place, even after the conclusion of war, yet not thereby render the place "domestic."

Finally, three additional opinions, also decided between 1901 and 1922, perhaps belong in the series: *Porto Rico v. Rosaly;*[8] *Porto Rico v. Tapia;*[9] *Porto Rico v. Muratti.*[10] In *Rosaly,* a suit against the government of Puerto Rico and several individuals for the recovery of property, the Supreme Court held that Puerto Rico's government "is of such nature as to come within the general rule exempting a government sovereign from being sued without its consent." Citing *Kopel v. Bingham,*[11] one of the *Insular Cases,* as the source of Puerto Rico's status, the Court explained that, at least for purposes of sovereign immunity, Puerto Rico was like the incorporated territory of Hawaii (because the relevant question was whether Puerto Rico had a three-branch government, which it did). The latter two cases held that the Fifth Amendment right to an indictment by a grand jury in a criminal prosecution does not apply to Puerto Rico.[12] As noted by an author writing on the *Insular Cases* in 1919, all of these "clearly [approved of] the doctrine of non-incorporation."[13]

Notes

1   Efrén Rivera Ramos provides the most complete list, containing twenty-three opinions. It includes nine decisions handed down in 1901: *De Lima v. Bidwell,* 182 U.S. 1 (1901); *Goetze v. United States,* 182 U.S. 221 (1901); *Crossman v. United States,* 182 U.S. 221 (1901); *Dooley v. United States,* 182 U.S. 222 (1901) (*Dooley I*); *Armstrong v. United States,* 182 U.S. 243 (1901); *Downes v. Bidwell,* 182 U.S. 244 (1901); *Huus v. New York and Porto Rico Steamship Company,* 182 U.S. 392 (1901); *Dooley v. United States,* 183 U.S. 151 (1901) (*Dooley II*); and *Fourteen Diamond Rings v. United States,* 183 U.S. 176 (1901); a second set of cases decided from 1903 to 1914: *Hawaii v. Mankichi,* 190 U.S. 197 (1903); *Gonzales v. Williams,* 192 U.S. 1 (1904); *Kepner v. United States,* 195 U.S. 100 (1904); *Dorr v. United States,* 195 U.S. 138 (1904); *Mendezona v. United States,* 195 U.S. 158 (1904); *Rassmussen v. United States,* 197 U.S. 516 (1905); *Trono v. United States,* 199 U.S. 521 (1905); *Grafton v. United States,* 206 U.S. 333 (1907); *Kent v. Porto*

Rico, 207 U.S. 113 (1907); *Kopel v. Bingham,* 211 U.S. 468 (1909); *Dowdell v. United States,* 221 U.S. 325 (1911); *Ochoa v. Hernandez,* 230 U.S. 139 (1913); *Ocampo v. United States,* 234 U.S. 91 (1914); and a 1922 decision: *Balzac v. Porto Rico,* 258 U.S. 298 (1922). See note 4 of Rivera Ramos's essay in this volume.

Other essays in this book cite several of the opinions as examples, rather than provide a full list. Cabranes cites, as examples, five cases from the years 1901–5: *Downes, Rassmussen, Dorr, Mankichi, Balzac* (see note 9). Weiner identifies the *Insular Cases* as a set of opinions dating from 1901–4, as well as others "including" *Rassmussen* and *Dowdell* (see note 80). Trías Monge cites the nine opinions handed down in 1901 as a "basic" list (see note 1), while Torruella identifies, "strictly speaking," the first six cases decided in 1901 (see note 14).

2 Usually, authors cite several of the opinions as examples, identifying as the rest a series culminating in *Balzac.* See, e.g., Marcos A. Ramírez, "Los Casos Insulares: Un Estudio Sobre el Proceso Judicial," *Revista Jurídica de la Universidad de Puerto Rico* 16 (1946): 121, at 121 n.1 (listing as "the most important" *Insular Cases* a set of nine cases decided between 1901 and 1905); Jaime B. Fuster, "The Origins of the Doctrine of Territorial Incorporation and its Implications Regarding the Power of the Commonwealth of Puerto Rico to Regulate Interstate Commerce," *Revista Jurídica Universidad de Puerto Rico* 43 (1974): 259, at 263 n. 7 (listing as the "original" *Insular Cases* "three main U.S. Supreme Court decisions dealing with Puerto Rico" (*De Lima, Downes,* and *Dooley I*) together with three per curiam opinions, and "all decisions through which the doctrine of territorial incorporation was developed, culminating in" *Balzac*); José A. Cabranes, *Citizenship and the American Empire: Notes on the Legislative History of the United States Citizenship of Puerto Ricans* (1979), at 28 n.97 (citing, as examples, *De Lima, Dooley I, Armstrong,* and *Downes*); Manuel Del Valle, "Puerto Rico before the United States Supreme Court," *Revista Jurídica de la Universidad Interamericana* 19 (1984): 13 (citing, as examples, *De Lima, Downes, Dooley I,* and *Dooley II*); Raymond Carr, *Puerto Rico: A Colonial Experiment* (1984), at 36 n. 34 (citing, as "the relevant ones," *Downes* and *De Lima,* and noting that *Balzac* reaffirmed their doctrine even after the grant of U.S. citizenship to Puerto Ricans).

A record of materials relating to seven out of the nine cases was published by the government in 1901 under the title *The Insular Cases.* See Albert H. Howe, ed., *The Insular Cases: Comprising the Records, Briefs, and Arguments of Counsel in the Insular Cases of the October Term, 1900, in the Supreme Court of the United States, including appendixes thereto,* H.R. Doc. No. 509, 56th Cong., 2d Sess. (1901). That compilation (an invaluable source on these cases, including even full transcripts of oral arguments) was published before the opinions in the last two 1901 cases were handed down.

3 See Efrén Rivera Ramos, "The Legal Construction of American Colonialism: The Insular Cases, 1901–1922," *Revista Jurídica Universidad de Puerto Rico* 65 (1996): 225, at 240–41, notes 40–42. Rivera Ramos's list is reproduced here, supra note 1.

4 *Balzac,* 258 U.S. at 311.

5 See *Examining Board v. Flores de Otero,* 426 U.S. 572 (1976) (holding that due process and equal protection guarantees apply, either through the Fifth or the Fourteenth Amendment); *Calero-Toledo v. Pearson Yacht Leasing Co.,* 416 U.S. 663 (1974) (due process guarantees apply, either through the Fifth or the Fourteenth Amendment).

6 *Neely v. Henkel* (No. 1), 180 U.S. 109 (1901); *Neely v. Henkel* (No. 2), 180 U.S. 126 (1901) (per curiam). I have found only one author who includes *Neely* on the list. See James Edward Kerr, *The Insular Cases: The Role of the Judiciary in American Expansionism* (1982), at 57 (citing the first *Neely*).

7 *Joint Resolution for the Recognition of the Independence of the People of Cuba, U.S. Statutes at*

Large 30 (April 20, 1898): 738, at 739 (the "Teller Amendment"); *Treaty of Peace between the United States and the Kingdom of Spain, U.S. Statutes at Large* 30 (1899): 1754 (the "Treaty of Paris").

8   227 U.S. 270 (1913).

9   245 U.S. 639 (1918) (per curiam).

10 245 U.S. 639 (1918) (per curiam).

11 211 U.S. 468.

12 For brief discussions of these, see Juan R. Torruella, *The Supreme Court and Puerto Rico: The Doctrine of Separate and Unequal* (1985), at 96; Rivera Ramos, supra note 3, at 268.

13 Pedro Capó Rodríguez, "The Relations between the United States and Porto Rico" (part 4), *American Journal of International Law* 13 (1919): 483, at 498 n. 91.

Notes on Contributors

José Julián Álvarez González is a professor at the University of Puerto Rico School of Law. His publications include "The Empire Strikes Out: Congressional Ruminations on the Citizenship Status of Puerto Ricans," *Harvard Journal on Legislation* 27 (1990): 309, and "The Protection of Civil Rights in Puerto Rico," *Arizona Journal of International and Comparative Law* 6 (1989): 68.

Roberto Aponte Toro is a professor at the University of Puerto Rico School of Law. He is a former member of the House of Representatives of the Commonwealth of Puerto Rico and was Executive Director of the U.P.R. School of Law Trust Fund from 1991 to 1998. He is the author of *Amor a la Americana* (1994).

Christina Duffy Burnett holds a J.D. from Yale Law School and an M.Phil. in Political Thought and Intellectual History from Cambridge University. She is the author of "The Case for Puerto Rican Decolonization," *Orbis: A Journal of World Affairs* (Summer 2001). She recently served as a law clerk on the U.S. Court of Appeals for the Second Circuit, and is currently a Research Associate in the Program in Law and Public Affairs at Princeton University.

José A. Cabranes is a judge on the United States Court of Appeals for the Second Circuit. His publications include *Citizenship and the American Empire* (1979), a legislative history of the United States citizenship of the people of Puerto Rico, and *Fear of Judging: Sentencing Guidelines in the Federal Courts* (with Kate Stith) (1998).

Sanford Levinson is the W. St. John Garwood and W. St. John Garwood, Jr. Regents Chair in Law at the University of Texas Law School. He is the author of *Constitutional Faith* (1988) and *Written in Stone: Public Monuments in Changing Societies* (1998); the editor of *Responding to Imperfection: The Theory and Practice of Constitutional Amendment* (1995); and a co-editor, with Akhil Reed Amar, Jack Balkin, and Paul Brest, of *Processes of Constitutional Decisionmaking* (4th ed. 2000), and, with Jack Balkin, of *Legal Canons* (2000).

Burke Marshall is Nicholas deB. Katzenbach Professor Emeritus of Law and George W. Crawford Professorial Lecturer in Law at Yale Law School. He was the Assistant Attorney General of the United States in the Civil Rights Division of the Department of Justice from 1961 to 1965. He is the author of *Federalism and Civil Rights* (1965) and the editor of *A Workable Government? The Constitution After 200 Years* (1987).

Gerald L. Neuman is Herbert Wechsler Professor of Federal Jurisprudence at Columbia Law School and the author of *Strangers to the Constitution: Immigrants, Borders, and Fundamental Law* (1996).

Juan F. Perea is the Cone, Wagner, Nugent, Johnson, Hazour, & Roth Professor of Law at the University of Florida College of Law. He is the author of *Race and Races: Cases and Resources for a Diverse America* (2000) (with Delgado, Harris, & Wildman), and the editor of *Immigrants Out! The New Nativism and the Anti-Immigrant Impulse in the United States* (1998).

Ángel Ricardo Oquendo is a professor at the University of Connecticut School of Law. His publications include "Re-Imagining the Latino/a Race," *Harvard Blackletter Law Journal* vol. 12 (1993): 93, reprinted in *The Latino/a Condition: A Critical Reader,* ed. Richard Delgado (1998); "La cultura nacional puertorriqueña frente a los Estados Unidos," *Revista Jurídica Universidad de Puerto Rico* 67 (1998): 1033; and "Der national Staat in pluralistischen Gesellschaften," *FBRW F.U. Berlin Fasch-bereichstag* (1999): 1.

Efrén Rivera Ramos is a professor at the University of Puerto Rico School of Law. He is the author of *The Legal Construction of Identity: The Judicial and Social Legacy of American Colonialism in Puerto Rico* (2001) and "The Legal Construction of American Colonialism: *The Insular Cases* (1901–1922)," *Revista Jurídica Universidad de Puerto Rico* 65 (1996): 225 (of which a version in Spanish appeared in *El Otro Derecho* 22 [1998]: 9).

Rogers M. Smith is professor of political science at the University of Pennsylvania and the author of *Citizenship Without Consent: the Illegal Alien in the American Polity,* with Peter Schuck (1985) and *Civic Ideals: Conflicting Visions of Citizenship in U.S. History* (1997), which was nominated for the Pulitzer Prize in History.

E. Robert Statham, Jr. is a professor of political science and Chair, Division of Behavioral and Social Sciences, at the University of Guam. His publications include *The Constitution of Public Philosophy: A Synthesis of Freedom and Responsibility in Postmodern America* (1998), and *Colonial Constitutionalism: The Tyranny of the United States's Offshore Territorial Policy and Relations* (2001).

Richard Thornburgh served two terms as governor of Pennsylvania, and also served as Attorney General of the United States and Under-Secretary General of the United Nations. He is currently counsel to the law firm of Kirkpatrick & Lockhart, LLP, and is a member of the American Bar Foundation, the American Judicature Society, and the Council on Foreign Relations.

Brook Thomas is a professor in the Department of English and Comparative Literature at the University of California, Irvine. He is author of *Cross-Examinations of Law and Literature: Cooper, Hawthorne, Stowe, and Melville,* and *American Literary Realism and the Failed Promise of Contract,* and the editor of *Plessy v. Ferguson: A Brief History with Documents* and *Literature and the Nation.*

Juan R. Torruella is the Chief Judge of the United States Court of Appeals for the First Circuit. He is the author of *The Supreme Court and Puerto Rico: The Doctrine of Separate and Unequal* (1985).

José Trías Monge served as Chief Justice of the Supreme Court of Puerto Rico from 1974 to 1985. His publications include *Historia Constitucional de Puerto Rico* (1980–1983 and 1993) and *Puerto Rico: The Trials of the Oldest Colony in the World* (1997).

Mark Tushnet is Carmack Waterhouse Professor of Constitutional Law at the Georgetown University Law Center. His publications include *Central America and the Law: The Constitutions, Civil Liberties and the Courts* (1988), *Comparative Constitutional Federalism: Europe and America* (1990), and, with Louis Michael Seidman, *Remnants of Belief: Contemporary Constitutional Issues* (1996).

Mark S. Weiner holds a J.D. from Yale Law School and a Ph.D. in American studies from Yale University. He is currently working on a book for Alfred A. Knopf that examines significant public trials of black Americans.

Index

Library of Congress Cataloging-in-Publication Data
Foreign in a domestic sense : Puerto Rico, American expansion,
and the Constitution /
edited by Christina Duffy Burnett and Burke Marshall.
p. cm. — (American encounters/global interactions)
Includes bibliographical references and index.
ISBN 0-8223-2689-2 (cloth : alk. paper) — ISBN 0-8223-2698-1 (pbk. : alk. paper)
1. Constitutional law—United States—Territories and possessions. 2. United
States—Territories and possessions—Politics and government. 3. Constitutional
law—Puerto Rico. 4. Puerto Rico—Politics and government.
I. Burnett, Christina Duffy. II. Marshall, Burke, 1922– III. Series.
KF4635 .F67 2001   342.73'083—dc21   00-047644

Please remember that this is a library book, and that it belongs only temporarily to each person who uses it. Be considerate. Do not write in this, or any, library book.